ARCHER'S DIGEST

Rick Sapp

Front Cover
The target archer will be well served with the PSE Mach II. The model show on the cover is equipped with the N.V. System, Vector wheel and a Vibracheck Fatfree Freestyle Stabilizer. Arrows are held in place by a Cavalier drop-away rest. Aiming is done with a Cobra Competition Sight and a Bull's Eye 6x with optic fiber reticle. The color is PSE's Good Vibrations pattern.

For the hunter, the PSE Nitro with the Centerfire Cam and N.V. System works especially well with the PSE Pro Series Tempest Sight and Cavalier Avalanche drop-away rest and a PSE quick-detach eight-arrow quiver and Vibracheck Isolator stabilizer. The color is PSE's own Brush Camo.

For more information contact:
Precision Shooting Equipment
P.O. Box 5487
Tuscon, AZ 85703

Published by

krause publications
An F+W Publications Company

700 East State Street • Iola, WI 54990-0001
715-445-2214 • 888-457-2873
www.krause.com

Please, call or write us for our free catalog of publications.
Our toll-free number to place an order or obtain a free catalog is 800-258-0929 or please us our regular business telephone 715-445-2214.

ISBN: 0-87349-561-6
Library of Congress Number: 2003108679
Printed in the United States of America

Edited by Kevin Michalowski
Designed by Brian Brogaard

CONTENTS

DEDICATION

To Isa, Hugh, Marge, Sally, Lemmer, Morgan and Don.
You know who you are.
You know what you did.
Thank you.

FOREWORD AND ACKNOWLEDGMENTS

Archery is a deceptive hobby. Like a multi-faceted gemstone any way you turn it, something else sparkles and is revealed. The historian can study it for a lifetime and never have all of his questions answered about how Turkish archers shot their heavy bows accurately from the backs of running horses. Even today, no practitioner could ever master all of its tools and games. Archery continues to change. In the 25 years that I have been shooting a bow, almost everything has undergone a remarkable evolution, except the basics.

The basics of archery never change because they have nothing to do with the tools. Even when the bow and arrow were used for warfare, as they often were, or murder, as was the case with the "Ice Man," the tools maintained a core mystique that separated them from the finality of their use.

The bow and arrow both defy us to master them and define us as humans. Symbolized by the beautiful, arcing flight of an arrow and the dramatic inspiration of impact, the basics of archery have always been honesty, integrity and respect.

Archer's Digest is a nuts and bolts gear book. It covers a lot of technical ground. You may find that it is not perfect, but it is a good synthesis of the available information and speculation about what has become a complex subject. I have learned that technical or even "scientific" data can be used to support opposing meanings or can even be used to give an unusual spin to political interpretations.

I have made a sincere effort to give the reader an overview of each side of the archery gem. In the chapter covering release aids, for instance, I wanted to explore not only what is available and how it works, in theory and in practice, but also why many archers choose to shoot with release aids and why some do not. I interviewed several manufacturers and archers about every issue, but the final synthesis, the final choice of "slant" has been mine. If there are errors of fact or perhaps misinterpretations, they are mine alone.

Still, not every subject or manufacturer is covered evenly. Some manufacturers replied with copious information; some did not reply at all. To those who did reply and who sent information and photos, thank you. I am in your debt. To those who did not, I look forward to learning from you for the next edition.

Rick Sapp
November 2003

INTRODUCTION

ARCHERY AND THE 21ST CENTURY: YOUR ACTUAL LIFE IN REAL TIME

This book is titled Archer's Digest. In the larger sense, it is not about archery. It is about our ability to make thoughtful choices in a world and at a time that permits us to enjoy bountiful recreation opportunities.

It is a mantra of Western civilization that our work defines us and in the United States, worker productivity and time on the job is apparently on the rise … just as the time we workers spend in vacation, recreation and leisure is on the decline. Surveys suggest that some of that decline is even voluntary. Isn't that odd? The time we want to spend shuffling meaningless papers or operating the mindless machines of industry is growing while the time we spend playing with our children decreases. Is this the legacy we wish to leave to our children; that we chose to work? At some point, we are becoming slaves to consumerism.

Archery is one of many choices we have for our leisure hours. Today, it seems that everything is possible; everything is practical. If we work longer hours to please our corporate masters, we can afford the Jet Ski and the trailer to pull it (although finding a day to take the family to the lake is impossible). We can buy the second home at the beach, but we take our laptop and do a little work while everyone else splashes around in the water. We can live in a huge home that is more like a museum than a cozy cave for the comfort and protection of our family. But while we are in that home, careful never to spill a drink or allow the cat to toss a hairball behind the sofa, we live isolated in cubicles with electronic boxes playing games or communicating with a world-wide community while ignoring the hearts beating in the room on the other side of the wall. Okay, we are working harder, collecting more nice stuff, but it appears that we have chosen to enjoy our stuff less than ever in history. Is this really the choice we want to make? Work over play. Work over family. Are we nuts?

Today, archery is more than just shooting the bow and arrow. It is a symbol of who we are and where we are going. It is a symbol of where we have come from, too. Archery is all about mastering a very special set of tools, a special language and finding the time to put it all to use. If that isn't what sets homo sapiens apart from the birds and apes and whales – who also, in numerous identified circumstances have some elementary tool-using abilities, there may not be one single other thing that does. Tool use. Chipping flint. Programming the VCR.

Let's accept that mastering the path to the Selenitic oasis in the latest version of Myst requires concentration. It takes effort to navigate in an alien landscape where there are pitfalls and hidden terrors and wonderful surprises. But is it better to experience, to participate in these emotions and sensations vicariously on-screen or in real life? Doesn't discovering the hidden riches in a computer program leave you just as poor as you were the day before?

If you love the skill and strategy and suspense of navigating in an alien landscape, you will certainly enjoy archery, because it has everything that a great computer game has programmed into an imaginary, electronic world. Learning to change draw weight and how that affects the tune of a modern compound bow is a minefield of competing opinions and semi-scientific analyses. Navigating successfully through the shooting ranks with competing manufacturing claims and the large egos of top professional archers on today's international tournament shooting circuits involves as much skill and intrigue as any electronic alliance ever could. And at the end of the day, you could walk away with real money and expensive prizes.

And then there is the question of life and death. Left click the mouse or press the "A" tab and you can reduce the Chief Gremlin to a mass of dripping blood and shredded flesh. Well, that's exciting, right? But try stalking a brown bear or hunting African lions, animals that can turn on you in a flash. If reality doesn't make your heart pound with breathless excitement, you need an electronic implant to make sure it is still ticking.

Life and death. These are facts, concepts, realities that many of today's "extreme sports" come to grips with in their own, and often antiseptic and highly imaginative manner. Flying a motorcycle over the Grand Canyon … oh, right. Flipping a skateboard along the edge of the marble bench outside the county court house can give you a nosebleed. Challenging space monsters in a paintball scenario game with the fate of the earth in the balance? Running marathons. Swimming the English Channel. These are immense tests of your individual skill and commitment, but there is no real blood.

Even today, blood is what makes archery different than other extreme sports, because although there are several national and international archery competition venues including the Olympic games, archery in the U.S. would virtually disappear were it not for bowhunting and, to a lesser extent, bowfishing. If there are about three million archers in North America, 90+ percent of them are hunters first and foremost. Of the remaining ten percent, most hunt and shoot their bow competitively. Few are solely competitors, but no one looks askance at someone who only shoots recreationally. Nevertheless, most (but certainly not all) of the equipment discussed in *Archer's Digest* is gear for hunters. After all, that's what makes archers different. Whether they choose to hunt or not, they have that option in every state and province north of the Rio Grande. Should it be this way? Who knows? It is simply a fact and it relates us to the path from the invention of the bow to today and tomorrow.

The bow was invented in Africa sometime before 25,000 B.C. We think. There are no magazine articles or videos from that period to confirm this educated hunch and because early bows were certainly made from wood and the fibers of animals – dried, greased sheep intestine strings, for instance – there is nothing left like a fossil to testify to the imaginative, skillful and thoughtful individuals who brought the bow along with or about the same time as the spear thrower or atl atl.

In its most elemental form, the bow is nothing more than a lever. Bows lever arrows through the air toward a target. The spear thrower did the same thing although it used the arm as a lever and the spear thrower was simply an extension of the arm giving it a longer radius of action and thereby increasing the distance and the force with which a spear could be chunked.

By around 18,000 B.C., dates confirmed by carbon dating (the rate of decay of radioactive elements like carbon 14) as well as other methods, fire-hardened arrow tips were being replaced by stone heads fastened to the fronts of arrows. A weighting and stabilizing factor such as bird feathers, some early Einstein discovered, helped put their arrow tips on target.

Now, Homo sapiens were off and running. With fire and complex language and stone-tipped arrows under their collective belt, it was only a matter of time before humans created the Mercedes Benz, banana-flavored Popsicles and the hanging chad on Florida electoral ballots. In a general sense, humans became masters of their universe.

Complete bows have been found buried in peat bogs in Denmark that date to about 9,000 years B.C. Were they not so delicate, these very bows would not raise an eyebrow at a get-together of traditional archers: yew and elm staves that were properly "tillered" which essentially means they would shoot straight.

We know that by about 5,000 B.C., the Egyptians used the bow and arrow in battle with the Persians. A couple thousand years later, the descendants of those warriors developed the first composite bow … the first that we know of, anyway. These bows tipped with horn and backed with pounded animal sinew, were so strong that it took two men to string them and any target within 400 yards was in danger.

Mastery of the planet, certainly, had its dark side. Just a dozen years ago, a man was discovered in the Alps who had been dead for about 5,000 years. He was called the "Ice Man," because he had fallen into deep snow and ice which preserved him and his gear. Evidence suggests that he may have been an itinerant coppersmith and shepherd. Indeed, he carried a copper ax, perhaps one of the first ever made, a bow and a quiver full of arrows. He also carried an arrowhead in his back and it must certainly have killed him.

And crossbows? Apparently these bows were developed in China … and they have been the source of controversy ever since.

The longbow and the crossbow were used in battle in Europe until the mid 1600s when they were supplanted by gunpowder. Around the world, various people (often organized into tribes called "Losers") continued to use their bows to hunt and to confront invaders with firearms for several hundred years with universally predictable results.

Thereafter, for several hundred years, the bow languished as hot burning gunpowder proved to be more effective at launching projectiles than did a wooden stick. Still, here and there, a few people continued to make bows and even hold small tournaments until an unusual thing happened early in the 20th Century. A lonely, starving man stumbled out of the mountains of California.

The starving man was called Ishi, although that was not his given name. Ishi was the last survivor of the Yahi tribe, a people who lived near Mount Lassen and who had been driven to extinction by the indifference and cruelty of the people who invaded their homeland. The man was named Ishi because his real name was forbidden to be spoken aloud. He was adopted by the two anthropologists at the University of California, Berkeley and lived his final years, before dying of tuberculosis, as caretaker and quiet, friendly gentleman-in-residence at the museum. While he was there, he befriended a doctor named Saxton Pope and the two men made bows and shot arrows together. A few years after Ishi's death, Pope met Art Young and the seed of modern archery was born.

Eventually, Pope and Young hunted together in Alaska and Canada and even in Africa, making bows in Ishi's fashion and making movies! It was one of their movies, Alaskan Adventures, which stirred the imagination of an auto-industry patternmaker in Detroit, Fred Bear, and thousands of others.

Archery began to grow in popularity. Slowly. Dozens of individuals were making bows by hand, but it was Ben Pearson from Arkansas, who is credited with mass-producing them in 1938. It is said that at one time Ben employed as many as 800 people. His mechanical inventiveness and astute business practices earned Ben Pearson Archery a reputation as the largest archery company in the world for the next 30 years. It was overtaken by Bear Archery and, eventually, by many others.

In the past 100 years archery has come out of hiding, but for our purposes, it has only been the past 40 that have been truly remarkable. With Holless Allen's patent on the compound bow filed on December 30, 1969, archery has undergone a rapid period of invention and application. At the turn of the 20th Century, practically no one shot a bow that they did not make themselves or have made by hand especially for them. By 1980, millions of people were shooting bows for hunting, in summer camp, in competition and just for the sheer fun of it.

No one knows exactly how many people shoot a bow these days, either traditional or compound or crossbow. A reasonable estimate in North America, where archery is highly concentrated, is about three million people. Perhaps another couple million shoot once or twice a year at camp or as part of a program such as the Boy Scouts. In spite of the vagueness and probable inaccuracy of our census, we know that archery is part of the lives of hundreds of thousands of people in every country around the world, because there is no corner of the globe where this ancient art is not practiced.

Archery is one of those sports with an amazing variety of gear to play with. The style of bow and arrows you choose can be either as primitive as the European "Ice Man" carried 5,000 years ago or as modern as computer-aided design and manufacturing can make them. You can choose arrows from wood or from the latest space age composite. Shoot with sights; shoot without sights; it literally does not matter what you choose. There is both a venue and a group of people to shoot with.

If your interest leans to the historic, you can build a longbow from yew and chip arrowheads out of stone. (That's called "flint knapping.") Archers who enjoy traditional shooting eschew modern aids to hitting their target, whether it is paper on a bale of hay or a whitetail deer browsing nearby. Perhaps their aim is to maintain the connection with the Ice Man, with 25,000 to 50,000 years of human heritage. These are the period re-enactors of archery, the people who joyously keep us in touch with our instincts as survivors and predators. These are people who enjoy the do-it-yourself ideal of self-sufficiency.

At the other end of the archery spectrum are people who choose to shoot the very newest gear available. These folks were the first archers on their block to buy fiber optic sights, to use a mechanical string release aid, to understand the lines on a draw force curve. They were the first to buy a one-cam bow that shot more than 300 fps. These are the folks out in front with the pioneers, looking to the future and experimenting with the very latest gadgets. And still, their archery object is the same as the man or woman using little more than a stick and string; to hit what they are aiming at precisely and efficiently.

The archery game has evolved technically, but perhaps not so much in the range of its application. Certainly, in the U.S. and Canada, most archers are hunters and some of them compete. Around the world, it is the reverse; most archers compete and a few hunt with their bow. As an Olympic sport, archery is governed by the Federation Internationale de Tir a l'Arc (FITA, the International Bow and Arrow Federation) and a separate international tournament circuit, the International Field Archery Association (IFAA), thrives for shooting at paper targets.

In the U.S., a peculiar brand of competition has sprung up since the development of the life-like 3-D big game target. Two large associations, the International Bowhunting Organization and the Archery Shooter's Association, promote competition circuits that attract thousands of archers to these shoots. The foam targets are molded and painted to look like commonly hunted North American big game animals such as deer and bear and turkeys, with the occasional leopard or space alien thrown in for fun.

Because there is so much equipment to play with in archery and there are so many styles of shooting, competitions are divided into classes. People shooting the hottest compound bows are not matched against longbow shooters who do not shoot against the crossbow shooters. Except in specified cases, FITA permits only recurves on the line for international competition.

So, archery is moving forward and backward in time at the same moment. What distinguishes it from the world of electronic entertainment with which we compared it earlier is that, like other extreme sports, it requires that the participant get up and become a physical actor in real time. The trophy deer will only come within shooting range once. The opportunity to light the Olympic torch with a flaming arrow in front of 100,000 spectators and millions of television viewers is a physical act that requires both practical skill and intense mental alertness.

Choose to get up and get going. Choose to get away from the phone and computer and get into archery. Live your life in real time. The skills you learn and the friends you make will last for all time.

THE MECHANICS OF SHOOTING A BOW

Archery is a highly individual activity. It is not a team sport although you can join a team or shoot in leagues and international competition features both individual and team events. But the act of shooting a bow and hitting your target is entirely personal. You can hire a coach and take instruction (in fact, that is recommended) but when it comes to releasing an arrow, it is only you, yourself, on the line. Performing well, hitting the target consistently, requires that you have equipment that is matched specifically to your personal taste, your body style and your comfort level.

Many novice archers start with hand-me-down bows or equipment that is "just like dad's." Good shooting gear certainly is not cheap, but unlike a .22 rifle, for instance, which can be passed around a room and shot successfully by dozens of people if they tweak the sights a little, a bow and arrow set-up has to be matched to you personally: to your "dominant eye," to your "draw length" or how far you will pull the string, and then to your preferred "draw weight" which is a function of your strength and the bow's design.

YOUR DOMINANT EYE

Bows are built to fit right-handed or left-handed

Immediate determination of your dominant eye will ease the equipment selection, tuning and learning process. Typically, but not always, a right-hander will be right-eye-dominant and vice versa for left-handers. To determine your dominant eye, use either the pointing (above) or "moving hole" methods.

individuals and your choice is based on eye dominance … not, it will surprise you to learn, on hand dominance. Just as people write, brush their teeth or eat with a fork right-handed or left-handed they also have a dominant eye, sometimes called a master eye. For most of us, hand and eye dominance are same-sided, but sometimes a right-handed person will have a dominant left eye or vice versa.

There are two ways to determine your dominant eye.

METHOD ONE: Point your index finger at a distant object with both eyes open. Now, close your left eye. If your finger still appears to be pointing at the object, you most certainly have a dominant right eye. If your finger appears to shift to the side when you close your left eye, you probably have a dominant left eye. For confirmation, point again with both eyes open and then close your right eye. If, while you are looking with your left eye only, your finger still points at the object, you can feel certain that your left eye is dominant.

METHOD TWO: An optional method which many people find less optically confusing uses both hands at the same time. First, place your hands together at arm's length from your eyes, palms facing out so you are viewing the backs of your hands. Now, touch the tips of your thumbs and forefingers and swivel your hands together so that the "V" between your thumbs and your forefingers forms a hole. Pick out some object on the far side of the room and center it in the hole. Slowly move your hands together so the hole becomes smaller and smaller and, while you are doing this, bring your hands and the hole back to your face. You should end up with the hole circumscribed by your hands in front of your dominant eye.

Hand-eye coordination is simplified if your dominant eye matches your dominant hand. If this is the case, simply choose a bow configured for your dominant side. For example, a right-hander with a dominant right eye will choose a right-handed bow.

If your hand and eye dominance are mismatched however, you should select a bow based on eye dominance rather than your hand dominance. A right-hander will probably feel awkward at first shooting a left-handed bow, but in the long run you will shoot better and more comfortably this way. Most successful archers sight with their dominant eye. Hand dominance in archery is simply performing the manual operations called for in order by the brain. This allows them to aim with both eyes open and that gives them better depth perception for distance estimation and a better "feel" for the target. To aim with your weaker eye, you need to close or cover your

dominant eye.

DETERMINE YOUR SPECIFIC DRAW LENGTH

The length of your arms and the width of your shoulders determine your draw length. Basically, your personal draw length is the distance between the bowstring and the grip when you hold a bow at full draw, or pull the string all the way back to what is called your "anchor point" or just "anchor." Draw length is a specific personal measurement that will govern your bow selection. Do not confuse it with arrow length, because while there is a relation, arrows can be shorter or longer than your draw length.

You can be measured for draw length at any archery pro shop or you can get a friend to help. Bear makes an ultra-lightweight Draw Check Bow that is ideal for determining draw length. This thin fiberglass recurve is fitted with a yard-stick that is permanently attached to the string and the riser. You simply draw, hold and have a friend read the numbers from the scale on the yard-stick arrow. If a Draw Check Bow is not available, use a lightweight bow and nock an arrow onto its bowstring. Then, draw the bow. As you hold comfortably at full draw, have your friend mark the arrow directly above the pressure point (the "V" formed by your thumb and forefinger as you grip the bow) of the handle. This spot should be even with the center of the arrow rest hole (the rear hole if there are two) in the sight window of the bow.

Add 1 ¾ inches to that measurement to determine your draw length for a compound bow as specified by the manufacturing governing body that sets standards for this industry. (Formerly called the Archery Manufacturers and Merchants Organization or AMO it is now known as the ATA or Archery Trade Association.) So, if the measurement is 29 inches from

Archers without an Allen Wrench Set (Hex Wrench Set) in their backpack are looking for trouble if anything in their bow and accessory set-up loosens in the field. If you change your draw weight for tuning or just for comfort, you will need the proper hex wrench.

the string to the pressure point at full draw, your draw length – your true draw – would be 29 + 1 ³/₄ = 30 ³/₄ inches.

Most compound bows allow for some draw length adjustments – from 26 to 31 inches, for example on the

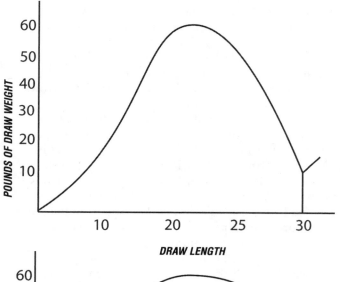

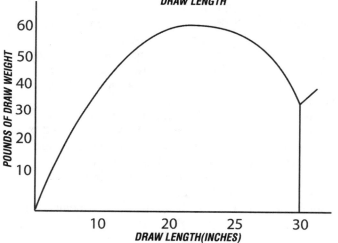

Force Draw Curves: A force draw curve (also called a "draw force curve") charts an inch of draw length (on the horizontal axis) against each pound of draw weight (on the vertical axis). The result is a visual representation of the way a bow "stacks" or stores kinetic energy and how much can be harnessed. In this respect, using standardized measurements of draw length and draw weight, bows can be compared and the "valley" or the point at which the archer reaches total let-off and begins to pull heavier weight can be charted. A force draw curve will show you how smoothly the bow pulls to peak weight by the steepness of the initial line, how long – by the horizontal length of the line at peak poundage – you must pull at peak weight before you reach full let-off and how steeply the bow lets off to its holding weight.

new Martin Onza II with Fury-X twin cams. You can usually make minor adjustments (+ ¼ inches or so) to draw length by changing the end of the bowstring from one post to another on your cam or cams or by moving the string spool from one position to another as on the Darton Storm with their modular PFC Single Cam System. Significant adjustments of more than a couple inches require you to install a different draw length module on the cam (a quick and easy job) or even to change cams, as cams come in different proportional sizes, but that is a more complex operation and usually requires the type bow press found in archery pro shops.

If your bow does not quite match your draw length, you can make additional adjustments by twisting or untwisting the string to change the draw length by up to ¼ inch. This is a more complex operation than changing a module or even a cam and should be performed with a bench-mounted bow press and, at least the first time you try it, with a certified bow mechanic. On compound bows with synthetic (rather than metal) cables, you can twist the cables tighter to increase draw length. A combination of twisting or untwisting the cables and strings gives you a virtually unlimited range of precise draw lengths. Keep in mind however that twisting the cables can throw a twin-cam bow out of tune, meaning, among other things, that the cams roll over unevenly. Some older style compound bows with metal cables have slotted harness attachments or yokes that allow for quarter-inch draw length changes. These kinds of adjustments will alter your draw weight as well as draw length. Lengthening the string increases draw weight while shortening the string reduces draw weight. It is exactly the opposite for lengthening and shortening the cables.

Reconsidering your draw length: Many archery coaches and pro shop owners believe the average archer would do well to reduce his draw length, because typically they are too long. Anyone beginning to shoot with fingers and then switching to a release, a low wrist grip and/or a string loop definitely needs to consider an appropriate drop in their draw length, as much as an inch to an inch and a half.

Canadian archery writer Tom Doyle believes today's archery instructors are systematically reducing their student's draw lengths and this actually helps them improve their accuracy. A shorter draw turns a shooter into the bow and target. It produces a more relaxed stance, opens up the distance between the shooter's chest and the string. For people wearing bulky cold weather clothing, this is a bonus. With the bow arm unlocked in this stance, another bonus is there's less stress on the elbow joint and tricep muscle.

If your draw length is too long, you must do at least one of the following to pull the string into the bow's valley: overextend your bow arm's elbow; push your shoulder unnaturally out toward the target; or anchor too far back away from the front of your face – sometimes to the point where the hand isn't even touching the face. Many archers with too long a draw length also take a stance that causes them to lean back away from the target. With these errors in form, an archer just cannot expect to shoot well?

FINDING A COMFORTABLE DRAW WEIGHT

Unless you are an inveterate shopper – and men with an avid pursuit such as archery sometimes are

Archers who try to draw too much weight are "over-bowed" and they are readily identified on the target range because with a grimace, they struggle to pull their bow to full draw, often lifting it well above the target as they do so. Being over-bowed will result in rapid fatigue of the muscles in your hands and arms that draw and hold steady. Drawing too much weight can eventually cause target panic, a situation where it becomes nearly impossible to place your sight on target and release

within the narrow confines of their avocation – archery is not about selecting a bow, buying equipment and getting gaga about camouflage patterns. Archery is about enjoying shooting the bow and arrow. Nevertheless, one of the parameters that govern your choice of a bow is peak draw weight, the maximum amount of pounds needed to draw the bow at any given setting.

Go to any shooting range and you will see archers (mostly men in their teens and early 20s) struggling to draw their bow. They exert extreme effort and this causes them to raise the bow over their head, grimace, grunt and sweat. If you have to raise a bow over your head for leverage when drawing, it is too heavy. If you cannot draw the string straight back to the side of your face without trembling or hunching your shoulders with the strain, you are trying to pull too much weight. It is macho to make a great shot, not draw a great weight. Reduce the draw weight on both limbs equally until you can easily draw straight back and then, as you improve in mechanics and perhaps strength, gradually ease the bow back toward a heavier draw weight if that is what you prefer.

It is impossible to come up with a precise formula for estimating your draw weight accurately, because comfortable draw weight varies according to each individual's physical build and strength. You ought to be able to draw your bow without significant difficulty, to hold your sights on target and pull the string straight back to your anchor without a lot of straining and shaking.

Shooting in a hunting situation is a lot different from competition shooting or practice on the range. Bowhunters used to sneer that competition archers "couldn't hit hair," but the rise of 3-D shooting has disproved that self-congratulatory phrase. As uncontrollable factors like fatigue, cold, buck fever and irritation at "things going wrong" take their toll on your body and your mind, it becomes increasingly difficult to draw your bow to its peak weight. Perhaps this is not so different from stepping up to a shooting stake on a hot day and trying to estimate yardage while you brush away mosquitoes. Anyway, if you have to strain to draw your bow when you are practicing, you may find that you cannot draw it at all when the pressure is on. The solution is to buy a bow with a draw weight you can easily handle under any circumstances.

A smooth draw is not the only reason to choose a bow with a given draw weight. Thousands of archers suffer chronic shoulder and elbow injuries, including tendonitis and bursitis. No one knows whether such ailments are caused by shooting bows with heavy draw weights over a period of years or whether heavy draw weights just aggravate a pre-existing condition. Maybe both. Certainly, these "overuse injuries" can be caused by repeatedly drawing a bow at any draw weight, but the added strain of heavy weights can irritate the problems significantly.

Drawing and holding very heavy bow weight can also contribute to target panic, the bane of many archers. (For a longer discussion of target panic and how it could affect your shooting, see the chapter on Release Aids.) A heavy draw weight bow, particularly one coupled with ultra-light or poorly spined arrows in a set-up tuned to extreme speeds rather than shooting comfort, sends harmful vibrations throughout a bow and your arm and elbow. Improvements in and changes to design and materials in modern bows and vibration dampening accessories have greatly reduced breakage and limb de-lamination problems, but the greater the stress on a bow, the greater the potential for damage. (That is a good reason to let the draw weight down if you will not be shooting for any significant length of

Properly supervised and instructed with a bow that fits, experience and research show that young people take quickly to archery. Remember to keep your instruction fun, but safe.

time.)

Modern compound bows that draw around 60 pounds are heavy enough for all North American game animals except perhaps for musk ox and the greater bears such as Kodiak, Polar and brown bears. Draw weights above 60 pounds may give your arrows a slightly flatter trajectory, a benefit at longer and unknown distances, but increasing weight does not significantly improve arrow penetration at a distance.

So, how do you determine your comfortable draw weight? You need to pull several bows of differing draw weights and choose one you can draw easily. If you can easily draw 70 pounds, then select a comparable bow, but most shooters are more comfortable in the 60-pound range. Remember that a bow that advertises a peak weight of 60 pounds, for instance, like the Buckmaster G2 from North American Archery Group, is fully adjustable from 50 to 60 pounds. So, if 60 pounds is a slight effort, you should back the bow down five to ten pounds and work your way to the point you feel comfortable. It is usually not recommended to back a bow down in weight beyond ten pounds because its efficiency begins to suffer.

Here is a recommendation by archery and hunting writer Bobby Worthington: "If you cannot sit flat on the floor, hold your bow straight out and draw it without straining, your draw weight is too heavy. If most arches would take five to seven pounds off their draw weight, they'd be amazed how steady their sight picture would become."

STEPS IN LEARNING TO SHOOT

Begin by facing your target and then turn your feet about 45 degrees to one side: counter-clockwise for a right-hander and clockwise for a left-hander. This is the classic "open stance." It offers several practical advantages both for hunting and competition. First, it helps move the bow and string slightly away from your arm and chest. This is doubly important because a few slaps of the string on your forearm can be enough to make a strong man squeal with pain. Second, if you are layering or wearing a down jacket on a cold day, the string is less likely to hang up on your clothes. If it does hang up on the zipper or some fold of clothing, you will not hit what you are aiming at.

The open stance allows hunting archers to shoot down from their treestand without bumping their leg against the bow's lower limb. The limb will naturally bend between your knees no matter how steep your shot angle becomes.

At some point in your shooting career, you may find yourself gravitating toward a more closed stance. This will give you more power as it aligns the bones, muscles and joints with the pull of the string, but it does have the disadvantage of bringing the bowstring close to your chest and clothing.

Whether you are a finger shooter or use a mechanical release aid, to achieve a good grouping of arrows around the bull's-eye consistently you must draw to the exact same spot on your face every time. You can touch your middle finger to the corner of your mouth or lock your index finger with a release under or along the side of your jaw. Establish an anchor point that aligns your eye with the string. If your eye is too far to either side, either left or right, your accuracy will suffer because you will be looking across your arrow and sights rather than at zero-angle.

Most accurate archers, whether they are hunters or competitors, use a string-mounted peep sight. A peep is essentially a black plastic blob with a small hole in it through which you look at your pins in reference to the target downrange. The peep forces a consistent anchor position because otherwise you could not see through it. To find the correct place on the string to mount your peep, close your eyes, draw your bow to anchor and then open your aiming eye. Have someone slide the peep down the string to your eye, never the other way around (trying to mount it too low will interfere with your center serving), and then serve it securely into place.

Grip your bow with a loose, relaxed hand. If you are drawing too much weight, this will be impossible. Go back to Step #1 and reduce your draw weight until you can draw without grimacing and grunting and gripping the bow with all your might. All that useless expended energy will only cause you to miss.

A wrist sling such as a Cavalier Ultra-Soft combined with a relaxed hand grip is an excellent performance characteristic, especially when you are shooting from a treestand. Relaxed, you can leave your fingers open or away from the bow riser as you draw and execute the shot. The sling is not there necessarily to catch the bow after you shoot, although it will. The purpose of the sling is to give you the confidence that you will not drop your bow and that confidence allows you to hold the bow in the fork of your thumb and forefinger without torquing it, even on (some would say, especially on) shot follow-through.

Aiming and follow-through are one step, one set of body and mind mechanics. Get on target the same way each time. Either bring your sight pins up and count the distance as you go or bring them from the side or top. It does not matter as long as you make the action repeatable, because if it is repeatable, it becomes more automatic and less error-prone. Then, when your pin is properly located on target, release the string or trigger your release smoothly and quickly. The longer you stay

at full draw with your pin on your target, the greater the chance that you will experience "target panic" or that you will begin to feel muscle fatigue. Draw, aim deliberately, breathe and shoot. Then, give yourself the luxury of a relaxed, but disciplined follow through. That means leaving your bow sight right on target until your arrow hits what you are aiming at or at least not consciously moving aside to look at the result. If you do this well, your arrow will always clear the set-up cleanly, no matter how excited you become. Your bow is naturally going to recoil or rebound following the shot, but that should not be a problem because the arrow is gone and … you are wearing a wrist sling.

If you "peek," twist your head immediately following release to see where your arrow hits, you will move the bow in a manner that is not conducive to good follow-through and as peeking gets to be a habit, your left-right accuracy will suffer.

Archer Michael Braden has written a 25-step "shot sequence" for releasing an arrow at a 3-D stake. This sequence may seem extraordinarily picky to bowhunters, but for 3-D competitors it is an excellent routine. If bowhunters could follow something similar ("Address the stake!" What is that all about?) under the stress of the moment, at least think through his shooting sequence during practice, more game would end up on the table than bounding away from an arrow stuck in a nearby tree.

1. Address (put your foot against) the stake or line.
2. Confirm the distance and select your pin or adjust your sight.
3. Check your stance.
4. Load and nock the arrow on your string.
5. Pick a spot with your binoculars.
6. Align your feet in relation to the target.
7. Hook the release on the string or the D-loop.
8. Place your hand in the grip. (This is a crucial Step #1 and must be done precisely, Michael says.)
9. Take a deep breath.
10. Lift and draw while watching the arrow.
11. Set initial tension against the wall of the bow's draw force curve.
12. Locate your primary anchor point by feel. (Crucial Step #2.)
13. Wrap your finger around the trigger and apply pre-load pressure.
14. Exhale breath.
15. Inhale about three-quarters of a breath.
16. Lift your head and lower your nose to touch the string.
17. Squint your left eye, center the scope inside the peep (Crucial Step #3.), level the bow and open the left eye.

18. Locate the desired point of impact through your scope.
19. Let the pin settle on the target.
20. Focus on the center of the spot (the last conscious effort) your effort is going to hit.
21. Begin the shot process by gradually pushing the pin into the target with the bow arm while pulling against the wall of the bow with the release arm. The force of the pull should be felt going straight back through the elbow of the release arm. This is a completely subconscious effort.
22. Maintain your aim while focusing on the center of the spot.
23. Be patient and wait for the shot process to fire the bow. (Crucial Step #4.)
24. Follow through.
25. If for any reason your focus is lost, let down and start the sequence over from the beginning.

While this may seem terribly tedious and too Zen-like for most of us pretty average bowhunters, remember that most 3-D competitors are

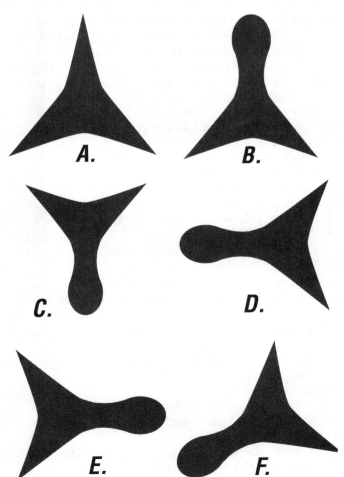

A.

B.

C.

D.

E.

F.

bowhunters, too!

TUNING YOUR BOW FOR ARROW FLIGHT

The most daunting aspect of archery is probably tuning your bow for effective arrow flight. While everyone understands that consistent arrow flight is highly desirable and most of us have read at least a couple articles in archery magazines about tuning, we do not believe that we can actually "tune" our own bow.

Tuning with feathers or vanes: The paper test is the most commonly used bow tuning test for archers using compound bows with release aids. (The same principles apply for bare shaft tuning.)

Use a picture frame style rack to firmly hold a sheet of 24-inch by 24-inch paper. Position the center of the paper about shoulder height. Make sure there is a target mat about 6 feet behind the paper to stop the arrows.

Stand approximately six to eight feet from the paper and shoot a fletched arrow through the center of the paper with the arrow at shoulder height (parallel to the floor).

Observe how the paper is torn. Tear (A) indicates correct arrow flight. The point and fletching enter the same hole. Tear (B) indicates a low nocking point. Correct by raising the nocking point. Tear (C) indicates a high nocking point or a vane clearance problem. Correct by lowering the nocking point. If the problem repeats, the disturbance is mot likely caused by lack of clearance. Tear (D) indicates a weak arrow spine or clearance problem for right-handed archers. Left-handed archers will have an opposite pattern. To correct, move the arrow rest in toward the bow riser or increase your peak weight or use a heavier arrow point or use a lighter string (a string with less strands) or use a weaker-spined arrow or try decreasing cushion plunger tension or using a weaker spring if you are shooting with a shoot-around rest. Tear (E) indicates a weak arrow spine or clearance problem for right-handed archers. Left-handed archers will have an opposite pattern. To correct try one or a combination of these procedures: decrease peak draw weight, decrease arrow point weight, increase bow string weight (more strands), move the arrow rest out away from the bow riser, use a stiffer-spined arrow, increase cushion plunger tension or use a stiffer spring on shoot-around rests. Tear (F) shows a combination of more than one flight disturbance. Use the procedures that apply to the tear pattern and combine the recommendations for correction, correcting the vertical pattern first, and then the horizontal.

There seems to be a mystery about bow tuning, perhaps an air of elitism as if the only people who could do it properly were professional archers or members of a secret society. This is certainly not the case. Anyone with a little time to tinker with their gear and perhaps a workbench and place to shoot can tune a bow. Regardless of all the technical jargon you hear about design elements in your bow, tuning for good shooting is not rocket science! Here are some tuning steps and ideas that will almost always work well for compound bows.

Your arrows are the most important elements in your shooting gear. Only a few of all the aluminum and carbon arrow shaft sizes made have the correct "spine" (think of this as the amount they flex when shot) to shoot well from your bow. You simply select proper arrow sizes –such as a 2117 size Chuck Adams' Signature XX78 Super Slam for an Easton aluminum shaft or a Beman ICS 340 size in Trebark camo – from an arrow manufacturer's shaft-selection chart by plugging in your personal data: draw weight, draw length and type of wheel or cam. It helps to know the type of bowstring material (from your bow owner's manual) and the weight of the broadhead or arrow point you plan to shoot. You certainly know whether you shoot with fingers or a mechanical release aid. After you purchase your arrows, spin them over rollers like those on the Arrow Inspector from Pine Ridge (the kitchen table will not do!) and never shoot any shaft-broadhead-nock combination that wobbles even slightly.

You will then need to find the right arrow rest. Finger shooters must use a side-control rest like the New Archery Products CenterRest Flipper or Cavalier Flipper rest. A finger-released arrow bends side-to-side as it leaves the bow, requiring left or right oscillation control. This horizontal porpoising is caused when the string leaves your fingertips in a semi-circular manner. By comparison, arrows shot with a mechanical release tend to oscillate vertically and require a launcher rest like Golden-Key Futura's TM-Hunter, QuickTune 3000 Micro, Golden Premier or Bodoodle PRO-Lite. A fall-away rest like Muzzy's Zero-Effect might also be an excellent choice if you use a release because it offers superior fletching clearance during the shot.

Your best string-release strategy is one that allows

Installing kisser buttons that touch the exact same spot on the lips and on the tip of the nose in addition to a served-in peep sight helps NFAA competitor Gene Goldacker focus on the essentials of good shooting form.

you to let the string go cleanly. How an arrow leaves the bowstring affects its down-range flight and penetration performance. For example, an arrow that attaches to the string underneath a clamp-on nocking point will not tune or shoot quite the same as one that is cradled within a tied-on release loop. Similarly, an arrow released by an archery using a high-friction finger release will not fly the same as one released by an archer who drops pressure from his top or bottom finger before he shoots.

In general, the best accuracy and easiest tune with a mechanical release comes from a soft, tied-on release loop or hard metal yoke on the string. Ask your archery pro shop about options currently available when you are ready. With fingers, the best shooters I know draw with three fingers and then relax the top or bottom finger pressure for a smooth, accurate two-finger release. For the cleanest finger release, use a tab, not a shooting glove.

Select your accessories and set up your bow before tuning. Any change you make to your bow or arrow setup can throw a monkey wrench into the tuning process. Attach your bowstring silencers, peep sight, kisser button, stabilizer, quiver, Limb Savers and any other accessories before you tune. Try to make a decision on a comfortable draw weight and tune the bow to that poundage. Finally, don't change the length or weight of your arrowhead after you finish your tune-up or you will need to review what you have just done.

To polish the tuning process, shoot through butcher paper or newspaper stretched between uprights or across a frame. The simplest paper setup is two arrow shafts jammed into the ground with paper alligator-clipped between them at all four corners. A large square of plywood with the center cut out works fine as does a good-sized picture-frame (or one built from boards).

Shoot your first arrow through the paper from about three feet away. The target on the other side needs to be at least three feet behind the paper or your arrow will hit and flip to the side before it exits the paper. This will result in a false paper tear.

Bare shaft tuning is the most reliable way to use a paper frame to figure out if your arrow is coming straight out of the bow. With no fletching to straighten the arrow's flight, the farther it travels, the more you can expect it to move in the direction and orientation it originally started when it left the bow.

Set the goal of tuning your setup so that a bare shaft will fly straight into the target at 20 yards (although you will not begin shooting at that distance). If you can do that, you can be comfortable assuming

that your fletched arrows will come out of the bow straight – assuming there's no fletch contact with your cables or arrow rest. If your arrow leaves the bow straight, the fletching will not have to work so hard to stabilize it and straighten out its flight. The minimal task remaining then is to keep the arrow on its original course. If you tune with a bare shaft first, arrow flight problems should disappear. Thereafter, you can put the issue of tuning aside and worry about something else, if you have to worry, but there is practically nothing else you can do you're your bow and arrow set-up to make it more accurate.

Before you begin bare-shaft tuning or any fine-tuning process, set the bow's basic adjustments as close as possible to "real" conditions: draw length and draw weight, install the D-loop and the silencers on the string, etc. Do not be concerned about getting them perfectly in place. Your bow surely is already set up well enough for bare-shaft tuning.

Here is another tip to make bare shaft tuning more effective: wrap duct tape around the arrows where fletching was removed until they weigh the same as your fletched arrows. Finally, do not mount broadheads on the bare shafts. While some archery engineers such as Mathews' Gary Simonds who is not a hunter think the concept is foolish, most tuning experts suggest that you use field points of the same weight as your broadheads. Their argument is simple. "They are available so why not eliminate one small tuning variable." That makes sense even to a non-engineer.

When you are ready to shoot, take your time. Think about your best form and with your bow set up for competition or hunting, shoot the bare shaft(s). Without moving from your position or stance, check to see how the arrows are sticking into the backstop. If the shafts are not sticking absolutely straight in, they did not leave the bow straight and some adjustments will be needed.

Begin by tuning your arrow nocks, either low or high. Look at the arrows from where you shot. If the arrows' nock ends are lower than the points where the arrows entered the backstop, your arrows are leaving the bow with the rear end low. You can fix this. Move the nock locator up on the string or else lower the arrow rest's launching platform. Either adjustment should have the same effect.

If the nock ends are too high in the backstop, adjust your nock locator in the opposite direction. If your string's brass nock locator is too low, the arrow's nock ends could very well kick up when they come off the rest, causing them to be very high in the target butt. This can falsely indicate that the string nock locator is too high.

Adjust the string nock locator up and down the string until the arrows are leaving the bow with the rear end neither high nor low but straight. Next, adjust for arrows leaving the bow with the nock end to the left or right. If the nock ends are to the left or right of the entry hole in the backstop, move the bow's center shot by moving the arrow rest to the left or right. Continue shooting and moving the rest until the bare shaft's nock is on the same vertical line left and right as the entry hole.

Some shooters will need to adjust the bow cast to the arrow spine difference. This will be necessary if, while tuning, you have to move your center shot away from your power stroke more than 1/4 inch to straighten shafts hitting severely left or right of the nocks. Changing arrow point weight might correct the problem by changing your arrow's spine, but if that isn't sufficient, you might need to change draw weight or use a differently spined arrow.

After you have tuned your shafts to enter straight into the backstop at three to five yards, shoot at 10 and 20 yards. You might once again see, as you move back, that you need to do some additional tweaking of your set-up. If your shafts were a little off at six yards, they will be off farther at 20 yards.

At 20 yards, the force of gravity will begin working on your broadheads so you should not tune for the height of the arrow nock to be exactly the same height as the arrow's entry hole in the backstop.

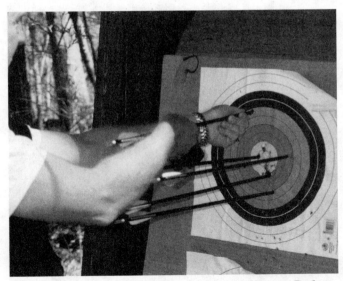

Numbering your arrows, as trophy bowhunter Dale Larson recommends, is a good way to find the one that consistently flies erratically. Information then action. Because arrows are expensive, you can probably remedy this "flyer" by replacing the nock or checking the alignment of point and nock, and even changing cock feather.

Because the arrowpoint is heavier and there is no fletching to raise it when you are bare-shaft tuning, the point gradually will pull the front end down. The entry hole normally will be lower than the shaft's nock by a couple of inches at around 20 yards.

In the end, tuning is nothing more complicated than moving your arrow rest and adjusting your nocking point. When an arrow tears a hole larger than the diameter of the broadhead, shaft and vanes, you will want to make some adjustments. Traditionally, a perfectly tuned bow is achieved when your arrows slice through the paper and leave what is known as "bullet holes" – holes shaped like a "Y" for three-vane arrows and three-blade broadheads or an "X" for four-vane arrows. These holes will not be any larger than the broadhead and fletching, with no tear at all. Typically, all you see is the neatly cut "footprint" of the broadhead blades and vanes. But, do not expect this result immediately.

Here is how to begin making adjustments based on the paper-tune results. If your arrows tear tail-high or tail-low, move the nocking point or release loop on the bowstring the opposite direction from the tear. If you cannot tell where the broadhead enters compared to the vanes and nock, smear a little lipstick on the tip of the broadhead. This should clearly indicate the arrow entry point on subsequent shots.

If your arrows tear tail-right or tail-left, move the arrow rest in the same direction as the tear. For a tail-right tear, for example, move the arrow rest to the right.

Adjust both the nocking point and the rest to deal with "combination" tears. For example, for a tail-high and tail-right tear, move the nocking point down and the arrow rest to the right. Then, shoot again and continue tweaking rest and nock position as needed. The same tuning instructions apply to right-handed and left-handed shooters.

If your arrows do not respond with gradual tuning adjustments from three feet away, you may have a couple readily identifiable and easily "fixable" problems: either your arrow is incorrectly spined and/or your arrow's vanes might be hitting your arrow rest when you release.

To check a collision problem, dust an arrow's vanes with talcum powder or common foot powder and shoot the arrow into the target again, but without the paper. Scuffs in the powder or residue on the rest will let you know if and where you have a problem with rest clearance. Rotate your arrow nocks or try a different rest to cure vane-to-rest interference.

Fall-away rests like those from Trophy Taker are becoming increasingly popular with finger and release shooters. These rests are designed to prevent any potential collision and the loss of a perfect tune. As a last resort curing rest-vane interference, try shooting with feathers instead of plastic vanes. Feathers are fragile. They are also a little noisy and prone to wilt in damp weather, but they do flatten on contact with any rest, thereby preventing problems.

After you are tuned-up with three-foot shots, step back to ten feet and repeat the paper-tune process. A little more tweaking of your rest and nock might be required to further refine the tune and finally, shoot through the paper at 20 feet. Once you are shooting bullet holes from all three ranges, your arrows will be flying true and remember that the purpose of going through all this effort is to hit what you are shooting at consistently.

SPECIAL TUNING DIFFICULTIES

Are there bows that cannot be tuned? Generally, the answer has to be "No," but in specific cases because archery is such an individual sport and equipment needs to be personally fitted to each shooter's physique and style, there will, every now and then, be a bow that could give a team of engineers fits.

Sometimes no matter what you do, it seems like your bow is designed like your three-wood on a par five hole with a fickle cross wind. No matter how you approach, it feels like it is impossible to hit the fairway for any distance. You check the cams for lean and then make sure your cable guard is as close as it can be set to give you fletching clearance and minimal side torque. These days, cam lean is something that an archer serious about pinpoint shooting will think about, because cams have become much larger. Or say the arrow has a consistently inconsistent left-right impact point and your buddy, who watches you shoot, swears you are not "peeking."

There are some things you cannot fix. A few risers have been produced that, coupled with the highest possible bow weight, will flex slightly. This can defeat any tuning effort except turning the weight down or replacing the handle. But how would you know if this is happening? It may be visible by an observer paying close attention or you may notice a manufacturer's Technical Bulletin on the Internet or a printed Product

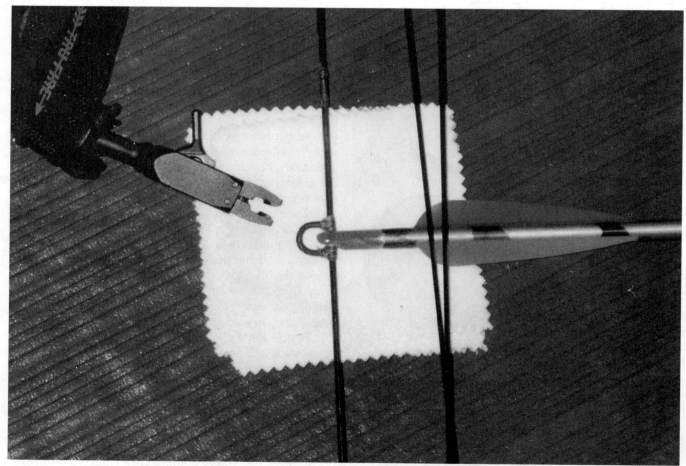

Installing a D-loop on the bowstring will help keep you from applying torque to the string with your release.

Recall notice in an archery or hunting magazine. This is rare however and chances are, it will never happen to you.

If your bow is not equipped with a split-harness system, you may want to take it to a qualified archery shop to discuss an installation. It is not expensive and a split-harness is supposed to help equalize the pressure on either side of the limb tip. If something there is out of balance or inappropriately assembled, this can definitely help. On twin-cam bows, a split-harness will stabilize both the top and bottom limbs. On one-cam bows, just the top limb with the idler wheel will be helped. These days, if your bow is new or even relatively new, it will come with a split harness system installed.

What about worn bushings? For archers who shoot a great deal – a great deal – this could eventually become a problem. You can check by having a pro shop put your bow in a bench-mounted bow press and take the pressure off the strings and cables. Try wiggling the cam or cams. If they wiggle "a lot" – obviously this is a judgment call, but movement of $1/8$-inch in either direction is significant – you can replace the bushings for a good, tight fit.

It never hurts to have a cushion plunger or arrow rest that incorporates a cushion plunger installed if you are shooting erratically. The cushion plunger, normally a feature of finger shooter's rests, provides padding for arrows that may not be leaving the bow straight. It helps modulate or cushion this movement.

If all else fails, if the pro shop eventually reaches the end of its patience, if paper tuning just seems to make everything worse, contact the manufacturer. A bow that cannot be tuned is like a car that will not drive forward. You can drive it only in reverse, but surprises will abound at every turn in the road. An un-tunable bow is extremely rare, but when it happens, you will not be able to live with it.

Now, Forget About Bow Tuning

Many archers seem discouraged with shooting the bow and arrow because frankly, they spend too much time worrying about paper tuning and cam lean and brace height and centershot and properly spined arrows. For most of us, hitting a pie plate consistently at 20 yards is just fine … really. It IS good enough to hunt with that level of accuracy and if you are exacting with your shot selection, you WILL often be successful. Of course, we need to be conscious of the ethics of taking the life of an animal, but archery games are supposed to be fun. We hunt because we love to hunt, not because we love to take an animal's life and whether it is a "game" or not … depends on your point of view.

Competition – 3-D, NFAA and FITA – is different. In those games, pinpoint accuracy is how you define success, how you measure yourself against the competition and it is only natural to worry about the most microscopic aspects of tuning and shooting.

It is a widely-accepted rule that archers have trouble hitting what they are shooting at, whether it is a deer, a 3-D critter or a painted gold circle on a target. Perhaps the primary problem with accuracy is that we spend too much time worrying about something called "tuning" and not enough time just getting outside and having fun.

It may amaze or puzzle you to understand that virtually any adult bow sold today is capable of better accuracy than is the person shooting it. So here is a rule of thumb for bow buying and accuracy: buy the bow you like, the one that feels good to you, one you will be proud to shoot and, when you being to tune it up and put on accessories, expect that – like Michaelangelo freeing his masterpieces from the raw stone – you will find a level of accuracy that you are comfortable with and go with it. Otherwise, the whole bow tuning issue can drive you to distraction and even kill your enjoyment for the sport. After all, archery is not about the bow and not even about precision, pinpoint shooting, it is about you the archer.

Tuning a bow has less effect on your shooting accuracy than practice and a consistent performance agenda. Pro shops will admit that you can change your bow's tiller by as much as four to six pounds on either limb and still shoot excellent, bull's eye groups on their range. Archery experts such as engineering writer Norbert Mullaney and pro shop owner and technical subject writer Emery Loiselle have checked this fact with their shooting machines and found that it is true enough although they do not recommend putting such a strain on your bow. So, basically you can quit worrying about the old argument that, if your limbs are unbalanced they will fight each other, thus disrupting level nock point travel in a significant manner because they will not be affixed to the riser at the same angle (or with the same weight). Measure your tiller, get the poundage at the limb bolts close and then forget about "tiller."

Wheel or cam "timing" is about the same. Timing or wheel roll-over should be close (or set at least initially to the manufacturer's recommendations) on a twin-cam bow, but this is a virtual irrelevancy on a one-cam bow. But all else being equal, if your wheel timing is the same on each shot, your arrows will hit in the same pattern. You can change centershot up to almost 1/2 inch and, with the bow in a shooting machine it will fling arrows into the same holes at 20 yards as it did before you made the change.

Dale Larson is a trophy bowhunter and a skilled craftsman when it comes to setting up a bow for precision arrow flight. Dale numbers his arrows and, among other things in the tuning process, is careful to note any arrow that consistently flies outside the grouping. This helps him identify and correct specific problems … and, with trophy whitetails like this to his credit, he apparently has few specific problems with tuning.

Archery gear gurus like Bobby Worthington say that "the string's nocking point is more crucial to accuracy than the other adjustment." Worthington writes that he has "often moved a nocking point up the bowstring 1/8 inch and greatly improved an archer's accuracy. I then might move it another 1/2 inch with no further effect." This defies conventional tuning wisdom.

For accurate shooting, you want to pay attention to two straight-forward ideas: select the bow that is right for you and then help your arrows leave the bow straight when you release the string.

For straight shooting, begin with straight, matched arrows. Spin check and weigh your arrows either before the season or before a major tournament. Spin checkers are not expensive and they have multiple uses from checking straightness, nock and broadhead alignment, and even cresting your arrows. Unless you want to buy your own grain scale from Martin or Apple Archery, any well-stocked pro shop can help

you weigh your arrows and components. First, spin your arrows with no point or nock attached to make sure the shaft is straight. Then, progressively add elements such as fletching or cresting, the nock, the insert and then your points or broadheads. It is a progressive system, but it is a logical system and it almost takes more time to write and read about it than it does to do it. It is easy to heat the insert glue in an aluminum arrow and turn the point until the arrow spins straight. (Do not overheat the shaft; heat it only enough to loosen the insert. Watch out here, because many composite shafts cannot be heated like this. Check with the manufacturer first.)

Note that not every arrow you spin will prove to be straight or well balanced, especially after a few practice sessions, pulling your arrows out of tight foam targets or uneven hay bales. Discard them or take them to a pro shop to be professionally straightened. Even then, you should mark these as strictly practice arrows and when you need to drill what you are shooting at,

Archery coach and bowhunter Terry Wunderle says the mental side of archery is extremely important, perhaps as important as the equipment and physical attributes of the archer.

We call it "bow tuning," but it is just as much "arrow tuning," because the whole point is to have your arrows hit what you are aiming at. A bow square is useful in practically all steps of the tuning process.

use your straightest and most balanced arrows.

The broadheads and arrow points you add to your arrow must be straight with the shaft. Do not be concerned about your broadheads being aligned with your fletching. That idea, truly, is irrelevant in spite of what some manufacturers are selling in their advertising.

With broadhead-tipped arrows, you do want to get weight as close as possible. Whereas some professional archers argue that a "two-grain weight difference between arrows will cause a three-inch difference on impact point at 50 yards" we have to ask if this matters. If you are shooting the length of a football

field in FITA competition or hunting skittish caribou on the open tundra, perhaps the answer is "Yes." Otherwise, the answer is certainly, "No."

The bow/arrow setup must be tuned so the arrow consistently comes out on a straight path in the direction the bow is pointing. Yes, the arrow will be flexing or oscillating as it leaves the bow, but it should be flexing along a straight path in the direction the bow is pointing. When the flexing ends, the arrow will be headed straight toward the point of aim.

Note that we are referring to your arrow's being straight when it leaves the bow, not downrange after the fletching has straightened it. If the arrow leaves the bow in a crooked manner and the fletching must move the shaft back and forth to correct it, the shaft might no longer be headed exactly toward the aiming point, and it will certainly lose velocity and kinetic energy. The fletching should not have to horse the arrow around to straighten its flight, only keep it on the straight path it started on.

If you are like most archers, you will spend some time tuning up your bow, hitting a paper plate consistently out to 40 yards and then, just as you are feeling confident and hunting season begins in a few days, you realize your broadheads do not hit the target anywhere close to the same spot as your field points. In fact, they are only consistent in the erratic nature of their flight. With less than a week to the season's opening day, you are frantic. Take a few minutes – yes, again – to paper tune. Arrows that do not leave your bow straight probably cause this problem. Broadhead blades have a wider surface than a field point (which has virtually none and which most archers shoot regularly before a hunting season). Consequently, if the arrow begins its flight crooked, your broadheads will tug against the directional stability of your fletching. The broadhead (even a small, vented blade like the Muzzy 100 grain three-blade) will move the arrow more in the direction it starts before the fletching can straighten it.

Once arrows leave your bow straight, provided the

broadheads are properly aligned with your shaft, you will no longer need to switch to broadheads before the season to adjust your sights. Both broadheads and field points now will impact at the same spot.

Shooting form problems or essential bow set-up cause some shooters to pull their hair out during the tuning and sighting-in process. If you twist the bow, for instance, your arrows will not begin their flight straight. If you shoot a super fast bow with arrows that are improperly spined for your draw weight, you could even have problems with bare-shaft flight. But, with a little attention or perhaps some coaching, most archers can adjust their set-ups so arrows will leave the bow just fine.

Five elements of set-up may (some would say "will") greatly simplify bow tuning, improve arrow flight and, ultimately, your accuracy:

1. Install a D-loop on the bowstring behind your arrow. This inexpensive device, which can be made from string or metal, lets you release the string from directly behind your arrow. When a D-loop is used, you will not twist the string or pre-load the arrow to cause the arrow to leave the plane of the bow in a crooked manner.

2. Consider switching a fall-away arrow rest. A fall-away rest is designed to hold the shaft in position for the first few inches of travel – most of the good ones are adjustable for length of travel – and then drop away before the back end of the shaft and its fletching reach it. These rests typically use the forward movement of the cable guard or the downward movement of the buss cable to move the rest out of the arrow's path. These rests are especially useful if you shoot large, helical fletching. Finger shooters will have very little trouble, because normal left-right arrow flex should move the fletched end of the shaft out and away from the riser.

3. If you are shooting aluminum arrows, try carbon or carbon-composite arrows. Carbon shafts are not as critical to the cast of the bow and will generally fly straighter from a greater variety of setups than aluminum arrows.

4. If you are a finger shooter, it is time to try a release aid. Every testimonial says that you will significantly improve your accuracy with a release. There are several styles of string-holding jaws – double or single calipers, rope, bars or levers, ball bearings – and all will work just fine. There is no evidence that any difference results from one style or another. Typically, however, rope releases are preferred in competition and almost any other style in bowhunting, because it takes a little more manual dexterity to hook a rope release and, under the pressure of a shot at a big game animal, this can become an almost impossible task.

5. Do not buy into the movement to light, mass weight bows. It has been something of a well-guarded secret among competition archers that a heavier bow – heavier mass weight, that is not draw weight – results in a steadier sight picture and tighter groups. If your bow is light, it will feel good as you carry it to your deer stand; however, it also will float around as you try to aim. If your bow is light and you are struggling with accuracy, consider mounting a heavier stabilizer, but try to get that weight close to the riser or perhaps with a set of "V" bars, behind it.

MORE TUNING TIPS
NUMBER YOUR ARROWS

Kansas trophy bowhunter Dale Larson suggests that, if you are having any tuning or arrow flight difficulties, you might try numbering each of your arrows and then shooting that numbered arrow at its own target. This practice works for him.

"This will eliminate a lot of guesswork in identifying the 'flyers,'" he says. "Arrows that are not hitting their respective targets might be corrected by simply rotating the nock to another cock feather or realigning the broadhead or insert."

Broadhead alignment is easily checked with a set of rollers or an arrow straightener with rollers. Simply position the tip of the broadhead on a reference line and turn the arrow on the rollers. Even the smallest alignment problems are noticeable.

Another of Dale's tips is to put a strip of masking tape on his bow square, the one he carries in his tool box on hunting trips. He records his bow and accessory settings (nock point height above center, peep sight position, sight and rest positions) on the strip so that, if something disastrous happens when he is bowhunting moose in Maine, he has a complete record of settings available to set up his back-up bow.

Several products are available to help you inspect your arrows for straightness. Apple Archery makes two inexpensive arrow checkers. Their Arrow Inspector helps you visually check your arrow's shaft straightness, nock alignment, vane and feather balance and broadhead balance and alignment. They also have a more serious version called their Pro Series Arrow Straightener with smooth, nylon arrow rollers and a precision indicator gauge that lets you check and straighten minor problems with your aluminum arrows. Of course, this straightener and the virtually identical instrument from Arizona Archery are useless with carbon shafts except as a spin tester for broadhead and nock tuning. If you are serious about archery, you would do well to invest in one of the less expensive spin checkers from Apple and let your neighborhood pro shop buy the expensive arrow straighteners for frequent everyday use.

Game Tracker makes a 6 ¼-inch aluminum bow square with dual clips for precise nocking point measurement and positioning. It works without having to move or remove any other bowstring accessories (peep, nock point locator, silencing whiskers, etc.) that may be in place. The spring steel clips will hold the square in place while you make any necessary adjustments. The bow square is also useful for setting tiller and nocking point. BPE builds a unique mini-square complete with a built-in 5/16" nock that screws into the arrow point insert and is useful for an instant visual check of your arrow nock in relation to the nock locator on the string. This one is especially handy for a day pack.

Tune for Centershot

World class archery coach and bowhunter Terry Wunderle has suggested an easy and interesting way to use your arrow rest to tune for centershot. "Shoot at a dot from 10 yards," he says, "then leave those arrows in the target and shoot at the same dot from 35 yards using the same sight pin. The arrows will of course hit low. Now, if the low arrows are left of a perpendicular line from the top arrows, move the rest to the right. If the low arrows are to the right, move the rest to the left. Repeat the process until the bottom group is directly below the top group."

Golden Key-Futura makes a popular and very specific tool for centershot determination called its TruCenter Gauge. "For many years, archers have been eye-balling centershot," says Golden Key's Freddy Troncoso, "but our TruCenter Gauge does the work for you."

The Game Tracker EZ CenterShot Tuning Tool is quite different from the Golden Key tool. Game Tracker's mounts to the hex key of your bow's limb bolts and suspends a small gauge on top of your arrow for calibrated adjustments.

Broadhead Tuning

With more than 50 years of archery hunting, competition and coaching experience, archery coach Terry Wunderle suggests that you select six matched and fletched arrows for broadhead tuning. Equip three of them with field points and three with the broadheads you will be shooting in the field. "Shoot each broadhead at a separate dot," he says, "then shoot a field point at each dot. This is a process of adjusting your nocking point and draw weight so your broadheads hit in the same place as your field points."

There are some general parameters to keep in mind when you begin fine tuning with this shot-by-shot method. If the broadheads hit high, Terry says, move the nock point up a little and try again. If they hit low, move the nock point down. If the broadhead hits directly left or right of the field point, adjust the weight of the bow. If the broadhead is to the right, decrease draw weight. If it is to the left, increase it. "It won't hurt arrow flight if the broadhead is a bit to the left side," Terry says, "but if it's to the right, it will certainly affect your grouping."

Several tools are available to help move your nock point without damaging your string or crimping the nock point. Saunders makes a set of pliers specifically designed for putting a nock point locator on your string. These pliers have two hole (or cavity) sizes for smooth crimping of different size nocks. TruFire's E-Z Pliers let you to remove or loosen the nock point without damaging the serving and or the nock. Unless it becomes scarred in the tuning process, you can then reuse the same nock a number of times.

The necessary tool in every archer's tool kit is a Bear Hex Wrench Set with nine hex keys (or Allen wrenches) that can be positioned at any angle. Although the steel is not especially hard and the keys are prone to strip their angled edges against the hex-slots in ultra-hard accessories (or even your bow's limb bolts), they fit most archery accessories. The Fletcher Field Tool has eight hex keys, a flat blade and Phillips blade screwdriver, an open-end adjustable wrench and a three-blade broadhead wrench.

TODAY'S COMPOUND BOWS

"It was only a few years ago that the compound bow was the ugly duckling of archery," Emery Loiselle wrote in his 1976 edition (since updated) of *Doctor Your Own Compound Bow*. "Being so radically different from the conventional recurve, archers shied away from the intricate appearing mechanism of the compound. Its appearance is also lacking in aesthetic appeal. Then again, archers like most people are leary (sic) of something too new."

Most North American archers shoot compound bows. We tend to think of compounds as the normal kind of bows. The regular kind. You know, Bows! Nevertheless, a highly vocal, but significant minority still enjoy the challenge, aesthetic appeal and perhaps the oddity of being different of doing archery "the hard way" with more traditional style recurves and longbows. Like Howard Hill or Fred Bear or Glenn St. Charles. We will discuss traditional equipment in a later chapter.

There is a distinctive difference between compound bows, bows that use cams and cable linkages to reduce the effort needed to pull the string to full draw and hold it there while you sight at your target, and all other bows. This reduced effort is called let-off. It allows you to hold a compound at your anchor at full draw to aim much longer than you could hold a longbow or a recurve that do not have let-off.

So, here is essentially how a compound bow works. Let's say your bow is set up at 65-pound draw weight and has cams that give you 75 percent let-off. That means you need to pull the string to 65 pounds, but then the cam or cams roll over and you are left holding only 75 percent of 65 pounds or 16 1/4 pounds at what is called full draw. Most young archers can hold 16 1/4 pounds and adults should be able to hold that weight for some time while they steady their breathing, select the proper sight pin and slowly, inexorably squeeze the trigger of their release aid. Certainly, you must pull through the peak weight of 65 pounds, but this normally takes only a moment before

Emery Loiselle has been writing about archery equipment for more than 35 years and bowhunting for a half century. Emery built the target bow in the photo almost 50 years ago and equipped it with a swiveling grip to reduce torque. His wife and partner in their pro shop, Eryleen Archery, eventually won a Massachusetts Field Archery championship with it.

you reach full draw and peak let-off.

On the other hand, to pull and hold your 65 pound recurve at full draw takes a full 65 pounds of effort. There is no let-off with recurves or longbows and holding a drawn bow at 65 pounds for any length of time while maintaining a decent sight picture is a very difficult task. Most traditional shooters have very little pause between the time they reach full draw and the time they release their arrow.

Since the significant difference between compounds and other bows is the eccentric, cabling and let-off arrangement, we will discuss that engineering marvel first.

The eccentrics or cams or wheels attached to the limb tips of a compound bow act like pulleys. They allow you to hold a compound at full draw using less force than the bow's rated draw weight. This reduction in draw force is determined by the design of the cam or cams. Not very many years ago, 33 percent let-off was standard and 50 percent let-off was thought of as high, as the maximum for a bow's best shooting properties. Designs have improved. Now, bows with a let-off as high as 80 and 85 percent are now common.

"Maximum arrow speed or higher break-off – bows with less let-off store more energy than identical bows with a larger percentage of relaxation – at the expense of having to hold more weight at full draw. Choose a Tamerlane or Alaskan with 33 percent let-off to gain feet per second in arrow travel, or a Polar LTD or Whitetail Hunter with 50 percent let-off for the ease of holding on target at full draw for a longer period of time." Bear Archery Catalog 1977.

When you are considering the purchase of a compound bow, you should be aware that some states, lobbied by advocates in the traditional archery

Unlike a compound bow, a recurve does not have cams or cables. Consequently, there is no let-off and at full draw, you are holding 100 percent of the recurve's draw weight. This deflex riser Hoyt Gold Medalist has a 25-inch die-cast magnesium alloy riser and you can change grips to match your shooting style.

With a slightly reflex riser, the Golden Eagle Raptor has the look of a "conventional" compound bow. The machined OneCam has 65 percent let-off. So, with a draw weight of 65 pounds, when you pull the cams over to full draw you end up only holding 23 pounds.

community, have considered limitations on let-off in the same manner that they have considered limiting electronic shooting and hunting aids. This outspoken minority of archers has successfully lobbied the Pope & Young Club, a private archery-only big game record-keeping club, to limit trophy entries to bows taken with no more than 65 percent let-off. That club's big brother however, the prestigious Boone & Crockett Club, has no such restriction and it is rapidly becoming home to many archery trophies. While its thresholds for entering big game trophies are higher, the Boone & Crockett Club's scoring system is the recognized authority for most other clubs.

As a group, you can visualize compound bows by thinking about the eccentrics or wheels (We will generally refer to them as cams.) around which the bowstring and cables are wrapped and attached. For 20 years, the dominant compound bow design featured two irregularly shaped cams each machined or molded to mirror the other. This twin-cam design has gradually fallen out of popularity. Since the early '90s as Matt McPherson's personal one-cam bow revolution gained momentum and designers worked out the kinks in one-cam performance: initial one-cam bow speed was relatively slow and nock travel – after release you want the nock to travel forward in a straight line – was inconsistent. One-cam shooting systems have a single, eccentrically shaped machined cam on the bottom limb and a perfectly round, balance wheel, called an idler, on the top limb. All major compound bow manufacturers offer bows in one-cam versions except for HoytUSA's 2003 bow line-up which features TEC bows only with their unique "Cam and ?" Performance System. (Examining the bow company catalogs for 2003, it is curious that twin-cam designs are quietly sneaking back into their line-up. Either there are new cost-benefit reasons – which would be trumpeted in their advertising and we have so far failed to notice – or archery manufacturers are simply looking for ways to avoid paying the one-cam inventor's tariff.)

The most attractive feature of single cam bows is that "timing" or synchronizing wheel rollover is eliminated because there is only one cam. A one-cam bow cannot go out of time with itself. With twin-cam bows, cams have to be roughly in-sync to prevent the nock point from moving forward in a jerky and uneven manner. On out of sync bows, the nock point locator can be charted moving forward in a series of hills and valleys through the power stroke. This, obviously, provides less than excellent propulsion to your arrow, which then flies erratically. (The function of the idler on the top limb by the way is not to just provide a rolling surface with minimal friction, although that is important, but with its twin grooves or string tracks it is supposed to help insure a balanced shot and straight-line nock and arrow travel.)

When you look over the new bow offerings, whether you are thinking of purchasing from a specialized archery pro shop or a sporting goods store with an archery department, you will normally be looking at a one-cam bow. It has not always been like that, however. One-cam bows have only recently supplanted two-cam or twin-cam bows in popularity and there is some evidence that two-cam bows are on the way back.

Whether you are hunting (or just practicing) from a ground blind or a treestand, stalking through the deer woods or hiking toward the high elk meadows, several trends in modern compound bow design will be beneficial: faster arrows, less shock and vibration and shorter axle-to-axle lengths.

Why then do you visit your local mass merchant and find two-cam bows in boxes on their shelves when most of your buddies bought a one-cam bow from a sporting goods store? The answer lies in two functions of mass merchants and one idea pounded home through the archery press during the past ten years. A mass merchant delivers a huge volume of goods effectively, but at very low prices. Service is not a mass merchant's specialty and archery is very hands-on; for young or novice archers to shoot effectively, they need lots of coaching and servicing. Because twin-cam bows have gradually fallen out of favor (demand has declined), the price a manufacturer can command for them has dipped. Ergo the usefulness of the mass merchant.

Over a corresponding time, the late 1980s and early 1990s, the general archery and shooting sports press has become much more equipment oriented and much less "let's have fun" oriented. Some would argue that the gear emphasis supplanting the experience emphasis is a blatant attempt to wring more advertising revenues out of the manufacturing community. To do this, popular magazines have become filled with articles on tuning and timing, with new equipment suggestions and analyses of equipment styles, all designed to do the same thing. Much of the material is simply lightly warmed-over press releases from manufacturers. We, as a community of archers, have become convinced that archery is more about learning about the spine of an arrow than it is about enjoying the limited time we have available in the field.

So wherever you buy, when you study the two-cam

Archery equipment is not "one size fits all." It needs to be fitted to your specific physical dimensions and strengths. A good relationship with an area archery pro shop will always result in better shooting and greater satisfaction.

compounds, be aware that there are three different wheel styles. Twenty-five years ago, manufacturers built bows with precisely round wheels and offset the axle holes from the center to give you let-off. By the mid to late 1980s round wheels were largely supplanted – except on entry-level compounds – by more sophisticated, oblong wheels often having dramatic cutouts. Today, we refer to them generally as cams. The outer rim of a cam has two tracks – one for your bowstring and the other for your cable. Around any campfire, you will be able to describe your bow as having a soft, medium or hard cam, depending on its shape and expected performance, and you will be understood.

SOFT CAMS: These cams are often referred to as energy wheels. They feature a rounded lobe over which the bowstring travels and a smooth, but irregularly shaped lobe for the cable. On energy wheels, the rounded string lobe is what gives you the smooth, easy pull. The oval cable lobe allows you to coerce more speed and striking power out of your bow than a fully rounded lobe. According to archery engineering expert Norb Mullaney, soft cams store about 1 foot-pound (ft-lb) of energy for each pound of draw weight you pull and hold. This means a bow that is drawing 70 pounds stores about 70 ft-lbs of kinetic energy. That is enough to win 3-D competitions and to hunt big game.

MEDIUM CAMS: Both the string and the cable sides of these cams have oval lobes. These are more dynamic cams, but they still allow a relatively smooth draw. Medium cams give you more energy storage and more speed than energy wheels. Mullaney says that as a general rule, medium cams store approximately 1 1/4 ft-lb of energy for each pound of peak weight you draw. Consequently, your 70-pound bow stores 87.5 ft-lbs or so of energy.

HARD CAMS: Hard cams may also be known as hatchet cams because they have a severely elliptical shape or lobe on both the bowstring and cable sides. Archery expert Mullaney says these cams store as much as 1 1/2 ft-lbs of energy per pound of peak draw weight if everything is configured properly. So, your 70-pound draw weight bow can potentially store more than 100 ft-lbs of energy. Twin-cam bows built with two hatchet cams can be very fast … and can also be very hard to manage, so they are not recommended for beginners.

THE DRAW FORCE CURVE

"The Compound Bow is a major change in one of Man's oldest sports. Unlike the conventional bow, which increases in weight as you draw back the string, the Compound Bow reaches its heaviest draw, or peak weight, shortly after you start to pull back the string and then relaxes to a much lighter weight to hold at full draw. This allows you to hold longer at full draw to take the best shot while bowhunting and provides for less muscle fatigue when target or field shooting." Bear Archery Catalog 1977.

An engineering drawing called a draw force curve (sometimes referred to as a force draw curve, but either way it means the same thing) gives a pictorial representation of one hard fact and three implementing actions. The fact is the total stored energy in a compound bow's set-up from rest to full draw and even beyond. The actions are: the increasing muscle strength you will need as you pull toward full draw; how long you must pull the bow at its full weight or at your chosen draw weight; and how rapidly the bow lets off and how much.

Upon first inspection, the draw force curve is a simple plot on the horizontal X-axis of "inches of draw length" against "pounds of draw weight" on the vertical Y-axis. The area beneath that curve (and you can construct a draw force curve for a recurve, a longbow or a crossbow) is the total stored energy or foot-pounds (ft-lbs) that could possibly be sunk into your arrow when you shoot. No bow transmits 100 percent of its stored energy to the arrow, but the more efficient your set-up, the greater will be the percentage of energy that is transferred and the greater your arrow's striking power.

The effort required to draw a bow like the PSE Beast with Synergy Pro cams (which are essentially energy wheels or soft cams) builds gradually, peaks sharply and then slides gradually into the "valley," the point where the holding weight is least or let-off is maximized. World-renowned archery trick shot artist Bob Markworth shoots a bow with this style soft cam because it is easy for him to manage when he is shooting balloons off his assistant's head!

Curiously, you can usually draw a compound bow – single cam or twin-cam – beyond its valley, but this is not recommended. Pulling up the other side of the valley or against "the wall" as it is called causes the bow to shoot inefficiently as thrust against your arrow increases, then decreases and finally increases again before it leaves the string. You can imagine how this affects arrow flight.

With hard cams such as the Centerfire on the PSE Nitro, your drawing effort will increase sharply, extend perhaps for a dozen inches at peak weight, and then drop rapidly into a short, steep valley. Unlike the Beast with soft cams that drop you smoothly into the valley, if you are unused to shooting a hard cam, you will feel

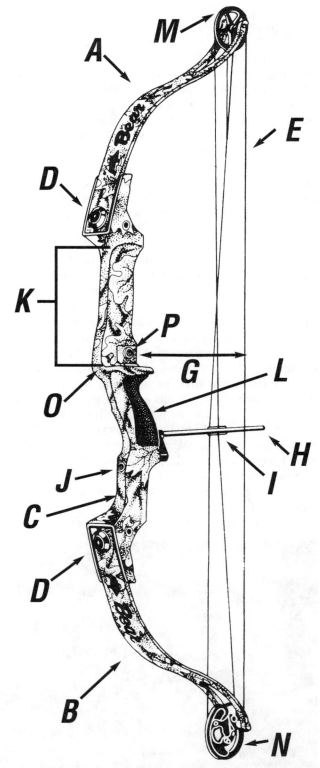

A. Upper Limb, B. Lower Limb, C. Riser or Handle, D. Limb Adjustment or Draw Weight Adjustment Bolts, E. Bowstring, F. Cables, G. Brace Height, H. Cable Guard, I. Cable Slide or Saver, J. Stabilizer Mounting Hole or Converta-Accessory Insert, K. Sight Window, L. Grip, M. Upper Cam or Idler Wheel, N. Lower Cam or OneCam, O. Arrow Shelf, P. Rest Mounting Hole.

a distinct – many archers say it is surprising and unpleasant – jerk when the Centerfire cam drops into its valley. What this also means is that even though a hard cam bow needs less holding force at full draw, it requires greater or more prolonged effort to draw through the draw force cycle. Bows equipped with medium cams such as the Inferno cam on the PSE Nova, fall somewhere between these two extremes.

Hard cams typically give you greater arrow speed than soft cams, but for the reasons mentioned above, many archers find them less pleasant and more difficult to shoot accurately. A hard cam's short valley, just a couple inches or so, demands that you hold the bow at full draw with discipline; the slightest bit of let-down or anticipation can either cause you to release prematurely or else can alter the arrow's impact point by several inches. At any distance at all, that is enough to miss your target completely.

In the past, bows equipped with two (or one!) hard-cam have often had a shorter brace height (the distance from the string to the deepest point of the grip on the bow handle before the bow is drawn). Short brace heights lengthen the string's power stroke. That puts more energy into your arrow and increases arrow speed. Unfortunately, because it also allows the arrow less time to straighten out as it leaves the string and passes the arrow rest, hard cam bows can be more difficult to tune and shoot with consistency. Since the average bowhunter is accustomed to 20 to 30 yard shooting, this may not be a dynamic worth spending much time reviewing, but for the competitor, it is one of the small things that can make a difference in

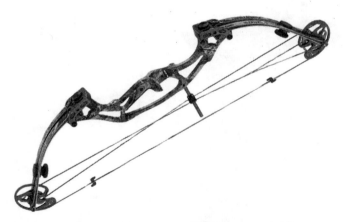

Hoyt USA raised the bar in bow design when they recently brought out the TEC riser design. The RazorTec is 33 inches axle-to-axle and, despite its heavy appearance, weighs less than four pounds. Hoyt says the TEC riser design eliminates noise, reduces shock and provides a more accurate shooting platform because the offset rear "strut" helps stiffen the riser design and acts like a shock absorber.

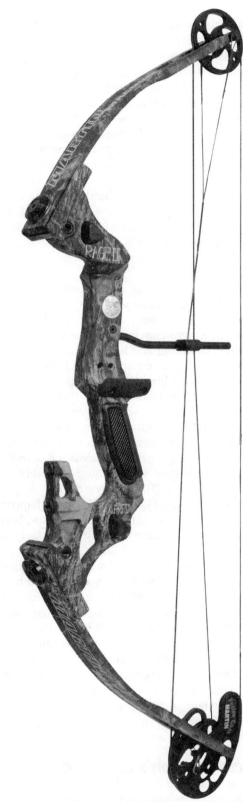

The Rage II Magnum Fuzion is built with Martin's "elevated stabilizer wing" on a radically reflex riser. At just 32 inches long, this remarkable bow has a 7-inch brace height.

finishing in the money or way down the list.

Increased speed can actually cause problems. Faster bow set-ups, for instance, are definitely more temperamental than slower ones. Slight flaws in your release will be exaggerated by the way your arrow absorbs energy. In other words, "columnar loading" (the mechanics of applying an energy vector only to the base of an arrow shaft rather than consistently throughout its length) initially makes the nock end of your arrow want to fly faster than your target point or broadhead end!

Finally, even a well-tuned hard-cam bow is going to be noisier than a soft-cam bow. Why? Hard, angular cams transmit a greater amount of energy to your arrow … but also to the bow and to your arm, too. This causes vibration, noisy vibration and what is known as "riser buzz."

Because it is a high-energy system and leaves some of that energy within your arm and the bow after a shot, a sophisticated hard-cam bow built with a single-cam or a twin-cam, requires continuous maintenance, tinkering and tuning. So, if spending time paper-tuning your equipment and checking it regularly at your workbench is not a problem, a hard cam bow may be just right for you. Typically, more experienced archers, people who want fast arrows, gravitate to a high performance bow with hard cams. For long shots at unknown distances, increased arrow speed and decreased trajectory may offer advantages, but the trade off is time spent tuning your set-up. The average archer taking 20- or 30-yard shots will certainly be more successful (and perhaps happier as well) with a soft-cam or a medium-cam bow, because they are quieter, smoother-shooting and easier to keep tuned.

A Note About Variations in Let-Off: This will not be a precise figure with many compound bows. Let-off varies slightly depending upon the modular arrangement of a bow's cam or cams. It may vary as much as seven percent above and below the advertised rating. Let-off typically varies over this range with changes in draw length and draw weight. So, if you test your Darton Rampage Express on an accurate bow scale and find that your holding weight varies by half a pound or so when you ramp it up from 50 to 60 pounds, remember that this is a normal condition of compound bows.

Your Compound Bow's Component Parts

The Handle (also called the riser): No matter where you anchor when you pull to full draw or how fast your bow shoots or how many accessories you attach, the handle you grip in your bow hand, the central portion of a compound bow called the riser, is

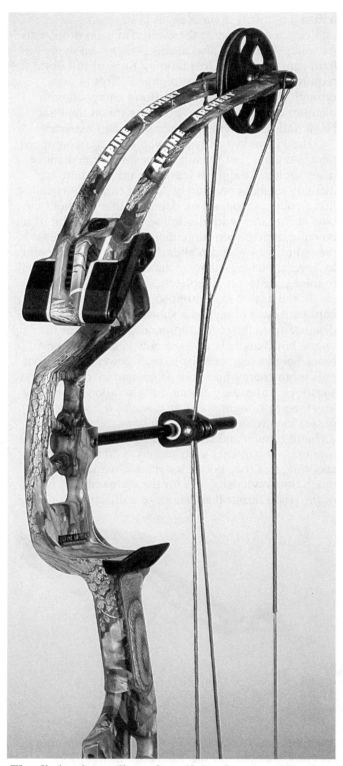

The distinctive styling of an Alpine bow is evident in the ultra-short, 28-inch, 4-pound Ravage, which has a high-mount carbon cable guard. A short bow is maneuverable, but at the higher speeds expected by archers today, it is more critical of shooting form errors than is a longer axle-to-axle bow.

going to remain functionally and fundamentally unchanged. The riser is the basis of your shooting system and your shooting success. It provides a handgrip, anchor points for the bow limbs or their mounting brackets and mounting holes for accessories such as your arrow rest, cable guard, overdraw, stabilizer and sights.

It is estimated that more than 90 percent of all adult bows for competition and hunting have risers that are machined from a solid bar or billet of aluminum. The aluminum in your bow riser may originally have been soda cans or aluminum window frames because a high percentage of aluminum is remanufactured from recycled materials and, since the 1960s, recycling of this common mineral has become cost effective. A recycled aluminum billet is identical in composition and properties to a virgin billet.

Aluminum was not the original choice for bow risers. It has only become so over the past dozen years, replacing die-cast magnesium-alloy handles which, along with laminated wood, were the original choices for compound riser materials.

Wood was the original material for bow risers. Wood was chosen because it was customary to use wood. It is readily available and easy to work. Besides, wood had a warm feel and properly laminated, a wood riser is a thing of beauty. But wood has virtually disappeared from the compound bow market, replaced by various forms of metal and even carbon composite.

For years, die-cast magnesium dominated the handle market by virtue of its light weight, reasonable cost and durability, but it, too, has been replaced.

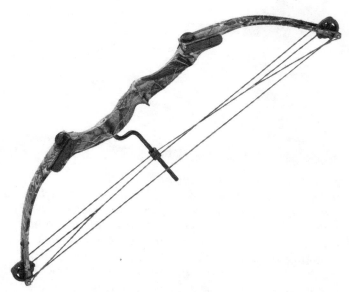

Hoyt built the 32-inch Banshee exclusively for young people. At less than 3 pounds, the magnesium-handled bow is available in draw weights of 25 or 45 pounds

Aluminum is king.

Bow risers come in three recognizable shapes: straight, reflexed and deflexed. On straight handles, the limb pockets at the top and bottom of the riser lie in a direct line with the handle. On deflexed bows, the limb pockets are designed behind the grip and the riser bends out and away from the shooter. On reflexed bows, the limb pockets are out in front of the handle so that from the side, the center of the bow appears to bend backward, toward the shooter.

Today, deflex risers on compounds are generally reserved for beginner bows. The Fred Bear "Little Delta" by North American is a good example of this styling. With their higher brace height (7 1/8 inches for the Little Delta), deflex handle bows are popular among young people and parents because they are easy to tune, easy to shoot, easy to learn with and more forgiving of a novice's shooting form errors. A high brace height contributes to introductory ease by giving arrows a little more time to straighten out before the arrow nock leaves the string and passes by or through the arrow rest. On their own, deflexed bows will usually tip back toward the shooter's face after a shot – which is considered desirable – and for this reason alone, most archers shooting deflex handle bows need a stabilizer to regulate the bow's in-hand balance.

While some very short bow designs like Pete Shepley's exceptionally reflexed PSE Firestorm Lite (30 inches axle-to-axle, 300 fps IBO and a remarkably large eight inches brace height) certainly defy the accepted rule, bows built with straight or reflexed handles are typically recognized as having lower brace heights than bows with deflexed handles. (Perhaps this is obvious since, by definition, "brace height" is measured from the curvature of the grip between the thumb and forefinger to the string when the bow is at rest.) Some highly reflexed bows have brace heights of six inches or less, compared to straight bows with brace heights of seven to eight inches. Traditionally, these straight and reflexed handle bows are faster than the deflex species.

But as is the case with the PSE Firestorm Lite, bow engineers are now finding ways to give archers both the forgiveness of a longer brace height and the speed that comes with a dramatically reflexed handle. The McPherson Hornet only measures 31 3/8 inches axle-to-axle, but this reflexed riser bow is rated at 302 fps IBO with a remarkable 7 7/8 inch brace height because Tom McMillan's team at McPherson Pro Shop Bows designed the riser to accept long, 14 1/2 inch split limbs and increased the limb take-off angle in the riser's machined limb pockets.

Compound bows with a short or low brace height have been faster over the past ten years because, although it sounds counter intuitive, they have a longer power stroke. The arrow stays longer on the string and accepts or loads a greater amount of energy. In the McPherson line, for instance, the new 35 inch axle-to-axle Raptor VX has the highest IBO speed of any bow in the McPherson line – a really screaming 325 to 330 fps – while its brace height is a short 6 1/8 inches. A bow like the Raptor VX with a 30 inch draw length and a six inch brace height will have a power stroke three inches longer than a deflex handle bow with a nine inch brace height. A power stroke that much longer will shoot significantly faster.

So, a bow with even a slightly reflexed riser and higher limb take-off angles such as the Alpine Fatal Impact has the benefit of greater arrow speed. Reflexed and straight risers also have excellent balance in your hand. To say that they will remain standing straight up in your hand following a shot or even tip forward slightly – which would be ideal – without the use of a stabilizer is straining to make a point, but their tendency to swing back quickly and pop you in the eye is lessened.

Bow mechanics once claimed that the lower brace heights of reflexed bows reduced the stability of your arrow, because the arrow "has less time to straighten out in the time between leaving the string and clearing the arrow rest." This is no longer a hard and fast rule as recent bow and cam designs have moved tirelessly in the direction of rapidly stabilizing arrows.

A few years ago, most bow risers were machined with an offset or a "cut-out" because many archers wanted to use an overdraw. The offset in the riser was a response to the interest by archers in shooting faster arrows. This interest and the manufacturing response meant that shorter arrows and broadheads which normally extended in front of the handle by an inch or so were being drawn back toward the archer a couple of inches and this gave the shooter a short overdraw effect, even when using the standard arrow rest mounting hole in the riser. (In a few extreme instances, the broadhead was actually drawn behind the bow riser in line with the shooter's wrist, a very dangerous set-up.) The offset riser design gave the archer a great deal of leeway adjusting for centershot and assured excellent broadhead clearance and fletching clearance for even the largest vanes. Today, with increasingly sophisticated short, fast bow design, an offset bow riser is less important and manufacturers are moving away from them.

Martin Archery writes, "With a full inch and a half of wrist clearance, the new Onza II will never interfere with your shooting style. Many bows like it on the market just simply do not have enough room. We have tripled the amount of clearance of other brands. This means no matter what your grip style, the riser will not touch you." For 2003, Martin is talking about wrist clearance on its "bridged riser," not broadhead clearance. This represents a clear difference in bow design and archer preference.

Above the riser's arrow shelf and any offset is a zone known as the sight window. You aim through this zone. For 20 years, the rule has been, short axle-to-axle bows have relatively short sight windows and longer bows have longer sight windows. This is no longer the case. The new Golden Eagle Obsession for instance has a full, 8-inch sight window even though it is only 34 inches axle-to-axle. If you anchor below your chin and your on-the-string peep sight is served high, six inches or more above the nocking point, you could have difficulty using a pin sight on a short bow. When you are shopping for a bow, before you make a purchase verify that you have selected one with a sight window greater than six inches high; a sight window that is shorter than this could obscure your top sight pins, the very ones that you will most need for those 20 to 30 yard shots.

When you anchor at the corner of your mouth or above, this effectively moves your peep downward on the string toward the nock point. In this instance then, you can probably manage with a short sight window.

THE GRIP: One of the greatest 3-D World Champions ever and a man who is a consummate bowhunter, Randy Ulmer, says that placing your hand on the grip is one of the most important steps in shooting a bow.

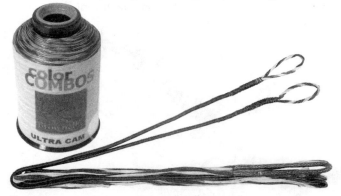

String material is available on spools from manufacturers such as Brownell and BCY. This 1/4-pound spool of Ultra Cam offers string material with outstanding strength from the thinnest diameter, in this case .013 inch. Ultra Cam has a single strand breaking strength of 120 pounds. From such a spool, a string is built to a specific length for your bow. The center of the string (where you nock your arrow and place your nock point locator) is then "served" (counter-wrapped) with nylon or Fast Flight as are the ends near the string loops that slip over the posts in the cam or cams.

He says the primary pressure point between your hand and the bow's grip should be perfectly in-line with the center of the two bones that make up your forearm.

"You can find this exact spot easily," Randy says. "Bend the wrist of your bow hand slightly and use the index finger of your other hand to press firmly on the palm at various points. Stay relaxed. Your wrist will fold or hinge when you press on every spot except the one that is perfectly in line with the forearm. That is the point that should feel the most contact pressure against the grip at full draw. Any other hand position is more likely to introduce tension and torque.

"Let your hand relax fully as you aim. Tension not only has the effect of turning the bow when you release the string; it also creeps into your bow arm and destroys your ability to hold a relaxed and steady aim. Let your fingers hang naturally. Trying to force your hand to stay open will create just as much shot-destroying tension as clenching it closed.

"Be diligent in making sure you place your hand on the grip exactly the same way every time. Spend the extra two or three seconds needed to ensure consistent hand placement. Eventually it will become instinctive.

"Many archers buckle their wrists and even slide their hands around on the grip as they pull the string and reach full draw. This may put them in a more powerful position for drawing the bow, but it undermines consistency. Once your hand and wrist are set in place, leave them alone. If you can't do that, you're probably shooting too much draw weight, or you're not placing your hand correctly to begin with."

All you have to do is study a current bow catalog

While perhaps 95 percent of all bows built in the US are painted in a popular camouflage pattern, lightweight limb covers such as these from NEET may be the ideal combination of camouflage and straight-line-confusion for bowhunting.

to see that the grip portion of the riser varies extensively from bow to bow. Some companies even specialize in grip replacement designs (Shrewd, Hicks, Coffey). Indeed, if you will think of how often you have watched people stand at a shooting line and shift the bow in their hand searching for their precise comfort zone, you will understand how and why the grip is important.

Even though the original Allen compound bows had bulky wood risers and many bows since then have had similar thick grips, it is not necessarily true that grips have gotten smaller over time. Some of the original Jennings compounds and many early Astro and Bear bows were built with thin, stylish metal risers and plastic grips. Typically and curiously, compounds with wood risers have big, meaty grips, but recurves drawing 65 and 70 pounds do not.

For comfortable shooting, you want a grip that fits pleasantly in your hand and feels "natural." This is a very subjective, very personal decision. Remember too that on cold days, you will often be shooting with a glove on your bow hand. Some archers believe that thick grips contribute to erratic shooting, because with a big handful of bow riser, there is a tendency to twist or torque the riser both before and after the shot and it is harder to duplicate your precise hand position for each shot. At the highest level of 3-D shooting, competitors rarely use a thick grip. Indeed, they often remove any wood or plastic grips provided by the manufacturer and simply wrap the "keel" of the riser with leather for warmth or shoot directly off the keel itself.

Higher end (more expensive) compound bows typically outfit the riser with attractive checkered wood grips, but that is not uniformly true. Although the new Golden Eagle Obsession has a warm, two-piece laminated wood grip, the rest of the bows in the 2003 Golden Eagle line have a one-piece, soft black "Elasto-Polymer" (plastic) grip. On the other hand, the two-piece wood grips on the 31-1/2-inch Hoyt HavocTec and the 36-inch Browning Eclipse SLX are very thin and highly stylized. About the single-piece wood grip on its new Legacy bow, a grip which features the laser engraved Mathews name, Mathews writes that it is "… sculptured from a solid piece of fine black walnut."

Today, low end (the 38 inch PSE Deer Hunter, for instance) and novice or beginner compounds (like the 32 1/2 inch PSE Outlaw) usually come with hard plastic grips. One version of a plastic grip that is not quite hard, but not quite soft either, is used by many companies such as the 302 fps IBO Jennings Rackmaster's "Vibration Suppressing" grip (34 3/8 inches axle-to-axle – with an offset riser!).

THE LIMBS: Not long ago every quality compound was built with laminated wood limbs. The multiple layers of wood, some dyed, and glue looked classy. Only less expensive models had solid Fiberglas limbs. "Choose laminated or Fiberglas limbs – Tamerlane, Alaskan and Polar LTEs feature hardrock maple and Fiberglas laminated limbs, while the Whitetail Hunter uses Bear's exclusive Thermal Bonded Epoxy Resin Fiberglas limbs." Bear Archery Catalog 1977.

Today, most high performance bows for hunting or competition feature limbs that are heat and compression molded and made from wraps or layers of Corning Fiberglas yarn inside a bath of liquid resin. These limbs are highly resistant to extremes of heat or cold, to moisture and other natural problems that often plagued laminated wood limbs, especially if those limbs became damaged by being dropped or banged up.

These days, some manufacturers claim that their "laminated" bow limbs incorporate layers of carbon as well as Fiberglas. Carbon would theoretically improve the performance of thin limbs by acting as a "stiffener." This would allow the limbs to be made narrower or thinner without sacrificing strength.

But, a layer of carbon, pure carbon, would be very expensive and we know that the amount of carbon or graphite varies considerably in fishing rods because manufacturers occasionally advertise comparisons. So, before you make a purchasing decision based on any carbon or carbon-related limb layers try to find out exactly how much carbon the manufacturer is talking about and then ask yourself if it is worth the additional cost. Technically, the scratch of a common, No. 2 pencil could qualify as having carbon in the limb and that could be shortened to a "carbon limb" at an advertising agency's copywriting desk. ….

Some bows feature recurved limbs that give them an appearance similar to your basic recurve bow. Most high energy, speed bows however rely on straight limbs. Recurved limbs may have more eye appeal, but in terms of performance, solid straight limbs will deliver more energy to your arrow and will stand up better to the rough handling of a typical shooting season.

Although all limbs on a compound bow appear to be curved, only the re-curved limbs are actually built with a curve. Straight limbs are only curved because they are under tremendous pressure, even at rest. (If you do not believe this is the case, try compressing an adult compound bow with just your hands and arms.)

Split or quad limb bows have been around for years. The TSS (Total Shooting Systems) QuadraFlex bow with angular split limbs was popular in the mid-80s. Now, these limb styles are back.

Whether they are straight or recurved, split or quad limbs have less mass than and weigh less than solid limbs. Some archery engineers suggest that like your arrow, just because quad limbs are lighter, they are also faster. They further suggest that split limbs offer advantages in balancing the forces at the limb tips, because typically, on high end bows like the 310 fps IBO Hoyt RazorTec or the Mathews Legacy with the "Roller Guard" instead of a standard steel or carbon cable guard, the harness splits about six inches below the idler wheel on the upper limb (or, in the 2003 Hoyt USA case, below the Cam & a half). Unless you are a 3-D competitor who is seriously interested in winning cash on the national 3-D tournament venues, the difference between solid and split limbs will be absolutely immaterial. It will not make any difference in your shooting, so buy what you like, what looks and feels good to you.

There is nothing split about split limbs by the way. So-called "split" limbs are not cut or ripped or sliced or much less split off a larger chunk of Fiberglas. Just like their straight cousins, the quad limbs, split limbs are molded as is. Knowledgeable archery designers would never try to sell actual "split" limbs because they would quickly splinter and sharp Fiberglas fibers would protrude from the limbs like hair on a cartoon character just after it had put its finger into an electrical socket. Perhaps the misleading technology began with early TSS models because the limb was molded as a single unit and shaped like a "Y" with six inches or so of the base (the end attached to the riser) actually attached.

There has been a significant change in bow limb styling recently away from recurve limbs, like those you find on the 36-inch Fred Bear TRX (Team Realtree Xtreme). On high-end bows, straight limbs are the passion because they are typically shorter, faster, easier to keep straight (they were often subject to twisting) and much more durable. Neither Hoyt USA, nor Browning or Pearson for example offers a single recurve limb bow. Less than 10 years ago, most high-end bows featured recurved limbs. Why the change?

Recurved limbs look good, but straight limbs are a little easier to manufacture and stress on a drawn limb is more evenly distributed. At one time, when it was still open at the Bear Archery manufacturing facility in Florida, the Fred Bear Museum displayed a bow limb that had undergone more than one million complete flexes (pulled to full draw and then relaxed, not drawn and released) in the Bear factory. It was a short, compression molded straight solid limb, not a recurve limb and not a set of quad or split limbs. While some engineers believe that the straight limb delivers more energy to the arrow than the recurve limb, the difference is quite small. The biggest difference in favor of straight limbs, whether solid or quad, may be in limb reliability and durability.

CABLES AND STRINGS: Early compound bows used strings made from Dacron and steel cables that were wrapped in plastic. Dacron strings were excellent for 70-pound bows with 60 to 75 pounds of stored energy, for instance, but as cams became harder and archers demanded greater arrow speeds, Dacron proved to be inadequate for the load.

Today, very few bow companies use steel cables on any bow. (The short draw – 21-to 25-inch – Fred Bear Badge with twin, 65 percent let-off MidasCams is an exception.) Virtually all manufacturers have replaced Dacron strings which, according to Brownell, have a single strand breaking strength of only about 50 pounds, with more advanced synthetic materials such as Western Filament's Spectra with a 90-pound single strand breaking strength or even Brownell's Dyneema D-75 (125-pound single strand strength) or S-4 (165-pound single strand strength). By reducing weight and string diameter and eliminating string stretch or creep, these all-synthetic systems are credited with increasing arrow speeds by as much as 10 feet per second. With new generation synthetic materials like Fast Flight, 450 Plus and DynaFlight 97 the bow tuning process has also simplified.

Early Fast Flight (95-pound single strand breaking strength and .015 inch diameter) string-and-cable systems developed a poor reputation because the strings and cables continually stretched and so the tune of the bow could never be guaranteed. Fast Flight and other of these man-made materials do stretch to some degree, especially in the hot weather on a summer 3-D range, but the number one problem with early "new generation" string materials was not stretch but creep – string materials were so slick that they would slip beneath the end servings. Improved manufacturing techniques have by and large eliminated that problem and today's all-synthetic riggings are very stable.

Regardless of the material, any bowstring sold as part of a compound bow will come with a string designed and manufactured to standard lengths. According to the Archery Manufacturer's Organization (AMO) which recently changed its name to the Archery Manufacturer's Association, "Compound bowstring length shall be designated by its stretched length as determined by placing the string loops over 1/4 inch diameter steel pins and stretching with 100 pounds of tension. Measurement is taken from outside of pin. Tolerance is + 1/4 inch after 20 seconds under tension load."

In an effort to eliminate string and cable stretch, in the early '90s manufacturers began to experiment with a material called Vectran, which does not stretch. Vectran however frays easily. This is a real shortcoming and a Vectran string can break after just a few thousand shots. Every two steps forward in the development of new string materials yielded a step backward.

Seeking the best of both worlds, string makers braided materials like Fast Flight with Vectran to make durable, low-stretch string materials called 450 Premium and S4. Today, many bows use one of these materials, or even Fast Flight, for their strings and cables, but many have moved to materials like BCY 452, which has the same strength as in half the diameter.

Here are the names you will hear used currently:

450 Plus – offers total stability with no creep. Good arrow speed and no fuzziness.
452 – very smooth and half the size of 450 Plus. Fast, small diameter and no creep.
DynaFlight 97 – the original high-strength Dyneema. Rugged, low creep, very durable.
Formula 8125 – high speeds with low creep and stretch. Smaller diameter than Dyneema.
Dyneema '02 – designed for recurves. Strong, low creep and stretch with extra light smooth wax.

Among string makers, the following general rules hold:
• The higher the number of strands the faster your arrow,
• Larger strands yield slower arrow speeds than thinner strands and
• The best combination for speed and durability is a small string wrapped by a thick serving.

Reserving your string: If you attach your release aid directly to your string, it is a given that your string's serving will eventually break or wear out. It is not a matter of "if," only when. You need to become familiar with the methods required to reapply the string's center serving. A simple serving jig and a spool of replacement material are all you need. One common replacement serving is BCY Halo. It is constructed of 100 percent braided Spectra and is nearly three times stronger than #62 Braid, the traditional standard for center serving. You have to serve Halo tight to keep the slick Spectra solidly in place on your string, but its extra durability makes it worth the additional attention needed for a good job. (Finger shooters by the way, love the way the slick-feeling Halo slips off the fingertips. As if it were oiled.)

Once you have your string re-served, Brownell's Liquid Lok is designed to lock the new serving material in place. When it dries, the adhesive prevents slippage and separation. Brownell's Cam EZ is a lubricant that goes on over the end serving where it slips into the grooves of the cam to prevent damage from wear. Both products are useful to help maintain a durable and accurate bowstring.

Serving Saver is an over-wrap that goes on the end serving of your string or buss cable to protect the serving from damage by the rotating cam. Serving damage is a common problem with many cam designs and particularly so on large single cams. Serving Saver can be applied by hand, but is best applied with a serving jig.

CABLE GUARD: The cable guard holds a compound bow's cables to the side to prevent interference with the arrow's fletching. You do not want this rigid rod to stretch the cables any farther to the side than necessary or excessive wheel lean and unnecessary torque could result.

In one form or another, a cable guard comes standard on all compound bows. Typically, it is an adjustable offset rod of either solid carbon or steel and the cables actually ride on a grooved plastic or Teflon slide that either slips over the rod or is held in place by the intense side pressure exerted by the cables. Teflon is an ideal material for a cable slide as it minimizes friction during the shot sequence.

Ideally, your cable guard would be positioned in the center of the bow, directly between the axles. And, it should move the cables aside just far enough for your fletching to pass without contact. With most bow configurations however, this is not possible and the guard must be positioned either above the arrow rest by 1 to 3 inches or below the rest by a half dozen or so inches. The Pearson 38 Special, for instance, positions its straight, carbon cable guard about 1-1/2 inches above the arrow rest hole measured center-to-center.

There is a safety factor as well as a technological factor to keep in mind when you look at cable guard placement. High-mount guards were standard until the early 1990s when low-mount guards became the norm, perhaps for no other reason than a change in style. Let go of a bow – not the string, the bow – that has a high-mount, above-the-rest guard and it can slam back and hit you in the eye or punch through the thin bones of the nose and head. Either spot will have disastrous results. Let go of a bow that has a low-mount, below-the-rest guard and it can slam back and hit you in the chest leaving you with a sore spot. All of these things have happened more than once.

Nevertheless, the best spot for the cable guard seems to be the high-mount position as from there, an adjustable rod can move the cables aside just enough to prevent interference and yet remain very close to the arrow. Minimal side movement of the cables means minimal torque on your bow and minimal pressure on the cam(s) or idler to lean. The ultimate result is maximum potential of your shooting platform to support your shot and your desired results.

So, is a carbon cable guard better than a steel rod? Carbon rods are straight, always. Steel rods can be straight or designed with a bend or offset. Both types will flex and then return to their original position. Unless there is some flaw in bow design – an exceptionally rare occurrence, but it does happen – both steel and carbon are entirely adequate. Under "normal" shooting conditions though, carbon will retain its strength and flexibility for a greater length of time than steel. Is it worth paying more for a carbon rod than for a steel rod? Probably not.

And what about the new Roller Guard on bows like the Mathews Legacy? Is it smoother? Do the machined wheels eliminate the friction of cables sliding through a Teflon cable saver or slide? Does it minimize the possibility of cam or idler lean? Perhaps the questions actually are: Will other bow manufacturers immediately follow suit and does it really matter? Yes, because of Mathews' significant marketing power, other manufacturers will certainly follow the Mathews lead and, as far as our shooting is concerned, no, it probably does not matter to our shooting in any measurable context.

BOW LENGTH: There has been a trend for compound bows to grow shorter and shorter over the past decade. Archers have wanted – and manufacturers have supplied – short axle-to-axle bows that aloow increased maneuverability in ground blinds and on treestands and increase arrow speeds. Today, the average length of a bow is probably 36 to 38 inches (axle to axle) and manufacturers now make some models that barely measure 31 inches! Just a few years ago, this would be unheard of and the bows would be roundly criticized as unstable and unpleasant to shoot.

A look through the archives of archery magazines give us a long-term snapshot of the bow length trend.

In the February 1982 issue of *Bow & Arrow,* which features a C.R. Learn bow report on the new 45-inch Bear Delta-V, the ad for the new Bear Kodiak Magnum notes that it is 46 inches long.

In the February 1989 issue of *Archery World*, which features a Norb Mullaney bow report on the new Pearson Spoiler 295, Norb writes: "Short bows are favored by a great many bowhunters. They are easier to maneuver in brush and in treestands, easier to transport in motor vehicles, trains or aircraft, and much less difficult to handle aboard a horse or when backpacking. But short bows generally have some disadvantages, too. They are subject to greater finger pinch, usually suffer in performance and shooting characteristics, and in the compound type, are more susceptible to hand torque. So when the folks at Pearson undertook to develop and produce a short, high-performance hunting compound, they were accepting a distinct challenge." Although Norb reports on almost every possible statistic and measurement for this bow in his six-page report, nowhere does he report the axle-to-axle length! (In this issue, Darton claims "At over 228 feet per second there is no production bow in the world faster than the DARTON 60MC.")

When the June/July 1997 *Bowhunter* arrived in the mail, the trend to shorter bows had begun. McPherson trumpeted that at 86 percent, its 36-inch axle-to-axle Mark VIII was the "highest let-off dual-cam bow in the world," but Mathews ignores the length of its new speed bow, the 320 fps IBO Z-Max

By the October 2002 issue of *Bow & Arrow*, Mathews brags about its 37-inch Icon, Reflex about its 34-inch Denali and, in his bow report on the High Country Triple S Pro with a lightweight carbon riser, Emery Loiselle writes that the 33-inch bow is "the answer to an archer's dream."

Short bows are generally faster than long bows. For any given draw length, the wheels on short bows are larger than on longer bows. This increases wheel rollover speed. Leverage is what is at stake. Imagine using a very short bar (the small wheel) to pry up a large stone. You will have a problem until you switch to a longer bar (a larger wheel). Archers with draw lengths of less than 28 inches will gain more speed from this principle than will people who have longer

The 34-inch Alpine Fatal Impact features a 7 1/4-inch brace height and an 8 1/2-inch sight window. Standard let-off for the Fatal Impact is 80 percent, but 65 percent modules are available.

draw lengths.

Of course, for every action, there is an equal and opposite reaction. We have long known that a short bow is more susceptible to hand-applied torque than a longer bow, probably because the longer and heavier bow is just more difficult to twist. Experienced archers who understand bow tuning and the elements of good shooting form will easily be able to enjoy the lightweight maneuverability of a short axle-to-axle bow. If you are still on the rapidly rising side of the archery learning curve or just do not have time to work on tuning and shooting form, a short bow can be more difficult to manage than the benefits it conveys.

Finger shooters need longer rather than shorter bows. A bow like the 42 7/8-inch Martin Scepter III rather than the 30-inch PSE Firestorm Lite, because when the bowstring is pulled to full draw, the acute string angle of a short bow pinches the fingers, even if you drop one below the string. The severity of this finger pinch will depend on your draw length, but with bows shorter than about 40 inches you should consider using a release aid. The 10 to 20 percent of archers who still shoot with fingers find that bows measuring 42 to 44 inches make it easier for them to become proficient.

PHYSICAL WEIGHT: Although archery technicians are gradually squeezing out the ounces, the physical or mass weight of a compound bow usually falls in the 3- to 4-pound range. Renegade's new Non Typical XL weighs 3 pounds, 15 ounces. With accessories and a load of arrows in a bow quiver, the weight can climb to 7 to 8 pounds. All this makes little or no difference if you spend your day sitting on a tree stand. If you are hiking through the Arizona desert and glassing for Coues deer however or wandering Western mountains day after day, a heavy bow can be a real chore to carry. Some of the new (but so far not well accepted by the shooting public) carbon-handle bows from Diamond or High Country weigh less than 3 pounds. Many slender aluminum-riser bows now weigh less than 4 pounds without their accessories and even HoytUSA's striking TEC Riser Designs, bows like the RazorTec and the SuperTec, come in under 4 pounds.

The decision you want to make between a heavier mass weight bow and a lighter bow does not really concern your fatigue during a day spent hiking the Rockies for elk. After all, we are probably talking 8 to 10 ounces or so. The essential difficulty with a light bow is its ability to deal with the kinetic energy left in the shooting system (the bow and attached accessories including your hand, wrist and arm) after a properly spined arrow absorbs its 80 or so percent. For a fine, high-end bow like the Darton Rampage Express, that means that 15 ft-lbs of energy are left in the bow to become riser buzz and arrow rattle, vibration and noise. That much leftover energy is equivalent to dropping the bow from chest height. After an afternoon of shooting it makes a difference in how your elbow and shoulder feel and in whether your accessories are subjected to screw-loosening, sight pin-rattling vibration.

It is easier for a heavier bow to deal with leftover energy. It is the same principle as dividing fighters into weight classes, heavyweights to fly weights. Given the same amount of stray energy, a lighter bow will make more noise and rattle your sight pins and arm much more than a heavier bow. So, if you opt for the purchase of the lighter bow, look for solid, stable accessories to help you deal with the leftover energy. Be aware of Loc-Tite to help keep your sight and arrow rest properly fastened. If you opt for the heavier bow, your accessory range will be larger.

CAMOUFLAGE AND COLOR: Function always comes first. A sharp shooting bow painted glaring lipstick red is preferable to a mediocre machine in any camouflage pattern. In fact, that candy-apple red bow will probably do quite well in 3-D competition and on the shooting line at the Atlantic City and Las Vegas Championships. Many companies build the same bow and offer it in either a range of competition colors or camo.

Browning's Eclipse ZLX and Adrenaline SX are excellent examples of bows dressed in competition colors and in camouflage. The competition handles can be shiny blue or red and the limbs are black with white graphics. Competition hardware, like the idler wheels or the limb pocket cups, is silver (not "real" jeweler's silver, but just not anodized black and dipped in clear coat for protection from the weather). Hardware on the hunting bows is anodized black.

A new and perhaps temporarily popular pattern is the US flag wrapped around metallic handle risers. HoytUSA for instance offers a variety of competition colors: faded red or green or blue, plus black, flame (Yes, like flames. Very cool.) and flag in red, white and blue with stars and stripes. The HoytUSA camo pattern is Realtree High Definition Green.

Perhaps the most interesting new competition colors are applied to PSE bows. Their Kolorfusion process applies a snakeskin pattern in Python Red or Blue. The multi-color "Good Vibrations" pattern is strikingly psychedelic.

There are two types of camo patterns that manufacturers apply to bows, their own or one of the mass marketed patterns from Realtree and Mossy Oak. If a salesman hands you a bow painted in an unusual pattern and with a name you do not recognize –

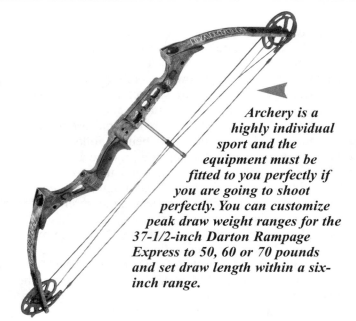

Archery is a highly individual sport and the equipment must be fitted to you perfectly if you are going to shoot perfectly. You can customize peak draw weight ranges for the 37-1/2-inch Darton Rampage Express to 50, 60 or 70 pounds and set draw length within a six-inch range.

Raccoon Mask or Monkey Vomit, for instance – it is a proprietary camo applied by the manufacturer who saves $10 to $15 per bow for its licensing fee. Whether that savings is passed along to you or not is debatable.

Nevertheless, a good non-reflective camo pattern that matches the vegetation in your area and is well-applied (painted) to a bow's riser and limbs makes it feel like it fits into a hunting situation – like it is ready to walk out of the store and into the woods. With new patterns every year, you can find bows in virtually every major and many virtually unknown camouflage patterns. For 2003, Ben Pearson Archery's McPherson Pro Shop Series has a new camo pattern called "Caged Cat" that it applies to its short draw SDS VX and its Diva VX. Caged Cat camo looks either like a spotted leopard ready to pounce or a faux leopard throw on a round bed in a mirrored motel room in Las Vegas. Leopard … or jaguar?

In an effort to haul the historic Bear Archery from the brink of insolvency, the North American Archery Group applies a different camo pattern to each of its four trademarked lines of bows. Golden Eagle bows like the new, 34-inch Obsession, are painted in Mossy Oak's new Break-Up camo with black hardware. Fred Bear bows such as the 32-inch TRX (Team Realtree Xtreme) 32 wear Realtree Hardwoods High Definition camo. Buckmasters bows such as the 35 inch G2 XL and Jennings bow such as the 40 ? inch GrandMaster wear Bill Jordan's Custom Realtree Hardwoods camo.

Believe it or not, deer and other big game animals do not care one way or the other about the camo pattern on your bow. Millions of trophy game animals were taken with solid green and solid black bows before the old World War II green or Jim Crumley's original Trebark camo were thoughtfully applied to our hunting bows.

CARE AND MAINTENANCE OF COMPOUND BOWS:
The Wyoming antelope hunt was a huge success. I took a record book buck at 20 yards, but the Oneida Eagle took a lot of punishment from the wind and blowing grit, which never stopped, day or night. The fresh pit blind was a hot and miserable hole, and difficult enough for us to dig through the hard-packed earth near the waterhole. Then, the buck came to water. I had marked the yardage and the bow performed perfectly.

Returning home, I noticed that the bow had collected dirt in places that would almost require

The 32-inch Fred Bear TRX (Team Realtree Xtreme) is a maneuverable hunter that is rated at 303 fps IBO. 75 percent let-off is standard, but 65 percent modules are available.

The 34-inch Golden Eagle Obsession comes with the exclusive Shock Stop string cushion to eliminate noise, vibration and string oscillation.

complete disassembly to clean. I shook it and wiped it and sprayed it. Nothing helped.

Finally, I called the Oneida factory, which was then in New York, and spoke to the inventor, John Islas who was the company's vice president. "I can't get your bow clean, John," I told him. "It makes quite an ugly racket with all that dirt I can't get out. Am I going to have to take it into the shower with me or find a hot tub?"

John laughed and replied that under the circumstances it would not hurt a thing to take it in the shower for a thorough cleaning, but just be sure to carefully dry it afterwards and give all the moving parts a very light coating of oil.

Like any fine shooting instrument, your bow needs to be treated with care and it will benefit from an occasional check-up. Excessive heat can damage any kind of bow, whether it is made from wood, Fiberglas or a carbon composite. Never leave your bow in the trunk of a car or hang it on the gun rack of your pick up truck if it is exposed to direct sunlight. Heat will cause the glue between laminates to crystallize and lose its bonding strength. It will also cause your stronger-than-steel synthetic cables to stretch. Your bow can lose its ability to shoot where you so carefully tuned it to hit and delaminate. Most manufacturers would give you some credit if the bow was not too old, but every bow brochure and owner's manual explicitly warns against such careless treatment.

Mud and blowing dust will adhere to any oil around the axles to the point of increasing your draw weight and reducing arrow speed. To prevent such ill effects when you are using the bow often, oil the axles and wheels every now and then. Use lightweight machine oil or a Teflon-based lubricant like Super Lube. Super Lube will not react with rubber, plastic, wood, leather, fabric or paint, so it is an ideal archery accessory. Tink's Gun and Bow Oil from Wellington, offers completely odorless oil for hunting and fishing gear.

Eventually bowstrings and cables fray from the extreme tension of a shot and from rubbing against branches and other abrasive surfaces. To reduce fraying, regularly lubricate your string and cables with a wax designed for this purpose. Every archery sales outlet including most mass merchants should carry a bowstring wax and one tube will usually last for years.

If you nick a string with your broadhead or a knife or if you detect any visible fraying, you should replace it right away. You should always carry a spare bowstring, one that is set up exactly like the current one on your bow. With the spare string, carry a simple bow press. Some bows will allow you to relax the bow limbs enough to change the string with only a hex

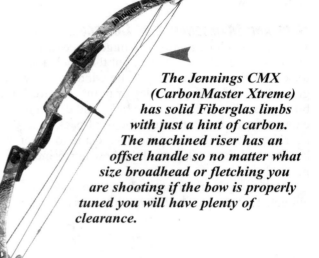

The Hoyt ProTec with the TEC riser is available in camo or a variety of colors including black, flame and flag. You can choose the 41-inch XT 3000 (pictured) in 30- to 70-pound draw weights and with Hoyt's own Cam & A Half System or AccuWheel. The ProTec LX Pro measures 46-1/2 inches axle to axle and is ideal for finger shooters.

The Jennings CMX (CarbonMaster Xtreme) has solid Fiberglas limbs with just a hint of carbon. The machined riser has an offset handle so no matter what size broadhead or fletching you are shooting if the bow is properly tuned you will have plenty of clearance.

wrench, but not very many.

Never dry-fire a bow. Normally when a bow is fired, the arrow absorbs as much as 80 percent of the energy released by the limbs, leaving only 20 percent in the bow itself. If you dry-fire a bow by drawing and releasing the string with no arrow on the string, the bow and your hand and arm will absorb 100 percent of the energy – as much as 100 ft-lbs of impact, like being bounced off the canvas by The Incredible Hulk – and the stress of vibration through the limbs, handle, cables and string can blow your bow apart. Dry-firing a bow has injured many unfortunate beginners and it usually voids your warranty.

Shooting light, underspined arrows can produce a similar effect to a dry fire, because light arrows absorb a smaller percentage of the bow's energy. To be safe, always adhere to the AMO guidelines or the manufacturer's suggested spine recommendations for arrow selection.

- Oil axles every few days when in the field.
- Avoid smearing insect repellents on the surface of your bow. The chemicals in these products can damage the finish.
- Carry a spare shot-in bowstring and a portable bow press when on a trip.
- Carry a set of Allen wrenches and check for loose accessories before shooting or hunting.
- Inspect the bowstring before shooting; Frayed strings should be replaced.
- Lubricate your bowstring regularly with a commercial bowstring wax.
- Keep your bow away from heat. Laminated bow limbs can come apart after only a few hours in a hot vehicle.
- Store your bow in a cool, dry area out of direct sunlight. Never store it hanging by the string or

cables. Hang your bow by the riser; lay it on a flat surface, or store it in a bow holder.
- Relax the tension on the string and cables by backing out the limb bolts before storing your bow for the season.

ALPINE

The 295 fps IBO Fatal Impact, Alpine's new 34-inch axle-to-axle bow has a very slightly reflexed machined handle. With high limb take-off angles (called parallel limb technology) this short bow also has a high, 7¼- inch brace height.

For 2003, Alpine is not talking about speed or durability, however, choosing to talk about how well its design quiets your shot and dampens vibration. "Our new Inter-Loc limb mounting system [for the parallel quad limbs) incorporates a nylon pocket liner to reduce vibration and limb movement," Rich Walton writes for Alpine. "This is accomplished by tightening both pockets and liners together with the pocket clamping bolts, after the weight has been adjusted. Zero limb movement is maintained with this innovative system."

The Fatal Impact has a relatively long riser for its length and one of the benefits is an extended 8-1/2-inch sight window so, no matter where you anchor, you should be able to easily see all of your sight pins. This new bow features a high-mount carbon cable guard, removable extended arrow shelf and a two-panel laminated and checkered wood grip. The Fatal Impact is available in peak draw weights of 50, 60 and 70 pounds in draw lengths from 27 to 31 inches. Let-off for the Perimeter Weighted One-Cam is 80 percent, but 65 percent modules are available. At 4.2 pounds mass

Archers who have seen copies of the high-speed film Easton developed 10 years ago will appreciate that a metal handle flexes during a shot. The handle (or "riser") of the Martin Onza II is designed "super stiff" with an offset strut or bridge that minimizes flexing. The Onza II Elite Fury is almost 40 inches axle to axle and is equipped with Vibration Escape Modules to help ease the vibration from 305 fps and 75 percent let-off.

weight, the Fatal Impact is a smidgen on the heavy side.

BOWTECH

Meet the Black Knight: 37-1/2 inches axle-to-axle and 4-1/4-pounds mass weight. It is available in peak draw weights of 50, 60 and 70 pounds with a draw length range that varies slightly with brace height.

BowTech advertises this twin-cam bow as the fastest production bow in the world, launching an arrow a truly stunning 350 fps. Actually, the Black Knight is available in two set-ups and both are amazingly fast, even at 65 percent. The 5-1/2-inch brace height (accommodates 26-to 30-inch draw lengths) model is advertised with an IBO speed of 344 to 350 fps while the 6.5-inch brace height (accommodates 27- to 31-inch draw lengths) Pro Series model is a nice and easy 333 to 339 fps. Wow!

BROWNING

Browning bows are now built by Precision Shooting Equipment. This brings Browning's archery division into line with the balance of their marketing enterprise because for many years, Browning actually built the bows they sold, unlike the clothing, knives, rifles, shotguns, accessories and even fishing gear that bears their name and their logo. No matter who builds it though, the Browning name still carries the imprint of quality.

The new 36-inch axle-to-axle Eclipse ZLX has an IBO rated speed of 305 fps. It weighs 4-1/3 pounds and is built on a reflex, machined aluminum riser with solid Fiberglas limbs. The Cyber-ZX adjustable let-off cam is standard with 75 percent let-off, but is

adjustable with modules to 65 percent. Browning reports that the Split Harness One-Cam system on this bow is the solution to one-cam wheel lean and serving wear. This one cam bow has adjustable draw lengths of five inches without modules. The wide-body string track reduces serving wear and provides a positive draw stop. Draw lengths are adjustable in the cam from 27 to 31 inches and peak draw weights are 60 and 70 pounds. The Eclipse ZLX is available for hunting in Mossy Oak BreakUp or in red or blue with black limbs for competition. The suggested retail price for the Eclipse ZLX is $799 for the hunting bow and $850 for the competition model.

BUCKMASTERS BY JENNINGS

Depending on the year, the North American Archery Group (NAAG) builds four or five lines of bows, but their Buckmasters bows have proven to be very popular in recent years. The G2 (short for Generation 2) and the G2 XL are virtually identical except for their length. Draw weights are available from 40 to 70 pounds with draw lengths of 28 through 30 inches. The original G2 featured 309 fps IBO/232 fps AMO arrow speed and was equipped with the exclusive, Shock Stop Kraton string bumper mounted on the carbon cable rod to break up the harmonic vibration of the string and thus lessen noise and vibration after a shot. These good-looking bows use compression-molded carbon-Fiberglas quad limbs and place Sims Riser Dampener units in the machined aluminum risers. The let-off for the 31-inch G2 and the 35-inch G2 XL is 70 percent, but modules are available for 65 percent. Like most high-end bows, these red-accented models have sculptured wood grips.

CHAMPION

The new kid on the block, Canada's Champion

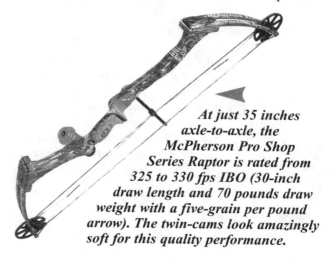

At just 35 inches axle-to-axle, the McPherson Pro Shop Series Raptor is rated from 325 to 330 fps IBO (30-inch draw length and 70 pounds draw weight with a five-grain per pound arrow). The twin-cams look amazingly soft for this quality performance.

Bow Company, has an eminently respectable line up and it also produces several bows under the "Buck Bows" label. Champion says its Mustang, Contender and all-new Spitfire one-cam bows "push the performance envelope" (shades of Chuck Yeager!) with carbon/Kevlar RST (Reverse Stress Technology) laminated limbs. They consider these "reverse curve" limbs and are designed for both long life and boosting the speed of your arrow.

Champion has not forgotten finger shooters. It machined the long, slightly reflexed riser for the surprisingly fast (301 fps IBO) Contender out of machined aluminum and now attaches its own reverse-mounted stabilizers – ISO Bars, the folks at Champion call them – on the shooter's side quite high and low on the riser near the limbs The Champion has a long, 8-inch brace height and measures 41-1/4 inches axle-to-axle. The draw length range is 26 to 32 inches and the peak draw weights are 60 and 70 pounds. The bow weighs 4-1/4 pounds and it is available in camouflage or competition blue. Ask for 80 or 65 percent let-off, your choice.

DARTON

The Rampage Express is equipped with versatile, modular Darton Controlled Power System (CPS) Cams. The CPS was introduced in 1995 because Darton wanted its own one-cam system rather than license the rights to build one-cam bows from patent owner and inventor Matt McPherson who owns Mathews Archery. The CPS System added a track to the upper idler as an answer to the tendency of nock points on one-cam systems to wander vertically after release.

The slightly reflexed Rampage riser is machined

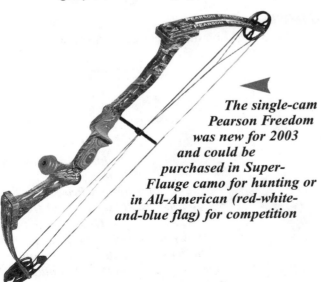

The single-cam Pearson Freedom was new for 2003 and could be purchased in Super-Flauge camo for hunting or in All-American (red-white-and-blue flag) for competition

from 6061 T6 aluminum. The high mount 3/8-inch carbon composite cable guard is not adjustable and the two-piece grip is a soft black rubber. Limbs are solid and straight. With the right draw length modules draw lengths cover a range from 25-3/8 to 31-3/4 inches at let-offs from 75 to 80 percent. Modules for lower let-offs, from 65 to 70 percent provide a slightly different draw length range. The string and cables are made from BCY 450 Plus and three Nok Sets are shrink-wrapped to the string just above the power cam to act as speed nocks and help dampen string oscillation during the power stroke. The Rampage is available in draw weights of 50, 60 and 70 pounds with a 10-pound downward adjustment.

During recent tests by archery engineer Norb Mullaney, a 60-pound Rampage Express shot 236 fps with a 540 grain arrow and 281 fps with a lighter 360-grain arrow.

DIAMOND

Although it started out a few years ago to build the perfect, lightweight carbon handle, Diamond has made the move to aluminum: the metal is cheaper, less engineering headaches, a known quantity and all-in-all, a pretty doggone good riser material.

The 33-inch axle-to-axle Diamond D.O.A. (Dead on Arrival?) claims 319 fps IBO (70 pounds draw at 30 inches with a 350-grain arrow) with a seven inch brace height. Diamond's Internet site at www.diamondarchery.com does not give much information about its bows, but it allows you – if you have the patience and Adobe Acrobat – to download their catalog.

The D.O.A. is built with 14-inch straight, solid limbs a modular cam system and shipped at 80 percent let-off although it makes 65 percent modules available. The D.O.A. is available in 25 to 30 inch draw lengths and 50-, 60- or 70-pound draw weights. This little speed demon currently carries a suggested retail price of $589!

FRED BEAR EQUIPMENT COMPANY

The 36-inch TRX or Team Realtree Xtreme was developed to celebrate the 100th anniversary of the birth of bowhunting legend Fred Bear. Consequently, the TRX is rigged with a lot of "bells and whistles" such as a custom checkered wood grip with an inlaid compass and a yellow/black TechTwist string. The TRX modular Perimeter OneCam allows a full 75 percent let-off (65 percent modules are separately available) and, combined with the balanced and fiber-aligned carbon/Fiberglas quad recurve limbs, provides an IBO speed of 305 fps and an AMO speed of 230 fps.

The low-mount carbon cable guard on the TRX is equipped with the exclusive Shock Stop string cushion that cuts noise and vibration resulting from string oscillation at the source. The brace height is 6-5/8 inches. Draw weights peak at 50, 60 or 70 pounds and the draw length range with optional modules is from 24 to 31 inches. The bow comes from the factory with a pair of speed buttons attached to the string a half-dozen inches above the one-cam and a rubber shrink wrap over and around them to keep them securely in place.

GOLDEN EAGLE BY NORTH AMERICAN

The new Golden Eagle Obsession is sold in Mossy Oak's new Break-Up camo. It has all of the advantages of these names too, featuring fine quality design and safe, but solid performance. With the exclusive Shock Stop string suppressor included, the 34-inch Obesssion is a quick, reliable shooter.

The Obsession is founded on a slightly reflexed machined aluminum riser equipped with a two-piece checkered hardwood grip with a quiet, interior leather wrap. The riser accepts a two-piece quiver as well as all standard archery accessories. The straight carbon cable guard is mounted above the grip, but the riser is machined to accept the cable guard (either straight carbon or the North American SwingArm cable guard) below the grip, too.

The modular Gold Dot Perimeter OneCam provides moderate power through the compression molded quad Fiberglas limbs and it is balanced with a large, four inch ball-bearing mounted idler. Draw lengths with optional modules allow adjustment from 27 to 31 inches and draw weights may be selected in three ranges, 40 to 50 pounds, 50 to 60 pounds and 60 to 70 pounds. The Obsession is shipped with a 75 percent let-off module on the medium (almost soft) cam, but a 65 percent module is available. Brace height is listed as a long, 7-7/8 inches.

HIGH COUNTRY

High Country is turning up the technology heat with its carbon risers. The new Carbon Lite Pro is built on a carbon riser that High Country calls its CR3 for Reflex, Super Carbon Riser that it says is Ultra lightweight and ultra strong with woven carbon/graphite. Not to be outdone by any other manufacturer's advertising, High Country says its limbs are the "World's Strongest, Fastest, Quietest, Lightest" limbs available anywhere and anytime. It does offer a lifetime (or 10-year, depending on whether you refer to the advertising or the Internet site) warranty on its Vibra Flex Armor V-Split Limbs which are designed to dampen sound and vibration and which

it claims are the "most expensive in the industry."

The Carbon Force Extreme, built with the reflex carbon handle, weighs slightly less than three pounds and is 35 inches, axle-to-axle. It has two one-cam options and comes with a two-piece wood grip. Peak draw weights are 60 or 70 pounds and draw lengths are 27 to 31 inches. High Country does not list arrow speeds for these bows.

HOYT USA

Everyone is getting on board the shock and vibration bandwagon including HoytUSA, but in typical Hoyt fashion, they have done it with an attractive and attention-getting advertising campaign, but – perhaps until 2003 – without much concern for cutting-edge arrow speed, opting instead to maximize other shooting qualities. Their new TEC bow series is a bit of a throwback to old riser designs (practically every company has tried some form of this design over the past 15 to 20 years), but this time it has a whole new approach and the bows are fast, too.

According to Hoyt, the unusual shape of the Hoyt TEC riser accomplishes more than getting people's attention. The rear (behind your wrist) riser truss stiffens the riser and performs like a shock absorber, dampening vibration, and leaving the front or grip truss, vibration free. Hoyt says that because the grip area is most vulnerable to stress and vibration, they designed the TEC riser to be widest at the grip and that it takes 2-1/2 "traditional" risers to match the TEC strength and stiffness. The rear truss allows for much less backward and forward flex of the riser during firing and this increases the bow's stability and consequently its accuracy as well. They compare the design to a suspension bridge with support trusses that prevent it from flexing. Without trusses, traditional risers bend and vibrate most at the grip area. Hoyt claims that TEC riser performance is backed by test results using bows set at (an extremely high) 104 ft. lbs. of stored energy with a 30-inch draw AND with dry fire durability equipment.

Whether any of this really makes sense to the layman is debatable, but Hoyt is building compounds and recurves with the TEC riser. Simon Fairweather, 2000 Olympic Gold Medalist, now uses a Hoyt TEC-riser recurve in his quest for world titles.

One of their latest compounds is the HavocTEC, which the company maintains, eliminates noise, shock, vibration and "most of the (axle-to-axle) length" while retaining the accuracy. (Hoyt says "…short bow manufacturers have never truly delivered on accuracy. Until now." And we always – and apparently mistakenly – thought accuracy was the archer's input into the system.)

The 31-inch axle-to-axle HavocTEC has a 7-3/4-inch brace height and an IBO rated speed of 308 fps. It is founded on the TEC riser for 23- to 31-inch draw lengths and has upper and lower machined holes for attaching a two-piece quiver and a center hole for a built-in, straight carbon cable guard. The HavocTEC comes with split limbs and two Sims Limb Savers.

Of special interest is the new Cam & a half Performance System available in either 65 percent or 75 percent let-off and with draw weights of 40 to 80 pounds for hunting (in camo) or 30 to 70 for competition. Curiously the Cam & A Half Performance System is a twin-cam design that Hoyt says eliminates cam timing (synchronous roll-over) problems because the top and bottom cams are symmetrical.

JENNINGS BY NORTH AMERICAN

California's Tom Jennings, who was building recurves at the time, was the first true convert to Holless W. Allen's crazy-looking compound bow in the late 1960s. Holless filed for a patent on June 23, 1966 and was granted patent number 3,486,495. Tom became his first licensee and generally staked his company on the compound bow. Jennings Archery enjoyed a dozen years of prosperity until a disagreement with the Allen family eventually forced him to go out of business and then sell his manufacturing company to Bear Archery in the early 1980s.

The GrandMaster is a 300 fps IBO rated (228 fps AMO) top-of-the-line compound bow produced under the Jennings name today. With a slightly deflexed aluminum riser, torque-resistant carbon twill straight solid limbs and a perimeter weighted one-cam with 70 percent let-off (of course, a 65 percent module is available), the GrandMaster was designed to display the Jennings by North American technical artistry. (Included with each purchase is an upper mount carbon cable guard for archers who prefer that style.)

Accented in blue, the long 40-inch axle-to-axle GrandMaster is equipped with a SwingArm Cable Guard tipped with the exclusive North American Kraton Shock Stop string oscillation suppressor. Small, vibration-absorbing Sims LimbSaver riser technology tames additional vibration in the machined riser. The GrandMaster features a blue/black TechTwist bowstring, factory-installed speed buttons and titanium-styled hardware. For competition, it is available in a Deep Sea Blue. Brace height is 7-1/2 inches and mass weight is almost 4-1/2 pounds. Jennings provides the GrandMaster in peak draw weights of 50, 60 and 70 pounds. Optional modules for the one-cam allow draw length adjustment from 26 to 33 inches.

KODIAK

Kodiak is also new to the bow building business and once you have seen one of the stylized cutouts in their machined aluminum reflex handles, you can recognize them from a distance. Their KO Series one-cam bows, which currently include the KO 32 (because it is 32 inches long) and the KO 36 (yep, 36 inches long), have solid, straight limbs, a high mount steel cable guard and attractive, two-piece wood grip plates.

The KO 32 and KO 36 each weigh about 3 1/3 pounds, as the difference is the longer limbs on the 36. Draw lengths and peak draw weights for each are similar: 26 to 30 inches and 60 or 70 pounds.

MARTIN

The name Cougar Magnum has been a part of the Martin family for some time, as has a track record for innovative approach to archery design. The Martin family builds traditional bows in their Damon Howatt and Nirk lines and developed an early one-cam bow design called the Dyna-Bo. Martin is quiet, but effective.

The Gold Series Cougar Magnum measures 36-1/2 inches axle-to-axle. Its 22-inch machined aluminum riser is slightly reflexed and the plunger hole is slotted for infinite positioning adjustments of the arrow rest. A significant feature is Martin's VEM or Vibration Escape Module silencing system installed through each end of the riser. These soft, black rubbery buttons look

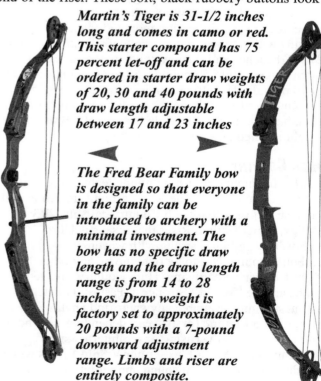

Martin's Tiger is 31-1/2 inches long and comes in camo or red. This starter compound has 75 percent let-off and can be ordered in starter draw weights of 20, 30 and 40 pounds with draw length adjustable between 17 and 23 inches

The Fred Bear Family bow is designed so that everyone in the family can be introduced to archery with a minimal investment. The bow has no specific draw length and the draw length range is from 14 to 28 inches. Draw weight is factory set to approximately 20 pounds with a 7-pound downward adjustment range. Limbs and riser are entirely composite.

a lot like those from Sims Vibration Labs.

The limbs on the four pound Cougar Magnum are 14-inch, solid-glass composite. Because the limbs are thicker at the ends where the cam and idler are fastened through them, this bow does not need reinforcing buttons to prevent the limbs from splitting.

Martin calls its one-cam a Fuzion Cam. Let-off can be changed to either 65 or 75 percent with a change of module. The cable guard is a simple bent steel rod and it may be installed either above or below the grip. The Cougar Magnum arrangement allows positioning the cable to a minimum offset so that the cable and forward portion of the string come off the grooves of the cam with the least amount of angle.

Peak draw weights are 50, 60 and 70 pounds while draw lengths range from 26 to 32 inches. The bow has a limited five-year warranty.

As tested by archery pro shop owner and writer Emery Loiselle, the Cougar Magnum stored 68.7 ft-lbs of energy at 50 pounds draw weight (30-inch draw length) and 82.4 ft-lbs at 60 pounds draw weight with a brace height of between 6-7/8 and 6-3/4 inches. Limb tip travel is a short 1-5/8 inches and according to Loiselle writing for ArrowTrade magazine, "A short limb travel uses less of the stored energy for limb recovery at the shot." The bow performed 226 fps AMO and 289 fps IBO. One interesting calculation that Loiselle makes is energy efficiency or how well the bow uses its energy at any particular setting. "The range of efficiencies," he writes, "ran from 64.3 percent with the lightest 250-grain arrow at 55 pounds to a high of 76.2 percent with the three heaviest arrows at the same draw weight."

The manufacturer's suggested retail price for the Cougar Magnum is $688.86.

MATHEWS

Utilizing an innovative marketing strategy, Mathews has given every other bow company a run for the heart and soul of archery during the past decade. At 308 fps IBO and 235 fps AMO, the new 34-inch axle-to-axle Legacy has been the hottest selling Mathews bow ever, founder Matt McPherson says. A 25-inch, lightweight machined aluminum handle and short, Fiberglas "parallel" limbs" make the Legacy a speedy shooter, but with the Mathews "extras" and a 7-1/2-inch brace height, this is a very forgiving bow, too. According to Mathews, shorter limbs dampen vibration more quickly and as limbs approach parallel (or horizontal), their inherent vibration tends to be cancelled out.

Mathews has addressed the current widespread interest in damping noise and vibration with String Suppressors and Harmonic Dampers. The String Suppressors are rubber bumpers that attach to the Legacy's axles and "stifle the ringing vibration driven by the bowstring at its source, the limb and string." The Harmonic Dampers are removable rubber inserts with brass weights that are set into the fat part of the handle riser near the limb attachment bolt. In theory, these Harmonic Dampers absorb vibration (which is nothing more than stray energy that is not absorbed by your arrow) and pass it along to their centered brass weights.

The interesting aspect of the Legacy however is that Mathews has gone back to a 1970s system for moving cables out of the way of your arrow. The above-arrow, riser-mounted Roller Guard minimizes the friction of cables rubbing over a cable guard/cable saver by rolling the cables over a pair of machined wheels.

McPHERSON

McPherson Pro Shop bows are a division of Ben Pearson – or perhaps it is the other way around since the owners of McPherson Archery actually purchased the Pearson name. Whatever. The 35-inch McPherson Raptor VX illustrates an interesting move by several manufacturers back into the twin-cam market. One cam bows have dominated archery for ten years because a single cam on the bottom limb balanced by a wheel (or idler) on the top limb essentially eliminated cam timing concerns (concerns that the cams rolled over in properly timed sequence for fully effective shooting). One-cam bows may eliminate timing problems, but they have raised concerns about straight-line nock travel. Matt McPherson, who started McPherson Archery and sold it and then started Mathews Archery, which he currently owns and operates, basically invented the one-cam bows. One-cam bows have many functional advantages, but they are usually slower than hot twin-cam bows. Speed is an issue.

At 325 to 330 fps IBO, the McPherson Raptor VX is long on speed. It is built with a long riser, relatively flat 42-degree limb pockets and short limbs, too, all of which are creeping design features in archery since the advent of highly maneuverable, but hard to manage 31-inch speed bows. With stainless steel ball bearings in the twin Raptor cams, efficiency lost to friction in this bow should be minimal.

PARKER

"Short and sweet," archery technical expert Norb Mullaney has written. "Parker's Ultra-Lite 31 is a finely designed hunting bow. I can say without question, this is the lightest compound I have ever placed on a scale."

The 31-inch Parker Ultra-Lite 31 is built on a machined, 6061-T6 aluminum riser that is slightly reflexed and outfitted with a one-piece walnut grip. The limbs are Gordon Power Tuff, solid and straight. The machined one-cam comes in a box at 80 percent let-off but with the proper module (available on request, Parker says), it is quickly converted to 65 percent. The fixed, upper cable guard is carbon composite. And – it weighs slightly less than three pounds!

Dressed in Superflauge Camo by Lynch with a brace height of 7 inches, the Ultra-Lite 31 achieves IBO rated arrow speed of 310 fps and AMO rated speeds of 240. Draw weights are 50, 60 and 70 pounds and the draw length range is 23 to 30 inches. Parker offers a Lifetime Warranty to the original purchaser, excluding strings, cables and the finish on the bow.

PEARSON

Do you call this company "Pearson" or by the name of its founder and the name it operated so successfully under for half a century, "Ben Pearson?" Its current ownership rescued Pearson from a dusty warehouse about a dozen years ago and today, its innovative characteristics and bow presentation are as good as it gets. Two years ago, Pearson designed a new riser with an built-in vibration reduction chamber below the grip and named it their VIB~X System. The company claims that independent testing at the University of Alabama College of Engineering shows that VIB~X reduces noise and vibration levels after a shot by as much as 40 percent.

The VIB~X riser chamber accepts a molded insert, a "formulated polymer gel" called Vibasorb which is supplied exclusively by Vibracheck. Tom McMillan, president and owner of Pearson, says that most bow companies place dampening devices around the limb pockets or out on the limbs, but by manufacturing the riser with VIB~X immediately below the grip where bow vibration is centered, the result is a higher level of silence and shooting comfort. The rod in the center of the molded gel is threaded to accept a stabilizer that is thereby effectively insulated from direct metal-to-metal contact with the riser. Following a shot, a shock-absorbing stabilizer is free to "stir the gel" and this makes it much more effective.

The Pearson Freedom comes in two versions. One is a hunting model in SuperFlauge Camo by Lynch Worldwide. This 35-3/16-inch axle-to-axle hunter has a 6-11/16-inch brace height. Let-off is standard at 75 percent, but 65 and 85 percent modules are available. Draw lengths are also modular. The Freedom will fit shooters from 23 to 30 inches with peak draw weights of 50, 60 or 70 pounds. The machined aluminum riser

has 42-degree limb pockets for its 12-1/2 inch split limbs. The arrow rest shelf has a quiet velvet antler finish and this one-cam bow comes with the Pearson Lifetime Guarantee. The Freedom is IBO speed rated at 310 to 315 fps (30 inch draw at 70 pounds with a five grain per pound arrow).

The Freedom Pro is decked out in a red, white and blue flag design that Pearson calls its "All-American Camo." While the ball-bearing mounted Z-Cam and Accu-Trac Idler are polished instead of black and the VIB~X is black rather than the brownish-gold of the hunting model, the Freedom Pro is essentially the same bow as the Freedom.

PRECISION SHOOTING EQUIPMENT

Best known as PSE or "Pete Shepley Enterprises" for its rugged and innovative founder, Pete Shepley, PSE says it holds more archery patents than any other manufacturer in the archery industry. Pete's patents include such things as a bow handle with offset sight window (November 2000), pivoting limb pockets (January 1994), molded bow limbs (March 1987), method for stringing a bow limb (August 1988) and compound bow having offset cable anchor (May 1994). And chances are, Pete and PSE are not finished yet.

PSE offers new cam options and a new lightweight riser design for its Nitro bows for 2003 … and they are offered in either OneCam or Twin-cam versions. Both versions of the Nitro share many similar features. Both of these bow risers are available in PSE's own PSE Brush camo or in three competition colors: snake scale patterned Python Blue or Python Red, or the red-white-blue Good Vibrations. Both are built on a relatively lightweight, reflex machined aluminum handle riser with pivoting limb pockets and slim wood grips. Both bows are equipped with the PSE-Sims Vibration Lab NV System strategically placed at the limb bolts to minimize vibration and shock before it reaches the riser. (The NV System, by the way, will mount on many different bows which use the AMO Standard 5/16-18 flathead limb bolt for attaching the limbs to the riser. According to PSE, the NV System "greatly reduces shock and vibration in today's high performance bows." The NV System shock absorbers are available in PSE Brush camo, black and polished or Brite for competition.)

The 36-inch Nitro Centerfire OneCam is available for draw lengths from 25 to 30 inches and peak draw weights of 60 and 70 pounds. The bow is shipped with a high, 80 percent let-off, but 65 percent modules are available. With a short, 6-inch brace height, the Nitro OneCam achieves 315 fps IBO.

The 36-inch Nitro Maxis-Plus TwinCam is available for draw lengths from 26 to 31 inches and peak draw weights of 60 and 70 pounds. The bow is shipped at the Pope & Young maximum 65 percent let-off. With a short, 6-inch brace height, the Nitro OneCam achieves 308 fps IBO.

REFLEX

Reflex is a division of Hoyt ... which is a division of Easton ... and famous archery writer and archery hunter Chuck Adams has been part of the family there for many years. Chuck is a believer in relatively "safe" speed bows that result in quick-enough, forgiving shooting. Accuracy, he says, is a whole lot better than speed.

The 34-inch axle-to-axle Denali is a new Reflex bow which features split Fiberglas limbs, a reflex machined aluminum riser and a straight, lightweight carbon cable guard. The let-off is adjustable from 60 to 75 percent and the draw length is adjustable from 27-1/2 to 30-1/2inches. This single-cam hunter has a long, 8-1/2-inch brace height and draw weight ranges from 50 to 70 pounds.

RENEGADE

The 41-inch Renegade Non Typical XL is a unique bow in this day of marketing for speed, short bow length and release shooting. It is designed for finger shooters. The machined, offset deflex aluminum riser is 18-7/8 inches long and it is equipped with a high-mount, adjustable composite cable guard and a symmetrical, one-piece walnut grip.

The Non Typical has Fiberglas limbs and Renegade's 1-Cam. The solid, straight limbs are machined from blanks of Gordon Power-Tuff unidirectional Fiberglas. The modular 1-Cam permits draw lengths from 29 to 36 inches and let-off of 80 and 65 percent. The bowstring is braided Fast Flight while the cables are made from Brownell's Ultra-Cam material. Peak draw weights are 60 and 70 pounds. Renegade also offers the Non Typical with a smoother drawing EZ-1 Solo Wheel. Recalling that this bow was designed for finger shooters, its modest arrow speeds should not be a surprise. The Non Typical rates 205 fps with a 30 inch draw at 60 pounds and a 540 grain arrow. With a lighter, 360 grain arrow, testing achieved 241 fps. The brace height on this compound bow is a remarkably high 9 1/2 inches.

STORM

Storm is a newcomer in the business. You may recall it as Clearwater or even Clearwater-Storm, but in October 2001 Jerry Rathburn purchased it from founder David Powers and one year later, simplified the name. Storm!

These bow models are competitive, fast and pleasantly forgiving. Led by five-time 3-D IBO World Champion and 22-time National Champion Burley Hall, Storm is promoting "Storm-Line Technology." This "technology" presents a compact front bow profile just 4 inches wide, including the integral Storm two-piece five-arrow quiver, pin sight with level and shoot-through arrow rest. Burley says this is about half the width of conventional bow and accessory set-ups. While there may certainly be some small maneuverability or balance benefit to this, many other factors would take precedence in order of shooting importance.

The new Storm F-28 bow is built around a dramatically reflexed machined aluminum riser and their machined, P-38 modular one-cam that is adjustable for let-off with its draw stop post from 65 to 80 percent. With speeds "in excess of" 310 fps IBO and a thin two-piece grip, the 36-inch F-28 can be purchased with variable draw lengths from 26 to 30 inches. Burley says the brace height is an "easy to work with" 7-1/4 inches. The suggested retail price of the Storm F-28 hunter in camo is $659 and the optional, integrated accessory package is an additional $117. The F-28 dressed for the competition line in either Windswept Blue or Windswept Black costs $100 extra.

TRU-FLITE GENESIS AND FRED BEAR FAMILY BOW

The 36-inch axle-to-axle Genesis bow, crafted originally by Matt McPherson's Mathews Archery, has an innovative cam that eliminates let-off and thereby fits all draw lengths from 15 to 30 inches. Practically anyone can shoot it. The Genesis is the first bow that accommodates young, beginning and adult archers alike. Since let-off is eliminated, the Genesis stores and releases energy comparable to a 35-pound recurve (when set at 20 pound peak weight). It has a machined aluminum riser and an aluminum, Genesis one-cam system with aluminum idler. The brace height is 7-1/2 inches. These bows also have composite limbs, a molded grip and a stainless steel cable guard. Each measures 36 inches axle-to-axle. Zero let-off! Matt says this bow was developed and is sold at about cost to help the next generation get into archery.

Following the Mathews lead, Fred Bear by North American has a 33-inch Family Bow with no specific draw length. It will fit archers drawing from 14 to 28 inches and is factory set at a light 20 pounds draw weight with a 7-pound downward adjustment range. "The light holding weight is necessary to ensure that the string will pull away from your fingers upon release," says North American's Joe White. Limbs and riser are composite and of course let-off is zero. (Unfortunately, at this time these bows are only available for right-handed archers.)

BOW RISERS: THE AUTHOR'S TRIBUTE TO MATERIALS AND ENGINEERING

When I began bowhunting in 1978, my first recurve was a Bear '76er Take-Down Recurve with a magnesium-alloy handle painted green. Within a year, I bought a 50 percent let-off two-wheel Browning Safari, my first compound bow. The riser on the recurve was thin and the grip was easy to manage whereas the handsome, laminated wood riser on the compound was a real handful. Today, I shoot a Pearson Anaconda, which has a machined aluminum 20-degree slant riser.

What accounts for the materials change when some of the original Jennings compound bows were magnesium and virtually all of the Allen-produced bows were wood handles?

Certain types of hardwood have properties that make wood very interesting for bow risers and totally acceptable – even desirable – for many styles. Unlike metal, it is warm to the feel. This quality is important when you are outside in cold weather. Hunting in Minnesota and the Dakotas in sub-freezing temperatures in December taught me the value of a warm handle.

Wood is also much lighter than a comparable chunk of metal and it looks better, too. Of course, now that we are insisting that virtually all or our archery products come with a popular camouflage pattern applied, a bow's "good looks" is less a function of color than it is of structure.

My first cam (as opposed to a wheel) bow was a relatively short axle-to-axle wood-riser compound that I drew to about 65 pounds. It was built by Ken Laird's American Archery. On a successful caribou hunt to northern Quebec in 1986, it performed flawlessly and was a real hunting buddy. On returning home however, I was disappointed to discover that it had begun to crack. The next time I went hunting, I had switched to an Oneida Eagle with a cast magnesium riser.

Wood was gradually replaced by metal for risers as bows became faster and stored more energy. What limits are appropriate for wood compound risers depend on the design and the quality of wood selected. Private manufacturers are still building excellent wood handle recurves and longbows with heavy draw weight.

Nevertheless, although it is lighter than metal, the properties of wood can be inconsistent and any imperfection in the finishing process can create a handle that absorbs water which will immediately cause it to begin the process of warping. Anyone who works with wood knows that the grain, however beautiful, can take irregular turns and the hardness varies from spot to spot through the cross-section. Laminating risers, cutting and gluing thin strips together, perhaps with a colorful section of Fiberglas between them, rather than cutting whole risers out of a single block of wood helps significantly with structural integrity. Still, the failure and perhaps the injury rate for wood risers would be very high if we mass-produced compound bows with 100 ft-lbs. of energy to shoot 300 fps arrows. Manufacturers are not interested in building equipment (even cheap, low end equipment) that fails because you would ask them to make repairs and their legal liability for any injury in these sue-happy days would be extraordinary.

Many of the same things said about wood are true for magnesium, even though it is a significant improvement over wood for high-energy shooting. A magnesium riser can withstand the 100 ft-lbs. of strain in a hot-shooting bow, because it is a stronger material. Magnesium is more consistent in cross section. Still, manufacturing often causes a couple of problems with cast magnesium-alloy handles. When hot molten metal is poured into molds, tiny air bubbles can form as it cools. These bubbles create weak spots. Although they are much stronger than laminated wood risers, magnesium handles do occasionally bend and sometimes break, especially when high draw weights are combined with light arrows. When a metal handle breaks or snaps, the result can be catastrophic. Cast-metal handles also have a tendency to warp as they cool. This can potentially degrade riser tolerances enough to affect bow performance.

So, for these reasons, aluminum risers have essentially taken over the high-end bow market. Aluminum risers are cut or machined from a solid aluminum bar, often with the computer programmed assistance of extremely expensive milling machines. Computer control means that today's aluminum risers are built to precise standards and tolerances and they are extremely strong. Machined aluminum handles are heavier than magnesium risers though and they are more expensive.

Compared to magnesium, aluminum can be highly uniform in cross section. For the scientifically minded, the atomic weight and density of magnesium are 24.312 and 1.74 respectively while the comparable figures for aluminum are 26.981 and 2.70. Both of these materials are abundant in the earth's crust.

Several companies (Forge and PSE) have experimented with forged risers, but they have not yet "caught on" with the archery public, because there is no obvious benefit at this time to the greater price charged for forging. In the forging process, aluminum billets are compressed (mashed or stamped!) into a handle-shaped mold. Machining adds finishing touches such as de-burring and cutting weight-reduction holes. Manufacturers claim that forged aluminum handles are stronger than handles machined from a bar so they can be slimmer and lighter without sacrificing strength.

Diamond Archery and perhaps High Country have also experimented with carbon risers. The obvious benefit to an archer is carbon's light weight. After all, we shoot carbon arrows, why not a carbon bow? High-end carbon bows can weigh as little as three pounds, even when they are completely outfitted with a rest, sight and quiver full of arrows. If you do a great deal of stalking or still hunting, especially "out West" on the plains for mule deer or in the mountains for elk, saving a few pounds is important, especially with a bow which is hard to sling over your shoulder or carry anywhere but in your hand.

In spite of some arguable benefits, carbon risers made a brief splash on the market a few years ago, but have since virtually disappeared. Their appearance, compared to the angular styling of most of today's reflex risers is inelegant. Plus, basic riser shape is limited because of the nature of the woven carbon materials. Aluminum and magnesium can be reflexed or deflexed, but carbon offers an essentially straight riser. Unlike a metal riser, carbon-based risers – which are primarily Fiberglas – need inserts and outserts to attach accessories and while the threads of a drilled and tapped aluminum riser can relatively easily be stripped, this is not common

THE TORQUE REDUCING CABLE (TRC) SYSTEM

Winner's Choice Custom Bowstrings has a product it believes really helps accuracy with one-cam bows. The Torque Reducing Cable or TRC System eliminates "between 60 and 80 percent of side torque generated by standard cable guards," says President Tom Nealy. "This helps reduce left-right arrow problems caused by buss cable induced torque, improves bow stability and enhances forgiveness."

Shooters occasionally notice that their sight pins are not in alignment with the arrow when the bow is at rest and the cause is cable guard torque, Nealy claims. This is one visible sign of cable guard torque.

"The buss cable on the single cam bow is responsible for a disproportionate amount of torque," Nealy says. "The TRC System splits the buss cable into two sections on either side of the arrow leaving both sides of the buss cable in a torque-free state. The splitter itself is length adjustable to enable the distance between the cable's two sides to be easily manipulated to attain a free-floating state. While one side of the cable still routes through a cable slide for guidance, it is essentially floating free in the groove, imparting no torque to the cable guard or bow. While the cable slide is still necessary to hold the return side of the string out of the arrow plane and does impart some pressure on the cable guard, this is reduced because the return side of the string can run in the 'closest to the arrow' position. And because this system operates above the bow arm, arm clearance is not a problem."

The TRC System works on most conventional single cam bows that use an above the rest cable guard. It is also recommended for bows with at least four inches between the grip and the nearest buss cable for total arm clearance. Nealy notes that the TRC System will not fit on some bows with oversized idler wheels such as the Mathews Q2XL and with Hoyt's dual track idler.

ARCHER TO THE STARS

Bob Markworth has shot the bow and arrow in 56 countries and in front of millions of people since he became a professional archer in 1954. He has performed live and on tape for television dozens of times, beginning with the famous Ed Sullivan Show, and has often launched arrows behind the scenes for movie stars. Prior to his ascension to international acclaim, he won the American amateur archery championships three years in a row, from 1951 trough 1953. Bob is indeed the 20th Century Robin Hood.

"I have the only professional archery act in the world that tours night clubs, hotels, theatres, sport shows and circuses," Bob says. "I began with a recurve, of course, and now shoot a compound, a recurve and a crossbow."

Bob's act on stage consists of a variety of trick shots, some of them phenomenal. He cuts cards in half – lengthwise – shoots aspirin out of the air, bursts balloons which his partner holds in her mouth and on her head and he will shoot multiple arrows at one time – with extreme precision.

Originally from Glendale, California, his first full-time job was selling advertising space for the Glendale

continue on next page

ARCHER TO THE STARS CONTINUED

Independent newspaper. "Once I began taking archery lessons though, it was all I wanted to do. I never looked back," Bob says. When he is not on stage or on a bowhunting trip, Bob tours extensively, demonstrating the bow and arrow for school programs.

On stage, his small-wheel, deflex handle compound may only be set to 40 pounds, but as a bowhunter, Bob usually has bigger game in the sights of his heavier bows. He has successfully hunted on six continents: tigers, leopards, pythons and crocodiles in the Orient and most species of North American and African big game.

Bob Markworth's bowhunting articles appear regularly in U.S. archery magazines and he has recently produced – in cooperation with some of America's greatest archers and bowhunters – a hugely enjoyable 70-minute video called *The Arrow Master*, which he says is "an in-depth look at every aspect of the sport of archery from its primitive origin to the remarkable and diverse sport that it is today."

One of Bob Markworth's great shots is to shoot an apple off the head of his assistant, Mayana, blindfolded! During his archery act, Bob shoots a low poundage compound wheel bow. Light and forgiving.

In spite of his "archer to the stars" reputation, Bob Markworth is a bowhunter at heart. His new video, The Arrow Master, is a fascinating and in-depth look at the sport of archery from its primitive origin to the diverse, complex sport that it is today

Bob Markworth, Archer to the Stars, has logged hundreds of thousands of miles giving archery trick shooting demonstrations that are entertaining and amazing. Here he shoots two arrows at once.

RECURVES AND LONGBOWS

"Traditional does not mean antique," write the developers of the 2003 Fred Bear Traditional Archery Equipment catalog. "Traditional means that the bow and its styling are classic. Traditional means that the methods of shooting and hunting with it conform to a worldview of man as a predator and the chase as a natural phenomenon in nature. Life and death are one.

"Recurves and longbows are not for everyone, but if you are called, you understand the commitment that is necessary to be effective with the stick-and-string. You understand the requirement for time to become proficient, the true limitation of your shooting distance. If you are called, you understand The Code."

Not an endorsement, just well stated. One of the fastest-growing segments of bowhunting today is traditional archery. We have heard this mantra ever since the compound bow took over the marketplace and it is a mixture of wishful thinking and persistence on the part of those addicted to what they consider "real" archery, archery without wheels.

Traditional equipment, longbows and recurve bows, all but disappeared in the 1970s with the

Traditional archery customarily means shooting with recurves, longbows, back quivers and wood arrows ... and without overdraws, fiber optic sights and releases. Is traditional shooting growing in popularity? Perhaps it is, but the question should be: With the development of high tech archery gear, why hasn't traditional archery gone away? Could it be more fun? More challenging? More satisfying? Traditional shooters believe these questions can be answered with an enthusiastic, "Yes!"

This is the classic style recurve. The Martin Hunter is available in draw weights from 30 to 70 pounds with a mass weight of a little over two pounds and AMO length of 62 inches tip-to-tip. The riser includes black dyed laminates of hard maple, bubinga and zebrawood with white maple highlights. The limbs are made from laminates of maple and black fiberglass with bubinga and black fiberglass overlays.

appearance and rapid rise to popularity of the compound bow. But in the 1980s, interest in traditional "stick bows" was reborn – modestly at first, but gradually "traditional shooting" gained a respectable following. Today, the stick bow movement shows no signs of halting and indeed may actually be growing.

The hunter who carries a recurve or longbow typically is an experienced archer who has mastered the modern compound and is looking for an additional challenge. Some chose stick bows for aesthetic reasons; recurves and longbows are simple and beautiful, without the "mechanical gadgetry" that is required to make a compound bow work. All longbows and many recurves are still wood laminates and the structure can be elegant, a work of art. Instinctive shooters are also drawn to traditional bows for their light weight and smooth draw.

But be aware that traditional bows are more difficult to use. They cannot be tuned and sighted with the same precision as compound bows, and they require more force to hold at full draw. Chances are your 60-pound longbow will reach 60 pounds before full draw with no let-off, while a comparable 60-pound compound bow with 75 percent let-off requires only 15 pounds of holding force.

The differences between a recurve and longbow are obvious even though there are several popular styles that have limbs that curve in recurve style. Recurve bows have limbs that curve back toward the front of the bow while most longbows have limbs that form a smooth curve toward the string. Which type do you chose? It's mostly a matter of personal preference. The recurve is probably the best choice for an archer already familiar with modern compound bows. Except for the let-off feature, the compound bow and the recurve are similar in some respects. Both are medium-length bows with pistol-style grips and with some models their performance characteristics can be comparable. With practice, basic proficiency with a recurve is easily attainable for those making the transition from modern equipment.

The longbow closely resembles the classic bow used by Native Americans and medieval archers. Although it is pleasurable to shoot, the longbow is a more difficult transition for an archery accustomed to shooting a compound. The longbow is extremely light for shooters conditioned to modern compound tackle, and the handle style is quite different. In fact, most shooters first gain experience with a recurve before turning to the longbow. Many experienced traditionalists however enjoy shooting both types of stick bows.

RECURVES

Even if you are used to a compound, today's recurve bow is fast, quiet, stable and a pleasure to shoot. Each limb on the recurve has two power curves that bend as the bow is drawn, thus storing energy. This gives the recurve more potential energy and faster speed than the typical longbow, which has a single power curve for each limb. Some recurve bows are even comparable to compound bows in speed, although admittedly at the lower AMO ratings of 200 to 225 fps range, NOT the 260 to 310 fps range. And the recurve draws smoother and has less hand shock than the longbow and some compound bows, too.

LENGTH: Recurve hunting bows come in a wide range of lengths, from 46 to 72 inches, but the most popular lengths are 60 and 62 inches. Bows below 58 inches are typically for specialty uses, or for young people or shooters with shorter draw lengths. Most shooters prefer bows over 64 inches with draw lengths exceeding 30 inches. Because of the limb design, a short recurve will usually be more comfortable to shoot than a short longbow.

When choosing a recurve bow, match the bow length to your individual draw length, as shown in the general recommendations chart below:

Draw Length	Bow Length
27 inches or less	56-58 inches
28-29 inches	60-62 inches
29-30 inches	62-64 inches
More than 30 inches	64-66 inches

When deciding on a bow length, consider your personal preferences and how you will use the bow. Bowhunting in open country or by stalking will allow the use of a longer bow. Because of the possibility of banging your bow against the stand and maneuvering while tied to a tree, stand hunters generally prefer a shorter bow, as do those hunting thick cover. Some archers prefer the feel and comfort of a longer bow; others like the balance and maneuverability of a shorter bow. It is entirely a personal decision based on the indefinable concept "how it feels to me."

DESIGN: Recurves are available in solid one-piece style or in takedown models. Takedown longbows are available, too, but are rarely seen at club shoots or in the field, perhaps because there is a sentiment among traditionalists that the takedown or take-apart concept goes against the traditional grain. One-piece bows have a fixed length and bow weight; while takedown recurves consist of three pieces – two limbs and a riser section – and takedown longbows break at the grip.

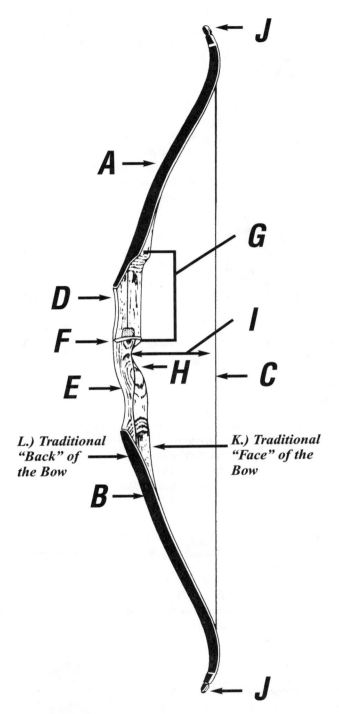

L.) Traditional "Back" of the Bow

K.) Traditional "Face" of the Bow

A. Upper Recurve Limb, B. Lower Recurve Limb, C. Bowstring, D. Handle Riser, E. Converta-Accessory Insert (Stabilizer Mount) – Optional, F. Arrow Shelf, G. Sight Window, H. Grip, I. Brace Height, J. String Notches (on either side of reinforced limb tip), K. Traditional "Face" of the bow: toward the archer, L. Traditional "Back" of the bow: away from the archer

An alternate and popular method used by many traditional shooters to carry their arrows into the field is a back quiver.

You will need a way to carry arrows and one common method is with a two-piece quiver that attaches to your recurve's riser.

A recurve bow stringer will help you set up to shoot safely.

Placing a bow tip protector over the tips of your recurve will help keep it intact when you are stringing and throughout a day in the field.

At the end of the day, a soft protective case keeps your longbow from getting banged up on the trip home.

Rubber, serve-on or tie-on string silencers placed six inches or so from each limb tip will help silence any noise from your shot.

Traditionalists take pride in their cedar shafts, often decorating them with individual paint jobs called "cresting."

A leather, lace-up armguard with shoe-hooks to hold the laces tight.

Brush buttons run over the string and nestled against the limb keeps your recurve from snagging in the undergrowth and picking up leaves and branches in the acute pinch between string and limb.

Traditionalists are finger shooters. They wear gloves or tabs to grip the bowstring, or shoot with bare fingers.

One-piece bows have a more traditional appearance that some archers prefer and they generally are lighter and have better balance than takedown bows, but the takedown recurve is considerably more versatile. By changing limbs on some takedown bows, you can alter their length and draw weight, a distinct advantage, especially for a beginning archer. A newcomer who begins with a 64-inch, 50-pound bow, for example, may decide after a year or two that a 62-inch, 55-pound bow is more appropriate. Rather than buy a new bow, the archer can simply purchase a new set of limbs and mount them on the original riser.

RISER: The length of the riser is a major factor in the length of the sight window, which often determines the type of sight you can use (if you use a sight) or your aiming method. In combination with the limbs, the riser is basic to the design and "feel" of the bow.

Some hunters prefer a longer riser section because it allows a longer sight window. This affords a better view of the target. But a longer riser usually means shorter limbs, which will affect the way the bow shocks your hand when you shoot it. For this reason, many archers prefer the combination of a short riser and longer limbs. If the bow is canted slightly to the side when shot, a longer sight window is not needed. Selecting the right length is best accomplished by shooting many bows with different riser lengths and choosing the one that feels best for your shooting style, the bow you believe you will be most successful with.

Limbs are usually laminated using fiberglass and a variety of woods. Risers can be made from a wide selection of materials from lathed and laminated wood to machined aluminum to modern formed carbon composites. While some modern recurves do have cast or machined aluminum risers, these materials are most often used in competition bows. (It is exceedingly rare to see a wood-riser at any but the lowest levels of international competition.) Most hunting recurves – and all longbows – have wood risers, either solid or laminated and these are often customized with inlays. Most recurve risers are designed to accommodate the use of arrow rests, stabilizers and sights, similar to those used on compound bows. Of course, whether these are actually attached or not is strictly a personal decision.

DRAW WEIGHT: It is impossible to overemphasize the importance of selecting a traditional bow that you can draw and shoot comfortably. The most common archery "shopping error" is choosing a draw weight that is too heavy and expecting that with a little practice you can "grow into it." The average man can manage a traditional bow in the 45- to 50-pound range, while women should choose 30 to 35 pounds to begin shooting.

A reasonable draw weight is particularly important when you first begin shooting with a recurve. Beginners can be taught to shoot adequately in a few sessions if they are drawing moderate weight; using bows that are too heavy, they may give up and never learn to shoot correctly.

Longbows

A few years ago, the longbow was an oddity and archers who shot them like the renowned Howard Hill were few and far between. Today, the longbow is a common sight in hunting camps and on archery ranges all across the country. For many, the longbow represents a return to the roots of archery in the US. The Native American Indians shot longbows, as did the first archers of note in this century, including Art Young, Saxton Pope, Maurice and Will Thompson, and Chief Compton.

Longbows do not shoot as fast as recurves or compound bows, and they require more practice for an archer to achieve proficiency. They are also rougher in the hand and produce a good deal more hand shock. But these "primitive" characteristics are precisely what devotees of traditional archery find so appealing.

But longbows have merits, too. Because they use longer limbs and have limbs with a single curve, longbows are particularly stable launching platforms. Often equipped with specially constructed Flemish

The Mountaineer Longbow from Martin is 68 inches long and has the classic longbow styling with a simple leather grip. Its slightly deflexed limbs remove hand shock and stack without affecting its natural aiming characteristics. Draw weights from 30 to 70 pounds are available and the bow's mass weight is 1 lb. 5 oz. The riser is exotic zebrawood and the limbs are laminations of red elm and fiberglass.

Traditional bowhunter Tom Brunofsky took this 6 x 6 Colorado bull elk with a 60-pound Wing Recurve, a Grizzly broadhead and self-made cedar arrows in 1996. Traditional equipment is suitable for hunting any big game animal in the world, but it is the hunter behind the bow who needs practice, practice, and practice.

strings, they are also very quiet. Many archers find the combination of stability, silence and tradition ideal for hunting and recreational shooting.

Although today's longbows are mostly built with modern materials, including fiberglass and new laminate bonding agents, there is a tiny segment of the longbow fraternity that builds and shoots the self bow, which is made entirely of a single piece of wood.

BOW LENGTH: Because a longbow limb is a single power curve – as opposed to the recurve's double curve – the limbs must be longer in order to achieve the necessary efficiency to launch an arrow with penetrating ability (kinetic energy). The most popular longbow lengths are 66 and 68 inches, but modern materials are now making it possible to create 62- and 64-inch longbows that have excellent performance. If tree-stand hunters switch to longbows in any significant numbers, shorter bows will likely become increasingly popular and more readily available through other than custom manufacturing outlets.

As with the recurve, the ideal bow length depends largely on your draw length. Keep in mind that the typical longbow shooter's draw will be about one inch less than with a recurve, and about $1\frac{1}{2}$ to 2 inches less than with a compound bow. Draw lengths exceeding 29 $\frac{1}{2}$ inches are rare in longbow shooters. Draw length recommendations are based on an average shooter and a longbow of standard modern design.

Draw Length	Longbow Bow Length
26 inches or less	66 inches or less
27 to 29 inches	66 inches
More than 29 inches	68 inches or more

DESIGN: Most longbows use a one-piece design. Some two-piece takedown models are commercially offered, but even though traveling with a 66-inch longbow is difficult and can be hazardous to the integrity of the bow, takedown longbows make up a small portion of the total longbow market. In contrast to the takedown recurve, which is aimed at versatility, the takedown longbow's appeal is mostly a matter of convenience, making the bow shorter.

The limbs on most longbows are a combination of fiberglass and other materials, usually wood laminates, and there has been much debate among manufacturers as to the best combination of these materials. Limbs that incorporate bamboo, maple, yew, Osage, black locust, hickory, tamarack and other woods are all available. Although some materials draw easier than others and some transfer less hand shock, in truth, there is little difference in the performance of these materials. This is because most of the limb power in

today's longbow comes from the fiberglass, not the wood laminations. In the modern longbow, performance is determined mostly by bow design and construction.

Self bows on the other hand, which are made without fiberglass, may significantly be affected by the choice of limb material.

DRAW WEIGHT: Because longbows are slightly less efficient than recurves or compounds, some archers make the mistake of compensating by choosing an overly heavy draw weight. That is a beginner's mistake. The poor shooting that results from being over-bowed is often blamed on the longbow. As with any bow, select a longbow weight which is comfortable for you and easy to shoot.

WHY?

We are a technological species. Perhaps the extent to which we make and use tools is what separates us from the other animal species, even from the other tool using animals, and there is beginning to be quite a list of those that even includes a few birds!

So, why do some members of our species deliberately turn away from the latest technology? Why are there people who move to Alaska to homestead with only an axe, a box of matches and a gleam in their eye? Why do people still drive buggies, even refusing to put the warning triangles on the back that might save their lives on dark nights? Why do some people choose to shoot less efficient, slower bows that pack less kinetic energy punch and have wide arcing trajectories to reach targets at any distance beyond 25 yards? Why indeed.

Tom Brunofsky shoots a 60-pound, 64-inch Bob Lee longbow that he draws to 28 inches. "I'm just a bowhunter," Tom says. "I've taken 40 or so whitetails, mule deer and elk, all with the longbow. When you shoot traditional, you have to shoot a lot to stay sharp. I have a treestand in my yard and I shoot year-round. Of course, I don't draw and aim. Just like Fred Bear, I'm all instinct, a snap shooter – but wouldn't necessarily recommend that style to anyone – but it is kind of unconscious and I never know when the string is going to release."

As far as archery goes, Tom says, "I think the longbow and recurve are more efficient than compounds because they are so much simpler and they can be just as effective, but the choice of a bow is a personal preference. With me, anything inside 20 yards is in trouble. Beyond that range, it's a matter of making a slow, careful decision about whether to shoot or not. I say a slow decision rather than a quick decision because even though I can get an arrow – several arrows in fact – off quicker and more accurately than someone shooting a compound, I want to take the time to be sure I can make a lethal shot. Hunting the way I do though with a real primitive weapon, I still get excited when I see a deer. I get a little rush of adrenaline."

Tom believes that "complexification" sometimes makes it difficult to hunt effectively. "A lot of archers miss when deer are closer than 20 yards," he says. "Under stress, it is easy to make a mistake and pick the wrong pin or to shoot at the whole deer. When I shoot a longbow – without sights, of course – I concentrate on one thing only, the spot on the target I want that arrow to hit. And moving deer are tougher for a compound with sights than with a longbow, because the longbow is instinct, not metal mechanics."

Like most traditional archers, Tom uses homemade wood arrows with feather fletching and shops enthusiastically at Three-Rivers Archery Supply, which does a thriving business in traditional gear and accessories.

You will not necessarily save any money shooting a traditional bow because name-brand, hand-made traditional longbows and recurves can easily cost between $500 and $1,000. You will save hundreds of dollars on the accessories you will not purchase – sights, shoot-through arrow rests, and releases – but few of North America's scores of thousands of traditional shooters do it because it is cheaper. They do it because it interests and challenges them on a more personal, even a more intimate level than high tech archery and that is what should motivate you, too, if you become curious about the boys in buckskin.

BLACK WIDOW

For a long time, Black Widow has been THE name in quality hunting recurves and Ken Black has built more than just a one-at-a-time custom traditional shop.

Ken's Ironwood (MA V) take-down recurve is handsome, sturdy and, for a recurve, fast enough. South American ironwood is two to three times harder than oak and it is this dark, maple-colored wood in the handle that makes the Ironwood take-down superior. The handle is cut $1/2$-inch past center and gives you a 5 $1/2$-inch sight window. The arrow rest shelf is radiused and, upon request, Black Widow will insert brass inserts for a Black Widow quiver, sight and stabilizer. Brace height is 8 $1/4$ to 9 inches and the mass weight is 3 $1/4$ pounds for a 60 inch bow, but the Ironwood can be ordered in 50, 60, 62 or 64 inch lengths.

Vertically stacked, tapered bamboo laminations in the take-down limbs enhance durability and performance, especially when they are reinforced with a strikingly handsome red woven glass core. Limbs are

Although its styling is anything but traditional, the deflex riser AeroTec from Hoyt USA is still a recurve at heart. Built on the same TEC riser design for eliminating noise and shock as its compound bows, the versatile takedown AeroTec is available in different colors, with different length risers and limbs.

faced with transparent Bo-Tuff Fiberglass and they are strung with a Flemish twist DynaFLIGHT 97 string. The limbs attach squarely with a dual-pin take-down alignment system.

The Black Widow Ironwood comes with: string, bowstringer, string silencers, shelf rest, tip protectors, nock points, a video and an Owner's Manual. It can be ordered right- or left-handed. Custom-shaped grips are available for an additional $70 and you must specify your preferred draw weight from 30 to 80 pounds in one-pound increments! Black Widow bows are not sold in retail stores, but the Ironwood may be ordered from the factory for $940.

FRED BEAR EQUIPMENT COMPANY

Of course, this was Bear Archery at one time, but times change. Bear was purchased by Victor Comptometer in the '60s, purchased Jennings Archery in the '80s and thereafter follows a tale of one fish swallowing another. Currently, a group of recognizable names – Bear, Jennings, Golden Eagle, Satellite – and additional brands – Brave (youth equipment) and Buckmasters (includes crossbows) – are enmeshed in a single corporate enterprise, The North American Archery Group (NAAG).

To its credit – even though it has sold the Fred Bear Museum to Bass Pro Shops – NAAG has continued and even expanded the traditional Fred Bear recurves and longbows. NAAG enlisted versatile archer Byron Ferguson to design and help market two signature longbows, the 64 inch Patriot and the 66 inch Royal Safari.

The classic recurve in the Elite Series is the Fred Bear Take-Down. This bow was Fred's own

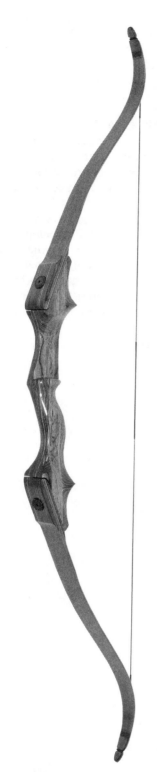

The 60-inch Gail Martin Classic takedown recurve from Martin Archery has a brace height range of 7 ¹/₂ to 8 ¹/₂ inches and a mass weight of almost three pounds. At 28 inches AMO, the draw weight range available is from 30 to 70 pounds.

masterpiece and shooting it was easy on the old fellow's lanky frame. Its patented limb latching mechanisms provide a tight, secure fit and it can be completely assembled in less than a minute. The Fred Bear Take-Down was Fred's "ultimate weapon" and he used it almost exclusively for many years. The bow still has a crowned shelf with a Bear Hair arrow rest, an inlaid compass and fiberglass reinforced limb tip laminates. The riser's hard-rock maple laminates are faced and backed with multiple layers of black and white fiberglass. This bow is available in two handle lengths, the classic "A handle" for a 56 inch bow and the longer "B handle" for a 60 inch bow.

The Fred Bear Take-Down is available either right- or left-handed at peak weights (measured at 28 inch draw length) of 45, 50, 55, 60 or 65 pounds.

HOYT USA

Hoyt USA and the other divisions of the giant Easton family enterprise are just about all success stories. Owner Jim Easton has always been interested in promoting the competition and target side of archery – as well as bowhunting – and even served his friend Peter Ueberroth as mayor of the Olympic Village for the Los Angeles Olympic Games in 1984.

Hoyt currently features three deflex-handle, takedown competition recurves, the AeroTec, Matrix and GM (Gold Medalist). Although they are available in six competition colors (including the US flag print), each of the handles is styled differently. The AeroTec is designed around the highly stylized (and extremely functional, Hoyt claims) "vibration free" TEC handle that Hoyt seems to have bet the company on. The handle comes in two lengths and, with three length limbs, this bow weighs a little more than 2 ¹/₂ pounds. Consequently, you can order an AeroTec in tip-to-tip lengths from 64 to 70 inches. The Matrix is just as versatile, but is more conventionally styled. The GM, Hoyt says, is "the ideal bow for someone just beginning to shoot a recurve."

Hoyt's recurve limbs use multiple laminated layers of fiberglass, woven carbon and hard foam. In addition, its Kinetic and Edge limbs also include hardwood maple wood laminates. Each set of Hoyt limbs tops out at 50 pounds draw.

MARTIN

The 60-inch Gail Martin Signature Take-Down recurve is named for the man who started this fine company. A glossy coating covers contrasting laminates of bubinga wood and maple. The limbs include a layer of red elm and the tips are reinforced with layers of bubinga and fiberglass. The string grooves are hand carved for a Flemish bowstring. Buy this bow and it comes with a traditional rest, Flemish string, bowstringer and silencer pad. Martin will install sight and stabilizer bushings if you request them. With draw weights of 30 to 70 pounds, this bow is available for right-handed or left-handed shooters. Brace height is 7 ½ to 8 ¼ inches and it weighs 2 ½ pounds.

Martin says its 68-inch Mountaineer Longbow was designed with the "seriously hooked" traditionalist in mind. It has slightly deflexed limbs to help eliminate hand shock and stacking while "preserving its natural shooting characteristics." The riser is made from zebrawood and the grip area has a leather wrap. The limbs are made from laminates of red elm and fiberglass overlays in clear and black. The Mountaineer draws from 30 to 70 pounds and weighs less than a pound and a half. Brace height is 6 ¼ to 7 inches. The handle is slightly cut out for an arrow shelf.

Arrow speed? You should be ashamed to ask.

Ed Eliason, a terrific recurve competitor, teamed with Dan Martin's team to create the very sharp

looking 3 ½-pound Aurora competition takedown recurve. Colorful deflex machined handle and superb laminated limbs. Available lengths for the Aurora are 65, 67 and 69 inches, tip to tip. The brace height is 8 to 8 ½ inches and the draw weights at 28 inches are from 30 to 50 pounds.

PRECISION SHOOTING EQUIPMENT

Pete Shepley's PSE has a standing interest in building quality recurves and to further that interest, it purchased the old Carroll recurve line a number of years ago. Today, PSE builds both competition and hunting recurves.

"Development of our new X-Factor take-down recurve began four years ago," Pete Shepley says. "Our engineers began researching exactly what features are important at the highest levels of international competition and then applying that knowledge to the new deflex machined aluminum X-Factor riser. "

The foundation of the X-Factor is PSE's patented

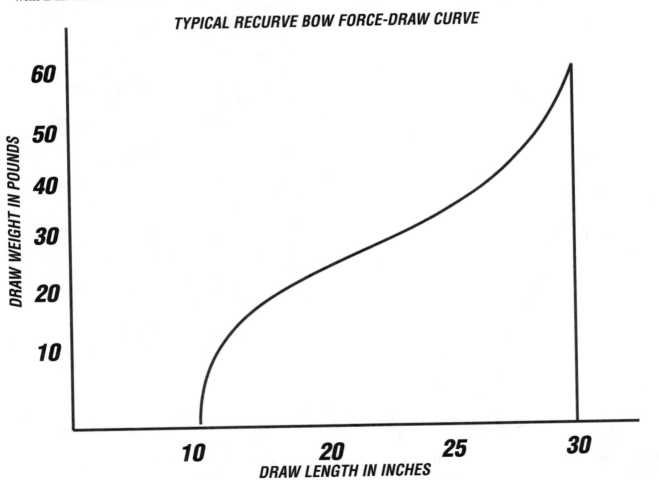

TYPICAL RECURVE BOW FORCE-DRAW CURVE

limb alignment system. "We achieve a natural balance," Pete says, "by strategically locating weight over the grip's pivot point. The slight centerflight offset on the X-Factor provides extra clearance and the cushion plunger holes have been moved closer to the pivot point of the grip to minimize the effect of bow hand torque. The main stabilizer mount has also been moved toward the pivot point of the grip and we believe this maximizes stabilizer effectiveness. Reduced overall mass weight provides the archer with increased flexibility of balance for the most accurate recurve ever made."

The X-Factor take-down recurve weighs 2 $\frac{1}{2}$ pounds and has a handle length of about 25 inches. It is available in PSE's snakeskin pattern Python Blue and Python Red.

PSE builds several hunting recurves. The top selling Coyote take-down is 60 inches long and is founded on a machined aluminum riser. The bow is finished in PSE's exclusive PSE Brush camo and it accepts PSE's two-piece quiver. This lightweight recurve is available in five-pound increment weights from 35 to 55 pounds. Recommended brace height is between 5 $\frac{1}{2}$ to 6 $\frac{1}{4}$ inches.

The 58 inch Kudu is a multi-layered, laminated, wood (walnut, imported paduk and maple) riser take-down recurve. Accessory inserts are solid brass and it is available in five-pound draw weight increments from 35 to 60 pounds. Recommended brace height is 7 to 7 $\frac{1}{2}$ inches.

SNAP SHOOTING AND THE FORCE-DRAW CURVE

Snap shooters are most commonly traditional archers. Snap shooters typically release the bowstring early, before they get to full draw. It is a form of target panic perhaps caused by the dramatically increasing weight of the bow and the registration of this strain in the muscles of your arms and back and, eventually, to the sensory triggers in your brain. The problem with snap shooting is that the arrow, not being fully drawn, does not have a chance to be aimed well, not even for a split second. Accuracy suffers and the arrow does not have a chance to absorb all of the kinetic energy it would absorb if released at full draw. The result is often poor arrow flight and poor penetration. Successful archers like Fred Bear just learn to compensate.

Unlike a compound bow which has let-off, some of them as much as 85 percent, neither recurves and longbows have cams and their force-draw curve is a relatively flat line at something like a 45 degree angle rather than something resembling a bell curve. The flat line means that the more pressure or strength you exert, the greater the weight you are holding. With a 60 pound, 65 percent let-off compound bow you reach peak weight just before full draw and then drop down to hold at 21 pounds. With a 60 pound recurve or longbow, you hold 60 pounds at a designated point, say 28 inches and if you draw beyond that – and most archers do – to say 30 inches and anchor at the corner of your lips, you might actually be holding 60 to 65 pounds. Obviously, you won't hold this very long.

For studying recurves and longbows, the archery manufacturers established a draw length of 28 inches as the standard at which all adult bows can be compared for industry purposes. A force-draw curve for a traditional stick bow will have a steep initial slope in the neighborhood of our or more pounds per inch of draw length, says industry standards guru Norb Mullaney. After four or five inches of draw this changes smoothly and gradually decreases over the next four to six inches of draw to a slope near two pounds per inch. For a smooth drawing, non-stacking characteristic, the two to three pound per inch slope will be maintained almost linearly through the 28-inch standard draw length to 30 inches or beyond.

FINDING A BOW FOR YOUR KIDS

There is some question whether we should call this a "bows for kids" or perhaps "short-draw bows" chapter. Both phrases have their defenders, but women typically have shorter draws than their spouse, father or – it may be sexist, but here it is – the male partner or friend who introduces them to archery. The BOW, Becoming an Outdoor Woman, is wonderful and we applaud it, but it is a fairly recent phenomenon and

The object of every parent who is introducing their youngster to archery is to teach them the fundamentals, build their confidence and help them have fun. Properly fitting equipment is an important part of the equation.

even there, many of the instructors are still men.

As early human society grew more complex, roles became specialized. Some hunted, some gathered, some give birth and watched over the development of the children. All are and have been honored. But because men do not give birth or nurse, they have stood farther from the hearth than the women and have typically been the hunters.

Enough apologizing. Most estimates of numbers of women in hunting hover at about five percent … or less. It may be a little higher on the competition side. So, we are considering that short draw bows are designed first for young people and second, for novices of any age or sex. Besides being available in draw lengths in the low 20-inch range, the weight range for beginner bows is lower too, often maxing-out at 45 pounds, which is about the minimum recommended for deer hunting.

Look for a bow with a peak draw weight close to your youngster's physical strength. If they can comfortably pull a 42-pound bow, purchase a bow that has an advertised draw weight that peaks at 45 pounds. As they gain strength and confidence, you can usually tune this bow upwards or add modules that give you greater weight. Shooting just below the peak, the bow is usually most efficient – it puts most of the energy of a shot into the arrow. Shooting at the lowest end of the acceptability scale – say 42 pounds on a bow that peaks at 50 or even 55 pounds – and your kid will experience sloppy and inconsistent performance.

Bows that are lighter – as most youth bows are these days – are going to be easier for your novice shooter to haul to the range or into the woods in your footsteps. For their sake … and yours … do not just give them a hand-me-down adult bow and try to make it fit unless they are very close to you in size and strength. Even then, in this material world, unless the bow you are jury-rigging for them is something very special, it will not be a bow that a young person will be proud of today.

medium recurves are available and, to learn the fundamentals of archery – breathing, stance, terminology and safety – this may be the preferred way to go.

THE GENESIS BOW

The 36-inch axle-to-axle Genesis bow, crafted originally by Matt McPherson's Mathews Archery, has an innovative cam that eliminates let-off and thereby fits all draw lengths from 15 to 30 inches. This may be the place to start your kids and perhaps your spouse also, because practically everyone can shoot it. Matt's original thought was that you could buy a single bow at a reasonable price – $150 or so – and the entire family could use it to get interested in archery. Great idea!

The Genesis is the first bow that will accommodate young, beginning and adult archers alike. Since the design eliminates let-off, the Genesis stores and releases energy comparable to a 35-pound recurve (when set at 20-pound peak weight). It has a lightweight machined aluminum riser and a machined aluminum, Genesis one-cam system with aluminum idler. The brace height is 7-1/2 inches. These bows also

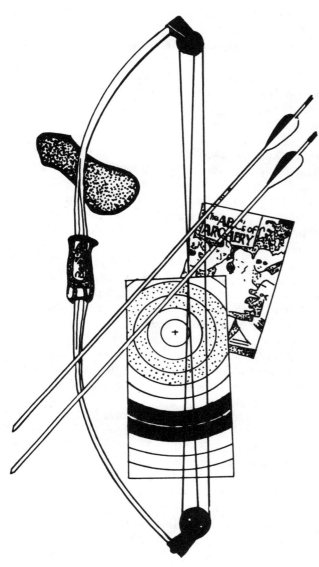

Many companies offer youth sets that are tailored to young archers. These sets typically are slightly more performance-oriented than toys, but are inexpensive and can provide young people with hours of shooting fun.

Smaller bows with short brace heights are probably going to be a difficult shot for your youngster. This brings up the question of whether they should start shooting and learn with a release aid. In the long run, if they enjoy archery and stick with it, it may not matter, but it is probably preferable to begin their shooting with fingers as very small bows, just barely larger and more powerful than toys, are available from several sources.

And the question of let-off assumes you will start your young shooter on a compound bow, but this is not necessarily right for everyone. Superior small-to-

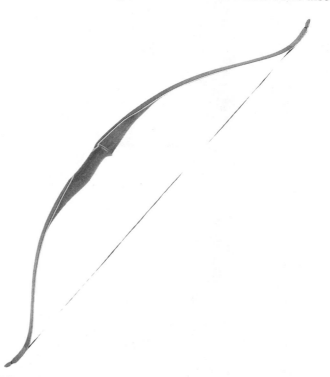

Many archers believe that a youngster learns best when he learns first with a recurve. The 48-inch Martin Prodigy comes in draw weights from 10 to 25 pounds. It only weighs 10 oz. so it will be easy for young people to handle.

have composite limbs, a molded grip and a stainless steel cable guard. And check out the zero let-off! The Genesis looks very much like a modern one-cam bow, but it is strictly for learning.

THE BOWS

We are going to look at a progression of bows from smallest to practically adult size to show the increasing complexity of archery on the one hand and, on the other, to show that no matter what the size or weight, a bow is a bow and what is expected of it does not essentially vary from the smallest kid's toy to the hottest competition set-up.

Very few manufacturers have as extensive a line-up for youth bows as the Brave bow line from The North American Archery Group (NAAG).

The 32-inch axle-to-axle Banshee from Hoyt USA is designed for short draw archers, but their catalog says "exclusively for kids." Draw lengths fit people from 16 to 23 inches and peak draw weights are available from 25 to 45 pounds.

Unfortunately, all three of the lower end or lightweight models are right hand only, thus ignoring the 10 percent of the population that shoot from the "other side."

Nevertheless, composite and fiberglass youth bows like the Brave Ranger, Lit'l Brave and Brave Sport provide increasing challenges for youngsters and increasing opportunities for their instructors. The Ranger is a lightweight recurve that almost any youngster can draw. The Lit'l Brave recurve is 45 inches long and weighs 1-1/2 pounds. It draws 13 pounds at 16 inches and 28 pounds at 24 inches draw. Finally, the 30 inch Brave Sport can be your youngster's first compound bow. Its draw length is 19, 20 or 21 inches and draw weight is 15 pounds with a 50 percent let-off.

NAAG's intermediate Brave compound bow is the 30-inch Scout. This composite, deflex, offset riser and solid recurve limb bow has draw lengths of 20 or 22 inches and adjustable draw weights from 17 to 22 pounds. The composite wheel offers 65 percent let-off. The Buckmaster's Young Bucks bow by NAAG is essentially a Scout in Realtree Hardwoods Camo with trimmed-out solid limbs to give it the look of a split-limb compound bow and to reduce the mass weight by about three ounces.

The step up to the 33-inch Brave Warrior and ultimately the Little Delta will depend on your young person's interest and ability. The Warrior's draw lengths are adjustable with modules from 23 to 28 inches and its draw weight range is 30 to 40 pounds. The twin RapidWheels do offer a high, 80 percent let-off.

The first "real" bow in the NAAG line or the last youth bow in the Brave line is the Little Delta, which has a magnesium handle and a composite, modular, 65 percent let-off twin cam. An interesting feature of the Little Delta is that its 28-inch Dacron string anchors in the cable harness with offset zinc tear drops, a design which basically passed out of existence 10 years ago with the introduction of single cam shooting systems. The Little Delta's look and feel is that of a "dad's bow" and its draw length is adjustable from 24 to 27 inches with 25- to 35- or 40- to 50-pound draw weights to choose from.

HoytUSA offers the 32-inch twin-wheel Banshee for short-draw archers (the catalog says "exclusively for kids"). Draw lengths available will fit people who need 16 to 23 inches and it still gives an IBO rated speed (at 45 pounds and 24 inches draw) at a very nice 235 fps. The cast magnesium riser is only slightly reflexed at 1/2 inch and the brace height is 6-1/2 inches. This fine little bow has a low-mount cable guard and weighs less than 3 pounds. It is available in draw weights of 25 and 45 pounds. The Banshee is available in camo for hunting or in red, black or blue for target shooting.

Parker has a couple of youth or short draw bows available. The Junior-Mag offers an offset, reflexed aluminum riser with a one-piece walnut grip. The twin Mini-Cams are machined and come with 80 percent let-off, which should please your novice shooter. Just like the "big" Parker bows, the Junior-Mag comes with a fixed, upper carbon composite cable guard. This bow measures 31 ? inches axle-to-axle and fits archers drawing from 19 to 24 inches with peak weights of 20, 30 and 40 pounds. At only 2-1/2 pounds and finished in Superflauge Camo, this bow is a little winner. It is also available in competition purple (ugh) with Italian marble limbs.

Parker has an interesting program for growing archers called "Grow Up With Parker." Simply return your bow to Parker and for just $50, the factory will upgrade the limbs and draw modules to accommodate your growing archer.

The 32-1/2-inch long Challenger is Parker's step up in length (23 to 27 inches) and weight (30, 40 and 50 pounds) from the Junior-Mag. It is their short draw one-cam bow and it too comes in either camo or competition colors: red or blue or purple with a one-piece walnut grip and marbleized white limbs. Incidentally, the hardware – limb bolts, one-cam and idler wheel – are anodized to match the color of the handle.

And how about the Recruit from ProLine? ProLine is now part of the Darton family of archery companies. The Recruit is a fine single cam bow for short draw archers. Its riser is unusual in that it is die-cast magnesium with a self-grip and a low-mount cable guard. In Version I at 32 inches long, it draws 21 to 24-1/2 inches, pulls a maximum of 35 pounds and has a 75 percent let-off. In Version II at 31-1/4 inches, it draws 22 to 25-1/2 inches, pulls a maximum of 45 pounds and has an 80 percent let-off. ProLine also offers the Recruit as a package with a quiver, sight and arrow rest.

Fore even shorter prospective archers, try the Sort Stop. It has the same magnesium riser and same solid straight fiberglass limbs, but the draw lengths are only 20 to 22 inches and the peak weight is 30 pounds, meaning that you can start a youngster at 20 pounds and, with the Tri-Draw composite wheels, it will let off 65 percent so they are holding a bare seven pounds!

PSE says its 2.2-pound 32-1/2-inch Outlaw is the "perfect bow to get young people involved in archery." The Outlaw Synergy-4 bow (S4) is fully adjustable from a 17-inch draw at 15 pounds to a 22-inch draw at 35 pounds. Brace height from the offset riser is 6-1/2 inches and let-off is a relatively low 65 (or 70, the catalog is not clear) percent which may be a little steep for kids at first, but like many bows with machined aluminum components (riser, limb cups and twin wheels) PSE's engineers may not have been certain that they wanted a youth bow, because the rated IBO speed is a very fast 210 fps. The low-mount cable guard is adjustable to let your young person's fletching clear the cables. The Outlaw has an all-synthetic cable harness and string system.

PSE's 46-inch Deputy takedown recurve has a unique shoot-through riser design that was pioneered long ago, but most recently by York Archery (no longer in business) for adult bows. This feature allows the

Remember to make shooting fun for your novice. Colorful targets. Balloons. Correctly sized equipment and fun.

bow to be used equally by left- or right-hand learners. It is available in weights of 15 or 20 pounds and has a recommended brace height of 6-1/2 to 7 inches. The Deputy is sold with a single pin sight and a shoot-around plastic arrow rest.

If your young people want to step up from the PSE Outlaw, they can do so with the 32-inch Browning Micro Midas 3, which is now made for Browning by PSE. At 2.6 pounds, the Micro Midas is a little heavier, but with a 70 percent let-off and Browning's new Hyper Max 10 twin-cams, it will fling an arrow down range at a very respectable 275 fps IBO. (The speed was calculated at 28-inch draw length, 40 pounds peak weight shooting a 200- or 250-grain arrow. The catalog is unclear on his point.)

The Micro Midas 3 is adjustable for draw length from 18 to 28 inches the catalog notes "without a bow press." The offset riser is aluminum and powder coated black; the limbs, finished in Mossy Oak Break Up camo, are fiberglass. The Micro Midas has a 6 ? inch brace height and is available in peak draw weights of 30 or 40 pounds. As a Browning combo package, this bow includes a two-piece, four arrow quiver, a two-track sight with three fiber optic tipped sight pins, a molded side-pressure plastic arrow rest, a nock point locator set and three 26-inch Micro Bullet Arrows. (Draw length adjustment above 26 inches on the Micro Midas 3 requires longer arrows than the arrows included in the combo set.) Browning suggests that the Micro Midas 3 retail for $229.95 and the combo set for $309.95.

Under the Buck label, Canada's Champion Bows produces an outstanding looking young person's or short draw bow called the "Buck Spike." At 33 inches axle-to-axle, it has all the features of a grow-up bow: machined modular one-cam, idler and riser. Draw lengths from 22 to 29 inches and peak draw weights of 35 or 45 pounds mean that most kids can begin shooting effectively at 25 pounds and work their way up, as they get stronger. Plus, this bow has a 7 5/8-inch brace height and a choice of let-off, too – 65 or 80 percent. The equivalent bow in the Champion line is the Badger, which is available in camo or competition red and blue.

THE CROSSBOW

In 1139 A.D., Pope Innocent II declared that the crossbow was an "evil" device and he called it "deadly and hateful to God and unfit to be used among Christians." Of course, the key word was among. Quarrelsome Christian warriors apparently used the crossbow to great effect during the era of the Crusades, fighting their way in and out of Europe and Asia Minor, slaughtering Moslems and other Christians by the thousands.

Early Chinese historical writing supports the contention that the crossbow was developed as a military rather than a hunting weapon. But its use precedes the first century B.C., perhaps by thousands of years. Pygmy hunters of central Africa and the Montagnards of the central highlands of Viet Nam use

Arguments for and against the crossbow may be rooted in medieval times and in mythology. The facts appear to be that the crossbow has little or no effect on healthy game populations when slotted into the regular archery season.

primitive – but apparently effective – crossbows for hunting. A large black and white photo hung in the Fred Bear Museum for many years depicting a very tall and very lean Fred Bear comparing notes with a group of pygmy hunters and the short men carried crossbows.

Whatever its history, it is as if the crossbow has somehow captured our imagination as a sinister weapon, something from the "dark side." The nasty orcs and goblins in the recent movies made form J.R.R. Tolkien's *Lord of the Rings* trilogy shoot crossbows whereas the men – both good and bad – shoot longbows. Go figure.

Early crossbows were huge, bulky and unwieldy weapons. Draw weights could range to several thousand pounds as enormous, wheel-mounted crossbows fired bolts of enormous size at enemy fortifications. Individual crossbowmen cocked the bow with a winch and while they were deadly, they were very slow to fire and not extremely accurate. Conventionally, it is recognized that an archer shooting a longbow could loose half a dozen arrows in the time it took the crossbowman to shoot and re-cock to fire again.

What is a crossbow? Today's crossbow is a horizontal bow. Or it is a cross-gun. It is either a threat to civilization as we know it or a unique possibility for outdoor enjoyment. It is a silent, deadly instrument of destruction in the hands of a dastardly poacher or it is just another tool in the outdoorsman's kit, especially for hunters who have exceptional physical challenges. Since it was adopted for use by the Medieval military, the crossbow has been extremely controversial, but perhaps with the realization of some of the crossbow's potential and its rather extreme limitations, it is becoming less so now. Whatever you think of it, personally, there is absolutely no question that today's crossbow is a technological marvel.

A crossbow is essentially a bow that can be shot in the manner of a gun. It is shoulder-fired and released with a trigger (much like a mechanical release aid). The bow mounts to and is held horizontally on the fore-end (the "prod") of a stock. The bowstring is drawn back toward the shooter into the trigger housing where the trigger and the crossbow safety hold it. A crossbow shoots arrows (or flat-end **bolts**) that kill by causing hemorrhage rather than shattering hydrostatic shock plus hemorrhage. Just like with any vertical bow, a recurve or compound, hunters shooting crossbows tell stories of lethal hits when the game animals do not so much as flinch until they suddenly sink to their knees, shudder and expire.

As you may know or have guessed, there have been deep divisions among archers, for and against crossbows being allowed in archery seasons. Here are some of the anti-crossbow positions:

- The crossbow is so powerful it is practically a gun, not a bow, and should not be used in archery seasons.
- The crossbow shoots an arrow (or a bolt) that is so powerful it does not have the arc of an arrow shot from a hand-drawn, hand-released bow. This simply makes it too lethal.
- The crossbow is a long-range weapon that will decimate the deer herd.
- Poachers will use crossbows to great effect, because they are silent, deadly killers.

Many of these concepts are founded on a study completed in 1987 by engineer Roy Marlow called "The Modern Hunting Crossbow – A Study of its Effectiveness Compared to the Handheld Bow." The study was funded by the Professional Bowhunter Society, which is rabidly anti-crossbow. Of course, Marlow began with the definition of a handheld bow

For turkey hunting, it is hard to beat a crossbow. Of course, you are only going to get one shot at a bird, but it will mount across your knees like a shotgun and carry the lethal punch of a hunting broadhead.

Shooting a crossbow under dad's supervision is an excellent way for a youngster to take the first steps along the hunting trail. A crossbow in the hands of your youngster will be less intimidating than a rifle or shotgun, but easier to handle than a vertical bow.

The 7-pound, 10-ounce Horton Legend SL compound crossbow features a composite thumbhole stock and comes with a peep-and-pin sight combination

as a vertical compound bow with eccentric wheels. Marlow's study has its good points and its arguable points, but here were his general conclusions:

- The crossbow is easier to learn how to use and can be mastered faster than the vertical bow.
- The crossbow can be shot from a rest position (like a gun).
- The crossbow's internal ballistics make it less likely to move while shooting, which is to say that the vertical bow has more possibilities for error.
- The crossbow shoots a faster arrow, has a flatter trajectory and delivers more energy on target than a vertical bow.
- The effective range of the crossbow is greater than a vertical bow.

When discussing crossbow hunting opportunities during a meeting of the Archery Manufacturers and Merchants Association (AMO) in 2002, AMO President Jay McAninch is quoted as saying, "Those discussing crossbow hunting opportunities should ask 'Why not instead of why.' AMO clearly must recognize crossbows as an archery product since they are produced by a wide variety of archery companies, are distributed by archery wholesalers, are sold by mail-order in the archery section of their catalogs and are

Because of the reduced movement needed to shoot and the fast arrow speeds you can expect from a modern crossbow, it can be shot effectively from a treestand or a ground blind.

Crossbow*	Power Stroke	Draw Weight	At 1 Meter	At 50 Meters
Great Lakes Durango	17.38"	165#	356 fps 113.1 ft-lbs KE	312 fps 86.9 ft-lbs KE
Horton Yukon SL	10.13"	150#	261 fps 60.8 ft-lbs KE	255 fps 60.3 ft-lbs KE
6 crossbows, each using 2213 arrow, average	13.77"	170#	315 fps 89.6 ft-lbs KE	276 fps 69.0 ft-lbs KE
6 crossbows, shooting 6 different arrows, average	13.77"	170#	299 fps 93.3 ft-lbs KE	267 fps 74.6 ft-lbs KE

*Blais and LaPointe chronographed six crossbows from a bench rest using six arrows: 2213 (402 gr.), 2117 (454 gr.), 2216 (462 gr.), 2315 (477 gr.), 2219 (495 gr.) and 2419 (539 gr.). The crossbows were the Great Lakes Durango, Horton Yukon SL, Horton Nitro Hunter, Barnett Quad-300, Excalibur ExoMag and TenPoint stealth X-2. The information presented in the above chart were the extremes of those tested, the Durango having the longest power stroke and therefore the greatest speed and kinetic energy, the Yukon SL with the shortest power stroke and the slowest speed and **kinetic energy** output.

sold by retailers in the archery sections of their stores. Whether or not crossbows would be considered historically and technically an archery product by everyone is a moot point and will never be resolved. Common sense takes precedence, in my opinion."

State of Ohio results should be conclusive for people arguing the case for or against the crossbow as an archery instrument. Ohio first allowed crossbows during the archery season in 1976 with a season that lasted two and a half months. That year, all hunters combined in the Buckeye State harvested 23,431 deer. Archers with conventional vertical bows took 1,638 deer while crossbow hunters took 27. A total of 138,946 hunting permits were sold which allowed deer hunting in 68 of Ohio's 88 counties. The ratio of deer harvested to permits sold was about 1-to-6.

By 1994, 18 years after the first year of crossbow hunting, the season was extended two weeks and the total harvest for all hunters grew to 170,527. The conventional bow harvest grew to 13,107 while the crossbow harvest grew to 16,283. Hunting permits sold went up to 385,068 and all 88 counties allowed deer hunting. By 1994, the ratio of deer harvested to permits sold increased to 1-to-3. By all accounts, Ohio's deer herd was healthy and growing.

TenPoint Crossbow's Dave Robb says, "The conclusions are clear. Over the 18-year span, crossbows did not decimate the deer population; the season was not eliminated or shortened; and crossbows did nothing to diminish archers' hunting opportunities or their chances of success. On the contrary, the opposite occurred. The deer population increased; the season got longer; more counties opened for hunting; more hunters participated; and their chances of success more than doubled."

THE ARROW'S CAST

Adapting his notes from a study published in

Vertical Bow	Arrow Length	Draw Weight	Arrow Used	At 1 Meter	At 50 Meteres
Mathews Ultra 2	27 1/2"	70#	Beeman ICS 400 Hunter (378 gr.)	298 fps 74.5 ft-lbs KE	267 fps 59.8 ft-lbs. KE
Champion Cobra	28 1/16"	64#	Easton XX75 2216 (550 gr.)	218 fps 58.0 ft-lbs KE	192 fps 45.0 ft-lbs KE
5 vertical bows shooting 5 arrows	28.26"	68#	Average arrow weight 438 gr.	264 fps 66.8 ft-lbs KE	237 fps 53.6 ft-lbs KE

*Blais and LaPointe chronographed five vertical bows, the Mathews Ultra 2, Champion Cobra, XI Legend, Fred Bear Epic Xtreme and Darton Cyclone. They tested only one arrow size each rather than the six they tested with the crossbows. Each vertical bow tested was fitted with its own size and weight arrow, so the results can not be directly comparable. Robb notes that the vertical bows tested were not representative of the variety of speed ranges available to today's archer and that these difficulties with their presentation makes the comparison of crossbow to vertical bow tentative only in their study.

The manufacturer's suggested retail price for the Horton Hunter XS is $875. This includes the 200-pound draw weight XS crossbow that delivers 87 ft-lbs of kinetic energy in Mossy Oak Break-Up Camo, a camouflaged 4x32 Mult-A-Range scope and rings, scope caps, camouflaged transverse 4-arrow quiver and a camo padded sling. The XS is 31 ¹/₂-inches long and 26-inches wide.

French in the Quebec publication *Aventure Chasse & Peche* by Christian Blais and Denis LaPointe, Dave Robb of TenPoint Crossbows concludes that the crossbow is in no way comparable to a muzzleloader or any other type of firearm. Crossbows, Robb concludes, work the same way as "vertical bows," taking game by causing hemorrhage rather than as a result of "knockdown" power which is a function of hydrostatic shock from a high-power centerfire rifle. Here are some of the interpreted and summarized crossbow data using a 2213 arrow weighing 402 grains except as noted:

*Blais and LaPointe chronographed six crossbows from a bench rest using six arrows: 2213 (402 gr.), 2117 (454 gr.), 2216 (462 gr.), 2315 (477 gr.), 2219 (495 gr.) and 2419 (539 gr.). The crossbows were the

Great Lakes Durango, Horton Yukon SL, Horton Nitro Hunter, Barnett Quad-300, Excalibur ExoMag and TenPoint stealth X-2. The information presented in the chart were the extremes of those tested, the Durango having the longest power stroke and therefore the greatest speed and kinetic energy, the Yukon SL with the shortest power stroke and the slowest speed and kinetic energy output.

TenPoint's Dave Robb has reviewed the information presented in the Blais/LaPointe study and while he says that scientific comparisons cannot be

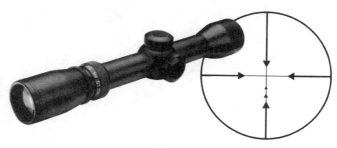

Distance	Fred Bear Epic Xtreme fps/ke	Horton Yukon fps/ke
1 meter	261 fps/60.8 ft-lbs	261 fps/60.8 ft-lbs
30 meters	248 fps/54.9 ft-lbs	246 fps/54.0 ft-lbs
50 meters	236 fps/49.7 ft-lbs	238 fps/50.6 ft-lbs
Each was tested with a 402-grain arrow		

Scopes on crossbows are subjected to tremendous shock during a shot and shots will normally be short range, 50 yards or less. Consequently, most archers believe that simpler is better.

drawn from the data, some informal themes or trends do stand out. "The summaries show that the average speed of all the crossbows using all the arrows was 35 fps faster than the average vertical bow measured at one meter and 30 fps faster measured at 50 meters," he says. "In the same comparison the crossbows produced 26.5 more foot-pounds of kinetic energy at one meter and 21 more at 50 meters."

The averages, he notes, show that the crossbows and vertical bows both held 89 percent of their initial speed and 80 percent of their initial energy by the time their arrows reached 50 meters.

"Because the crossbows tested were weighted way on the fast side of reality," Robb says, "it is safe to assume that a valid comparative study would have shown less difference in average speed and average energy between crossbows and vertical bows.

"Even without a more valid comparison however it is clear that crossbows and compound bows are ballistically similar. That is, they shoot with similar speed and hit with similar energy."

Based on the above information, Dave Robb concludes it is ludicrous to suggest that crossbows are ballistically comparable to any other type of firearm than modern compound bows. "Ballistics aside," Dave says, "there are some differences between crossbows and vertical bows, but they are not enough to warrant any discrimination in assignment of hunting seasons."

And speaking of the hunting situation, anyone who is familiar with both crossbow shooting and shooting a compound bow will recognize the difference the respective tools will have in the field. With similar speed ratings and effective shot distances, the

crossbow is a useful for hunting but it has serious drawbacks. The crossbow is a one-shot instrument, because the noise level from a shot is three to four times that of a silenced compound or vertical bow. The bang of a shot is enough to lay a wet blanket over the woods for a quarter mile in every direction!

In addition, the physical effort and amount of movement needed to cock a 150-pound crossbow is significant. This cannot be accomplished sitting down.

Horton's Steelforce recurve limb crossbow is built in 80-pound and 150-pound draw weights. 80 pounds is fine for target shooting and fun in the back yard, but 150 pounds is about minimum for energy delivery (43 ft-lbs) for a hunting crossbow. The limbs are tempered steel.

The Great Lakes Crossbow designers were thinking about balance and performance when they designed the Durango. It has a hard anodized Teflon-impregnated steel track and a 17-inch power stroke. It weights 7-1/2-pounds and is 28-1/2-inches from axle-to-axle. It is available in 150- and 165-pound peak draw weights and it will launch a 22-inch, 2219, 463 grain arrow at a blistering 320 fps or a 535 grain arrow at 305 fps.

Excalibur's Bill Troubridge demonstrates the power of his recurve limb crossbows by bringing down a moose, certainly one of North America's largest and toughest big game animals.

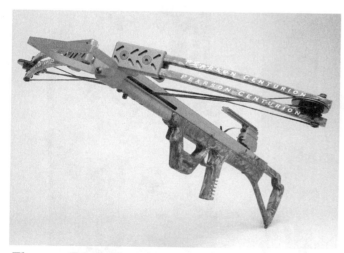

The new Centurion compound crossbow from Ben Pearson Archery comes with 165-pound split limbs that provide a 15 ½-inch power stroke that produces a 330 fps arrow with a 480 gr. crossbow bolt. It is built with a dry fire inhibitor to prevent accidental discharge. Available accessories: T-handle cocking rope, Direct Drive Winch, sling, five-arrow lateral quiver and Weaver-style scope mount.

Once you stand up on your treestand, fit your boot into the crossbow stirrup, bend over to grab the string, and then haul it up into the receiver, you have committed more movement than most vertical bow bowhunters need for an entire day on stand, including a couple shots at deer and squirrel

CROSSBOWS AND COMPANIES

Perhaps the crossbow name most frequently thought of in the US and Canada is Horton. A fine example of engineering is the Firehawk, introduced in 2002. This 200-pound compound crossbow shoots 310 fps and delivers 81 ft-lbs of energy with one of the Horton Carbon Strike arrows. The wide limbs, adjustable length of the composite thumb hole stock and what Horton calls its Dura-Tip integrated Yoke System all work together for shooting accuracy. Horton says the non-tapered profile of its fiberglass limbs distributes stress across the entire limb, rather than concentrating it in one or two high stress areas. This should make these limbs more resilient. The Firehawk weighs six pounds, eight ounces. It is 31.2 inches long and 26 inches wide. It comes with a 7/8-inch scope or

Bill Troubridge's Excalibur crossbows are all recurve limb bows. It is simply not true that the recurve is slower or less powerful than compound crossbows, Troubridge says.

sight base installed and a machined steel trigger mechanism.

The Buckmaster MaxPoint, made by The North American Archery Group is advertised at 175 pounds draw with a 340 fps arrow. The secret, says Vice President Joe White, is the zero percent let-off MaxWing Cams that allow the MaxPoint to store more energy than any crossbow ever made. The MaxPoint has carbon quad limbs and an aluminum riser with a 6 inch brace height. The MaxPoint weighs 7 pounds and as a set comes with four arrows, a four-arrow quiver and a 1 x 30mm Red Dot Scope.

Barnett bills itself as the largest manufacturer of crossbows in the world. It makes compound, recurve and pistol crossbows. The Trident II is a unique style of pistol crossbow. With a 75 pound draw weight, manual safety, a foot stirrup that folds back after cocking and hooks to help cock the bowstring, the Trident II is a unique and powerful shooting toy. Barnett maintains that none of its crossbows is a toy however and that all of them can be dangerous, even deadly if used in an improper manner.

One of Barnett's most currently popular compound crossbows is the Quad-300. It has a molded stock, aluminum rail and tough Gordon Glass limbs. The 150-pound Quad-300 has a 15.25-inch power stroke and propels an arrow downrange at 335 fps with a kinetic energy rating of 122.2 ft-lbs. The Quad-300 measures 31.5 inches wide and is 35.25 inches long. Both a hand-drawn rope cocking device or a crank cocking device is available and Barnett says that use of a cocking device reduces the strength needed to cock the crossbow by half. Barnett also recommends that to prevent string wear the archer rub its special Lubewax onto the center serving, cables and flight track. The manufacturer recommends 20 inch, 2219 Easton XX75 arrows weighing 450 gr. as a standard for accuracy and a long, trouble-free shooting life.

Barnett's recurve crossbows have often shown up

in movies. The Rhino has an ambidextrous sculptured aluminum stock and draws 150 pounds. With a 10-inch power stroke, it shoots 235 fps and delivers 50 ft-lbs of kinetic energy into the 16-inch aluminum arrows Barnett recommends.

Bill Troubridge in Ontario builds the Excalibur line of recurve limb crossbows although he consulted in a considerable fashion on the development of the Buckmaster MaxPoint. Bill says that recurve limbs deliver just as much speed and power with far less hassle and potential for something to go wrong than compound crossbows with cams and strings and cables. "Recurve limb crossbows are lighter and more reliable," he says.

The Exocet at 175 pounds and 300 fps and the ExoMag at 200 pounds and 330 fps are Excalibur's headliners. Each features a molded composite stock, machined trigger and ambidextrous manual safety.

The newest entry into the crossbow market is the 7.1-pound Centurion from Ben Pearson. Introduced in 2003, the Centurion features a hard anodized, Teflon-impregnated aluminum barrel assembly and a molded SuperFlauge camo stock with a pistol grip. The Centurion uses 165-pound Quadra-flex split limbs and has a 15-1/2-inch power stroke for a speed of 330 fps with a 480 gr. crossbow bolt, and we specify "bolt" rather than arrow as the Centurion requires a bolt with a flat base rather than an arrow nock. The patented manual safety is called a DFI or dry-fire inhibitor and

Most crossbow manufacturers specify the arrow spine you will need for shooting their bows. Ten Point recommends 2219 Easton Aluminum shafts or shafts of comparable weight.

The Carbon Strike from Horton is a tough, 20-inch pultruded carbon shaft with + .003-inch straightness specifically designed for heavy draw weight crossbows. Weight with a 100 gr. field point is 410 gr. with feathers and 426 gr. with vanes.

The Lightning Strike is a 20-inch Easton XX75 aluminum tube. Its weight with a 100 gr. field point is 414 gr. with feathers and 430 gr. with vanes.

it prevents accidental discharge. The Centurion comes with a three-pin front sight and a rear peep sight that fit atop the factory installed, universal "Weaver-style" scope rail. Fittings for manual and crank cocking devices are built-in. Pearson offers the Centurion with a Lifetime Guarantee that covers the stock, barrel, limbs and cams for the original owner.

Although they began producing crossbows only in 1994, TenPoint has become a leading name in the crossbow field offering Limited Lifetime Warranties on their state-of-the-art bows. The 185-pound TenPoint Stealth X-2 shoots 323 fps! Their Turbo Extreme features quad fiberglass limbs and an extruded aluminum barrel that is hard coated and Teflon

For an open-on-impact broadhead, Horton suggests the Gator 100 with high-carbon steel Trocar Tip and two .030-inch blades from Rocky Mountain. Weight is 100 gr. and cutting diameter 2 inches.

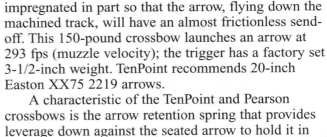

A modern crossbow with 150 pounds or so of draw weight will be able to shoot almost any hunting head accurately. The Thunderhead 125 from New Archery Products would be an excellent choice.

impregnated in part so that the arrow, flying down the machined track, will have an almost frictionless send-off. This 150-pound crossbow launches an arrow at 293 fps (muzzle velocity); the trigger has a factory set 3-1/2-inch weight. TenPoint recommends 20-inch Easton XX75 2219 arrows.

A characteristic of the TenPoint and Pearson crossbows is the arrow retention spring that provides leverage down against the seated arrow to hold it in place on the string. TenPoint's "Clawover" trigger assembly positions the string catch from above rather than below in order, the company says, to provide for better arrow flight. The Turbo Extreme features a molded thumbhole stock and a high cheek-piece. Since the same crossbow is essentially both a right-hander's and a left-hander's weapon (no shell is ejected into your face) the TenPoint safety can be operated ambidextrously.

Precision Shooting Equipment President Pete Shepley has long maintained a position that people who want to shoot and hunt with crossbows should be able to do so without harassment – certainly not by other hunters and archers. For 2003, PSE is introducing two new compound crossbows, the 165-pound Maxim and the 175-pound Deerslayer. Both

An instant detach 4-5 arrow lateral quiver for Ten Point crossbows. The quick detach feature is also available in the 2-3 arrow version.

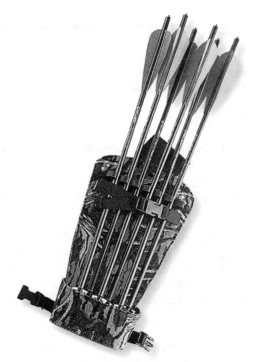

Here is a rugged hip quiver that holds six arrows securely in a foam-filled hood with a camo fleece exterior lining to eliminate noise. A leg strap keeps the quiver secure while allowing a full range of motion. Excellent for lowering the strain on your hands and arms.

crossbows have quad limbs, an anti-dry fire mechanism and a composite, thumbhole stock.

Darton's Great Lakes Durango Express features an unusual open style prod that allows its 17-inch power stroke to maximize this bow's down range energy delivery. Quad limbs and a skeletal stock minimize the mass weight allowing it to come in at only 7 ½ pounds. The Durango Express is available in 150 pound and 165 pound draw weights in several camouflage patterns. At 165 pounds, Great Lakes advertises that the Durango Express will deliver a 460-grain arrow at 330 fps factory measured muzzle velocity. It is 28-½ inches tip-to-tip and its pre-set trigger tension is a light 3-½ pounds. Darton outfits its crossbow with a patented dry fire prevention safety system and an adjustable arrow retention system. The Durango Express accepts three different cocking devices.

ARROWS AND BOLTS FOR CROSSBOWS

Does a crossbow shoot arrows or bolts? Bolt is an old term, dating to early Medieval times in Europe when the shafts were short and heavy, made from solid wood or iron. Steering, such as it was, was provided by

leather vanes. Bolts were also made from vane-less tapered shafts that were thicker at the arrowpoint end than the butt end. Crossbows were deadly, but depending on the age and style, were not very accurate. They were also almost impossible to load quickly for a follow-up shot because the crossbows themselves were heavy and the string had to be hand-cranked back into position with wooden gears and sinew fittings. Imagine.

For the purpose of learning about crossbows, let's consider that some modern crossbows are designed to shoot nocked arrows while some are built for arrows without nocks, arrows with flat bases and we will call these bolts. For numerous reasons – ease and cost of manufacturing, refinement of design and public acceptance – manufacturers are switching their designs increasingly to arrows.

Following a manufacturer's specifications, two types of arrows can usually be shot from crossbows, aluminum and carbon or carbon composite. Aluminum shafts are traditional in archery. They can be made exactly straight and are relatively inexpensive. Additionally, an archer has multiple spine or shaft stiffness options with aluminum. Of course, aluminum tubing bends and once bent just cannot be straightened if you want to shoot with great accurately. The best thing to do with a bent arrow is to save the head and snap the shaft so you will not be tempted to use it again.

Carbon shafts have been gaining increasing acceptance for practically 20 years. They are pricey, the shaft and spine designations are different than aluminum, and the method for fletching carbon is a little different than aluminum, so there is a learning curve. Still, carbon shafts offer an extremely tough arrow that is typically lighter and smaller in diameter than its matching aluminum counterpart and while it may snap, it will never bend. The "ding" that would put a permanent dent and then a crimp and finally a total bend and shaft failure in your Easton XX75

Scopes on crossbows are subjected to tremendous shock during a shot and shots will normally be short range, 50 yards or less. Consequently, most archers believe the simpler the better

Good crossbow shooting requires realistic practice with targets from Blue Ridge, McKenzie or Rinehart.

One accessory you will value if you take up crossbow sports is a padded sling. Typically weighing 7-8 pounds and bulky when outfitted with a scope and a quiver full of arrows, the crossbow will not become your enemy if you can sling it over your shoulder for some of the day.

aluminum shaft will not leave a mark on your carbon shaft.

Most crossbows today are manufactured to use a #22 or #22/64 diameter shaft, says Bill Troubridge of Excalibur Crossbows. Shaft diameter is important because if it is too big, it will not fit into the receiver or trigger unit and if it is too small, it will fall into or

wedge in the track on the top of the stock. Another issue when selecting arrows is alignment of the string to the centerline of the arrow. You want the string to push the center of the shaft and a shaft that is either too large or too small will receive offset thrust and this can cause poor arrow flight.

Troubridge says that light arrows like 2213s, 2216s or most #22 carbon shafts are fast flyers and because spine is less of an issue with crossbows, these can give you excellent flight and accuracy. As you make a shaft selection, verify the arrow specifications for your crossbow and try to fall well inside the range. For large game like moose or elk, Troubridge prefers a heavier shaft like 2219s, which have a thicker and sturdier wall. The 2219s may be a bit slower, but they typically deliver more kinetic energy than their smaller cousins.

For arrow stabilization, Troubridge recommends

small, straight vanes for competition, but for hunting he likes a vane or feather at least 5 inches long set helically or at an offset. He believes that feathers are slightly better for accuracy because they are rougher than vanes and cause more drag to keep the arrow flight in line. Plus, turkey feathers are lighter than plastic vanes by about 1/3 so they leave the bow faster, but then provide stabilizing drag faster, too.

Plastic vane proponents argue that vanes are more durable than feathers and are moisture-proof. Out to ranges of 50 yards, it probably does not matter, says Troubridge, who shoots feathers himself, applying a coating of anti-wetting agent for damp days.

Horton sells a line of pultruded carbon shafts and provides interesting information about carbon shafts on its web site at www.crossbow.com. Realizing that this is self-promotional and that no independent authority has published or verified the information, Horton suggests that its CarbonStrike carbon shafts, designed for 175-200 pound draw weight crossbows, transfer more energy on impact because the pultrusion process – carbon matrix drawn or squeezed under heat and pressure through small holes – results in parallel or unidirectional fibers as opposed to wrapped carbon shafts.

While it is easy to accept the claim that their straightness averages .003 inches for a 20 inch shaft, that the wall thickness is .035 inches and that the CarbonStrike shaft weighs 410 gr. with feathers and 426 gr. with vanes (including a 100 gr. broadhead), we accept "on faith" the "independent test results" which compare Horton arrows with "Brand A" and "Brand B." According to their test, Brand A carbon shaft actually consists of 11.7 percent carbon, 24.3 percent resin and 53.3 percent glass and inorganic oxides. For Brand B, the similar measurement for carbon is 59.7 percent. Horton's shaft registered 70 percent carbon. In theory, this makes the Horton shaft far superior in memory (the ability to retain its straightness) and flexibility.

SCOPES FOR CROSSBOWS

Typically, a crossbow is outfitted with a low power shotgun or handgun scope or a non-magnifying red dot scope. These mount to the crossbow's scope rail with adjustable scope mounting brackets. If you like a fixed or adjustable power scope, remember that a crossbow, just like a vertical bow, is a weapon with limited range, so your need for magnification is extremely limited and an index such as field of view (the maximum width of the area that can be seen through your scope) may be more important to your shooting success.

A lot of crossbow hunters do not believe they need a scope to make an accurate shot at a deer that is only 30 to 40 yards away. The "normal" sights – a rear peep and a front pin sight – on crossbows may not fit everyone well, especially two-season hunters who are accustomed to placing their cheek against the cheek-piece on a gun stock. A scope makes a crossbow hunter aim precisely, concentrating intently on making an accurate, clean shot. Many old hands with crossbows want to shoot with both eyes open (okay with a non-magnifying red dot scope) as if they are bird shooting and even experienced gun hunters, especially those partial to the shotgun, get excited and fail to tuck the butt stock tight into their shoulder. They may get away with this for a time with shotguns, but it can cause a very nasty shoulder or cheek bruise with a crossbow and will certainly cause them to miss what they are shooting at. With a crossbow, you must execute because it is a point-to-point aiming weapon like a rifle or a vertical bow, not an area weapon that you point like a shotgun. A scope makes a hunter shoot the crossbow more like a rifle.

Famous for their inexpensive approach to equipment, archers will tend to want to economize

Do not believe that a modern device does not require old-fashioned maintenance and care. String and cable wax and flight rail and trigger lube are critical to maintaining all crossbows in good working order and extending the life of your strings and cables. Ten Point claims that its Flight Rail Lube (right) will not freeze-up in cold weather or collect dirt which can make your trigger sluggish and impede its performance.

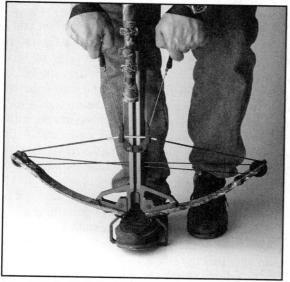

The EZ-Pull Cocking Harness reduces cocking effort by 50 percent. It is compact, lightweight and helps center the string exactly.

Carrying and cocking a crossbow can be challenging enough without the added weight and bulk of a cocking device permanently attached. Horton's EZ-Winder allows hunters to consistently and effortlessly cock your bow in 30 seconds with minimal effort.

with a crossbow scope, especially when the scopes are of relatively low power. Remember though that your best shooting will invariably arise in low light conditions so a variable intensity lighted aiming point, whether it is a dot or crosshairs, and a quality optical picture are important.

Speaking of low light conditions, Bill Troubridge of Excaliber says this is the number one advantage of scopes over peep sights. "Light gathering in the last 20 minutes of the day through a rear peep sight is a disaster," Bill says, "as there is a reduction in available light to see the target and the front sight pins. Low power scopes condense light during this important hunting part of the day and make the target, crosshairs and any obstructions more easily visible."

Many crossbow shooters believe that electronic red dot scopes give you faster target acquisition, especially in poor visibility or low light conditions, than do conventional crosshair scopes. Aimpoint of Sweden introduced a consumer red dot scope in the late '70s and today most companies have one or two in their line. Most are the "reflex" type, which means the dot is in a sense an illusion that is created when a beam of light is reflected off the front lens and back into your eye. Except for the Aimpoint, red dot sights are as susceptible to parallax error as other scopes. That means you lose accuracy if your eye is off the central axis of the sight. Aimpoint, incidentally, still manufactures red dot scopes and offers a 2x magnification. The CET diode on the Aimpoint 7000 can keep the sight lighted up to 250 times longer, the company claims, than standard LED reticles.
If you choose a red dot scope, be aware that some are designed to magnify and some are not, but almost all have a rheostat control that allows you to govern the intensity or brightness of the aiming dot. A brighter setting is used for daylight shooting while a dimmer setting is used for low light conditions. Use a bright setting in the evening and the intensity of the dot will prevent you from seeing your target. On the other hand, use a dim setting in the middle of a sunny day and you will not be able to see your aiming point.

To use a non-magnifying red dot scope, you need to shoot with both eyes open. Usually, if you close one eye, you can see the dot, but not your target, because the pupil of your eye is dilating.

Red dot scopes offer a choice of dot size. Select one that is big enough to see quickly, but not so big that it will block the target. A "three-minute" dot in a one-power sight is too small for many eyes, especially as we archers get older. An eleven-minute dot is too big. Something in a five- or six-minute dot for a non-magnifying scope or even a smaller dot, say a three-minute dot in a two-power scope may work. To keep the dot sharp, use the lowest battery or rheostat power setting that makes the dot easy to see.

Tasco's Propoint and Accudot are less expensive than the Aimpoint. Leupold/Gilmore sights are best known for their use on handguns, but like any red dot sight, they have unlimited eye relief and can be used on crossbows as well. BSA, Millett, Swift, Simmons, Burris and Bushnell also carry red dot sights.

Horton says its 4x32mm Mult-A-Range Crossbow Scope was specifically designed for use on crossbows. The unique feature of this scope is that the crosshairs are designed to zero at 20 yards. Below that horizontal zero point reference are four additional gradient lines for 30, 40, 50 and 60 yards. Five pre-determined reference points help eliminate some of the guesswork

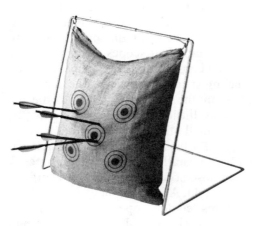

For backyard or even basement shooting in the winter, a nylon-filled crossbow target with metal stand such as this one is perfect for shooting field points.

in judging distance. This scope has a 2.5-inch eye relief, quarter-minute windage and elevation adjustment and fully coated optics for shock, water and fog. (Incidentally, the Horton web site notes that a modern crossbow sighted in at 20 yards hits a full 21 inches low at 40 yards.)

The Bushnell Holosight is not a red dot sight although it shares an illuminated, variable-intensity reticle. At six ounces, the Holosight is lighter than most red dot sights. It is also more compact and offers an unlimited field of view. As with red dot sights, which have tube diameter larger than a 1-inch riflescope, the Holosight's axis is a little higher than shooters may be accustomed to, so you must lift your face to see through it.

TUNING

No matter what brand or model you have, tuning your crossbow for most effective shooting is a simple, four-step process.

First, inspect the crossbow and check it for loose fittings. Wax the string. Lubricate the rail and the serving to lower the friction between the rail and the string.

Second, confirm brace height, tiller and retainer-clip condition. The tiller on a crossbow is correct (unless otherwise specified by the manufacturer) when the distance from the base of the limb on either side of the prod to the string is exactly the same. Even tiller creates equal pressure on the limbs. Now, check the arrow retainer clip to make sure it is not damaged, too tight or twisted off center. It should be only tight enough to lightly hold the arrow in place. If it is too tight or twisted, it can affect arrow flight and there is only one way for this clip to affect the flight of an

arrow – badly.

You may want to make sure here that when you go to the field, you are drawing the string exactly into the center of the trigger receiver. Bill Troubridge of Excalibur Crossbows believes that not drawing he string perfectly into the receiver behind the center of the arrow is the number one reason we miss. Some archers mark two spots on the bowstring at rest with a color marker (correction fluid works well.) and as they draw, these two marks indicate the outside of the trigger housing. If you do not pull directly back on center, it will be obvious.

Third, check your arrows: fletching should not be peeling off, the heads should be tight and the shaft should be straight. Decide what orientation your arrows will have to the shooting grove on the barrel and make them all the same.

Finally, double check the pin and peep sights or your scope for proper adjustment.

Now, head to the range. If you recall the question with which we began the chapter – archery or firearm – we recommended, for numerous reasons, that the crossbow be adopted wholeheartedly into archery. Shooting form however, is where we accept the good things from our firearm cousins. A crossbow can be shot from a bench or while you are sitting or even lying on the ground. Whatever your form, remember to breathe, squeeze and allow yourself to be surprised when the explosion sends the arrow down range. You want this shooting form eventually to become automatic, but in the meantime, remember to breathe.

Should you relax or unstring your crossbow when it will not be used for extended periods? A recurve crossbow should be unstrung, just like a recurve vertical bow. A compound crossbow's limbs are designed to withstand extended periods of stress, but if you will not be shooting for a while, go ahead and let off the weight to reduce the stress. It is not necessary to totally remove parts. Reducing the stress should be sufficient for most modern limbs to fully regain their "memory" and energy potential when next you pick up the bow.

SILENCING YOUR SHOT

On the subject of how to silence the noise a crossbow makes when it shoots, Bill Troubridge of Excalibur frankly admits that you cannot quiet the shot and maintain the excellent speeds that modern crossbows are capable of shooting.

At his Internet site, www.excaliburcrossbows.com, he specifically discusses each tool for silencing and notes the feet per second arrow speed lost to each. For example, Sims Limb Savers do help but they cost 12 fps.

As a result of the crossbow's extreme noise and conventional failures to silence a shot, he has designed a set of Dissipater Bars that help with sound and recoil suppression but do not cut arrow speed because they are not attached directly to the crossbow's limbs. Bill says his Dissipater Bars, which insert beneath and are held tight by the bow limb attachment bolts, reduce noise by as much as eight decibels!

HARD-SIDED TRAVELING CASE

Every traveling archer needs to protect his gear, because bows and arrows must be tuned and balanced. SKB was the first manufacturer to offer a commercial, hard-sided crossbow case.

The SKB-8000 Standard Crossbow Case handles most popular crossbow models. It is made from molded hard plastic with light aluminum straps and fittings and interior eggshell foam cushion. The bumpers and ribs of the SKB-8000 are designed to absorb shock and vibration, provide protection for exposed hardware and enhance the structural integrity of the case. Interior straps secure your quiver and arrows inside the case cover separately. Crossbow archers will like the fact that their bow does not have to be disassembled for travel.

Wherever you purchase your crossbow, you should be able to buy a padded case for it and this is certainly recommended. Two reasons of course, suggest that a padded case is necessary. First, it protects your investment and a case will often offer extra pockets for small accessories. Look for a case that protects your arrows in their quiver and perhaps one with a handle and carrying straps, too. Second, the crossbow receives a mixed reception in public and is often seen – even or especially by other archers – as a threatening weapon. So, keep your crossbow protected and free from controversy.

AMERICAN CROSSBOW FEDERATION

Archers interested in affiliating with other crossbow shooters and with building acceptance of crossbows may want to contact the American Crossbow Federation (ACF).

The ACF can be reached through Post Office Box 251/20 NE 9th Ave., Glenwood, MN 56334 or (320) 634-3660. A one-year membership is currently $16.95 US and $22.95 Canada. Of that membership, $11.95 goes to a subscription of Horizontal Bowhunter magazine, the official publication of the ACF.

CURRENT CROSSBOW REGULATIONS BY STATE

State	Current Regulations
Alabama	Permitted during archery seasons by physically challenged.
Alaska	Permitted during general season, but not permitted during archery season.
Arizona	Permitted during general seasons and during H.A.M. (Handgun, Archery, Muzzleloader) and for fishing.
Arkansas	Classified and permitted as part of the archery deer season. Also for small game, predators and fishing.
California	Permitted for big game during general firearms season. Permitted for small game.
Colorado	Permitted for big game during general firearms season and for small game.
Connecticut	Permitted for physically challenged during hunting season.
Delaware	Permitted for physically challenged for big game during general firearms and shotgun seasons.
Florida	Permitted for big game during general firearms season and for small game.
Georgia	Permitted during archery season and for fishing.
Hawaii	Permitted for big and small game on private land.
Idaho	Permitted during general firearms season for big game and for small game and fishing.
Illinois	Permitted for physically challenged during archery season. Permitted for fishing.
Indiana	Permitted during the late archery season and for fishing. Permitted for physically challenged in the early archery season.
Iowa	Permitted for physically challenged during archery season.
Kansas	Permitted for physically challenged during archery season and for small game.
Kentucky	Permitted for small and big game during crossbow season and general firearms season.
Louisiana	Permitted for physically challenged during archery season.
Maine	Not recognized as a legal hunting weapon.
Maryland	Permitted for physically challenged during archery season.
Massachusetts	Permitted for by permit physically challenged
Michigan	Permitted for physically challenged during archery season.
Minnesota	Permitted for physically challenged during archery season.
Mississippi	Permitted for physically challenged during archery season.
Missouri	Permitted during regular firearms and small game seasons. Permitted for fishing. Permitted for physically challenged in archery season.
Montana	Permitted for regular firearms season and for small game and predators.
Nebraska	Permitted for physically challenged during archery and regular firearms seasons.
Nevada	Not recognized as legal hunting weapon.
New Hampshire	Permitted for physically challenged during archery season.
New Jersey	Permitted for physically challenged only.
New Mexico	Not recognized as legal hunting weapon.

New York	Permitted for physically challenged during archery season.
North Carolina	Permitted for physically challenged during archery season.
North Dakota	Permitted for physically challenged during archery season.
Ohio	Classified in state's archery deer season. Permitted for fishing and all legal game except waterfowl.
Oklahoma	Permitted for physically challenged during archery season.
Oregon	Not recognized as a legal hunting weapon. Permitted for fishing and non-game animals.
Pennsylvania	Permitted for physically challenged during archery season.
Rhode Island	Not recognized as a legal hunting weapon.
South Carolina	Permitted during archery and firearms seasons (except in Areas 1, 2 and 4, and wildlife management areas).
South Dakota	Permitted for physically challenged during archery season.
Tennessee	Permitted for physically challenged during archery, general firearms and muzzleloader seasons.
Texas	Permitted during general firearms season.
Utah	Permitted for use by the physically challenged.
Vermont	Permitted for physically challenged during archery season.
Virginia	Permitted for physically challenged during archery season.
Washington	Not recognized as a legal hunting weapon.
West Virginia	Not recognized as a legal hunting weapon.
Wisconsin	Permitted for physically challenged during archery season and fishing.
Wyoming	Permitted during any legal season for legal game. Permitted for fishing. Permitted for use during any legal season for legal game. Permitted for fishing.

JUST FOR FUN

Barnett offers several crossbow pistols that are not powerful enough for hunting but are excellent for family shooting fun. The Nitro and the Trident II weigh about 1 1/2 pounds are finished in black and measure 14 inches long by 16 inches wide. The difference is that while the 35 pound draw Nitro launches a bolt at 130 fps, the Trident II is a heftier 75 pounds and its bolts travel at 165 fps.

Barnett's Bandit is a true toy, but is excellent for introducing children to the joy of shooting. The Bandit has a metal prod, lightweight skeletal frame and shoots safety darts with soft suction cup tips. The Bandit package includes three darts and a color target.

BUT IS IT A CROSSBOW?

Tom Sheffield began working on his Halfbreed bow 1989. Tom says it is a compound bow because it is hand held, hand drawn and hand released – with a release aid. Opponents say it is a crossbow. Perhaps it

is half vertical compound bow, half horizontal bow … and half slingshot.

In Florida where Tom maintains his factory, the 3.5-pound Halfbreed bow is legal during archery season. While the fore-end looks like a crossbow – with an aluminum prod housing, twin glass limbs and 70 percent let-off machined aluminum cams, and connectivity via a nylon-coated 500 pound steel cable – nothing else looks like anything you have shot before with the exception of a lower hand grip that looks like a slingshot grip.

Tom calls the tubular rear section of the Halfbreed bow a stabilizer unit. It provides a fixed guide for your hand and a machined button into which the modified release aid used with the Halfbreed is drawn and held. He has modified the handle of his TruFire ball bearing release for use with the Halfbreed. This release, he believes, is ideal because the head rotates in front of the index finger trigger. Tom recommends that you use the stainless steel wire string loop he provides and then sand off the rear protruding tip ends of your arrow nocks so the release does not squeeze the arrow off the string as you draw.

The Halfbreed works this way. Insert a 24-inch 2216 arrow or an arrow with comparable spine through the center of the prod housing; allow it to rest on the adjustable stainless steel wire arrow rest; and snap it on the cable. The Halfbreed provides 100 percent of its energy directly in line with the center of the arrow. Snap the release on the cable loop and draw it to the indexed base of the stabilizer unit. Fire at will.

Whether you enjoy shooting a crossbow or a vertical bow, the Halfbreed is unusual, to say the least. Tom says any experienced archer can learn to shoot it in 15 minutes. "It comes already tuned and equipped with our special silencers," he says. "I designed this bow for hunting, but when you learn to shoot it you can drive nails from 30 yards."

The Halfbreed draws from 45 to 85 pounds to a 6-inch brace height, but draw length is irrelevant Tom says, because the bow will virtually fit any adult and can be shot by right hand or left hand archers. With a 490 gr. arrow at 45 pounds, he says, you can expect an arrow speed of 190 fps. Maxed-out at 85 pounds, the Halfbreed shoots 260 fps. "I measured these speeds with a relatively heavy 490 gr. arrow," Tom notes, "and that included a 125 gr. broadhead and full, five inch feathers set in a straight, offset pattern.

The Halfbreed is 25-7/8 inches axle-to-axle and 29 inches from the front of the prod to the rear of the stabilizer unit and has 14-inch limbs. It is machined precisely with index slots for a quiver and sights or an optional crossbow scope. Incidentally, Hoppes has a relatively small molded case that is perfect for the whole bow and measures only 29 inches by 12 inches.

The suggested retail price for the Halfbreed bow is $279.00.

Tom Sheffield shows the shooting form he recommends for his Halfbreed bow.

Tom Sheffield's Halfbreed bow. Is it a vertical compound bow that is shot sidways or a crossbow? Sheffield recommends 24-inch 2216 arrows.

BOW ISSUES

LET-OFF

There is no question that compound bows with high let-offs are selling better than bows with lower let-offs, perhaps four-to-one. Of course, 20 years ago, a bow that let off 50 percent — holding 32.5 pounds after you drew 65 pounds — was about standard and it seemed high for the day. Today, the average bow sold has a 75 percent let-off and manufacturers make optional modules for 65 percent and even 85 percent let-off available. Some include them with a bow purchase and some sell them as optional accessories.

The Predator VX from Pearson is a good example of the trend to lower holding weights. Just 34-1/4 inches axle-to-axle with a 7-1/4 inch brace height, this 304 fps IBO rated speed bow is sold at 85 percent let-off with 65 percent let-off modules available to be purchased separately.

Once you reach full draw, a bow with a lower holding weight should be easier to aim and shoot effectively, allowing you to put your arrow right on the money. That is the conventional wisdom and it is true to a point, but high let-off bows tend to be finicky with steep draw-force curves which means that if you allow the string to creep only slightly, your bow's "mechanical mind" will want to let the arrow go — NOW. It is relatively easy to let down — not shoot an arrow after you come to full draw — with a low let-off bow, say 50 or 65 percent. Sure, you can feel the cams snapping over and the bow will give a jerk, but the snap is manageable. If you decide to let down a high let-off bow, say a 305 fps Browning Adrenaline with 70 percent Lightning Cams (These are hard or "hatchet" cams.), be prepared for an unpleasant moment wrestling with the string when you are sure your shoulders are going to snap together beneath your chin. Hold the string securely with your fingers and consciously move your finger or thumb away from your release's trigger or you could dry fire your bow and if you do, you could damage it and void your warranty.

The issue is not just comfort, however. The most widely accepted record book for hunting archers is the private Pope & Young Club. Founded in the 1960s by a fabulous group of archery leaders including Fred Bear and Glen St. Charles, the Pope & Young Club's record book was designed to honor trophy animals instead of the hunters and honor big game trophies in numerous classes from whitetail deer to Shiras moose to musk ox. This club was not independently modeled. Its founders studied and imitated most of the older Boone & Crockett Club's ideals, standards and measuring systems. Boone & Crockett was founded by Theodore Roosevelt at the beginning of the 20th century for gun hunters (there were no hunting archers at the time and no sanctioned game seasons for archery), but it consistently allows all game taken legally and ethically to be entered.

Unfortunately for archers around the world, a small group of elitists have hijacked the Pope & Young Club. Today, the club's structure prevents it from moving with the times and it has long been controlled by a self-aggrandizing group of self-elected archers who want time, equipment, equipment standards and fellow bowhunters to stand still or to hunt and shoot only in the manner they feel is acceptable.

The Pope & Young Club does not accept any trophy taken with a compound bow that allows more than 65 percent let-off. There have even been serious moves within the organization to limit entries to recurves and longbows (or even to separate trophies taken with compound bows) the small group of elitist voting members has questioned most equipment advances that are legal and ethical such as release aids and lighted sights. Crossbow-taken trophies are not allowed and a majority of the leadership would certainly ban compound bows except for the sure awareness that such a move would doom the club and its current leaders to the tiniest dustbin of archery history. If you have a lighted sight on your bow, any trophy taken is not eligible for "the book." If you are

The new Predator VX from Ben Pearson illustrates several recent trends in archery. Pearson gives the archer a choice of let-off, but delivers the Predator at 85 percent — 65 percent modules are optional — and the central feature of this bow is not just its 34 ½ inch length, but also the Pearson VIB~X System positioned below the grip to absorb vibration and reduce noise. A huge buck taken with the 85-percent let-off would not currently be eligible for the Pope & Young record books but the same deer taken with the lower 65-percent let-off would be eligible

If this marvelous whitetail buck taken by World Champion 3-D professional and avid bowhunter Jesse Morehead had been taken with a bow with an 85 percent let-off, the deer could be entered in the prestigious Boone & Crockett Club record book, but not honored by the smaller, archery-only Pope & Young Club record book.

drawing a bow with more than 65 percent let-off, any trophy taken is not eligible for "the book." If the senior and regular members do not like you personally, you may never advance in level or status within the club.

In November 2000 Xenia, Ohio bowhunter Mike Beatty shot the largest antlered whitetail buck ever killed by any modern hunter. Not just any archer, but any gun hunter, too. Mike's amazing 39-point Ohio non-typical buck scored 304 6/8 Boone & Crockett. It was not accepted for the junior Pope & Young record book because Mike's new Mathews bow was equipped with an 80 percent let-off module, which, to Mike's credit, he freely admitted.

This lack of respect for game animals by the Pope & Young Club has happened hundreds, perhaps thousands of times in the past dozen years and the club's tightly controlled decisions are absolutely impervious to change. Consequently, the Pope & Young Club is in danger of becoming an anachronism, a legend in its own mind.

So, when you go to the field with an 85 percent bow, be prepared to champion the movement for increased archery inclusion in the Boone & Crockett Club, the real book of North American Big Game Trophies or even the relatively new Buckmasters "Full Credit" scoring system. The Pope & Young Club may have outlived its usefulness to the sport of archery and to big game management in North America.

TUNING A BOW FOR SILENCING

Emery Loiselle, owner of Eryleen Archery in Burlington, Mass., says tuning a bow for silent shooting is a pretty simple operation. Essentially, there are five steps, says the 82-yearold archer and archery technical writer who still hunts with a 50-pound Mathews Legacy bow:

- Use a bow that is built for some noise and vibration deadening as well as speed or other shooting characteristics,
- Select the properly spined arrow shaft for your bow because not all arrows absorb energy in the same proportion,
- Use a good stabilizer, one that provides the forward balancing you want and some vibration and noise damping, too,
- Attach a pair of rubber string silencers and
- Experiment with all the new gadgets on the market designed to dampen noise, but especially Limb

Saver technology from Sims Vibration Laboratory.

FIRST, it helps to shoot a bow that has some special built-in mechanical advantage, one that specifically addresses the noise and vibration problem. In the "old days," slow bows were relatively quiet, Emery says, although every archer tied or served CatWhiskers from Rancho Safari onto his string nine to ten inches or so above and below the nocking point. Today's fast bows (not only the fast one-cam bows, but the hard cam or twin hatchet cam bows, too) can be noise and vibration terrors though, but most national manufacturers have worked to incorporate a silencing mechanism into the physical bow itself:

North American's Kraton rubber Shock Stop String Cushion on their Jennings GrandMaster is mounted on the cable slide. It is designed to provide an intermediate string contact point that immediately diminishes string oscillation — and therefore noise — after a shot. As much as 40 percent, claims North American engineer Henry Gallops. In cooperation with Sims Vibration Lags, North American also has developed a system of rubber, Adjustable Damping System (ACS) riser plugs, that help kill riser buzz.

The Mathews Legacy is equipped with String Suppressors on its StraightLine MaxCam and on the axle for its ball bearing mounted idler wheel. These String Suppressors function like small rubber traps to physically catch the string and dampen oscillation near the source, the contact point between the bow's cam and its string. In addition, the Legacy has two removable, center-weighted rubber Harmonic Dampers plugged into the riser itself near the limb pivot points.

Pearson's new Freedom Pro and the McPherson (by Pearson) 38" Special have a built-in vibration and noise reduction chamber manufactured into the riser that is filled with a rubberized polymer gel plug called Vibasorb from Vibracheck (R&R Enterprises). Roger Templeton, chief of research and development at Pearson says this system, called VIB~X, has been tested at the University of Alabama and is scientifically proven to eliminate more than 40 percent of noise and vibration following a shot. It also eliminates metal-to-metal contact between your bow riser and your stabilizer.

And, while it is debatable whether it is actually built-in or technically a factory add-on, the PSE Quantum features Sims Limb Savers designed into a special aluminum donut at each limb pivot. PSE calls this its NV ("no vibration"?) system.

SECOND for silencing, Emery Loiselle says, select the arrow shaft that is most suitably spined for your bow. The proper arrow shaft is the one that will shoot most efficiently. It will absorb most — but not all, it can never absorb "all" — of the shock of a shot, allowing the bow to do its work transforming potential energy into deliverable kinetic energy. Generally, the more energy an arrow shaft absorbs from the bow, the less troubling noise and vibration will remain in your shooting system. The less you will see and feel.

All arrow manufacturers provide information in the form of charts, graphs, catalogs and reams of brochures to help you make the proper shaft selection. You will want to spend "a while" studying these fascinating documents, especially the arrow selection charts, to learn your range of options.

As a quick example, if you know your draw length is 30 inches, your draw weight is 65 pounds and you have what you think of as a "moderate" cam on your Reflex Denali you still have to know what weight broadhead you are going to be shooting before you can make the right shaft selection. Let's say you decide on a 125 gr. Thunderhead from New Archery Products and move your finger down the column to … the 64 to 70 block … then across the line to the 30 inch block and select … 2219, 24 15, 2315 or 2512 shafts. Whew! There are XX78s and XX75s plus three types of carbon composite shaft. If you are normal, you will be confused.

At this point, seek the help of your local pro shop owner or some knowledgeable and more experienced archer, because while the bare 2512s are lighter at your 30 inch draw length (308 gr.) and will fly a little faster, the 2219s (413 gr.) should deliver a greater kinetic energy punch, but will fly a little slower … all things being equal, that is, and they never are.

The Kraton rubber Shock Stop String Cushion on the new Fred Bear TRX 32 works to break up noise and vibration at its source, string oscillation. The soft cushion absorbs the shock of the released string and virtually smothers the harmonics that cause wear and tear in your shooting system

Another add-on element to silence a bow is a good stabilizer. The Deadenator from TRUGLO uses Sims rubberized shock-absorbing technology along with the balancing of their stabilizer to help cut the noise and vibration after the string is released.

Chances are that without asking for help you will select a shaft size that has to be special ordered … and that is even before the pro shop owner prompts you about the dozens of different camouflage patterns on Easton's aluminum shafts … and then tempts you in buy (because of their higher price, some would say "invest") in carbon shafts. Until recently, carbon shafts had the basic good sense to come in your basic black. Now, they too are available in numerous camo patterns.

Number THREE, Emery says, is that once you have settled on a shaft size, you will want to look for a noise- and vibration- damping stabilizer. A modern stabilizer, such as a new, 7-inch, 7-ounce Vibracheck Icon, will both provide balance — hence the variation in stabilizer lengths — and some damping of stray system energy, too.

Specialty Archery Products offers a stabilizer in 5-, 7- or 10-inch lengths called the Dead Stix. The lightweight housing is filled with Sims Limb Saver material and a rubber Sims absorbing cap tops off the end.

The weighted body of Quiet-Tune's fully adjustable, rubber-mounted stabilizers float on an adjustable rubber bushing system for "complete omni-directional vibration and oscillation dampening." Quiet-Tune says their stabilizers reduce the decibels of noise from a shot by about 20 percent, which means as much as 35 to 40 decibels (dB) for a bow with no stabilizer to 29 to 31 decibels with a Quiet-Tune stabilizer.

The tried-and-true Vibracheck Isolator stabilizer is offered in 4-, 7- or 9-inch lengths. Filled with an exclusive, visco-elastic polymer gel, the stackable aluminum end weights are held in place by a rod that is actually molded into the gel along the length of the stabilizer. This isolates the metal end weights from other metal contact and allows them to "stir" the gel, which quickly absorbs and dissipates stray energy. The camouflaged, 1 3/8-inch diameter stabilizer tube is rubber-coated for additional silencing.

Again, according to Emery, step FOUR in silencing a bow is perhaps the most old-fashioned. Tie

something on or loop something into your strings that break up the oscillation and noise harmonic that results from a shot. Of course, the down side of a quieter shot from this step is a slower arrow. That's because anything, even a peep sight — anything except speed nocks, it seems — attached to a bowstring is going to slow down your arrow.

U-nique Archery Products makes a number of items that will help silence your shot, from its serve-on or tie-on rubber string silencers (Spider Leggs or Scorpion) to a variety of 100 percent Teflon cable slides and Teflon silencing sleeves to slide over the launcher arms of your shoot-through arrow rest.

Numerous varieties of string silencers are available — Tarantulas, NEET's Maxi Mufflers and Puffs — but some of these work best on traditional or even round wheel bows as the string tension of BCY's 450 Plus, 452 or Brownell's Fast Flight strings (advertised as "stronger than steel") can quickly destroy some brands.

(Incidentally, the speed buttons mentioned above might be something as simple as extra nock sets carefully and securely applied or they may be the specialty buttons manufactured by U-nique and NEET. Positioned properly within a few inches of your cam or wheel, a set of these buttons will dampen string oscillation and can actually increase your arrow speed by four to eight feet per second!)

Emery said this was a good place to mention that a

Three conventional ways to deaden the noise your bow makes are a tie-on or serve-on pair of rubber string silencers, each about 4 to 6 inches above and below your cam axles; cable silencers to prevent cable snap and vibration; and, oddly enough, speed buttons which enhance performance and deaden noise by dampening string oscillation. Speed buttons typically increase arrow speed by 4 to 8 fps.

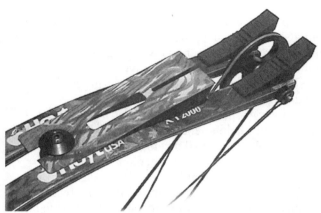

With more than a half-century of building, repairing and tuning bows, Emery Loiselle says that one thing the average archer can do to improve his all-around shooting is to watch for new possibilities entering the marketplace. One new accessory that offers advantages in deadening the vibration after a shot is Global Resource's Shock Fins for your bow's limbs.

way of reducing a small amount of torque on some bow models was to remove the cable slide and instead put a strip of Teflon tape from Coffey or Cir-Cut along the steel guard. This brings the cables closer to centerline and, with an adjustable cable guard, allows you to fine tune for exact fletching clearance. (For least torque, you want the cables as close to the center of the bow as possible without interfering with arrow flight or snagging on the fletching.) It also makes the trip down the cable guard as friction-free — at this time in the 21st century — as is humanly possible.

The FIFTH element in Emery Loiselle's silencing strategy is a recommendation that you look into the options coming on the market from new, innovative companies such as Global Resource on the east coast and Sims Vibration Laboratory on the west coast.

Just a couple years ago, Sims Limb Saver technology was the hottest archery accessory available through a pro shop, hands down. Since the introduction of the original Limb Savers, Sims has expanded its offering to fit virtually any compound bow limb (solid or split) ever made — and even recurve bow limbs! Sims recently introduced a String Leech string silencer that, SVL claims, delivers 80 percent reduction in string resonance with "minimal if any speed loss." The new Sims Insulator Wrap is a rubber strip that wraps around your grip and reduces hand shock and felt bow recoil. It is available with or without the "nodes."

Global Resource has designed a vibration damping system for bow limbs called Shock Fins, an interesting, butterfly-shaped string dampener (replicates the image

and motion of a butterfly, the company says!) and accessory dampeners with interesting light amplifying inserts that attach to your bow sight.

So, can you ever really silence your shot so that an alert deer will not or cannot hear it? Perhaps on a windy day or when you are hunting near a highway or an airport or a dam. Otherwise, probably not, Emery concludes, and certainly not if you are shooting a crossbow which is notoriously loud. Emery says he has had traditional archers shooting longbows say deer jumped their string and that does not give the speed bow shooter much hope except to make his shot as accurate and silent as possible and expect that his fast arrow will do its job.

FAST ... OR FORGIVING? AND MISCELLANEOUS NOTES

In the "old days," archers talked about a forgiving bow, as in "I would rather beg forgiveness than ask permission." A standard that individuals discussed was a bow with a 7-inch or greater brace height, the distance from the low point of the grip to the string when the bow is at rest.

The benefit of a greater brace height is thought of as improved bow efficiency. Today, a high brace height bow typically lets you shoot a lighter, thinner walled arrow and that gives you greater arrow speed. With the advances in bow design resulting from consumer demand for fast, quiet, short axle-to-axle bows over the past ten years, the traditional thinking about brace height may not be true across the board.

The true improvement has not so much been about speed as it has been about an arrow with a flat trajectory. At 240 fps IBO, which is a great speed for consistent, no problem shooting, you can misestimate yardage to a 40-yard deer by several yards and still place your broadhead in its vitals. At 300 or more fps IBO, you can misestimate by twice as much and still collect your trophy.

On the down side, faster usually means more tuning problems and you are probably shooting with a bow that is less efficient. Any "wasted" energy not transmitted to the arrow becomes noise and vibration ... and maybe a sore shoulder and elbow on your bow arm. A slower bow launching heavier arrows or with increased draw weight is usually more efficient.

Slower is usually quieter, too. Slower arrow speed not only means less time in the bow and bare shaft tuning process (essentially making your arrows fly straight), it means that there is less stray energy left over in the system after the arrow escapes.

Lightweight carbon-composite shafts are not necessarily straight with tolerances 50-100 percent below top quality aluminum or carbon composites.

What this means is inconsistent wall thickness 360 degrees around the carbon shaft, an inconsistency that is magnified by faster arrow speed. Still, you are looking at very minute differences that, unless you are an Olympic or top 3-D professional competitor, will probably not make any difference at all in your shooting.

Many pro shop owners believe that 250 to 260 fps arrow speed is about as much as average archer can tune for, even with feathers. After that speed range, the stress on your bow becomes so high that unusual things can happen that the average person cannot predict or prepare for: handle flexing, cam lean and so on. The typical paradigms react in a chaotic manner and hence the switch by hunters to mechanical heads that fly like darts. (How they hit and penetrate is another story.)

To counter the urge for a faster arrow, a rangefinder could be the difference between hours tuning your bow and shooting through paper to make small adjustments and enjoying archery. If you like to tinker with equipment, go for higher and higher arrow speeds. If you simply enjoy the pleasure of shooting a bow — hunting, fishing, competition or even something really different like archery golf — then

tune a little and shoot a lot.

If you have a need for speed, you probably want a short axle-to-axle bow with hard, aggressive eccentrics. You will shoot with a caliper-style release aid and use light, short carbon arrows tipped with 75- or 100-grain broadheads — or mechanical, open-on-impact heads — and fletched with short plastic vanes. In addition, you will want to draw as much weight as you can get out of the bow and then spend all the time you can getting our arrows to fly like darts.

Archery technical expert and bowhunter Norb Mullaney studies the new All-American paint job on a 37-inch Ben Pearson Freedom Pro which is equipped with the patented Pearson VIB~X noise and vibration reduction system in the riser below the grip.

When you shop for a bow, you may need to make a decision whether you want a fast bow or a forgiving bow. The average archer may occasionally be able to squeeze 300 fps out of a bow on rare occasions, but you should really expect a top speed of 250 to 270 fps. Bows like the Darton Rampage Express have a relatively long brace height (7 inches) and a long power stroke. It is a good compromise of speed and forgiveness with an AMO rated speed of 240 fps and an IBO rated speed of 310 fps

Your fast arrow set-up will eliminate some pin guessing errors and flatten your arrows trajectory so that distance estimation errors are minimized, too. Consider adding an overdraw that incorporates an arrow rest so that you can pull your arrow back behind the riser at full draw. Make sure you install speed nocks on your bowstring four to five inches above your one-cam for an equivalent speed increase of three to six feet per second. Position any rubber limb saver dampeners as far out on the end of your limbs as possible.

There is a well-accepted and general caution about fast set-ups. You will only achieve peak performance from your equipment if you practice and achieve peak performance form yourself. This means you must study good shooting form and your practice sessions should be disciplined

THE MASTER SET-UP

Among those individuals who are respected throughout the archery industry, Norbert "Norb" Mullaney is high on almost every list. He is an engineer who has been long-time archery technical columnist, commentator and consultant, a bowhunter and recently elected member of the Archery Hall of Fame.

Norb says he has shot everything, meaning every kind of bow from every company for the past 30 years, and still does. He has built his own bows and began hunting with a bow in 1956. From 1956 to 1968, Norb hunted exclusively with recurves. He has used lightweight compound bows to take kudu and various plains antelope in Africa, bows that most bowhunters would think of as dangerously light: 53 pounds of draw weight delivering just over 50 ft. lbs. of kinetic energy. At 71, Norb is no spring chicken though and he stayed

clear of Cape buffalo, elephant and rhino with this set-up.

"My bow preferences have changed over the years," he says. "These days I'm trying the Darton CPS (Controlled Power System) bows that Rex Darlington designed. (Rex is the owner of Darton Archery.) These cams let me make very small draw length adjustments. Most of my life, I have been a finger shooter, but I'm learning to shoot with a release." Norb shoots Easton Aluminum shafts with Thunderhead 100 or 125 broadheads. Mechanicals are here to stay, he says, because they solve some problems associated with tuning for accurate flight and they maintain a higher velocity down range with less fletching drag.

While Norb began shooting as an instinctive shooter who "visualized the path of the arrow," he has relied on pin sights for the past 10 years.

"Today, I shoot compounds exclusively," Norb says. "No recurve can approach a compound now for storing energy. Today's compounds have a high Stored Energy/Peak Draw Force ratio of 1.3 to 1.5. The best recurve made has a SE/PDF of about 1.1. On competitive testing at AMO Standards (30 inch draw, 60 pounds weight, 540 gr.), I have found that the fastest recurve shoots about 207 fps (that was a Bill Stewart model) and the fastest longbow about 201 fps (21st Century Longbows and the Stampers). The fastest compounds — by AMO, not IBO, standards — so far have been a couple of Martin and Mathews bows that registered 247 fps on my chronograph."

ALL ABOUT ARROWS

Should you choose a conventional aluminum shaft or one of the new generations of carbon shafts?

"Carbon has unquestionably grown in popularity," says Deb Adamson, Marketing Director for Easton Technical Products, which manufactures Easton aluminum and Beman carbon arrow shafts. "Carbon shafts are excellent and the price has fallen in the last few years – early versions from every company tended to be pricey as everyone worked out the technology – but, assuming they come from the manufacturer straight (a carbon shaft cannot be straightened) it is going to be hard to beat a carbon shaft for speed, accuracy and durability. The arrow shaft is what delivers your package on target. We at Easton and Beman don't believe you should economize there. Buy quality and that means level of straightness with tight-fitting components."

Nevertheless, Easton and other manufacturers offer almost perfectly straight aluminum shafts that, for the money, have proven themselves to be reliable in the most difficult hunting and competition situations. Aluminum shafts also tend to be less expensive than carbon shafts and for fletching and cresting, the technology is well established.

If either will do, the question of whether to buy aluminum or carbon may not be as critical as availability of a shaft in the spine ("spine" basically means stiffness) you need for perfect arrow flight with your set-up. Indeed, it matters whether you are shooting a 45-pound recurve or a 75-pound one-cam bow. That is why Easton and the other arrow shaft manufacturers offer what at first glance seems to be a bewildering array of arrows. Here is how the Archery Manufacturer's Association defines "spine:"
The amount of bend (deflection) in an arrow shaft that is caused by a specific weight being placed at the center of the shaft while the shaft is supported at a designated span. Or the recovery characteristics of an arrow that permit it to bend and then recover to its original shape while in flight.

This refers to the fact that an arrow shaft bends an amazing amount as it leaves the bowstring, recovering to its original straight shape several yards downrange.

Well-known archers like Chuck Adams are instrumental in field testing new arrows and gear designs around the world and then reporting their findings in the popular archery and bowhunting magazines. Chuck is not a "speed freak," preferring a bow-arrow combination that he can shoot precisely and manageably.

Shafts released using a mechanical release aid tend to flex in a vertical or up and down plane while those released with fingers tend to flex in a horizontal or side to side plane. A shaft of correct spine for your bow set-up will flex less and recover more quickly than one of improper spine, a critical factor in arrow flight.

Each arrow manufacturer has an arrow shaft selection chart that matches a specific shaft size (spine) with the finished arrow's overall length, the point weight being used, your draw length, the draw weight of your bow and the type of wheel or cam the bow has if any: round, hard twin cam, one cam, etc.

Generally, several arrow sizes will work with your bow. If you are fortunate enough to work with a competent archery pro shop, you may be able to shoot each size and see which flies best.

After you make a spine selection, your next consideration is weight. Lighter arrows fly faster with a flatter trajectory, but they squander energy and leave more vibration in the system which means you feel a shot more in the arm and your bow set-up needs to be checked frequently to be sure things do not rattle apart. Lightweight aluminum arrows have thinner walls and will therefore not be as durable as comparably spined heavier arrows. Also, heavier shafts will absorb more kinetic energy and this promotes penetration. That is not a factor necessarily for a competitor, but for a

bowhunter, it can be crucial to a successful blood trail.

Your arrow's overall spine rating is determined by its wall thickness and shaft diameter with diameter having the greatest overall influence. So, a larger diameter arrow with a thin wall can be made stiffer and lighter than a smaller diameter arrow with a thick wall. For example, a 30-inch 2315 aluminum shaft with a diameter of 23/64 inches and a wall thickness of 12/1,000 inch weighs 350 grains while a 30-inch 2413 shaft with a diameter of 24/64 inch and wall thickness of 13/1,000 inch weighs 312 grains. Both have a comparable spine, but the heavier of the two outweighs the other by 11 percent.

Typically, carbon shafts cover a larger range of spine sizes than aluminum shafts. This means that it is relatively simpler to choose the correct spine for a carbon shaft than an aluminum shaft.

Like good bullets, arrows are the link between you and the game you're hunting. You have control over the bow until the time of the release, but then the arrow is on its own and the entire outcome of your hunt depends on the flight of that arrow. So you want the most accurate and reliable arrow you can buy. Selecting the right arrows may be the single most important decision in archery and bowhunting.

Though many hunters do not realize it, no arrow flies perfectly straight. When shot from a bow, an

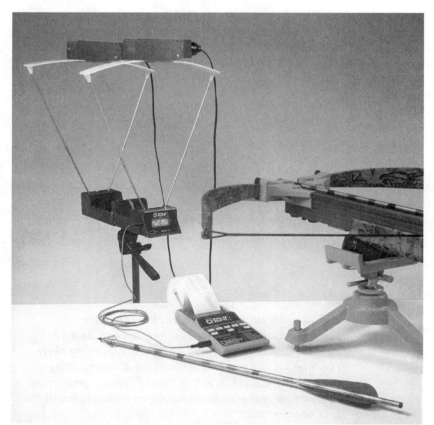

Archers talk about bow speed when they really mean arrow speed. Chronographs such the Shooting Chrony are reliable and are used at many archery events.

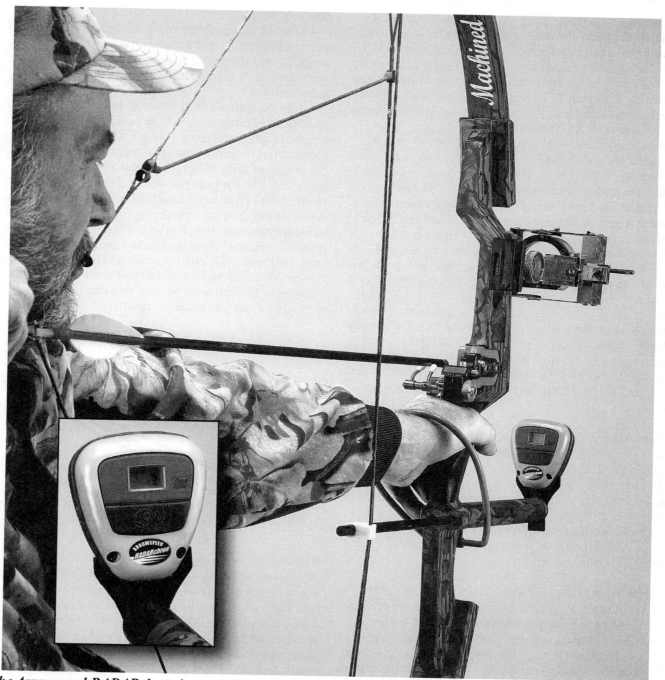

Easton Aluminum has worked with Chuck Adams for many years. The aluminum alloy XX78 Super Slam and Super Slam Select are named for Chuck's accomplishments in the field. The straightness tolerance of this shaft is plus or minus .0015 inches.

arrow bends dramatically and wobbles back and forth like a swimming trout. If this oscillation occurs at the right frequency, the arrow's path is relatively true; if not, the arrow flies poorly.

Manufacturers use the term spine to describe an arrow's stiffness, as determined by the amount the arrow bends when shot from a bow. When an archer has consistent difficulty making his arrows fly straight,

The Arrowspeed RADARchron is a small Doppler radar that uses microwave technology to measure arrow speed. It attaches to the end of most stabilizers or to an extension rod provided with the radar

it's usually because the arrow spine is mismatched for his bow.

The stiffness, or spine, of an arrow is governed by several variables, the most important of which are the diameter of the shaft, thickness of the outer walls, the length of the arrow and the weight of the head.

Generally arrows with a larger diameter and thicker the walls have a greater spine. Manufacturers use a four-digit number to identify the diameter and wall thickness of an arrow. In addition, the length of the shaft affects the arrow's spine; shorter shafts are stiffer than long shafts. For example, a 32-inch 2213 arrow will flex much more than a 26-inch 2213 arrow.

Finally, heavy arrowheads reduce an arrow's spine. That is, a 32-inch 2213 aluminum arrow with a 150-grain broadhead will flex more than an identical arrow equipped with a 100-grain head.

Other variables also can affect spine, or at least change the way a shaft behaves when shot. A large fletching, for example, makes an arrow stiffer in flight. And the spring tension setting of an arrow rest can affect arrow flight enough to effectively change spine value. Even the release method can affect the bending of an arrow; arrows released with fingers bend somewhat more than those shot with a release aid.

Use the chart on the following page as a guide to selecting the right shafts when setting up any new bow and arrow combination. Or, if your current bow and arrow setup is not shooting to your satisfaction, consult the chart to make sure your shafts are spined correctly for the draw weight of your bow. These charts are updated as new arrows are developed and bow technology evolves. Check with your dealer at the time of purchase and confirm that you are using current data.

Consistency: Not only must arrow shafts be matched to a given bow, but also they must be matched to each other. Small variations in length, diameter, head weight and fletching style can make it impossible to achieve consistent arrow flight. Your finished arrows should be identical in weight. Even with identical spine values, arrows with weight variations as small as 5 grains can have differing impact points at various ranges, especially with broadheads.

Arrow Wieght: As the spine chart shows, you have many choices of arrow weight within each given spine range. With increasing emphasis on speed, many archers choose the lightest shafts within the spine range. That's not a bad decision, but at some point the light-arrow game meets the law of diminishing returns, and you begin to lose more than you gain. Ultra light, high-speed arrows, particularly when equipped with

broadheads, are more temperamental than heavier, slower arrows. Unless the shot is executed perfectly, very light arrows are likely to fly poorly. And, more seriously, light arrows increase the chances for bow damage. Heavy arrows absorb as much as 80 percent of a bow's energy, but lighter arrows absorb much less, leaving more energy to vibrate through the bow. If this vibration becomes excessive, as in the case of a dry finer (shooting a bow with no arrow on the string), a bow can break.

The old standard rule of thumb recommended 9 grains of arrow weight for every pound of draw weight. For a 60-pound bow, that translates to 540-grain arrows (9 grains x 60 pounds draw weight = 540-grain arrows).

The old formula is antiquated, given modern bow and arrow construction, but the principle of using draw weight to determine arrow weight still applies. Some manufacturers recommend 6 grains of arrow weight per pound of draw weight – a good all-around guideline. The formula has been refined even further by the AMO (Archery Manufacturers and Merchants Association). The accompanying chart shows the AO's recommendations, which take into account not only draw weight, but wheel design and draw length, as well. Following this chart ensures a safe and reasonably efficient bow and arrow combination. Pushing to the extremes beyond this chart could yield explosive – and unpleasant – results.

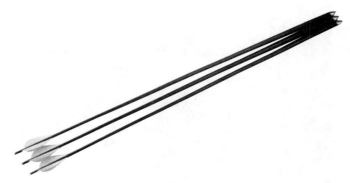

The carbon arrow has been coming on strong in popularity recently, and not just among elite archers. Once very high, the cost of a dozen arrows has fallen and the technology for straightness and consistency has improved. The Nitro Stinger .395 Magnum features an extra-fat-tip that, at 26/62-inches in diameter, is the same size as the largest aluminum shaft. The .395 gives competitors the line-cutting ability of an aluminum 2613 without extra speed-robbing arrow weight.

Just 10 years ago, carbon and composite shafts were only available in black. Today, many camouflage patterns have successfully been applied such as the Realtree Timber HD on this BlackHawk Vapor carbon shaft.

Many accessories, originally designed before carbon shafts became popular, were designed to work with larger aluminum arrows and need to be modified for carbon. PSE's two-piece pivoting pocket eight-arrow quiver will work with carbon or aluminum arrows. When you are outfitting your bow with accessories, be sure to ask about the details before you buy!

Adjustable shoot-through rests like the PSE Mongoose Universal must be carefully tuned to the flight of any arrow, but the smooth passage of small-diameter carbon shafts across the prongs and the resultant passage of the bottom vane through them is especially critical.

ATTACHING "THINGS" TO YOUR ARROW SHAFT

Once you have chosen between carbon or aluminum and made a shaft selection that is spined correctly for your draw weight and style of bow, you are going to want to attach things to that shaft: fletching to steer it on the rear end, nocks on the very back to hold it on the bowstring and, on the front, some type arrow point. Every shaft type has its own set of options and your archery club or pro shop will guide you through the selection and set-up process until it becomes second nature.

Whatever you choose, unless you have the pro shop set everything up for you or you buy ready-made arrows in a box, your new arrow shaft will be a flat stub. Wood arrows need to be tapered and there are special tools for this for both ends. Carbon and aluminum shafts need to have lightweight aluminum threaded inserts glued in for arrow points. Once the glue dries, you will be able to screw in any standard practice point or broadhead. The inserts should fit tightly and when you have applied the hot melt glue, you will want to press them into the empty shaft; rotate them to be sure the glue completely encircles the insert; then finally, press them onto a flat surface to be sure they are fully seated. You must buy the correctly sized insert for your arrow or all bets are off and if you glue the insert in crooked, well … your chances of hitting anything consistently are slim.

Not many years ago, about half the carbon arrows on the market used "outserts" rather than standardized inserts. With the increasing popularity of carbon over the past decade however, there has been a major push to standardize and today all main-line carbon shafts use carbon inserts of the same style as aluminum shafts, although the two will not be interchangeable because of the differing shaft sizes.

The beauty of the insert on the front end is that it allows you to screw in and then remove arrow points as often as you desire. On the back end of the shaft, you can experiment with different types of arrow nocks or even use one of the relatively new, stick-on tunable nocks that can be rotated to give you the best fletching-arrow rest orientation.

FLETCHING

Bird and turkey feathers have been used to stabilize arrows (and some spears) ever since men began shooting the bow and arrow. They are not so popular today because we rely so heavily on civilization's wonder drug, plastic. Most archers use plastic vanes for fletching. Some experts believe that 90 percent of all arrows shot use plastic vanes.

You could select plastic for its durability or because it does not become wet and heavier or because you are convinced that the two to four fps you will gain switching from feathers to vanes is important.

Whatever you use, the size fletching should be in proportion to your shaft diameter and broadhead size and weight. Remember, it is the fletching that steers

If you are careful, you can cut aluminum arrows to length in the garage with a hacksaw, although Easton and your local pro shop would be horrified. Still, this is not recommended since more arrows will be cut crookedly and damaged than will turn out right. NEVER try this with a carbon shaft, though. Carbon shafts require powerful cut-off saws such as this pro-shop model with blades rotating at 5,000 rpm. Cut carbon with a hacksaw and you will ruin 100 percent.

For years, archers have personalized their arrows to fit their own style. The process of dipping the ends of arrows in high visibility colors is messy and smelly. Now, with arrow wraps like Martin's Quick Dip, there is no mess at all. Just peel the colored vinyl off the protective backing and roll it carefully on the shaft. It is fletching glue-compatible, too

your arrow and once you have shot it, bigger fletching generally gives you the better kinetic energy delivery or impact on target than smaller fletching. Figure 4- or 5-inch fletching for most heavy aluminum arrows and 3- to 4-inch for your smaller carbon shafts.

MEASURING ARROW SPEED

The next time you study a bow catalog or read an equipment story in an archery magazine, you will be faced with the difficulty of understanding bow speed. The trouble thinking that way is that bows do not speed. Arrows speed. If your bow is speeding, you need to investigate a wrist sling.

Arrow speed is measured typically (and bows are rated for performance) in two ways. If you understand the two systems, you will have a standard against which you can tune your arrows and your shooting system. Remember that bow manufacturers from Mathews to Hoyt to Pro Line give you the peak arrow speeds their engineers can achieve, not something the average archer will experience with a bow out of the box. In fact, it will usually take a lot of work and some modification to match the arrow speeds manufacturers advertise.

Bow speed is measured in feet per second (fps). A bow that shoots 300 fps has become the bragging standard for manufacturers and a lot of archers, too. 300 fps is fast. We usually do not relate it to miles per hour (mph) – in the same way we do not measure the family car in feet per second – but an arrow traveling that fast is moving along at one million and eighty thousand feet per hour. Okay. That's a wowee number, but if you were traveling 204.55 mph in the family car, the wife and kids would be bug-eyed in terror.

The original speed rating was called "AMO" and it will always be the lower of the two numbers. This is the speed the normal archer can relatively easily attain. AMO stands for the Archery Manufacturer's Organization (now the Archery Manufacturer's Association) that oversees equipment standardization and lobbies in support of archery and bowhunting. A bow is AMO rated using a 30-inch draw length, a 60-pound draw weight and a 540-grain arrow. This standard requires nine grains of arrow weight per pound of draw weight.

Deluxe cedar arrows such as these sold by Martin Archery are designed for traditional archers. Made of premium Port Orford cedar, nine coats of stain and lacquer seal the shaft and hand cresting is applied for a terrifically good-looking arrow. This arrow is fletched with 5-inch shield cut feathers.

The newer and faster "IBO" speed rating is named after the International Bowhunting Organization and it is always the higher of the two ratings, the speed a bow is capable of producing. The IBO sponsors national 3-D tournaments and has an agenda for promoting bowhunting around the world. IBO speeds reflect a 30-inch draw length, a 70-pound draw weight and a 350-grain arrow. It is based on five grains of arrow weight per pound of draw weight.

Lighter arrows (five grains as opposed to nine) at heavier draw weights (70 pounds as opposed to 60) tend to fly faster. This is the reason archery manufacturers emphasize IBO rather than AMO. A typical high end hunting bow like the Jennings GrandMaster will shoot 223 fps AMO. The same bow

The nock's job is to keep your arrow on your string as you draw. The nock must be put on the shaft precisely as any lean to one side or the other or any misalignment can cause a problem with arrow flight. Snap-on nocks are popular and come in a variety of colors and sizes.

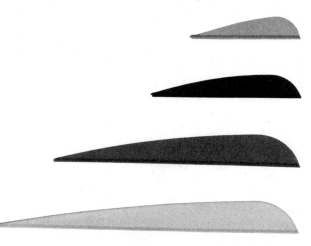

The argument about fletching with feathers or plastic vanes will go on for some time. Vanes for noiseless, all-weather durability. Feathers for a little more speed and forgiveness. Arizona Vanes in the parabolic cut have been used by top archery professionals for years. The soft material and lightly textured finish offers maximum arrow stabilization with a minimal amount of drag. They are available in dozens of colors.

tested on the IBO scale will shoot 300 fps. It will take some tuning, tinkering and proper equipment selection to get your arrows to approach this level.

THE CHRONOGRAPH

Arrow speed (velocity timing) is measured with a chronograph. Most good archery pro shops have one on hand and large tournaments will have one available for occasional random testing to ensure that all competing archers are shooting to standard. ASA and IBO, for instance, now limit arrow speed to 280 fps.

A chronograph works by timing how long it takes your arrow to pass over or through a photoelectric circuit actuated when the arrow interrupts a beam of light. This chronograph style can be set to the length of each arrow tested and then resets automatically. The ProChrono Digital from Competition Electronics works off a single nine-volt battery and will give readings from 22 to 7,000 fps in temperatures from 33 to 100 degrees. It is light, easy to set up and has an error index of just plus or minus a couple percentage points.

The Shooting Chrony works on the same principle and measures speeds from 30 fps to 7,000 fps with, the manufacturer says, 99.5 percent accuracy. Set-up of the 2.5 pound folding Shooting Chrony takes a couple

Several powder formulas are available to help your feathers repel water. Application does not add weight or odor.

A flu-flu describes an arrow designed for quick flight for a short distance. The feathers are full cut and will slow this cedar shaft down quickly. Use flu-flu arrows for bird hunting or small game.

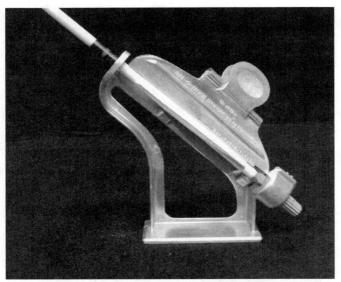

Nothing is more satisfying for most archers who, as a group, enjoy working with their equipment, than building arrows. The aluminum Bitzenburger fletching jig is the top of the line for adding feathers or vanes to wood, carbon or aluminum shafts.

minutes and it is powered by one nine volt battery. The LCD display and electronics are housed in one unit. The Master Chrony has a 16-foot phone cord to connect the chronograph itself to the digital display unit and the optional printer. The value of a separate readout and printer unit is that you can move the display and information elements to a separate table away from the actual shooting (important when you switch from your relatively quiet bow to a .30-06).

The Arrowspeed RADARchron by Sports Sensors is a small Doppler radar that measures the speed of an arrow as it is shot from the bow with microwave technology (high-frequency, short-wavelength 5.8-gigahertz energy). It attaches to the end of most stabilizers or to an extension rod provided with the radar. Unlike optical chronographs, President Al Dilz says, short-range microwave operation of the Arrowspeed cannot be affected by background light or shadows. The Arrowspeed is only 2.5 inches by 3.69

KE (FT. LBS) OF YOUR SET-UP	SUITABLE FOR HUNTING
Less than 25	Small game: rabbits and squirrels
26 – 41	Medium game: pronghorns and deer
42 – 65	Large game: black bear, elk and wild boar
66 and higher	Big Game: African plains game, grizzly and brown bears

inches and weighs 2.7 ounces. It is operated with one button, is powered by a three-volt camera battery and has a four percent error range (plus or minus 2%) between 150 fps and 450 fps.

MEASURING KINETIC ENERGY (KE)

Kinetic energy is an important concept in archery and especially so in bowhunting because it is one of our few relative measures of penetrating ability and that's extraordinarily important because without penetrating ability, you simply have no hunting ability. Penetration with a broadhead-tipped arrow means slicing and bleeding and that means a blood trail and big game animals that often expire in less than a minute with a good, clean shot through the heart-lung vitals.

It is no longer arguable whether you want a broadhead to pass completely through an animal or to remain inside it. In the old days perhaps, when Ishi and his brother archers around the world shot deer, their flint heads remained inside the animal. These hunters often used poison-tipped arrows however because their arrows did not pack enough power or kinetic energy to kill an animal like a deer or a giraffe quickly by hemorrhaging alone. It is different now. The idea that a broadhead should remain inside an animal and continue to cut and chew up its insides as it runs has been discredited by experienced and well known big game bowhunters like Chuck Adams and Bob Foulkrod.

The penetration standard today is an arrow tipped with a super-sharp broadhead that passes cleanly and completely through an animal. This gives you an entry and an exit hole, both leaking blood. Because most deer and bear are shot from treestands, it is important to have a lower exit hole for blood to drain out as more blood will typically pour out of the lower hole than from the hole higher on the body.

There is no widely accepted standard for determining how much kinetic energy is sufficient. Hunting archers believe however that the larger the game, the greater the KE required for a quick, clean kill. For deer, 40 to 50 foot-pounds will certainly do the job; less is acceptable with precise arrow placement. For larger, heavier animals like elk or caribou, you will need to step up your energy output. If you fly to Alaska for Kodiak bear or on safari to Africa, a dramatic increase in KE will be required for Cape buffalo or zebra or even the larger antelope species like eland.

On the face of it, the idea of kinetic energy (KE) is relatively simple. The formula for calculating kinetic energy in foot-pounds is speed (in fps) squared multiplied by total arrow weight (including your

Pete Shepley, founder of Precision Shooting Equipment, developed hand-wrapped, multi-layered Carbon Force Arrows that are available in black or camo and range from an amazing straightness of plus or minus .001 inch for the Competition Pro. Pete is one of the individuals who have significantly shaped archery and bowhunting for the 21st Century.

broadhead, in grains) divided by 450,240. A foot pound is the energy required to raise one pound one foot against gravity. Under controlled laboratory conditions, an arrow with 50 foot-pounds of KE will penetrate twice as far as an arrow with 25 foot-pounds of energy.

Studying the formula, some archers believe that a fast light arrow will give them greater KE. In a sense, the formula is deceptive and the poetic idea of balance comes into play, because a light arrow absorbs less energy than a heavy arrow.

Here is an example. You are shooting 250 fps with a 500-grain Easton aluminum shaft (with a 100-grain broadhead included) and switch to a 400-grain carbon arrow (with a 75-grain head included) and pick up 10 fps. The heavier projectile yields 69.4 foot-pounds of KE while the lighter arrow yields 60.0 foot-pounds. The lighter projectile has 16 percent less energy at chronograph or point-blank range than the heavier projectile! At close range, say 10 to 20 yards, this may

not be a significant difference, but as your shooting distance increases, the lighter arrows loses its energy faster than the heavier arrow. The same 500-grain arrow will have much more energy at 40 yards than the 400-grain arrow. All things being equal, that may mean and additional 6 or 7 inches of penetration and it is significant in terms of recovered game.

Shooting heavier arrows is one way to improve the punch, the KE your arrow delivers. Another way is to increase your draw weight. Increase the average compound bow 5 pounds and you will enjoy an arrow-energy increase of about 10 percent – and gain speed and a flatter trajectory, too.

We know from years of study and a half century of modern bowhunting experience that perfectly flying arrows out-penetrate wobbly arrows. For deepest penetration, you want your arrow's energy directed straight down the centerline of the shaft, because when a flexing arrow hits game, the shaft tends to whip to one side. This diminishes the amount of energy available to drive that shaft through your quarry. A perfectly flying arrow puts all its energy behind the broadhead. This is another issue with the current breed of mechanical or open-on-impact heads.

Jim Easton is the son of Doug Easton who founded Easton Aluminum. Jim has taken the lead internationally in developing arrows to serve all modern archery uses, from aluminum to carbon to composite. He has put together the largest archery company in the world and estimates suggest that Easton (which now owns Beman, HoytUSA and numerous other sporting goods companies) sells more than 75 percent of all arrows in the world.

Walking or running animals sometimes cause arrows to lurch sideways on impact. The broadhead enters, the shaft whips to one side and penetration suffers. For best penetration in game, you should never shoot an arrow at a running animal. Unless your bow is extra-heavy, you will probably fail to shoot completely through.

Once you know and understand kinetic energy, is there a formula for determining what game animals can (or should) be hunted with your bow set-up? No, but the following recommendations are taken from a technical bulletin from Easton Technical Products. The spreads are wide and obviously, this chart is only intended as a guide, but at the lower end of KE for each range, one has to wonder if the KE delivered is sufficient for lethal and ethical hunting. If in doubt, err on the high side remembering that heavier arrows deliver five to ten percent more KE than lighter arrows, both at less than 10 yards and out to 40 yards. The farther your shot, the more KE the heavier arrow retains.

How Far We Have Come

It is common to expect that we deliver more than 60 foot-pounds of energy on target with a modern, tuned compound bow.

In the 1979 edition of *Fred Bear's The World of Archery* a hardback book published by Doubleday in New York, they give the following example of calculating kinetic energy:

"In a test with a 48-pound conventional recurve bow 58 inches long, we found the following by using the following formula (for calculating KE):

304-grain arrow – 205.93 feet per second – 28.576 foot-pounds.
400-grain arrow – 187.95 feet per second – 31,200 foot-pounds (sic).

"The striking energy increased 9.2 per cent (sic) with the heavier arrow. This is because the heavier arrow absorbs more of the bow's energy. The conclusion is that, within the correct spine range for a given bow, light arrows with high velocity are best for target shooting, while the heavier arrow with more energy (striking power) should be used for hunting."

The Magnock: Several varieties of drop-away arrow rest use magnets. Now, there is a specific magnetic application in arrow release, an obvious spot, only requiring some enterprising company to invest the time in its development. That company is Aznat.

Magnock is a two-piece nock that makes a magnetic connection between the back of the arrow and a receiver permanently attached to your bowstring. Once you release the bowstring, the magnet in your nock releases your arrow at 4.5 ounces of pressure every time, regardless of the weather. Magnock's testing suggests that more conventional nocks have a release pressure that varies by as much as 20 ounces.

The polycarbonate Magnock receiver with the permanent magnet is served onto the string. Its inventors say the Magnock system works best with a string loop and release aid so that your point of release is immediately behind the arrow. Instead of nocks, you then attach an insert, with a small metal ball inside, to the base of your arrow. The insert also has an alignment ridge that slides into a slot in the receiver to ensure consistent fletching alignment.

Hunters will want to know what happens if your arrow falls off the rest. Will the Magnock hold it?

Magnock's inventor's say that it will.

Magnocks improve accuracy and even simplify bow tuning because of their consistent release tension and the elimination of some shaft flexing at release. Reduced shaft flexing means the flat sides of a broadhead and vanes will not plane against the air after you shoot. So, you can use smaller vanes and perhaps a lighter shaft, because there is less problem with arrow stabilization. Smaller vanes have less drag and create less turbulence. And, since there is no glue-on nock, you can usually trim about $1/2$-inch off your arrow. The result is smoother, more accurate arrow flight and a faster arrow, too! Check them out at www.magnock.com.

ARROW POINTS AND BROADHEADS

No arrow is complete without a specialized point. Shooting an arrow without a proper point or head at any target is a sure way to destroy the arrow and miss the target, too.

There are four categories of arrow point depending on how you intend to use them. For practice or recreational shooting, you would choose field, bullet or blunt points. For bowfishing, a subject we cover in a separate chapter, heads are designed with barbs to hook and hold fish. Elite national and international competition requires special points that are rarely-to-never used by the average archer. Finally, and probably most important to the three million archers in the US and Canada, there is a variety of hunting arrowheads or broadheads.

The point you choose will depend on the task you need done. An arrow must fly straight and then it needs to penetrate and stick in (or pass completely through, most hunting archers shooting broadheads would argue) its target.

RECREATIONAL AND PRACTICE SHOOTING

Traditionally, you will purchase a handful of field or bullet points when you buy a new bow or new arrows. You will keep a few of these points in your pocket, a few in your fanny pack, several in your archery tackle box and not less than a couple rattling around on the floor of the pick-up or in the glove compartment. You just never know when you will need to warm up and take a couple practice shots!

Practice points for recreational shooting come in several styles, but all are intended to accomplish one thing: make practicing easy and fun, thereby helping an archer stay in shape and tighten his shot grouping. Whether you choose Satellite bullet points or field

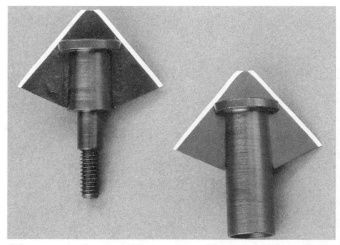

Magnus Archery produces these "blunts with a bite" just in case you decide to hunt squirrels or rabbits when you are stump shooting!

An arrow point like this brass glue-on from Ace is excellent for target practice, initial sight settings and recreational shooting

Many archers like to use a blunt tip for field shooting (also called stump shooting or roving) because it is less prone to stick deeply in stumps and slide or run beneath the grass. This makes it easier to find.

points or a hybrid head such as the Saunders Combo Point, the styling of these practice points is designed to fly precisely and pull easily out of any type target, foam, layered fiber or compressed hay bales.

For many years, the standard for recreational and even hunting accuracy has been hitting an eight-inch paper plate consistently at 20 yards, perhaps because that size approximates the vital area of a big game animal, a deer or a bear or even an elk. Commonly, any public outdoor shooting range is littered with shredded paper plates that had been fastened to hay bales with twisted sections of coat hanger. In this "accuracy environment," such technicalities as matching the grain weight of your practice points to the grain weight of your broadhead was not considered very important, given all of the other factors involved in taking and making a clean shot. Even some archery engineers thought matching practice points with actual hunting components was probably unnecessary.

Today, the bar of accuracy has been raised. Even novice archers understand the need for tight groups. Practice points are now available in multiple sizes to approximate the weight of a hunting head and to give the best flight characteristic to your draw weight and arrow spine.

Recreational arrow points are measured in two ways: diameter in inches (to closely match the diameter of your arrow shaft) and weight in grains. Typically, these machined and black anodized steel field or bullet points screw into a lightweight threaded aluminum adapter or insert in the business end of your arrow shaft. Should you choose to shoot a traditional set-up, glue-on field points are available for practice with wooden shafts.

A popular style of practice head that can also be used for small game hunting or a warm-up during the day while you are in the field (commonly referred to as "stump shooting") is the Zwickey "Judo Point." Practicing in the field traditionally meant that arrows

tipped with bullet or field points when shot would occasionally slide under the grass and therefore be hard to find, especially with the increasing popularity of camouflaged arrow shafts. The Judo Point was designed with a blunt tip and four springy wires to slow down the arrow's forward momentum and catch or hang up in grass or weeds. It is referred to in the company's advertising as an "unloseable miracle point."

Similar points or variations on the classic Judo concept are available from Zwickey, Game Tracker and Muzzy. All are designed to hit with a powerful punch and then snag with their exposed wire "arms." Every archer will want to have a few Judo Points or similar wire-arm-equipped arrowhead devices in their fanny pack.

An acceptable option for small game hunting or stump shooting is a rubber blunt. It is not recommended that you shoot at small game such as squirrels or rabbits with field points. While these heads will certainly kill small game, the tendency is for them to pass through an animal. Although it will most likely die from the hit, it may climb a tree or run into a hole before it expires and your arrow may end up dozens of yards from the original point of impact.

THE REAL THING: HUNTING BROADHEADS

If there is one item of hunting gear the typical archer is opinionated about, it is his broadhead. An archer will argue the pros and cons of broadheads until the proverbial "cows come home."

Archers seem to be more fanatic about their broadheads than about their bows or releases or treestands. Fortunately, there are practically as many broadhead brands, styles and weights as there are bowhunters, so there is much to choose from … and argue about!

Following the developmental path of the spear, the first broadhead may have been nothing more than a pointed rock fastened to the end of a wooden projectile. Certainly, the first man to accomplish that feat with a split arrow and a bit of twisted sinew, immediately got into an argument with his hunting

The popular Zwickey Judo Point (and its many imitators) are perfect for "stump shooting" and small game hunting. With their wide, flexible wire "wings" a Judo Point will catch and stand up in the grass rather than bury itself beneath it.

It looks like something chipped out of flint, but the 85-gain. Hawkeye four-blade – two of them are serrated – is actually a durable nylon small game head.

partner who was using a stick rubbed on a soft stone until the tip came to a sharp point. He had then held it near the fire to dry. This made it less flexible, but more brittle for better penetration. You can almost hear their conversation:

"What's that you're doing over there, Thag?"
"Hey, look at this, Gorp. I've put this pointed stone on the front of my arrow. I'll bet it penetrates better this way. Plus, if the arrow does not pass completely through those wild oxen we're hunting this afternoon, it will keep cutting internally as they run and that way will create a better blood trail. Our tracking job will be easier and we'll recover more of the animals we hit. Cool, huh!"
"Oh, right. Just wait until the guys see that. They'll laugh you out of camp. That stone is going to unbalance your cast. You won't be able to hit the broad side of a buffalo. It's way too heavy! There's too much weight forward. No cave bear steak for you tonight, Thag."

Arrowheads for hunting and warfare – today they are called broadheads – may date back 20,000 years or more, well into the Paleolithic or "Stone Age," before

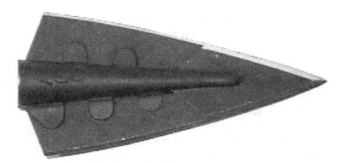

The Ace Standard is a fine example of a traditional broadhead. Such heads sharpen easily with a stone or file and ceramic touch-up stick. Traditional heads are durable and begin cutting the instant of contact. They are not usually recommended for high-speed bows however as their design can make them hard to tune for precision flight when shot from a bow with hard cams.

the arts of metal-working became widely understood. Once metal became available as refined copper and bronze and eventually as iron, it quickly supplanted stone as the material of choice for arrowheads. Frontier reports exist of Native American warriors taking the iron rims off wagon wheels and hammering and cutting that hard metal into arrowheads in the 19th century.

Metal caught on rapidly because it was harder and

Fred Bear's Razorhead (with insert) is only slightly different from the classic he patented in the 1950s. Today's 145-gr. Super Razorhead features stainless steel blades.

more durable than stone. With some touch-up to the edges, metal heads could be used repeatedly; and metal heads could (eventually) be manufactured almost exactly alike. It is true that stone heads, especially those made of superbly fine-grained materials like obsidian (a rare volcanic glass) could be made as sharp as any metal head – some would argue, sharper – but they were brittle, and delicate heads could eat up daylight manufacturing one at a time. But whether metal was superior to stone for an arrowhead may ultimately have been more a question of the availability of specialized materials, such as flint, that lent themselves to "napping" or chipping to create pointed heads. It could simply have been a matter of fashion, too, the endless argument about the best arrowhead. When Thag's ancestors strapped a metal head on their arrow, Gorp's ancestors, not wanting to appear backward, eventually followed suit … again!

Practical and philosophical arguments abound surrounding broadheads. Now, with the sudden rise in popularity of mechanical or open-on-impact heads and fast compound bows, those arguments have intensified.

TRADITIONAL FIXED BLADE BROADHEADS

What could be much easier than a broadhead that simply glues on your wood arrow shaft or screws into your aluminum or composite shaft? If it becomes dull, you sharpen it with a file, a ceramic stick or a sheet of fine grit sandpaper. If the tip hits a rock and the blade bends, you straighten it or throw it away. The only tricky part is your responsibility to keep these heads sharp, because no head less than surgically sharp should be shot at a game animal.

Single-piece broadheads are simple, nothing-can-go-wrong arrowheads. There is nothing that moves and there is nothing to replace. In practically any thickness (.040 inches is standard because the blades are typically wide, although the insert or bleeder blades may only measure .015 inches), they are suitable for taking any big game animal, including elephant and Cape buffalo, as Howard Hill, Fred Bear and Bob Swinehart proved hunting in Africa in the 1950s and '60s. Nevertheless, today, a minority of archers uses single-piece broadheads.

These days, "traditional" shooters gravitate to single-piece broadheads. Traditional archers shoot recurves and longbows and much of their archery enjoyment comes from simplifying their gear and even their methods for shooting and hunting. Traditional heads may represent as much as 10   percent of the total arrow head market.

Half a dozen names dominate the manufacture of traditional style broadheads – Ace, Bear, Magnus, Rothhaar, Wensel and Zwickey – and there are many additional styles available, too: Bonebuster, Burnette, Del-Ma, Eclipse, G5, Modoc, Phantom, Simmons, Steel Force, Whiffen and Wolverine & Grizzly.

Bob Mayo, the owner of Ace Archery Tackle in Forrest, Illinois purchased Ace Broadheads in 2000. A traditional bowhunter and a machinist, Bob estimates more than a million Ace broadheads have been sold since the company began in 1927.

"Traditional archers shoot more than people using compounds because they have more fun," says Bob.

"Since we usually glue heads onto wood arrow shafts, we like one-piece heads because they are tougher and last longer. We don't lose blades or tips when we practice shooting into ethafoam or hay bales."

While a traditional broadhead may appear simple to the uninitiated or those used to the more complex styles of heads with moving parts and replaceable blades, the actual construction of quality traditional heads such as his involves a number of precision steps:

1. raw steel selection. Bob says a high carbon steel1 with a hardness on the Rockwell Scale[2] of C-46 is ideal because this steel is very hard, but can be sharpened with a common metal file, although to sharpen curved blades, Bob likes to use a curved autobody file.

2. calibration of the punch press to stamp out the pieces of the broadhead. For the Ace Standard, available in 125, 145 and 160-grain weights, one blade and two ferrule sections are produced.

3. stamping the ferrule sections for desired roundness and for the traditional five-degree arrow taper. Ace

Arrowhead manufacturers use a variety of methods – some scientific and some anecdotal – to test the effectiveness of broadhead designs before they market a new style. Muzzy Products' Tim Mangum routinely shoots Muzzy heads through 55-gallon drums.

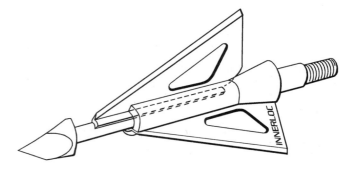

Well designed, mean looking and brutally tough. Jerry Simmons used his 160-grain Land Shark to take hundreds of big game animals while testing his heads during nearly 40 years of bowhunting. The Land Shark includes replaceable bleeder blades.

heads are sold without inserts. They can immediately be glued onto wood shafts or onto inserts that screw into aluminum and composite arrows.

4. spot-welding. Head parts are spot welded in place.
5. copper braising. In this elaborate strengthening process, the spot-welded heads are covered with a copper paste and heated in a vacuum to 2100-degrees Fahrenheit (F). The heat melts the copper which completely in-fills between the steel head components, thus making them one solid piece.
6. heat-treating. Heads are heated 1650 degrees F in a controlled-atmosphere furnace, excluding oxygen. Then, heads are "quenched," immersed in cold oil. This process makes the heads very hard and brittle.
7. tempering. Next, head are heat-treated and quenched again. This time they are heated only to about 500 degrees F before being doused in the cold oil. This process sets the desired Rockwell hardness and essentially makes the heads less hard.
8. painting.
9. sharpening. Edges are ground and factory sharpened.

Innerloc (Sullivan Industries) has worked hard to answer critics of replaceable-blade heads who say that blades can come loose from the broadhead ferrule on impact with a trophy deer's shoulder joint or perhaps the shoulder shield of a bear or feral hog. Unexpectedly encountering a loose razor-sharp blade with your bare hand as you are field dressing big game can become a terrible problem. Innerloc heads are designed to lock in place around a central steel core.

Traditional heads are usually sharpened with a file or on a stone. Bob Mayo glues his 165-grain Ace Express onto a wood arrow shafts and, holding his file stationary, draws the head toward him, base to tip. When using a sharpening stone, Bob recommends, begin with coarse and work your way to fine. A few drops of honing oil increases the effectiveness of this sharpening procedure. Touch up your traditional heads with a ceramic stick from the kitchen. (Three-blade Whiffen Bodkins and other styles with edges which lie flat, may be sharpened on a sheet of sandpaper lying on a tabletop. Because the steel of the Bodkin is relatively soft, it is easy to sharpen, but can lose its edge quickly.)

The orientation of broadheads on an arrow shaft is a much debated topic, especially with large, flat heads like the 160-grain., 1 $\frac{1}{2}$-inch wide Magnus, the 130 grain

Like many traditional blades, each 125-grain Magnus two-blade glue-on head needs to be oriented percisely on your arrow shaft for consistent shooting. Inserts can be purchased from Magnus or from a good pro shop to adapt these heads to aluminum or carbon shafts.

These replaceable stainless steel blades for an Innerloc broadhead are extremely sharp.

This classic Muzzy 100-grain four-blade head features a ferrule in Realtree Camo and the company's trademarked steel "Trocar Tip."

Zwickey Black Diamond Delta or the massive, 210-grain .048-inch Steel Force Premium from Ballistic Archery. Bob says he, like many traditional archers – and he mentioned famous traditional trick shot artist Byron Ferguson as an example – turn their blades to shoot vertically, a reasonable consideration given the normal porpoising or wallowing of an arrow shaft as it leaves the bowstring.

An interesting take on the argument about proper blade orientation is a style of broadhead with offset blades designed to spin or rotate independent of the arrow shaft. The 100-grain Razorbak 100 from New Archery Products features a .039-inch thick cut-on-contact main blade, a .020-inch bleeder blade and a 1 1/8-inch cutting diameter. Set in a tough composite core, the core and vented blades actually rotate around the ferrule during flight.

A survey of traditional heads suggests they run far ahead of the conventional replaceable-blade and mechanical heads in both size and weight. The super-heavyweight 200-grain Ace Super Express is one of the largest ever produced and sold commercially. "At the distances we traditional archers take game animals, 25-yards or less," says Bob Mayo, "the heavy heads won't substantially affect arrow flight. On the other hand, heavier arrows definitely penetrate better."

REPLACEABLE-BLADE BROADHEADS

Dozens of companies make replaceable-blade broadheads. Most of them are excellent. Since the '70s, this style hunting head has become the standard for archery hunters. A quality, replaceable-blade head will fly true, cut easily and penetrate rapidly. Blades lock securely in slots machined in the central shaft, called a "ferrule," which is usually structural aluminum, although various composite materials have been used. You must have a head that will not lose its blades if it encounters bone in elk or deer, too. (There are many stories about hunting archers who have unexpectedly found a loose or broken blade from their own arrow with their bare hand while field dressing

downed game! The result can be deadly.)

Replaceable blade heads usually come in a three-blade or a four-blade configuration. It is common that blades will be vented; that means, they have sections cut-out from their flat surface. Most archers believe a vented design helps prevent wind-planing of their arrow in flight and manufacturers claim that heads are designed so that the columnar loss of steel will not weaken a head's integrity or striking power. (On the other hand, some manufacturers of open-on-impact heads suggest that the vented sections create additional opportunities for wind interference and friction in flight. This, of course, if it is true, slows down your arrow.)

The number of blades in a broadhead, the thickness of those blades, whether they are vented or not and the style of tip on the head (chisel, cut-to-tip or conical) is far less important than obtaining good arrow flight or being able to put your arrow precisely into the vitals of game animals. As hunting archers, we know from experience that our quarry rarely stands still while we aim and invariably appears at less than the perfect time or angle. Nevertheless, the most common replaceable blade head in the deer woods is a three-blade style. A fourth blade on a head – and remember, this is the leading edge of your arrow – may require that you increase the number or size of the fletching on the back of the arrow for stabilization as your arrow rotates in flight. A rule of thumb is to match the fletching to the size and number of blades you are shooting.

The argument for open-on-impact broadheads is illustrated in this two-photo sequence of a 100-grain Sonoran three-blade head. First, the head is closed for flight. With a very low aerodynamic profile, this head should not wind-plane and ought to "fly like a field point." Upon impact, the cam-action of the blade mounting swings the blades out and fully open for devastating results. If all goes well, the archer experiences the best of both worlds: superior flight and penetration.

Stable, accurate broadhead flight is essential to penetration. Generally speaking, for traditional bows, the heavier the arrow and head, the better the penetration. With the advent of the speed craze in the early 1990s though, many archers began shooting smaller, lighter heads with low profile blades from their compound bows. Lighter heads and shorter, lighter arrows helped boost top arrow speeds above 300 fps – about 200 mph – but sufficient penetration became an issue and remains an issue today.

Speed, in itself, did nothing to promote desirable arrow flight or accuracy however and broadheads could no longer be determined to be mounted correctly if they simply remained on the shaft after a shot.

Properly mounting a broadhead of any kind means the tip of the arrow will be in line with the center of the arrow shaft. Upon release, your bowstring moves forward, pushing the arrow ahead of it. You want that thrust to load the column of the arrow or deliver the bow's stored energy to your shaft without angled force vectors to torque the arrow in any direction.

For years, archers have given their broadhead-tipped arrows the "spin test." Here is how it works: With the broadhead mounted on the arrow ready for a shot, place the tip of the broadhead on your flat, stretched palm or on a thumbnail. With the center of the shaft lying at a slight angle in the "V" formed by the intersection of the smooth nails of your opposite thumb and middle finger and the shaft standing relatively vertical, blow vigorously against the fletching. While it may require several attempts to learn the technique, a head that is mounted properly will spin in a more or less fluid manner. A head that is not in-line may wobble perceptibly. Caution is advised, because this is not an extremely accurate test. It will not be sufficient if you are serious about 3-D competition, for instance. On the other hand, however, it is a beginning and requires no equipment or additional investment. It may, in fact, be entirely sufficient for shots out to 20 yards.

The second test for arrow flight is natural: take your broadhead-tipped arrows outside and shoot, perhaps into a foam target, after you have grouped arrows using field points. Shooting broadheads into the hay bales that are customary on public practice ranges is dangerous for three reasons:

- an errant arrow could hit someone as you are working to make them group and this could cause serious injury or death;
- a broadhead-tipped arrow lost after it scoots along under the grass can be stepped on and cause terrible injury to a person's foot; and
- broadheads can not be withdrawn easily from hay bales. They often come out missing a blade

Broadhead practice is "a must" before you shoot at live game. The recommended target is one of the several varieties of durable foam sold commercially through sporting goods stores. Broadheads pull out of foam easily and the design of many foam targets, especially those used for 3-D competition, replicates the size and appearance of a big game animal. (Shooting broadheads into these targets will eventually destroy them, but repair kits and replaceable "kill zones" are available from the manufacturers.)

Practicing with the arrows and broadheads you will use during hunting season is the only reliable way to absolutely fine tune arrow flight for consistency. If you cannot shoot tight groups with your preferred broadhead or if it comes apart or bends after shooting you should try another brand or style. It is much less expensive to experiment with a number of broadheads to find one that suits your shooting style than it is to miss or wound a big game animal.

As if high-tech archery in the 21st century were not difficult enough, a recent technical question about arrow balance with a mounted broadhead has generated considerable discussion. Most hunting archers who are shooting within their comfort zone can ignore this controversy, but anyone who wants to compete successfully or who is obsessed with pinpoint shooting or is experiencing erratic or unbalanced arrow flight will want to study FOC.

FOC or forward-of-center balancing is one of many things that affect arrow flight, and it can be critical for high let-off, high draw weight, speed bows. It is easy to determine the FOC of your arrow set-up:

- measure your arrow from the nock to the tip of your installed broadhead
- mark the arrow at the center or half-way point
- now, place the arrow on the side of your finger or on some other thin balancing point and mark that point also
- Finally, measure the distance from the center of your arrow to the balance mark and divide that number by the total length of the arrow. It sounds complicated, but it is not.

For example, the center or half-way point of a 28-inch arrow is 14 inches. It will balance forward-of-center because the broadhead on the front is heavier than the fletching on the rear. If the arrow balances say, at three inches forward of the half-way point, you determine your FOC as 3 divided by 28. The result is 11 percent.

Most archery writers believe an FOC of 10-12 percent is about right for balanced and accurate arrow flight. (Some writers slice it thinner, recommending

The Vortex Pro Extreme 100-grain. expanding head relies on a super-hard chisel tip to punch into its target. Its twin, 32/1000-inch stainless steel blades are held against the ferrule by a rubber band which easily and instantly snaps on impact, allowing the blades to swing out and back to cut a large, 2 ½-inch wound channel.

higher FOC – 12-15 percent – for carbon shafts and lower FOC – 8-10 percent – for aluminum shafts.)

In the same example, if the balance point was 5 inches forward of the half-way point, the FOC would be 18 percent. You could predict that your arrow flight would be erratic. To stabilize the flight of your arrow, you would want to try a lighter broadhead, heavier fletching or perhaps a longer arrow – or some combination – but as we have learned, FOC is only one of many indicators that helps us learn to shoot a fast, accurate arrow that delivers all of its energy in-line through its tip when it hits its target.

Family owned for 25 years, Barrie Archery builds a versatile broadhead line that incorporates replaceable (and expandable) blade technology in several screw-in styles. The Barrie Rocky Mountain three blade is a hunting standard. In its "Ti-Line," Barrie machines a one-piece tip-and-ferrule from a solid block of titanium alloy. Slots for the .030 inch stainless steel blades are machined in alignment with the edges of the tip. The Ti-Line is available in three weights, each having a separate cutting diameter: 85-grain (1 1/8-inch), 100-grain (1 ¹/₈-inch) and 125-grain (1 ³/₁₆-inch).

Barrie is one of the few companies commercially producing a broadhead using titanium. Aircraft titanium is 45 percent lighter, but three-times stronger than basic steel. It is also more expensive and more

difficult to machine.

Founded in the early 1980s, Muzzy Products developed the idea that practice blades could be manufactured to fly with the same qualities as hunting blades. Today, matched-weight, unsharpened practice blades are available for standard Muzzy heads. They fly like the real thing, but are angled front and back to aid removal from targets. Today, Muzzy manufactures a wide variety of replaceable blade broadheads including four blade heads for wood, composite or aluminum arrow shafts. Muzzy blades are .020 inch thick heat-treated stainless steel and the four blade models have a 1-¹/₈-inch cutting diameter.

Muzzy broadhead ferrules are the industry standard machined aluminum and are available in a variety of colors and camouflage patterns. The screw-in, hollow ground high grade stainless steel Trocar Tip is resharpenable and replaceable. The Muzzy ferrule features an L-shaped locking groove that makes blade alignment easy and locks blades tight even if your shot hits bone.

A continuing innovator in replaceable blade broadhead design, Golden Key-Futura has experimented with blades set at angles in a central ferrule and manufactures heads with as many as six blades, their Dead Head 6 Destroyer.

OPEN-ON-IMPACT OR MECHANICAL BROADHEADS

Blades that move to open when a head meets its target define a class of broadheads collectively referred to as expandable, mechanical or, most commonly, open-on-impact. Theoretically, with all makes and models, these heads fly like a practice point, penetrate like a fixed-blade head and cut like a sharp replaceable-blade head. It is a wonderful idea. Archery engineers have worked on the concept seriously for a dozen years, studying concepts like "rotational momentum" and "gyroscopic stabilization" that mean little to the average hunting archer.

Regardless of their engineering and design, mechanical broadheads remain a controversial topic in archery. If the fundamental concepts actually work, the benefits to hunters (and perhaps, curiously, to game animals as well) are extraordinary. Still, the practical difficulties are large and the ultimate benefits are arguable.

PRO

Those who shoot open-on-impact heads argue they have several benefits that hunting archers need to be aware of when they select hunting gear:
• First, they are designed to fly like field points. This means your practice and set-up time will be

shorter, because the time required to tune your heads for true, consistent flight will decline dramatically. In an extremely time-conscious world, this is an important advantage.

- Second, arrows tipped with expandable heads should wind-plane less than any other type head. This means that, if you shoot within your effective range, you should have less misses and may also have less wounded game.
- Tipped with expandable broadheads on arrows that fly straighter to their target and hit with greater impact energy, hunting archers should feel they have made the sensible and the ethical decision when they shoot mechanicals.

CON

Archery may be a lifetime sport, the sport of kings, but archery hunting or bowhunting is a privilege that requires practice, patience and dedication because the ultimate aim is to take the life of an animal. As

such, these are the arguments against open-on-impact broadheads:

- First, they often do not work properly. While they may fly like field points, unless their impact on target is strictly vertical or perpendicular, these heads may … or may not … penetrate and cut as advertised.
- Because expandable heads often fail to work as advertised, they are responsible for many wounded and un-recovered big game animals, some of which will die from their wound. It is normally recommended that archers shooting open-on-impact heads draw heavier weight bows to insure that impact energy and resultant penetration are adequate. If this is true, this is a serious indictment of hunting archery.
- Because open-on-impact heads will fly like field points, archers are encouraged to shoot beyond their limitations. An archer who has a comfort range shooting out to 30 yards, will be

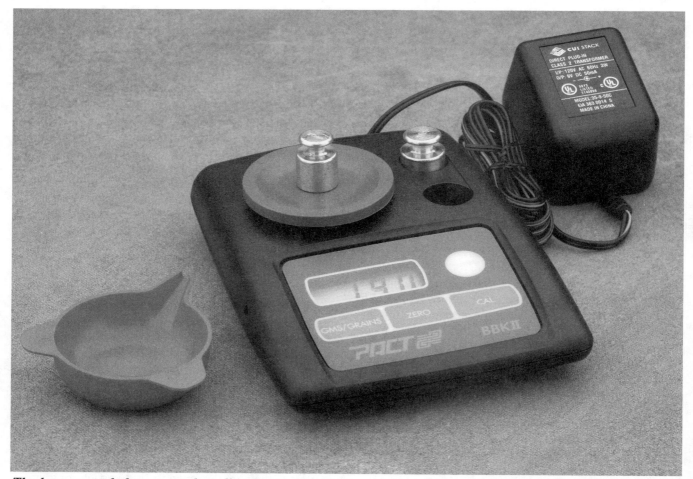

The best way to balance your broadheads, practice points and arrows is to weigh them on a digital electronic grain scale such as this on from Golden Key-Futura. This scale has a 750-grain capacity and is accurate to .20 grain. It is powered by a 9 volt battery or an included AC Adaptor.

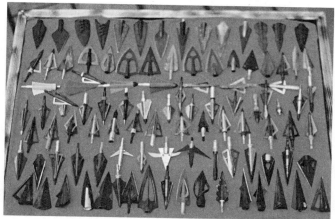

Broadhead collecting – whether modern or ancient – is a fascinating way to intensify your interest in archery and provides a personal glimpse into the evolution of bowhunting and the history of materials and design.

encouraged to try a 40 yard or 50 yard shot. At those ranges, the arrow has less dynamic energy for penetration and the margin of error is wider.

• Mechanical heads do not leave a significant blood trail because they often fail to cut

completely through a game animal. This means there is no exit hole. While many of these heads are designed to cut larger holes at the instant of impact and while they are fully deployed once they are inside an animal, the energy required to push completely through a heavy animal needs to be greater than with conventional heads. Expect blood to seep out of the entry hole, a spot usually higher on the body than the exit hole: seep, not run or pour, as it typically will from an exit wound. Tracking … and finding … therefore is harder.

• If it is true that expandable heads fly like field points and their set-up and tuning is fast compared to conventional heads, critics worry that archers are not spending enough time practicing with, getting to know their equipment. In this scenario, the short-term benefits are out-weighed by the lack of long-term interest and understanding. What makes hunting archery so special is the very fact that it is not easy!

What is certainly true about open-on-impact broadhead designs is that archers have taken to them by the hundreds of thousands. Estimates vary, but one hears that as many as half of all bowhunters shoot this type head today. Some established companies (Muzzy Products) refuse to manufacture any expandable head, but others (New Archery Products) has embraced the open-on-impact idea and placed its faith in superior engineering.

What is true for one hunting archer though may not be gospel for another. Still, common sense archery rules apply. If you choose to shoot an open-on-impact head, you need to experiment before taking them to the

Long-time archer Johnny Boatner enjoys the challenge of making arrow points and spearheads from a variety of stones and glass, a process called knapping. The results of his work are beautiful and prized by collectors.

field. Shoot into foam targets to test the type and weight head that works best for your set-up. Wait for quality broadside shots. Shoot within your effective range. Think of the animal at all times and remember that the objective is always a quick, clean kill.

Open-on-impact broadheads have most of the same qualities as traditional heads: size, weight, cutting diameter, number of blades, width and thickness of blades, type of point (cut-on-contact or punch-cut) and locking style. In addition, they have significant additional characteristics such as how the blades are attached to the ferrule and how they swing open.

Mechanical head weights vary from ultra-lightweight to moderately heavy. While most hunting archers shoot 100-grain heads a significant minority shoot light heads on composite arrows, stretching to reach arrow speeds in the 300 fps neighborhood. Two-blade head styles such as the Mar-Den Mini-Max have

a large, 2-inch cutting diameter, but weigh as little as 75-grain with .032 inch stainless spring steel blades. Newer Rocky Mountain open-on-impact heads are typically standardized at 100 grain and have three blades with a smaller, 1 3/8-inch cutting diameter.

Bloodtrailer broadheads are highly recognizable. The company has even developed a blunt 90 grain head in their characteristic four blade staggered style for turkey hunting. This, says Bloodtrailer developer Terry Austin, stops complete pass-through shots on turkeys making the tough birds easier to catch after a shot. Bloodtrailer, incidentally, began in the expandable-blade market and has recently marketed non-expandable, fixed blade heads in the same style.

One of the most versatile manufacturers of mechanical heads is Rocket Aeroheads. Rocket heads feature an offset, "deployable-blade" design, the company says, eschewing the open-on-impact label. Rocket's strength is its variety of lightweight heads for speed bows, even stating recommended "launch speeds" for some of its heads. From the small, 57 grain. Wolverine three blade to its giant, 150-grain Sledgehammer with a 3 $\frac{1}{2}$-inch cutting diameter recommended for 80-pound and over bows, Rocket has been an innovator in "deployable-blade" size and style. For archery hunters who can not make up their mind whether to shoot expandable- or fixed-blade heads, Rocket's Buckblaster 125 features both and may be shot with its "fixed" blades or without them.

If you choose an expandable blade head, you will want to be sure the Kinetic Energy (foot-pounds) delivered by your arrow will be sufficient to penetrate, fully deploy the head and cut a long, wide blood channel. Archery engineers who are also bowhunters recommend shooting at least 50 ft-lbs for moderate game like deer and up to 65 ft-lbs for larger game such as elk.

FOOTNOTES

1. Steel, an alloy of iron, carbon and small proportions of other elements, is classified by its carbon content. High carbon steel has great hardness and brittleness. Consequently, it is ideal for dies and cutting tools like knives and broadheads. Low-to-medium carbon steels are used for sheeting and structural components. Alloy steels add specific elements (aluminum, nickel, chromium, for instance) to produce steel with specific qualities. Stainless steel is a very high tensile strength, high chromium content steel that resists abrasion and corrosion. Stainless is a superb steel for many broadhead blades.

Judy Kovar believes that a traditional and resharpenable, one-piece broadhead such as the Phantom 100 is best for big game because it gives her more control over her shooting.

2. The Rockwell Hardness Scale is an international standard for determining hardness of metals and some plastics. With steel, the higher the Rockwell number, the harder it is, but with steel, harder correlates with brittle. Hardness is expressed as a number based on the depth impression of specific diameter steel balls or diamond cones. Hardness, of course, relates to tensile strength and a broadhead made from Rockwell C-46 steel, for instance has a tensile strength of 227,000 psi.

GRAIN WEIGHT

Most broadhead manufacturers sell their heads as a specific grain weight. The truth, however, is that the advertised grain weights are only approximations. Any given arrow head may vary five to 10 percent heavier or lighter than advertised. While most competition archers fret about matching total shaft weights precisely, this amount of variation is not significant for bowhunting.

Although we are not too familiar with weights expressed in grains outside our broadheads and bullets, according to the Internet site English weights and measures (at the address http://home.clara.net/brianp/) the "grain" is the "basic unit of weight in the British system," a system which has evolved over more than 3,000 years. Historically, the grain is based on the weight of one grain of English barley.

Today, the "pound avoirdupois" is what we typically refer to as a pound when we check a bow's draw weights or sneak a look at the bathroom scales after a big meal. Our pound equals 7,000 grains (abbreviated gr.). Therefore, an ounce – and there are 16 ounces in one pound avoirdupois – equals 437.5 grains and a 200-pound bowhunter actually weighs 1,400,000 grains!

So, why do we measure broadheads in grains? The development of mass-produced, commercially available broadheads is a 20th century phenomenon, but bullets were manufactured and sold by grain weight in the 19th century. Larry Whiffen thinks it was probably a copycat phenomenon. Larry, owner of Whiffen Archery in Milwaukee, Wisconsin is an excellent resource because his "archery pedigree" is outstanding. His father, Larry, Senior, who was inducted into the Archery Hall of Fame in 2002, participated in the development of the original Bodkin fixed-blade broadhead in 1946. Based on the results of field-tests by world famous bowhunter and manufacturer Fred Bear, Larry, Senior, modified the design of the Bodkin three years later. Larry designed straight sides for the

Trophy bowhunter and writer Eddie Claypool likes the tested and proven abilities of replaceable blade broadheads. Although he is a self-professed "elk-a-holic," Eddie will occasionally slow down for a mule deer! His preferred head on an aluminum shaft is a 100-grain titanium three-blade from Rocky Mountain. When he shoots carbon shafts, he steps the head up to 125 grain. These titanium heads feature a one-piece ferrule/tip machined from solid titanium.

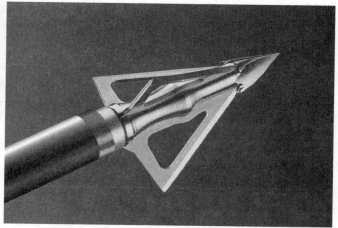

The Titanium 100-gr. three-blade broadhead from Rocky Mountain is very hard, highly machined and expensive.

Wayne Carlton championed elk calling when no one else was willing to try it. Today, this outdoor humorist, writer and seminar speaker believes mechanical heads have developed sufficiently in their design and construction to take America's biggest game animals.

blades and gave the ferrule a five-degree taper to accommodate standard wooden shaft mounting. Now, more than half a century after that final re-design, Larry's sons, Larry and Grant, sell a Bodkin broadhead that is manufactured faithfully to that 1949 design.

COLLECTING BROADHEADS

With so many commercial broadhead styles and manufacturers, there has always been a collector's interest. According to Greg Schwehr, membership chairman, the American Broadhead Collectors Club (ABCC) is a worldwide organization of collectors of archery and bowhunting memorabilia.

The ABCC produces a quarterly newsletter, Broadhead. In this publication, Greg says, members "will find information about old and new broadheads and manufacturers. There is also a section for members to trade heads."

At an annual meeting each summer, usually at one of the larger archery shoots in the US Midwest, a

"good number of collectors get together to do some serious trading."

The ABCC publishes five books on identifying broadheads: four volumes of Best of Broadhead and one volume of old broadhead advertisements. A list of members is available for trading and networking. Over the past 25 years, a master list of broadheads has been compiled which lists every head known to have been marketed: sizes, weights, date and manufacturer information is included.

"We have a designated member who buys a small number of all new heads," Greg says. "This individual then makes the heads available to other members at a low cost, thereby eliminating the need for every member to buy packages of three or six."

ABCC members collect more than just broadheads. Equipment catalogs, books, leather goods, bows, archery equipment and autographed arrows are other areas of interest and all of these can be traded for in the club.

ABCC membership is $20 for one year. If you are interested, please contact:

American Broadhead Collectors Club (ABCC)
Greg Schwehr, Membership Chairman
9717 W. Reichert Place
Milwaukee, WI 53225
(414) 463-8685
gregory.schwehr@med.ge.com

"BUILDING YOUR OWN"

For an archer, there are few hobbies as interesting and perhaps as fulfilling as making your own arrow (and spear) points. This activity is referred to as "knapping" and there is a large national community of hobbyists and collectors.

Long-time archer Johnny Boatner, who now lives in Arkansas, says knapping puts him in touch with people who are interested in keeping alive the knowledge and secrets of antiquity: building bows and arrows, tanning hides and making clothing, hunting and cooking game in a traditional or "primitive" manner.

"It's fun and there's a lot to learn about techniques and materials," Johnny says. "We think we're pretty smart with computer technology, round-the-world communication through the Internet and landing men on the moon, but all of this amazing stuff was built on some basic survival techniques that kept human beings alive for hundreds of thousands of years. Bring a Paleolithic hunter into our world and he would certainly be bewildered, but if we put ourselves in his world, we would be equally helpless."

To go hunting for additional information:

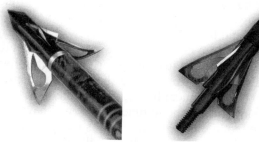

Unveiled at the 2003 Archery Trade Show, the Crimson Talon broadhead with curved EZ-Flex blades are designed to provide spin-stabilization on the front of the arrow. This way, Scott Mackie says, arrow stabilization relies less on the size and configuration of your feathers and vanes. The Crimson Talon weighs 100-grain and cuts a 1 ¼-inch path with its stainless steel blades.

- look for a local gathering of arrow-head makers, flint knappers and collectors called a "knap-in,"
- visit your favorite Internet search engine and enter such key words as knapping, flint knapping, survival techniques or even neolithic. You will find sites such as these filled with information and contacts: www.thegirs.com (the Genuine Indian Relic Society), www.primitive.org (Society of Primitive Technology), www.amasci.com (The Knapper's Corner) or even one of the hundreds of illustrated private sites such as George and Eloise Weymouth's www.weymouthwildlifeart.com or Mark Condron's www.thenaturalearth.com
- search your favorite book store for magazines that specialize in historic or traditional information and articles such as Mother Earth News or Primitive Archer (P.O. Box 79306, Houston, TX 77279 (713) 467-8202 www.primitivearcher.com)

ARCHERS ON BROADHEADS
TRADITIONAL HEADS: JUDY KOVAR

Native American seminar speaker and archer Judy Kovar of Illinois hunts with a 105-grain Phantom traditional broadhead (115 grains with the bleeder blade). "My ancestors depended on hunting, fishing, gathering and farming for survival and in school seminars, I emphasize that we are part of nature, that we – plants and animals – depend on each other," Judy says. Judy's husband Herman introduced her to archery in 1986:

"When it comes to archery … and life in general," Judy says, "I believe in the old saw, keep it simple. The more stuff you rely on, the more chances there are for

problems. Murphy's Law – whatever can go wrong eventually will – operates soon enough when you are juggling binoculars, a release aid, rangefinders and a cup of coffee in a treestand. With a good traditional, cut-on-contact head, there is just less that can go wrong.

"I orient the Phantom's blades vertically, north-to-south. This minimizes wind-planing. I rarely use the Phantom's bleeder blades because I want a fast cutting head that will slide around bone when my arrow hits a big game animal in the ribs. To control the head and stabilize my ACC composite shaft, I shoot four-fletch with feathers. Feathers are faster out to 40 yards and more forgiving of shooting form errors than plastic vanes."

REPLACEABLE BLADE HEADS: EDDIE CLAYPOOL

Shooting a bow since the mid 1970s, Oklahoma archer Eddie Claypool has made a name as a go-anywhere elk hunter. A pipe-fitter by profession, Eddie prides himself on being a blue-collar guy who likes nothing better than to climb in his pick-up truck and driving as fast as he can to Colorado or Wyoming or, if he gets drawn in their state lottery, to New Mexico and Arizona, to hunt wapiti. He chooses standard, tried-and-true, replaceable blade broadheads. Eddie says:

"Replaceable blade broadheads have been around for a long time. They are foolproof and I have never had a problem. When the replaceable blades – these days they are usually stainless steel – become dull from use, you just slide them out of the slotted ferrule and either re-sharpen or replace them. I'm not sold on mechanical heads even though they are supposed to tune easier and fly better. I have been in several hunting camps where people using mechanical heads lost animals because the heads did not properly open on impact.

"I shoot three-blade Rocky Mountain titanium heads from Barrie Archery. The one-piece titanium ferrules and tips are virtually indestructible. With aluminum shafts, I use a 100-grain head and with carbon shafts I step up to 125 grains. I stabilize my arrows with three, 5-inch plastic vanes. With my set-up, alignment of the blades in relation to the feathers or the vertical plane doesn't matter."

MECHANICAL: WAYNE CARLTON

Wayne Carlton is a transplanted South Carolinian who now lives in central Colorado. Wayne was the first person to successfully apply the calling techniques for wild turkeys to elk and bears. A hunter all his life, Wayne says:

"I always liked the old Fred Bear Razorhead, but it weighed 145 grains with the bleeder blade and that big surface tended to wind-plane even when I oriented it vertically on my arrow shaft. So, I switched to mechanical heads. I used a Mar-Den head successfully for years and now shoot the Game Tracker FirstCut EXP. Like most mechanical heads, the EXP flies like your practice points without any wind-planing. With a blade mounted on the tip of the head, it cuts on impact, too – like the Razorhead – and this reduces the energy required for penetration.

"A good expandable head gives you pin-point shooting. It gives you confidence as a hunter because you know your broadhead will fly just like a practice point.

"I've killed elk and deer with many sizes of expandable head, but there are several things you should watch out for with expandables. Be careful to choose a style that opens consistently. That was a problem for early models, but is not so much a problem today. And I like two-blade cut-on-contact versions like Game Tracker's FirstCut EXP rather than three-blade or chisel point heads because I believe it takes less energy for them to penetrate and open fully."

THE GRIZZLED VETERAN

Tink Nathan does not use his birth name. In fact, he has trademarked "Tink" and is known by that name throughout the world of archery. A bowhunter since 1949, a former manufacturer of scent and lure products and a first rate archery personality, Tink returned to Virginia in 2002 following nine years working as a guide in South Africa.

Tink has gone full circle with broadheads. He began archery with traditional broadheads, marketed an early generation mechanical head in the 1980s and now shoots replaceable-blade heads.

"Mechanical heads were available in the 1950s and 1960s," Tink recalls, "but I don't think they worked well with the equipment we used then. They were sold as 'scissor heads' and they could cut a really big hole.

"In the mid-80s, a decade ahead of its time, I marketed the Viper mechanical head. We had a three-blade and possibly four-blade version. The friction of the head entering a medium like a game animal, was supposed to make the blades pop open. I tested it on African game in 1983 and 1984 and it worked fine, but the market wasn't ready. I was way ahead of my time when I pioneered the Viper. Even though design and machining have improved since then, I can't honestly recommend a broadhead with moving parts.

"Today, I shoot Muzzy replaceable-blade heads. These heads are consistent. They work every time and nothing can go wrong. They are already open for contact.

"The idea that a mechanical head flies well is

bogus. According to the Pope & Young Club, most archers take game animals within 20 yards. Not much goes wrong within 20 yards. Anyone who knows archery should be able to make an arrow fly properly, because it isn't the head that flies, it's the arrow and fletching. The head is just along for the ride, to provide balanced weight up front on the shaft. When people say they use mechanical heads, you can bet that they aren't taking much time to tune their bow. I have come to believe that the mechanical head is designed to fix something that isn't broken. It's usually the novice who shoots a mechanical head, not the experienced archer.

"What made the difference in not selling mechanical heads in the 1980s and in their rush of popularity in the 1990s? Tons of advertising dollars to promote them.

"Mechanical heads can work. They can even attain 95 to 98 percent success rates for opening and working perfectly, but is that good enough? I don't think so."

BROADHEADS AND PENETRATION

One of the world's foremost bowhunters, Chuck Adams, says the average hunting arrow has less kinetic energy than a 40-grain .22 Long Rifle bullet and, on the surface, that does not seem like very much. Yet, your arrow will penetrate completely through a big game trophy if you have a tuned bowhunting setup … and often, even if you do not.

More than kinetic energy, Chuck believes, the design of a broadhead controls its ability to penetrate. He references both his own extensive experience and tests performed by broadhead manufacturer Satellite Archery (now, with Bear and Golden Eagle, part of The North American Archery Group) that offers several broadhead styles. A slender, two-blade head that cuts right to the tip will slice deep with minimal friction, Chuck says. A large, four-blade head with a bulky nose, while it appears more formidable, encounters a great deal of friction and resistance from bone, muscle and sinew. This causes it to expend arrow energy in all directions. Some open-on-impact broadheads shed energy as they forcibly unfold while penetrating the tough hide of game animals. To take advantage of all the energy of your flying arrow, Chuck says, it makes sense to use a reasonably low-friction head.

To Chuck, the key word is "reasonably," because penetrating ability is not the only desirable factor in a hunting arrowhead. Heads with sturdy chisel noses sacrifice something in penetration, but smash through bone with superior durability. Some mechanical heads might require extra bow power to drive deep, but they provide easy accuracy even from bows that you take out of the closet just a week before the season opens.

Consideration of factors such as weight, penetration and effective arrow flight for your set-up is a balancing act.

Chuck has written that cut-on-contact heads like the Zwickey Eskimo or Black Diamond, the Fred Bear Super Razorhead, the Patriot and the Chuck Adams Super Slam penetrate best because they slice through game like low-friction, high-energy knives.

Based on tests by Satellite, next in line are slender-tipped chisel heads like New Archery Products' Thunderhead 125 and the Rocky Mountain Premier. Performance seems to depend on how sharp and how slender the actual chisel edges are. The hollow-ground Trocar tips on popular Muzzy heads, for example, are relatively large, but actually slice deeply due to their unique hollow-ground styling.

Heads with large, edgeless nose cones perform the worst in most tests. Fortunately, Chuck says, there are not many of these designs still popular and available.

As far as penetration is concerned, open-on-impact heads are all over the place. Although they are becoming stronger and better designed each year, on average, they still come in last in terms of deep penetration by broadhead category and that can be a problem for big game hunters.

Not surprisingly, the test results from Satellite reinforce common sense.

- The more blades a broadhead holds the higher the friction and the poorer the penetration.
- The less streamlined the ferrule, the poorer the penetration. Ferrules with sudden steps or shoulders near the arrow shaft do not penetrate well.
- Ferrules with in-line grooves like those in the New Archery Products Pro Series and the Super Slam, penetrate well, perhaps because there is less high surface on the ferrule to create friction against flesh.

A common myth about broadhead penetration that Chuck feels is important to discuss has to do with arrow shaft diameter. Just because carbon arrows with small diameter penetrate better in foam targets, some archers assume they also penetrate better in game animals. Chuck's testing suggests this is incorrect. Flesh, unlike foam, does not seize or clamp down on the arrow shaft and stop a fatter arrow first. The broadhead cuts the hole and the shaft slides through well-lubricated hide and flesh with almost no friction. So, shaft size is almost irrelevant for a consideration of effective broadhead penetration.

Chuck Adams has hunted wherever bowhunting is allowed around the world. His analysis of equipment and of hunting situation is widely respected and published. Gregg Gutschow's book about the life and hunting philosophy of Chuck Adams *Life at Full Draw: The Chuck Adams Story* is now available from IHUNT Communications in Chanhassen, Minnesota (866) 837-3135.)

ALL ABOUT ARROW RESTS

On my first pronghorn hunt, a wonderful trip to Pierre, South Dakota the guide reached into the bed of his pick-up and when he pulled out his bow, the arrow rest was missing. Like any true outdoorsman, he improvised. Reaching into the glove compartment, he pulled out a yellow No. 2 pencil, broke off the eraser end and wedged it into the Berger Button hole in his compound bow. I was shooting a wooden handle Browning Safari with a Teflon sleeve over the wire arm of my Flipper Rest. Grunting in satisfaction we took off across the rolling prairie. We did not take a pronghorn that day or the next, for that matter. The year was 1983. Times have changed.

It would be easy to say that we know much more about the importance of the arrow rest to good arrow flight today than we did 20 years ago, but that may not be the case. The old Olympic sport of Pop-n-Jay, where simulated birds are shot off a tall pole by men wearing ties and women in long skirts, looks as difficult as hitting a running buck in the vitals. Surely those who came before, with their own style bows –Turks shooting short, laminated recurves from horseback, English yeomen facing down the overconfident and overweight French cavalry at the battles of Crecy and Poitiers with only their longbows, Japanese warriors drawing 8-foot longbows and Central African pygmy hunters with tiny crossbows – all understood how to hit their target as well as (and some would argue better) than we do with our sophisticated space-age synthetic equipment. Remember that the ancient warriors and hunters, men whose lives depended on making a killing or incapacitating shot, launched their arrows right off their fingers or their knuckles, without specialized arrow rests.

Today, the arrow rest is the most important piece of equipment that you will put on your bow.

To find out what kind of arrow rest works best for your kind of shooting, consider that there are two basic techniques, shooting with your fingers or with a mechanical release, and three basic arrow rest designs

with dozens of cross-over rests which feature one or two elements of other designs:

- The suddenly popular but not necessarily new "drop-away" arrow rest. This rest design holds or cradles the arrow until its nock is released by the bowstring. At that point the arrow has reached maximum velocity and absorbed all of the kinetic energy the bow is going to give it. When, within

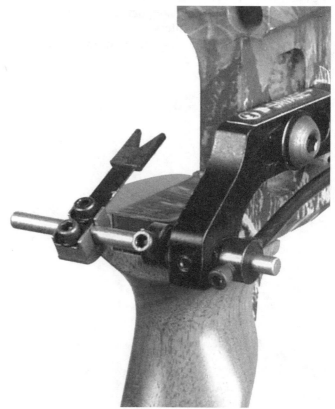

The Savage Derringer with V-Spoon molded Teflon launcher is an inexpensive, but adjustable drop-away arrow rest. When you shoot, the launcher drops. To reposition it, simply lift the bar with the thumb of your bow hand.

a few inches, the bowstring exits the nock, the rest drops out of the way of the flexing arrow and your approaching fletching.

- The basic "shoot-around" rest is just right for finger shooters. On release, the string rolls off the fingertips in a semi-circular motion and this causes the arrow to bend or wallow in the horizontal plane in a left-right pattern. The middle of the arrow bends in the opposite direction as the nock. About half way through the power stroke and while the arrow is still on the string, the nock swings in the opposite direction and the arrow bends again in the opposite direction. After all of this horizontal movement, your arrow usually stabilizes just a few yards down range. Whey you shoot, the rear of the arrow moves in a different pattern for a few micro-seconds than the front of the arrow. High-speed photography verifies that about a quarter of your arrow is actually in contact with the rest, as little as 6 to 8 inches of shaft. Typically used in conjunction with a Berger Button, a shoot-around rest allows your arrow to move into and through its natural cycle with minimum interference.

"Shoot-through" or launcher rests became popular when archers began to learn how shooting with a mechanical release aid caused the string, and therefore the arrow, to respond to different force vectors than they would when shooting with fingers. When a string leaves a mechanically triggered release (assuming there are no radical errors in shooting form), it moves forward in a straight line. True, force vectors cause a

mechanical phenomenon called "columnar loading" and this causes up and down bending in the vertical plane of the arrow, but the quantity of bending described from high-speed photography is much less than with fingers and the motion is described as "porpoising" rather than "wallowing." A good adjustable shoot-through rest will rock out of the way of the arrow and fletching although it remains in contact with the arrow longer than a shoot-around finger rest or a drop-away rest.

Let's take a closer look at the three arrow rest designs before reviewing the general availability of rest offerings from archery manufacturers. Before we do, however, remember that there are between 200 and 300 different rests commercially available at any one time. The cost ranges from as little as $5 for a simple rubber stick-on rest like the Bear Weatherest to nearly $200 for a micro-adjustable shoot-through like the Golden Key-Futura Infinity or $150 for a quality drop-away rest like Joe Angeloni's Zero Effect from Muzzy. With arrow rests it is absolutely true that you get what you pay for, but there are many fine and effective rests available in the $50 to $90 price range. Remember however that there are only two places where your arrow is in contact with your bow, the string and the rest. So, wherever else you compromise and economize, it is never a good idea to buy a cheap rest.

DROP-AWAY RESTS: THE ZERO EFFECT

A so-called "drop-away" rest cradles your arrow through the first moments of release – as your arrow moves from zero mph to maximum speed – and then gets out of the way. Because you can shoot virtually any fletching orientation with a drop-away rest, your bow is easier to tune. By the time the back of your arrow and the feathers or vanes reach the rest, it's gone, out of the way. Its function is fulfilled. Because drop-away rests move out of the way, they can be built to hold the arrow securely. There is nothing more aggravating than shifting position on a treestand only to have your arrow fall off the rest, twist off the string, evade your clutching grasp and bounce off your boot on its way to the ground. Finally, there is the not-so-minor matter of improved accuracy!

If drop-away rests have a downside, it is that they usually have more moving parts than conventional rests. "Moving parts" are never a good thing on a bowhunting trip where anything that can go wrong usually does. (That is a direct proportion distance function. The closer you are to home, the fewer things will go wrong.) Be prepared.

Of course, drop-away rests are excellent for archers who shoot with mechanical release aids which can, with a D-loop on their bowstring, release directly

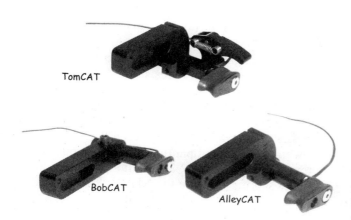

Copper John has introduced a line of drop-away arrow rests. The highly adjustable TomCAT retails for about $70. The TomCAT's unique arrow holder is designed for an auto-release when the bow is drawn back.

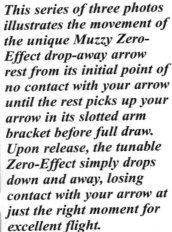

This series of three photos illustrates the movement of the unique Muzzy Zero-Effect drop-away arrow rest from its initial point of no contact with your arrow until the rest picks up your arrow in its slotted arm bracket before full draw. Upon release, the tunable Zero-Effect simply drops down and away, losing contact with your arrow at just the right moment for excellent flight.

behind the arrow. This minimizes side-to-side pressure. Drop-away rests are not considered desirable for finger shooters who need some stabilizing pressure such as a cushion plunger on the bow riser side, especially for that first and largest bending of the arrow.

An unusual difficulty when you are paper tuning a one-cam bow – and one-cam bows are the majority of compound bows sold now – is discovering that your bow pushes your arrows to the right. In extreme situations, a drop-away rest just will not work with this bow design and a rest that is designed with some side pressure will be necessary.

With a two-cam bow, you can alter cam roll-over timing to solve this problem, but the whole idea of a one-cam bow is to eliminate timing problems. As we know with a piece of equipment as complex as a modern compound bow, solving one problem occasionally causes you to discover something else to worry about. That is the case here.

Archery manufacturers generally credit Keith Barner with developing one of the first working drop-away arrow rests. His early '80s model relied on a magnetic strip, like the current Savage Derringer Drop-A-Way. Archers in the early 1980s were just becoming aware that they could shoot faster than 200 fps

however and drop-away rests never caught on. By the mid 1990s, archers understood that rests like the Derringer could solve some of the problems associated with increased arrow speed, shorter axle-to-axle bows and more critical shooting at speeds around 300 fps. A magnet embedded in the bar that holds the rest to your bow riser makes the Derringer work. It is a simple and effective design. The first downward pressure of the arrow following release pops the metal arm free from the magnet's attraction and the Teflon dipped "V" Spoon launcher drops away from your arrow. You reposition the launcher by lifting the metal arm back into the magnet's attractive field with the tip of your thumb.

Joe Angeloni's Zero Effect Arrow Rest offered by Muzzy Products is a spring-less, cable slide-driven drop-away rest. As you draw the bowstring, the cables move a slide coupled by an adjustable linkage to a plastic hook that grabs and lifts your arrow into firing position. When you release, the Zero Effect guides the arrow for only a few inches, before being driven downward by the synchronous movement of your bow's cables. This movement eliminates the possibility of contact between the rest and the rear three-quarters of the arrow where most of the flexing occurs.

The Zero Effect is not sensitive to arrow diameter or nock-to-fletching-to-string orientation. And because the rest is not in contact with your arrow when most bow torquing occurs, torque-related problems are drastically reduced. In some cases, they can be eliminated entirely.

The Zero Effect is designed with a wide, black plastic hook that lifts your arrow off the bow shelf and into firing position as you draw. An adjustable "V-groove" in the hook positions your arrow quickly for centershot and the wide hook itself ensures that no arrow will fall off or through the rest, no matter what its diameter or length, no matter what its fletching or what type or weight arrow head you are shooting.

Unlike some drop-away rests, the Zero Effect can not interfere with arrow speed and in most cases will ensure that you achieve maximum arrow velocity with your chosen set-up if properly tuned. Professional 3-D competitor Ginger Morehead has used the Zero Effect for bowhunting and competition. For the second year in a row, she won the 2002 3-D Nationals in Redding, California scoring 1,509 in the NFAA's Professional Female Freestyle Division. In Redding, she was dead-on with targets out to 100 yards. Ginger says your arrow speed may actually increase as a result of the Zero Effect's precision drop-away design which reduces friction by as much as 70 to 80 percent.

The elevation adjustment of the Zero Effect Arrow Rest consists of a self-locking, pointed set screw.

The adjustable APA Ultimate is a style of arrow rest that offers minimal contact with your arrow by the support wires. The wires completely enclose your arrow so it cannot fall off at a stressful moment. With a little moleskin or other silencing tape, this simple rest offers excellent shooting for hunting archers.

Windage adjustment is a simple split-clamp arrangement. This combination guarantees exact, repeatable arrow rest positioning with no horizontal movement, says Joe Angeloni, Zero Effect inventor, so tuning for broadheads is a snap.

A new model of the Zero Effect has been designed to fit the Mathews Legacy and Icon and other bows with a central pylon that eliminates the cable guard.

Drop-away rests give you the ability to experiment with fletching types and it is a basic tenet of archery that the arrow's fletching provides essential flight control and stabilization of a shaft in flight. Because the arrow rest and its arrow support arms basically cannot be in the way of the fletching, you are free to shoot a high degree of helical offset, typically thought of as the fletching style that provides the best in-flight stabilization. With a properly functioning adjustable drop-away rest you do not have to worry about the old bugaboo of cock feather up or down, either. It really does not matter.

Trophy Taker is one of the rising names in arrow rest design. Its drop-away rests seem simple, but elegant and effective. They give the archer the opportunity to shoot large, helical vanes – that yield superior down range stabilization – without having to worry about vane clearance. This is a benefit for people who want to shoot a large, fixed blade broadhead like the old Simmons Sharks, for example. Jerrod Lile at Trophy Taker says a fall away rest helps reduce the effects of post-release shooter form errors such as gripping the riser (and thereby causing torque) since the arrow only comes in contact with the rest for the very earliest moment of the shot.

The Trophy Taker is basically a big "Y" attached to

Finger shooters typically launch arrows that need side support. With so many archers shooting a release and so many accessories – quiver, sight, arrows, arrow holder and rest – attached to the side of a bow, the Berger Button has declined in usage. The two speed fins on the Bodoodle Timberdoodle are designed to give finger shooters 3 o'clock and 7 o'clock support for their arrows.

the bow riser on one end and to your cables on the other end. As you draw, a cord pulls your arrow holder upward and lifts your arrow. You adjust this rest's timing by changing the length of the cord (or tube) tied on your cable.

Trophy Taker's curiously named Shaky Hunter fall away rest has few moving parts and its adjustable stainless steel spring is fully enclosed for maximum protection and snag-free operation. The wide-mount, one-piece stainless steel launcher is anchored in a machined aluminum bar that rises and falls via a durable cord that attaches to your cable or cable slide.

Rick Bohl at Golden Key, which makes the adjustable Free Fall drop-away rest, believes arrows need some rest-guidance before their rest drops completely away. He relates this need to nock travel. If the arrow rests against the nock point locator, that little brass button on the bowstring influences arrow flight for a micro-second or until the arrow is off the string.

Julian Pinto's shoot-through Arrow Tamer rest from American Archery was designed for clean fletching clearance. Three adjustable spring-loaded plungers, tipped with stainless steel heads, offer complete clearance even with small diameter shafts. Silent silicon guides on the bottom lift the arrow off the plungers when it is drawn back.

If the rest drops immediately after you shoot, your arrow is naturally going to drop, too. Thus all the discussion about nock travel between one cam and twin cam bows.

"Use the rubber tubing provided with the Free Fall," he says, "and set the length of the tubing so the rest reaches its final "up position" when the string is five to eight inches short of full draw. As a result, the rest will fall more gradually and offer plenty of guidance to smooth out most nock travel problems. This helps tuning for almost any size arrow shaft."

Copper John offers three adjustable arrow rests in its CAT "drop-away" Series. With a bracket machined from aluminum, CAT Series rests rotate around a central point on a stationery horizontal arm. Copper John shrink wraps the launchers or rest troughs, in this case with a Teflon-coated polymer to eliminate noise and wear. In a sense, these are not true drop-away rests because the arrow rises away from the rest during the shot rather than the rest falling out of the way. The high end TomCAT features a unique CATtail spring-loaded arrow holder that automatically flips out of the way when you draw.

SHOOT-AROUND RESTS: THE CENTEREST

Shoot-around rests have fallen out of fashion because the percentage of archers who shoot mechanical releases has overwhelmed the market. Twenty years ago, a release shooter was rare. Today, for the 10-20 percent of archers who still shoot with their fingers, a shoot-around rest with a cushion plunger is still the answer to accurate shooting – for reasons we have already discussed, but primarily because the string moves faster than your fingers when you let it go. The string swings out and around your fingers, thereby causing the arrow to "wallow" or bend in flight like the body of a shark swimming overhead in a *National Geographic* documentary.

The Centerest Flipper from Andy Simo's New Archery Products combines the rest and cushion plunger in one simple unit. It is easy to install, adjust and replace. The shaft screws into your riser through the arrow rest (Berger button) hole and the head of the rest is then snapped in place. The head consists of a wire flipper arm with a silencing Teflon sleeve and a cushioned cut-out that acts as a set-off to cushion the flexing arrow as it passes.

New Archery Products' Bob Mizek notes that for accurate shooting, archers need to be conscious of nock point placement when they use a shoot-around rest like the Centerest. "When we mount a rest, we use a bow square and go high," he says. "We begin tuning by placing the bottom of the nock at least half the diameter of the arrow above center. A low nock just won't work."

Cavalier and Golden Key sell a variety of shoot-around rests. The Cavalier SuperFlyte mounts on the side of the bow with a cap screw. You adjust it vertically by levering the rest up and down with your finger as you tighten the cap screw. It adjusts horizontally via the long hex rod. The built-in, stainless steel side pressure plate acts as a cushion plunger. It may also be removed if you want to use this rest with a separate, spring-loaded cushion plunger. The wire arrow support arm has a smooth Teflon sleeve for silent, friction-free arrow passage.

SHOOT-THROUGH RESTS: THE INFINITI

One of the most adjustable shoot-through rests ever made is the new Infiniti from Golden Key-Futura. What makes shoot-through rests work is the in-line energy delivery of a release aid to your arrow and the orientation of your arrow's vanes so that the springy launcher arms of the rest will not interfere with them as the arrow passes in flight. Your cock vane can be

The Bear Hair arrow rest is designed for use on recurve bows. The synthetic bristles of the shelf rug are soft and the side plate is leather

A light, stick-on rest like this Bear WeatherRest is excellent for beginner shooting and very lightweight bows.

shot straight down to pass through the middle of the rest launchers or even straight up with the other two vanes (assuming that most archers shoot three-fletch feathers or vanes) at about the four o'clock and eight o'clock positions. For a shoot-through rest to work properly, the vanes must fully clear the rest's launcher arms.

The Infiniti is a good looking rest that has all the bells and whistles. The black mounting bar and housing for the springs are machined aluminum and they are accented with polished aluminum and brass. There is a full 1/2 inch of adjustability in the vertical and horizontal planes on the self-locking Micro Adjustment System. You adjust for vertical (for tuning and clearance) and horizontal (for centershot) positioning with small hex screws. Tuning gradients are marked in white. Ultra fine spring adjustment is accomplished with 12 tension-setting positions, with a separate increment gauge. The stainless steel launcher arms are independently adjustable with their own set screws and may be replaced with one of Golden Key's several dozen launcher styles (four sets are included with each rest) or covered with shrink tubing or Teflon silencing film. Vince Troncoso, who is in charge of research and development at Golden Key, says this rest will withstand "the punishment of 90-pound bows shooting lightweight arrows."

The Infiniti is equipped with an interesting Tuning Gauge that is supposed to indicate when the following tuning settings are incorrect: bad arrows, nocking point alignment, downward deflection, undernock pressure, vane deflection, arrow condition, arrow spine problems, arrow nock installation, centershot, spring tension and wheel timing. The gauge has red, yellow and green areas to indicate a problem, a marginal situation and "well-tuned." That is a lot to ask from a computer, much less a spring, so if you consider one of

these rests, be certain to get a thorough explanation about how the Tuning Gauge works. It is surely a cross between having your personal bow mechanic and relying on the "idiot lights" in your car.

The beauty of the Infiniti rest is its independently adjustable elements, but its drawback – especially for hunters who need rugged, nothing can go wrong gear – is that it may be a little too delicate for everyday use in the field. Plus, some archers find all this adjustment tedious.

S.G. Christian at Bodoodle developed his highly recognizable line of fully-machined, aluminum and stainless arrow rests to accommodate and modulate the initial bending of your arrow after a shot and thereby stabilize your arrow rapidly. A Bodoodle's twin stainless launcher arms are attached to an adjustable pivoting yoke that is designed to support your arrow with a minimum of force. All nine Bodoodle rests, from the 3.3-ounce Conquest II, with its heavy body and wide arrow catcher tray, to the lightweight Bullet, are built to the same basic plan and rely on an adjustable (but unprotected) spring for necessary launch support.

With its launcher arms set at 3 o'clock and 7 o'clock, the Timberdoodle accommodates left-right arrow flexing when shot with fingers. The Zapper 300 uses four launchers to fully enclose your arrow. This makes shooting downward or at an odd angle easier because the arrow will not fall off the rest, but it requires that you pay strict attention to the orientation of your fletching. The noise of an arrow passing over the steel launchers can be dampened with the easy application of a layer of Bodoodle's Teflon-coated "Smoke Quiet" tape to their tips.

One of the most popular arrow rest the past couple years has been the unique Whisker Biscuit from Carolina Archery Products. The Biscuit is a round, fully enclosed rest that supports your arrow in a 360 degree ring of synthetic black bristles. Using a Biscuit, you can launch an arrow quietly while shooting from the ground or hanging upside-down. The three Biscuit models are essentially the same. Each is manually adjustable and by simply moving the axle from one side to the other, the same rest will work for left-hand and right-hand shooters.

The advantage of this style rest is its simplicity: after set-up, it holds your arrow in position effortlessly and can be used with any orientation or number of fletching. Ike Branthwaite at Carolina recommends short, straight fletching. He says a loss of one to two fps can be expected with four inch straight fletch and a greater loss – up to 15 fps – with helical fletch. An archer should weigh the obvious benefits of this style rest against the loss of arrow speed before purchasing it.

The first time you look at an APA Ultimate rest, you will wonder if you have installed it upside down. The unique feature of the Ultimate is that it cradles your arrow from the overhead position. Set up properly, an arrow cannot fall off this rest. It will accommodate every size and style arrow. Fit the included cam fleece or some silencing material on the wire arms and this rest should be excellent for hunting archers because a broadhead can not slide or flip to the side and threaten your hand and arm at full draw. In addition, the Ultimate should shoot very quietly. For finger shooters, a wider wire armature is available for the left-right flexing of the arrow.

TRADITIONAL SHOOTING

In theory, a recurve or longbow could be shot with a mechanical release, but it might damage the bow or a wood arrow and it would certainly fly in the face of the spirit of traditional shooting. So, if you pick up a traditional bow, expect to shoot it with your fingers.

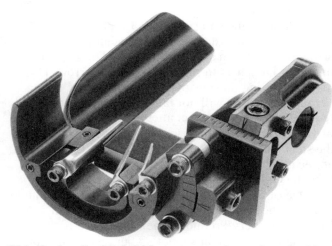

This Bodoodle PRO-500 arrow rest is equipped with a wide arrow catcher tray and an overdraw extension. The cradle of the PRO-500 floats on jeweled bearings that can be adjusted to give the arrow the correct support during launch.

The classic rest for traditional shooting is the shelf of the bow itself. With a recurve, there is typically a generous shelf. Often it will be crowned in the center and archers cover it with a piece of thick, but low-pile carpet or even a leather patch of some sort. In wet or humid conditions, the carpet can soak up water, but making sure it is synthetic and the pile is cut low will usually prevent any serious problem.

A standard traditional rest is the Bear Hair rest from Bear Archery which comes in two pieces: a lightweight, synthetic carpeting with self-adhesive backing that can be cut exactly to fit your bow's shelf and a leather side plate to keep the arrow slightly away from the wood riser.

Of course, any of the stick-on plastic rests such as a Bear Weatherest will work, although they are only recommended for beginner bows. Many shoot-around rests such as the Cavalier Super T-300 will also fit many traditional bows. The Super T has adhesive tape for instant mounting, a stainless steel spine and a Teflon-coated arrow support arm. The older style Flipper II rest from New Archery Products is also excellent because it has an adhesive backing, a Teflon-coated stainless steel flipper arm and a slick-surface nylon button which gives your arrow some offset from the bow's riser.

On rare occasions, an archer will shoot an arrow with plastic fletching from a traditional bow. You will not be able to achieve sufficient clearance for plastic vanes when you shoot off the shelf or from a stick-on rest. Plastic vanes will hit the bow shelf or the rest as the arrow flies by and this will cause erratic arrow flight. Soft, pliable feathers only. Please.

THE OVERDRAW

Nobody shoots an overdraw now. Well, strictly speaking that is not true. Strictly speaking, a huge number of archers shoot overdraws.

An overdraw is an extension of the arrow shelf and hence, the arrow rest, back toward the shooter. It allows you to shoot a shorter arrow than you would otherwise shoot if your launcher tips were in line with the arrow rest hole in the riser. With an overdraw, an archer drawing a 30-inch arrow can shoot a 28-inch or 29-inch shaft.

The theory of the shorter arrow is that it saves weight. Saving weight increases speed. Increasing speed flattens trajectory. A flatter trajectory makes distance judging slightly less critical. How much speed you can pick up and how flat your trajectory will become and how much distance error is "slightly less" depends of course on your bow set-up. It is common for an archer to pick up from 10 to 20 fps, however.

There is an arrow issue with overdraws, too.

World Champion archer and bowhunter Joella Bates was the first woman to take a Cape Buffalo with a bow in modern times. "Find an arrow rest you can reliably expect will perform every shot," she says, "but I do not recommend that most archers use an overdraw unless they really know what they are doing."

Archers with short draw lengths (say 28 inches) have a number of arrow shaft styles to choose from. The longer your draw, the less the arrow charts allow for smooth, effective shooting with other than large, stiff heavy shafts. If you can cut a couple inches off your shaft length, you can open up the arrow spine chart for shorter, lighter arrows.

Tennessee's Joella Bates is a professional wildlife biologist and a five-time 3-D World Champion. Today, she competes and bowhunts actively. She recently became the first woman to take a Cape Buffalo in Africa with a modern bow and arrow. A recipient of the Muzzy Products "TALL Man" Award for outstanding service to archery, Joella gives seminars, demonstrations and promotes the sport throughout the year.

"I don't recommend that a casual shooter put an overdraw on a bow," Joella says. "Unless someone

The Mariner roller rest from Bear Archery is designed specifically to hold the heavy arrows needed for bowfishing.

Before archers flocked to release shooting in the late '80s, millions of adjustable spring-loaded, Teflon-tipped cushion plungers like this Master Plunger from Martin were sold to help finger shooters control the left-right porpoising of their arrow.

shoots a lot and has very consistent form, an overdraw can cause more problems than it solves. An overdraw will magnify errors in shooting form and make your bow much less manageable. Overdraws got to be extremely popular before carbon arrows opened up additional size and weight opportunities for archers, but now, you never see one of the old fashioned black shelf overdraws on a 3-D range. When I go to archery shops to give seminars or help coach the shooting staff and teach bow set up, we don't spend much time talking about overdraws. They are kind of a thing of the past."

Joella has a 26-inch draw length and shoots a 25-inch carbon arrow, though. For competition, she likes a light, fat shaft, a "line cutter." For hunting, she uses a smaller diameter, but thicker walled shaft that delivers more kinetic energy.

One problem that arises as a result of the nature of the overdraw is that there is less space between the cables and string and the back of the overdraw shelf. During the peak of the overdraw craze in the early-mid 1990s, archers installed overdraws as long as 4 inches. They soon discovered that the string and cables hit the back of the shelf. This caused extreme difficulties with wear on the string and cables, noise and erratic arrow flight. The initial answer was to pad the back of the overdraw, but archers eventually discovered that for the short axle-to-axle bows with short brace heights that were becoming popular, a very short overdraw gave them maximum speed, increased versatility to choose arrow shafts and maximum bow "forgivability" or control. Today, it is widely accepted that a minimum of 2 inches of space needs to be available between the back of an overdraw and the cables.

To every rule there is an exception, but an overdraw cannot be shot effectively with fingers. The shorter the arrow shot from a high-energy bow, the more critical the release. With reduced space between the string and the back of the rest, the finger-released arrow is still in the middle of its initial bend when it crosses the back of the overdraw and this may cause

For years before the development of fully enclosed rests, archers looked for simple, effective ways to keep their arrows mounted on their rest. This lightweight plastic holder from New Archery Products attaches to the inside of the riser with the arrow rest bolt. It flips up and out of the way when you draw.

interference with your shot.

Today's high-end arrow rests such as the Micro-Adjustable QuickTune 3000 from New Archery Products have brackets configured for a short overdraw extension. Joella shoots a 5.3-ounce Bodoodle Pro-500 that can give as much as 2 inches of overdraw adjustability with its supplied bracket.

The final and perhaps most serious consideration when shooting an overdraw is safety. Because overdraws allows you to pull your arrow back behind your hand, perhaps even behind your wrist, it is critical that any overdraw be equipped with an arrow catcher tray. The wind, a slight twist of the bow, bumping the bottom limb against your treestand or jerking the release during a moment of tension can easily cause the arrow to fall off a shoot-through rest. If you trigger your release with the arrow improperly centered on your rest, you will certainly miss your target, will probably damage your bow and may hurt yourself seriously with a splintered shaft. (The author personally knows several archers who have had terrible accidents when shooting overdraws.) So, if you shoot with an overdraw, the rule is to be safe. Be thoughtful. Go slow.

Overdraw manufacturers such as Precision Shooting Equipment, Golden Key-Futura, North American Archery Group and Savage Systems automatically equip their products with side protective plates or arrow catcher trays to help prevent injuries. They are included for your protection. Do not disable, remove or alter them!

ARROW REST PARTICULARS

There are arrow rests for special purposes like bowfishing. The roller rest from Cajun Archery, for instance, is made from sturdy, water resistant Delrin plastic. Roller rests are simple in design and only adjust in and out from your riser. The "U-shaped" Delrin ring spins freely on an adjustable shaft that screws into the arrow rest hole in your riser. It is quite sturdy and designed for smooth flight of heavy, solid Fiberglas fishing arrows. After all, when you are

bowfishing you are only shooting 10 yards and that arrow is dragging a heavy fishing line. These rests work equally well in fresh or salt water.

A cushion plunger is a necessary accessory for a finger shooter. Used in conjunction with a shoot-around arrow rest, it will help control the flight of your arrow so that – with good form, a smooth release and complete follow-through – a finger shooter can expect pinpoint accuracy at close ranges and good shooting at a distance. Depending on the set-up, a cushion plunger can often be used to good effect by a release shooter with a shoot-through rest, too.

The cushion plunger screws directly through the arrow rest hole in your riser. It will typically have a couple of locking hex nuts and set screws to lock it firmly in place. The plunger is a hollow brass or aluminum sleeve with a spring inside. The end in contact with your arrow has a hard nylon tip. This

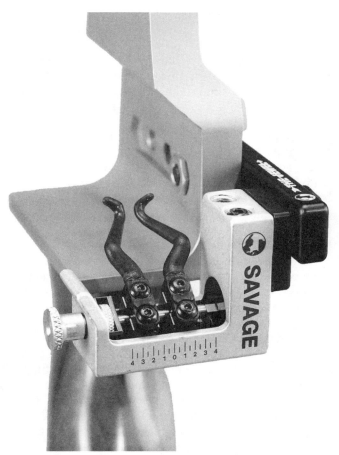

As one of the slickest materials – if not THE slickest – known to man, Teflon has practical applications in archery. Savage Archery has used solid, molded Teflon launchers for arrow rests for several years.

Teflon launchers and tape such as Bodoodle's Smoke Quiet wrap-on strips will help silence any scraping noise that arrows make when they pass over stainless steel launchers or speed fins.

allows your arrow to slide against it with the least

amount of friction. A quality bonus is a thin, internal Teflon sleeve for ultra-smooth spring movement. When your moving arrow slides against the plunger tip that gives slightly, compressing the spring inside the sleeve. This cushions your arrow's flight around the riser and moderates the left-right arrow flex that is typical of a finger shooter's arrow. Plunger barrels from Cavalier are stainless steel with an internal Teflon sleeve and a white nylon tip. You can expect to pay $40-$50 for their adjustable (spring tension and length) Master Plunger. Golden Key-Futura makes an economy plunger with a brass sleeve and black nylon tip that retails in the $15-$20 range.

Whether it is from a treestand or on the ground, archers who hunt know that one of the challenges they face is to keep the arrow on the rest in readiness for a shot. Of course, if you shoot an enclosed arrow rest like the Whisker Biscuit from Carolina Archery Products, the Funnel from Golden Key-Futura or the Zapper 300 from Bodoodle, this will not be a problem because the rest is designed to completely encircle your arrow.

Individual rest manufacturers like Bodoodle offer rest-specific solutions to this problem. (Bodoodle, for instance, offers a simple rubber band that is cheap and efficient.) The "old stand-by" arrow holders are the Saunders Kwik Lok and the Sta-Jac. These attach to your riser with double stick tape or via a pre-set hole for your cushion plunger and the holder's rubber arm reaches around to grab your arrow and hold it in place, ready for a shot. The difficulty using these is that your bow's riser style and rest may not accept their attachment and when you draw, their tendency of course is to hold on to the arrow and this pulls it off the rest toward your riser.

Golden Key-Futura has designed several arrow holders that are specific to its rests and others that are universal in design. Their popular Arrow Holder clamps under the rest mounting plate and, by a series of linkages, holds the arrow on your rest from the top. Its wide cup accommodates any size arrow and it works with any arrow rest, Golden Key says, plus an internal spring flips it up and out of the way within the first inch of draw so it will not interfere with the passage of large fletching. A less expensive version attaches to your riser with double-stick tape.

Within the past decade or two, as more and more archers have taken to the field to hunt, they have become increasingly sensitive to the noise an arrow makes as it slides across a rest's stainless steel launchers or wire. New Archery Products offered a Teflon sleeve with its Springy rest 20 years ago.

Shooting with stainless launchers, as hundreds of thousands of hunters and competitors do, and realizing how quickly a deer can "jump the string" or dodge down and out of the way of your arrow, it only makes sense to purchase shrink tubing which can quickly be heat-set around your launchers; Teflon tape which can be cut and applied directly to the point of arrow contact; or even special nylon tips.

An option, of course, for silencing any shot is to purchase a rest which has Teflon-coated launchers or a rest such as the adjustable Savage Systems Easy Rest which features solid, molded Teflon launchers. With a clean arrow shaft, that will be as quiet as shooting an arrow gets.

READING THE FINE PRINT

S.G. Christian, founder and president of Bodoodle arrow rests is fond of telling how his daughter Lee Ann helped him learn about the dynamics of arrow flight and arrow movement across an arrow rest.

In the 1970s, S.G. was interested in designing the perfect mechanical release aid, not arrow rests, but when Lee Ann, using a low draw weight bow was able to see visual evidence of the natural bending reaction of arrows during the launch sequence, S.G. changed his inventive focus. The result is a highly regarded line of shoot through arrow rests that are proven in world class competition and hunting.

"Lee Ann could red the fine print on an aspirin box from across the room," S.G. says, "and that's small. So I knew she could see the arrow nock and the string going forward."

S.G. concluded that archers needed an arrow rest that would use the natural flexing action of an arrow to deliver smooth, consistent flight. "One way or another, an arrow is going to flex," S.G. says. "There's nothing you can do about that. What you have to do with your arrow rest is to support the arrow for a moment – until it leaves the string – and then let it move out of the way of the flexing shaft and fletching. Our rest line is founded on that principle." The 5.3-ounce Bodoodle Pro-500 for instance is built with conical, jewel-type bearings that cradle a machined aluminum yoke and the attached stainless steel launcher arms. With the spring tension set initially so light that it will barely support your arrow, a Bodoodle is remarkably easy to tune.

TEFLON

According to the "*Guinness Book of World Records*," if you have a rest that uses Teflon, either as sleeves or tape (Bodoodle Smoke Quiet Tape) over the arrow rest support or launcher arms or as solid, molded support arms (Savage solid Teflon launchers), you are shooting your arrows across the world's most slippery substance!

A scientist named Roy Plunkett discovered Teflon at the DuPont laboratories in New Jersey in 1938. He was working with gases related to Freon refrigerants, checking frozen, compressed samples of tetrafluoroethylene that had spontaneously "polymerized" to a white, waxy solid called polytetrafluoroethylene or PTFE. DuPont eventually named this Teflon and patented it in 1945.

Teflon has some amazing properties. It is virtually inert to all chemicals and, of course, it is slippery. You could say it is self-lubricating. Since 1945, several variations on the original PTFE have been discovered and patented.

Wallace Carothers, a DuPont chemist discovered Nylon the same year that Plunkett stumbled onto Teflon. Oddly enough, DuPont decided not patent Nylon and company publicists declare that DuPont decided to "give it to the world." DuPont gave it to the world first as "nylons," women's stockings, because during World War II silk for stockings was almost impossible to buy. These days, Nylon is used in many archery products such as arrow launchers from Golden Key-Futura and others.

THE QUIVER

Ishi's quiver was made of a whole otter skin with the fur outside and was large enough to carry his bow as well as his arrows reports Theodora Kroeber in Ishi in Two Worlds.

The study of Ishi, the Native American hunter from the Pacific Northwest, provided great insights for those interested in bowhunting. Today, there are not enough otters to go around and our inventiveness in developing quiver styles might surprise and would certainly interest the "last wild Indian in North America."

The quiver holds your arrows and there is a different style quiver for every archery activity. Hip quivers hang from your belt and are popular with competitors. Bow quivers attach to your bow riser and are used by bowhunters. Traditionalists and hunters

Two-piece leather bow quivers are standard on many traditional bows. The two sections slide over the limbs and hold six arrows.

who make extended hunting and camping forays into national forests or wilderness areas often use back quivers. There is even a ground quiver that holds your arrows upright while you stand in one place shooting practice arrows.

The quiver is a utilitarian item, but it is an important utilitarian item and, for competitors, it can be a decorative item, too. The competitor's hip quiver is often part of an assembly of clips and zippered pockets in which he stores pencils and scorecards; perhaps a monocular and necessary spare items like field points or a set of Allen wrenches. The quiver needs to hold your arrows quietly and securely, and so they are easy to retrieve when it is time to "load up" and shoot. You don't want arrows rattling or scraping against each other and your razor-sharp broadheads need to be fully covered to protect your fingers from nasty cuts.

BOW-MOUNTED QUIVERS

More bow-mounted quivers are sold in North America each year than all other styles combined because most archers on this continent are bowhunters first and competitors, plinkers, recreational shooters second.

The bow-mounted quiver has been around since Fred Bear and others began experimenting with them in the '40s and '50s. Early bow quivers were more concerned with holding arrows rather than protecting the archer and they often left the cutting edges of the archer's broadheads exposed. Perhaps this is because earlier generation broadheads, sharpened by hand with files and stones, were simply not as sharp as the ones we use in the field today and the chance of getting a nasty slice from casual contact was less. (Fred said he preferred a broadhead with less than maximum sharpness as the very slight ragged edge promoted hemorrhaging by cutting a wound channel that was slower to seal.)

One of Fred Bear's earliest quiver styles (one that

is still seen among recurve shooters today) attached above and below a recurve's riser with sturdy wire. Most single-piece bow-mounted quivers fit recurves as well as compounds.

The direction in bow quivers is to build a style with the following qualities:

- It must be lightweight, but sturdy, and it must attach to the bow riser securely. You do not want it to rattle when you shoot.
- It must hold your arrows securely inside it. You do not want them vibrating following a shot and you do not want arrow fletching to be continually scraping against other fletching when you are moving. So, the farther down the shaft the gripper holds your arrows the better, although given the usual positioning of the quiver base above your grip and the length of your arrows – 26 to 30 inches – this causes practical design difficulties.
- The quiver should attach or detach easily and not interfere with the mounting of other accessories such as your sights or a backward facing V-bar stabilizer.
- The gripper slots should be properly sized to your arrows. Typically, smaller holes are necessary for carbon shafts than for aluminum shafts and this requires different grippers. In addition, the gripper needs to be made from a flexible product that holds the arrows securely, but not so tight that you could easily bend one

getting it out. The rubber quiver gripper must work as well in very cold weather as it does on a blue bird day in the early season.

- The hood should completely encase your broadheads and it should be adaptable to the kind of broadhead you are shooting. If you are shooting a large head like the two-blade Snuffer 125 which has a 1-5/16-inch cutting diameter, you need to be sure there is plenty of room in the quiver cup to hold the arrowheads. On the other hand, if you are shooting the mechanical Gold Tip Gladiator, you need to be sure that pressing the sharp blades up in the quiver does not qualify as "open-on-impact!"

There are two kinds of bow-mounted quiver, the single-piece and the two-piece. The classic single-piece quiver evolved from recurve days and superb examples are still made by virtually all of the significant manufacturers. The plastic Bear Hug Quiver from Bear Archery (now part of The North American Archery Group) has been essentially unchanged for decades. It holds seven arrows and attaches or detaches from the plastic bracket, that you more or less attach permanently to your riser, with just a twist. The generous cup fully protects your broadheads and the gripper holds your arrows at about their center, flaring them outward slightly so the fletching can be spaced apart. Many quivers are available in a similar style: the Kwikee six-Arrow Quiver, the low-hood-profile Bohning five-Arrow Jack Pine and the PSE Mongoose.

 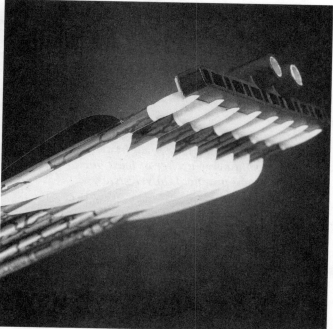

The patented Fine Line Hunter Quiver weighs 12 ounces and holds up to eight arrows. It is length adjustable and, unlike most bow-mounted quivers, holds arrowheads in a foam cup and the nocks over a lower bar (close-up).

The compact Axis 360 from TRUGLO carries up to six arrows. The rotational locking mechanism keeps arrows or bolts securely in place while the mechanism turns to release one arrow at a time.

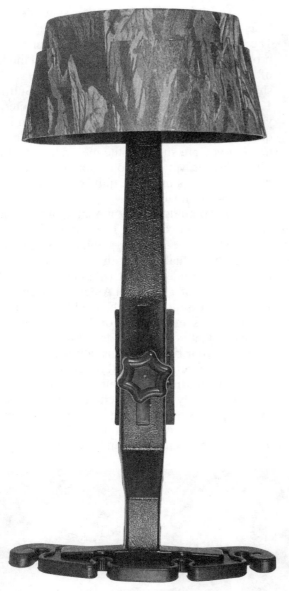

The standard style hard plastic detachable quiver for hunting archers holds four to eight arrows. Kwikee Kwiver has sold every archer at least one of these inexpensive and practical quiver styles.

The difficulties with the traditional one-piece quivers are rattle, proper arrow fit and their tendency to stand out from the bow riser by four to five inches. These are excellent, economical quivers for novices or for archers who take their quiver off the bow and hang or tie it on a branch when they hunt.

Most manufacturers build several grippers and one is certain to fit your type and size of arrow. This allows Bear Archery, for instance, to upgrade their inexpensive Bear Hug to the Super 7. In place of the molded rubber broadhead or arrow holder in the hood is a block of foam that is not supposed to dull your broadheads when you push them into place. Instead of the molded rubber gripper is a thicker gripper that is designed to hold both aluminum or carbon shafts. If you choose a foam-filled hood, you need to place your arrows with the same blade orientation into the same broadhead holes each time or you will soon chew up the foam and need to replace it.

If you like the simplicity of the one-piece quiver and its quick-detach benefit, ask for one with a low profile broadhead cup. In place of the bulky broadhead cup on the Bear Super 7, bowhunters have increasingly been interested in the low-profile cup style of a quiver like the Bohning Badger. Excellent, except that with the arrows in a row rather than in a circle around the stem of the quiver, the Badger holds three less arrows than the Super 7.

But how many arrows do you need? Unless you are one of those archers who like to carry a lot of ammo – on general principles or the theory that today just might be your lucky day – on any given outing, four arrows should be plenty.

The bow-mounted Martin Super Quiver has three small compartments in the quiver cup and a built-in broadhead wrench. The quiver includes two external arrow clips for extra arrows, which are great for flu-flu arrows, or blunts. The quiver cup will hold eight arrows.

Numerous differences in style make your quiver selection open-ended:

- Designed for open-on-impact heads, Kwikee's Mechanical 4 grips the arrows behind the head.
- The Hot Shot Quick Lock 7 Arrow Quiver's metal frame resists riser buzz and vibration after a shot.
- The Martin 10-Arrow Super Quiver has a built-in broadhead wrench and three storage compartments with snap-on lids and holds arrows nine and ten on special clips outside the quiver cup, thus exposing you to the broadhead if you choose to use these rather than the eight held inside the quiver.
- The Archer's Choice Pivoter Five Arrow Quiver is built with independent arrow holders that pivot for a smooth, silent arrow release.
- The unique Fine-Line Hunter will hold eight arrows. The twin center posts are adjustable to the length of your arrows. You simply push the head of the arrow into the foam-filled quiver cup and slip the notch of your arrow nocks over the bar at the bottom of the quiver.

The great debate with quivers is whether you are a

Hunting archer Jamie Ashley takes his quiver off his bow when he climbs into his treestand. "I practice with the quiver off," he says, "so I hunt the same way."

more accurate shot with one mounted on your bow or one that carries your arrows on your hip, leaving your bow free to balance down the centerline of your hand. While you can find good arguments for removing the quiver and its weight with a load of arrows and broadheads from the side of your bow, there does not seem to be a clear-cut answer to the question. Apparently, with diligence, you can learn to shoot properly with almost any handicap, including a loaded quiver mounted on your bow riser, if you execute your shot the same way each time.

Kentucky bowhunter Jamie Ashley uses the Kwikee 3-Arrow and 4-Arrow quivers, depending on whether a season for wild turkeys is also open during deer season. Jamie likes to keep an expandable 100-grain Rocket Sidewinder in his quiver for turkeys

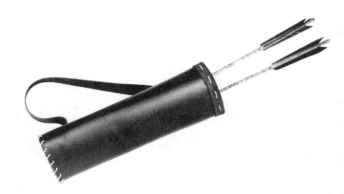

Traditional archers who want their arrows close at hand and immediately available, especially when they are stalking and still-hunting often prefer this style leather hip quiver from Gerry Kaufman's Wyandotte Leather.

Champion professional 3-D competitors like Jackie Caudle typically prefer a hip quiver. Back quivers are hot and awkward for this shooting venue and bow-mounted quivers add a pound or so of off-center weight that causes torque, just the opposite of what a precision shot needs to hit the 12-ring consistently.

alongside his replaceable-blade Muzzy 100-grain 3-blade heads for deer. "You don't need more than about three arrows for a day's hunting," Jamie says. "On a quality deer, you are only going to get one shot. It's rare that you will get a second shot. Anything beyond that, I'm too excited for another shot anyway!"

Jamie also takes his quiver off his Pearson bow when he reaches his Loc-On treestand. "Kwikee makes something they call a Bracket Kaddy," he says, "that lets you snap the quiver and arrows off your bow and hang them right on the tree. The Bracket Kaddy is built just like the quiver receiver you put on your bow and it has a screw on the back that you can screw into the tree trunk."

Jamie says taking the quiver off reduces the bulk he holds and reduces his silhouette. "I practice with the

quiver off. If I don't take it off, I have trouble sometimes with left-right arrow placement."

Having used one-piece quivers for decades, appreciated their convenience and put up with their shortcomings, many archers shooting compound bows switched to two-piece quivers in the mid 1990s. The two-piece quiver has a broadhead cup that attaches near the top of your riser and a separate gripper

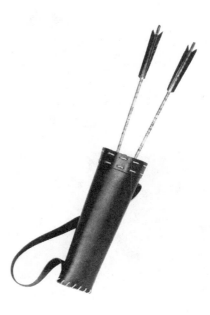

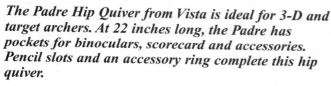

The Padre Hip Quiver from Vista is ideal for 3-D and target archers. At 22 inches long, the Padre has pockets for binoculars, scorecard and accessories. Pencil slots and an accessory ring complete this hip quiver.

Defining the style for traditional archers, Wyandotte Leather produces a rugged, good looking back quiver that is both safe and easy to use.

element near the bottom of the riser. These may be held in place either at a specially machined mounting holes or under the limb bolts. If the two-piece quiver you have chosen fits under the limb bolts, you will want a competent bow mechanic or a pro shop to assist with the set-up because the bow will almost have to be disassembled before the quiver can be mounted.

A relatively new quiver called AIS or Arrow Incased System has features of both a bow-mounted quiver and a back quiver. AIS is a plastic tube that holds five arrows securely and protectively via an inner rotational device, essentially a central spindle with a high-mount and a low-mount gripper. The patented AIS holds any type or size arrow or broadhead and weighs less than two pounds. It is available in 32-inch or 35-inch lengths and in black plus four popular camo patterns. The manufacturer sells an optional shoulder strap. Although AIS is bulky, it may be the answer for many bowhunters.

HIP (SIDE) QUIVERS FOR HUNTING AND COMPETITION

The hip quiver for hunting is still a rare item in the east where hunting archers walk to their treestands and wait to ambush a whitetail. In the west however where "the deer and the antelope play" and hunters frequently use the spot and stalk method, hip quivers are common

and are excellent for recurve and longbow shooters.

Hip quivers fasten over your belt and, with a tie-down strap, around your leg to keep them from flapping. The arrow heads fit inside a standard, foam-filled hood and the arrows are carried with the fletching pointed up and to the rear. Because most archers today were reared on bow-mounted quivers, the hip quiver may take some getting used to, especially the restricting feel of the tie around the leg. On a hot day, this tie-on can make the hip quiver a hot and sweaty accessory.

A number of manufacturers specialize in hip quivers for competition, but NEET makes several hip or side quivers just for hunting archers. Their Bowhunter in Mossy Oak or Advantage Camo attaches to your belt and holds six arrows. It comes with an adjustable web strap for mounting to a stand or tree when you reach your hunting location and want to take it off. The NEET Mechanical Broadhead side quiver holds four arrows suspended with the heads in a fully enclosed cup. The Vista Rustler will hold seven aluminum or six carbon arrows inside a rigid, camouflaged shell protected and silenced with a fleece lining.

For quivers, the marriage of beauty and function takes place in the competition quiver. These hip quivers hang or clip over your belt and present arrows angled nock forward for you to withdraw as needed. A right hand shooter hangs the quiver on the right side, a

Fine, hand tooled leather back quivers like this one from NEET and Wyandotte are standard accessories for traditional archers. The shoulder strap is adjustable and there is a one-inch foam bottom insert to cushion your broadheads.

left-hander on his left side. If you hang a hip quiver on the wrong side, it can interfere with drawing the bow.

Rigid, inexpensive tube quivers are fine for novices or for an hour of practice at a shooting range or even for league shooting. They are not designed for broadhead-tipped arrows or for tramping around a 3-D range, though. Depending on how tightly you pack them inside, the tube quiver will hold from six to ten arrows. The NEET Deluxe is 17 ? inches long and has a three inch opening with a belt clip attachment.

Vista offers a diverse line of competition hip or side quivers, both in camo and in bright, interesting colors and patterns. The Padre is 22 inches long and features a binocular pocket, large accessory pocket, arrow lubricant slot, score card pocket and a pencil slot. Arrows ride in individual tubes just like the tubes for clubs in a golf bag. Look for heavy Cordura construction in a handsome Southwestern motif.

BACK QUIVERS

Two types of archers like back quivers: traditionalists and folks who are packing heavy for either a tall climb or a long walk. For traditional hunters, the look and feel of leather complements their choice of additional self-limitation beyond what any modern bow and arrow normally provides. For hunters who are preparing for an extended stay in the outback or who are covering rough terrain and need their hands

free for climbing or glassing, light, durable materials are the best choice.

Gerald Kaufman, president of Wyandotte Leather, remembers when Fred Bear would come for dinner and work with his father developing patterns for leather archery accessories. Wyandotte opened its doors in 1943 after they began helping Boy Scouts earn their Archery Merit Badges. Today, the use of high quality leather for archery accessories is on the decline.

"Our leather back and side quivers are used by traditional style bowhunters or by people who just prefer the sturdy, quality look and feel of leather," Gerald says. "We use a much heavier leather than shoes. The leather in our quivers grades out at seven to eight ounces per square foot. In contrast, dress shoes are three to four ounce and work shoes are five to six ounce leather. A heavier grade of leather like ours is necessary for quivers that contain sharp broadheads. Nylon or some other synthetic could not withstand the continual cutting and abrasion like leather does."

Gerald says leather has some positive characteristics that an archer should consider before making a purchase. First, leather is "wearable." It lasts a long time. The older it is the better leather looks. On the other hand, leather is relatively heavy and although it is said to "breathe" it can be very hot on the back when you are climbing, hiking or stalking.

Wyandotte's quivers include a 24-arrow leather kit that needs to be assembled. "A lot of archers enjoy that," Gerald says. "It involves pride of ownership of building something with your own hands. And with 24 arrows in the quiver, someone shooting a longbow can reach back and pull out arrow after arrow in a hurry." Most leather back quivers also have small pockets for a file or knife and several are even camouflaged with a random coloration process Gerald likens to tie-dying!

In contrast to the more traditional leather products by Wyandotte, Rancho Safari builds several back quivers in its Cat Quiver line that use the latest materials and technology.

The Cat Quiver Mini is worn like a single strap back quiver. Its fletching hood and broadhead base – these quivers are all designed with the broadhead down and the fletching up which may require an adjustment if you are used to a bow-mounted quiver – are ABS plastic and are held together by an adjustable 1/2-inch aluminum slide bar so your arrows are held in by pressure. The Mini holds seven arrows. The shoulder strap is wide, padded and adjustable.

At the opposite end in terms of features is the camouflaged, seven arrow Cat Quiver VII which combines the quiver with a large, versatile back pack and a fanny pack, all in one unit. The ample, padded waist strap has two large side pockets and a water bottle pouch. The main compartment features padded back support and a private security pocket. A second bellows pocket has a side zipper opening. There are plenty of padded straps over the shoulders and around the waist to keep the packs and quiver tight. Arrows are drawn from the side of this Cat Quiver. These quivers are available in tough saddle cloth or lightweight twill fabric.

The Maverick back quiver from Vista even includes a pouch to carry a take-down recurve.

Whatever style back quiver you choose, make sure the arrows do not rattle around in a tube. This can be very disconcerting, especially when you are stalking.

MORE THAN YOU EVER WANTED TO KNOW ABOUT HOOK AND LOOP

Okay, so we customarily think of this category of fastener on our backpacks, our kid's tennis shoes and an abundance of hangers and fasteners as "velcro." Well, that would be wrong. It's Velcro with an ® or else it is some other brand and you cannot legally refer to it "velcro." Velcro is a company and a very specific brand of hook and loop fastener.

The story of "velcro" says that a Swiss engineer named George de Maestral, who was living in England, went for a walk with his dog one day in 1957. The dog picked up cockleburs and as George picked them off, he became curious about the manner in which the weed attached so tenaciously to his dog. George placed a cocklebur under his microscope and decided to see if he could replicate nature's tiny hooks and loops artificially.

Eventually, he was successful spinning the little hooks and loops and someone – the information from Velcro with an ® is maddeningly vague – combined the French words velour and crochet to make "velcro." An industry quickly rose around the invention and its subsequent knock-offs – thank goodness! – and today we use this little miracle many times each day without giving it a second thought.

CORDURA

Your camo backpack, the one with the single change of underwear for a week's camping, the one with the mule deer blood smeared on the side, began its life as a pair of silk stockings for a supermodel. Well not exactly, but there is a grain of truth in it. Cordura is a variety of "Nylon 6, 6" and spun Nylon replaced silk for women's stockings within a few years after Wallace Carothers discovered it in 1934.

Carothers worked for E.I. DuPont, the E.I. standing for Eleuthere Irenee, who was a French immigrant who began making gunpowder in the US in 1804. Certainly, there is more than a century between E.I.'s early black

powder factory and today's totally synthetic Cordura fabrics, but during that time, some very smart and very lucky people have changed practically everything about our lives, including the way we hunt and fish.

It all seems so primitive now. A Swiss chemist named Audemars dissolves the inner bark of the mulberry tree to produce cellulose and forms threads by the simple expedient of dipping needles in the solution and then drawing them out again. One thing led to another of course and 40 years later a French scientist named Hilaire de Chardonnet followed up thoroughly and produced Rayon threads and – shades of Rapunzel's hair – spun them into fabric.

It was another huge leap from Rayon, made from liquefied plant cellulose, to Nylon, which is actually a petrochemical (oil) by-product. Hence, DuPont's purchase of Conoco (That cost $7.9 billion in 1981 in case you were wondering.) to ensure a "petroleum-based feedstock" for its Nylon spinning mills.

Technically, your Cordura backpack is made from an "air-textured, high-tenacity Nylon" that is lightweight, abrasion resistant and ultra-durable. (After they are extruded, DuPont's public relations people exclaim, Nylon strands travel through the DuPont factories at more than 180 mph.) In other words, women's stockings. Enjoy!

With an umbrella for shade or rain, this could be the ultimate in comfort for a 3-D shoot and not so bad for a bowhunting ground blind, either. The portable stool has an underseat cargo compartment and a carrying strap. The hip quiver carries arrows with target points, but could be pressed into service to carry broadheads.

MECHANICAL RELEASE AIDS

When my buddy, Don Friberg, and I hunted pheasants with shotguns in South Dakota in the 1980s, he had the foresight to bring his dog, an energetic black and white Springer spaniel named Katy. I did not have a dog.

Naturally, when we spread out to walk-up birds in the expansive rolling hills along the Missouri River we were well apart to prevent any error in shotgun handling. Sometimes I could not see him or his dog, but I could always tell where Don and Katy were because the report of his booming 12-gauge arrived just a little quicker than his shouts, "Good dog! Good Katy! Work up that bird."

At the end of the day, Don returned to camp with a limit and I would skulk back empty handed. The difference of course was the dog (and the unmentionable fact that Don was a better shot). Katy ran along with her nose on the ground, casting back and forth, but staying close to her owner. That dog knew its business. The next time we went, I was either going to shoot that dadgum dog or take one of my own. I got a dog.

A release aid to an archer is like a good bird dog for a wing shooter. You can shoot a modern, high-energy compound bow without a release aid, but why would you want to? Sure, finger shooting is traditional and a good way (some would argue the best way) to learn to shoot. It is closer to the tradition of Robin Hood and Ishi and Fred Bear and Doug Easton. But with a release aid, you can shoot better than Robin Hood or Ishi or Fred Bear. Guaranteed.

We owe a debt of immense proportion to the generations – and there are hundreds of them – of archers who refined the bow and arrow since its invention. Certainly we understand the mechanics of wood today, but the truth is that we hardly know much that ancient archers and bow builders did not already know. Sure, we can put numbers on our understanding … or perhaps we have to. It could be a matter of the chicken or the egg, but we know that release aids have

Most experts agree that young people (and even older novices) should begin shooting with a finger release rather than a mechanical release aid. Starting with lightweight bows, they quickly learn the fundamentals of stance, draw, aim and follow-through. As they move toward adult-size or hunting weight bows (usually about 45 pounds draw weight) they can then make an informed decision to continue shooting with fingers or learn to shoot a release aid.

Fred Bear called his archery style "snap shooting." He was certainly strong enough to draw and hold his heavy hunting recurves at his anchor point, but he had developed a form of "target panic" that afflicts many archers in competition and hunting. Target panic prevents the archer from coming to full draw, holding, breathing, aiming, releasing and following through. The condition causes you to release before you are ready and the worse it becomes, the harder it is to hit what you are aiming at.

been around since Babylonian archers, Mongol warriors and the Japanese warlords.

Emery Loiselle, the writer and student of archery technology who owns Eryleen Archery in Massachusetts, built a release aid in the 1950s and called it the "Pincer." In those days, only one-piece releases were allowed on NFAA competition circuits.

Jerry Carter has been building releases since the 1960s and has been at it full time since 1989. He does not think often of the ancients, but he does remember that people used those releases with recurve bows. "I recall that Bob Jacobsen, who owns Jake's Archery Distributors now, won the Las Vegas Indoor Championships* the first year they switched to the three-spot target and he shot a Carroll recurve with a rope spike release."

Jerry says the beauty of the release is that it allows you to shoot the classic unanticipated shot. "It's like

learning to shoot a rifle," he says. "You breathe to steady yourself and then slowly squeeze the trigger. This technique, which they teach riflemen in the military, allows you to essentially be surprised when the shot goes off. If you anticipate the shot, an archer (or a rifleman) will often react to it before the shot actually goes off by flinching or snap shooting the release or peeking to see if you hit what you are aiming at. Before releases reached today's level of refinement, people shot clickers if they had any trouble with their release."

A mechanical release aid helps an archer overcome "target panic" by teaching how to eliminate flinching and freezing. The inability to release with the pin on target is one form of target panic. A second form is flinching or jerking the string. In neither case will you hit what you are aiming at. Because you – theoretically – do not know when the release will go off your mind can focus on perfecting your form and on holding steady. Jerry says that a back tension release like the Carter Solution 2, which works on rotation of the hand, is the best possible release for helping address target panic because you do not actually punch a trigger to make the shot go off.

It is generally believed that releases triggered by the pinkie or thumb rather than the index finger are better for helping cure target panic. While there is some speculation as to why this is so, no one knows for sure. It is a custom to trigger something or push a button with the index finger, so using the thumb or pinkie may set up a different set of muscular reflexes, a different "train of thought" and it thereby breaks a habit.

If you are looking for your first release, Jerry Carter has some thoughts to keep in mind. "Today, I think 99 percent of all target shooters use a thumb triggered release," he says, "while 99 percent of all hunters and especially folks who are crossing over from gun hunting, prefer an index finger release." Whatever style you choose, probably a rope spike release like the ultra-light, slim-line Carter Colby is best. This triggerless back tension release will fit any size hand and may be shot most successfully with a rope or D-loop on the string.

HOW A RELEASE ATTACHES TO THE STRING

One way to understand the hand-held mechanical release aid is to look at the way they grip your

bowstring or D-loop. There are three basic ways a release can draw your bowstring back: rope, jaws or caliper and ball bearing.

The rope release is the oldest style in general use now. A rope loops around your string and then is held tight by a cocked lever. The lever is a slight hook, smooth on every side, which is manually locked over the rope. The lever or jaw holds the rope in an open or in a closed manner, your choice. In the open style, like the Stanislawski Avenger or Jim Fletcher's Fletchmatic, the lever does not close tightly against the body of the release and this, at least potentially, could allow it to slip and fire prematurely. Some shooters prefer these because they believe they shoot faster and smoother as they have less distance to travel when you pull or push the trigger. It is debatable. The closed jaw release, like the venerable TruFire Crackshot, actually encircles the string with the jaw and the body of the release. Until you press the trigger, the string is held in place without the option of coming out unexpectedly.

New from Tru-Fire for 2003, the HC Hurricane's twin moving caliper jaws open when you depress the trigger and close when you let up on the trigger. Steve Tentler at Tru-Fire says the Hurricane uses a "free-floating, self-centering steel roller that does not slide over the jaws, but rolls along the inside of the jaws." Jaws are heat-treated and triggers are Teflon coated.

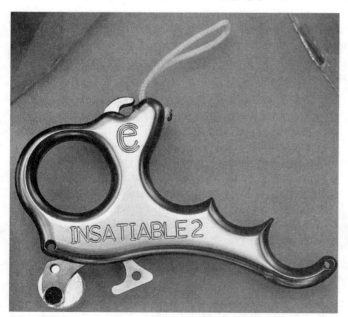

The Carter Insatiable 2 release includes a hole for the archer's index finger and fits all four fingers on medium to large hands. It is a reverse closed jaw and can be used with a rope or on a D-loop.

With distinctive styling, Greg Summers has managed to give his precision-designed T.R.U. Ball releases a high archery profile with a sure grip in the hand and on the wrist.

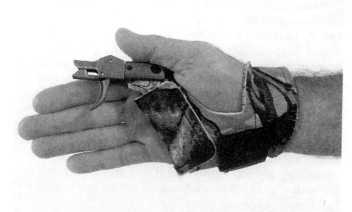

The Tru-Fire Badger is an excellent example of a single jaw caliper release. More than one inch of length adjustment is designed into the connector between the Teflon-coated trigger and the strap buckle. This accommodates different hand sizes or gloves.

Geary Garvison's Free Flight release aid styling is nearly a quarter century old, but its design was sufficiently forward-looking at the time of its development that, according to Geary, it is still being copied! "Free Flight releases are easy for finger shooters to use because the mechanism is held right on the hand. The draw length and anchor point come up naturally to the side of your face."

Rope releases typically can not be left on the string – they will simply fall off or fall down the string and hang against your lower cam – and they take some practice to get used to as they are a three step operation: put the release string around the bowstring, use your thumb to move the release string around the jaw and then lock the jaw. Whew! For people who do use rope releases, they offer most of the advantages of other styles, will never damage a string and can be shot very successfully without a D-loop because the rope loops compress to such a small dimension when you have drawn the bow that they almost can not put any torque on your arrow.

In some form or fashion, every modern release uses jaws or some version of a rotating sear pin. On a rope release, the jaw (singular) actually holds the release rope. On the other styles, the jaws hold the bowstring or your D-loop directly.

Perhaps the newest style is seen in the Freeflight Caliper Release from Geary Garvison at Winn Archery. The distinctive Freeflight has a single, rounded edge stainless steel movable jaw and is held deep in the hand, almost against the base of the thumb. This is unusual for release styles today that typically make you reach for the trigger. Geary says this deep hold gives you more control and the single jaw caliper keeps the serving "on plane." What's more, his releases are designed to give you a natural, comfortable draw because the strap is more of a glove than just a simple wrist strap. "It feels like you are drawing about 20

percent less weight this way," he says. "The strap distributes the pull around the grip, hand and wrist, not just the wrist. It's just gotta feel better this way!"

Geary credits Bill Scott, founder of Scott's Archery, with building the first caliper release. Today, the Scott Shark has a dual moving jaw design on a fully adjustable, aluminum pivoting head. The dual, heat-treated steel jaws completely encircle your bowstring. This style dual caliper is perfect for a D-loop because if the calipers are attached directly to the string, they can quickly abrade the serving and put pressure on the nock at the base or control end of your arrow. The beauty of the caliper release, whether it is a single or double jaw design, is that it holds your string-loop immediately behind the base of your arrow and whereas, technically, the bowstring does slide through

The Tru-Fire Badger is an excellent example of a single jaw caliper release. More than one inch of length adjustment is designed into the connector between the Teflon-coated trigger and the strap buckle. This accommodates different hand sizes or gloves.

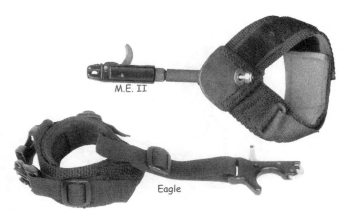

The Raptor line of release aids from Copper John includes the Eagle ($60 retail), which offers a natural resting place for the index finger and is triggered by the middle finger. The design of the M.E. II hunting release ($55 retail) was taken from the Stanislawski release line, which Copper John purchased two years ago.

Jerry Carter's black, open jaw Cheap Shot release comes with a sturdy black wrist strap that hunters will like. Trigger tension is adjustable and a thumb safety is built-in. This open jaw release shoots either with a D-loop attached to the string or using the rope that is included with a purchase.

your release jaws when you trigger the release, there is no sliding with a caliper. Bam! The jaw or jaws open and the string goes forward.

The b forwardzall bearing style release saw its height of popularity in the early to mid 1990s. A ball bearing release draws the bowstring or D-loop back between the rounded surfaces of two, upper and lower, ball bearings. This design provides a crisp release of the bowstring because there was so little surface area holding it. Unfortunately, the type release tends to damage the serving because the small ball bearings crush or separate the synthetic strands of the serving. With a D-loop however, there is no reason a ball bearing release cannot be entirely satisfactory.

TruFire makes a finely machined ball bearing mounted, swiveling release head. They mount it on a variety of releases in a SplitFire group: the finger-drawn Three Finger model, the full hand grip of the Custom and an economical hunting model called the Wrist Release. TruFire's Steve Tentler says they now chamfer the ball bearings in an octagonal manner to present a flat surface to the bowstring. This eliminates the pinching and string crushing from the round surfaces. Steve says that when archers switch from finger shooting to release shooting, they often like something to hold in their hand that replaces the bowstring and that is one reason TruFire has kept the ball bearing releases in its line.

RELEASES FOR HUNTING AND COMPETITION

Many archers believe that for hunting a release aid is a necessary evil. It is an unnatural gadget, some doggone thing you have to worry about working perfectly at the "moment of truth." Still, a mechanical release will, without a doubt, help you hit what you are aiming at and that may be worth the extra worry.

First, there is not a specific release that is a "hunting release" versus one that is a "target release." Typically, hunters rely on releases attached to a wrist strap while competitors use releases that are hand held or finger held. But these are only convenient ways to categorize releases. You could use a double jaw James Greene Gator Jaws release with wrist strap and win Vegas, Atlantic City or the NFAA Indoor Championship … and go out later in the year and hunt mule deer successfully with it. Conversely, you can use a metallic red, reverse close jaw Carter Insatiable 2 rope release to take deer and elk … and then shoot to win the three legs of the IBO Triple Crown.

A second generalization is that hunters tend to set their release with a little "give" in it while competitors like a release with almost a hair trigger. Geary Garvison of Winn believes hunters should have a little play or give in their trigger because they are often wearing gloves or mitts and they are shooting from unusual heights and at odd angles. A little play in their release trigger will help disguise the instant of the shot and should thereby help the archer avoid target panic. Jennie Richardson, a professional 3-D competitor, says she likes her Hicks XR7 because she can set the tension for 100 percent no-travel crispness. She touches the trigger with a hint of sincerity … and BAM! Her arrow is on the way.

Most hunters use a wrist strap release like the Copper John M.E. II rather than an older style concho (like the Fletcher Fletchhunter) or even a finger-held style (like the Carter Hunter). The concho style release, with a single tubular connection to wrap your hand

Competition is a gregarious activity and when stellar performers like Burley Hall become celebrities, they learn to autograph caps and shirts. "At times," Burley laughs, "it is flattering and at times it is a nuisance."

around, was popular in the 1980s. This change has come about because with all of the other things that the modern bowhunter has to worry about, dropping your release from your treestand is about the worst. If this happens, unless you have a backup in your pocket, you might as well just pack it in.

A wrist strap does not prevent all difficulties however. When you have to move a limb out of your bow cables or make some other last minute adjustment

Kentucky's Jennie Richardson is a 5-foot 4-inch professional archer and a leader in the recruitment of young people into archery. She was recently honored with the Muzzy Products 2002 TALL MAN Award presented annually to an individual in archery who "stands tall among their peers."

before you shoot, a forgotten, dangling metal release head and trigger on the end of a nylon strap can bang against your bow with results no more satisfactory than simply dropping it.

The release wrist strap is extremely important primarily because the wrist absorbs all of the pressure associated with drawing your bow. In a finger held or hand held style release like the TruFire Magnum, all of the tension is held by the grip of the fingers. This obviously puts a lot of strain on some of the smallest muscles of the body and with a higher draw weight bow that strain can cause your hand and fingers to shake. Releases held by your fingers or your hand are usually thumb-activated and work best with light draw weights.

With a wrist strap, look for total adjustability and plenty of room for a good fit over both a light cotton tee shirt and a pair of insulated coveralls. Most wrist straps are black and have plastic buckles for total adjustability and the good ones also have a Velcro strip for extra security. The very best wrist straps such as those on the Carter Lok Jaw 2000 are also padded. Look for smaller side buckles to take up the slack of the nylon strips when you tighten the strap. You sure do not want dangling nylon straps to get in the way of the bowstring and maybe send your hand down range following your arrow.

A down side to a wrist strap release is that, with a big game animal approaching unexpectedly, you will have to orient the release in your hand and then attach it – without a significant amount of fumbling – onto the string before you draw. A nervous hunter can have problems here. That may be the greatest benefit of a finger held release for bowhunters. Some finger held releases can actually be snapped on the bowstring or on your D-loop and left there. A nock placed on the string will keep the release from sliding down if you do not have a D-loop and shoot directly off the string.

With any release, it is always possible to trigger it too soon. For a hunter, one instance of this can ruin an entire season. Because most hunters shoot a release triggered by their index finger however, the essential safety feature is mental: keep your "trigger finger" away from or behind the trigger while you draw and then move it forward consciously at the right moment to trigger the shot.

Competition, whether it is 3-D outside in the rain or indoor spot shooting in a dimly lighted hall or even a Buckmaster pop-up round, is a gregarious activity. That is quite unlike bowhunting. During competition, archers analyze their equipment and each other, fiddle with their equipment, discuss the weather and do a lot of standing around. Who needs a release flopping around on their wrist with so much going on? Most

Renowned archery coach, technical writer and equipment designer Bernie Pellerite has successfully treated "target panic" which he says every archer – bowhunter and competitor – experiences because we begin to anticipate the shot sequence even including the impact of the arrow on target. Bernie's new book **Idiot Proof Archery** *is available in hardcover from Robinhood Video Productions (614) 933-0011.*

competitors hang their compact T.R.U. Ball Little Boss Talon or their Stanislawski Maxim releases on their belt quiver or just put it in their pocket as they wait to step up to the shooting stake.

With an estimated 3.5 million releases sold, TruFire is the largest release manufacturer in the world. Steve Tentler says that rope-style releases used to be the only kind of release that competition shooters would use, because the flexible rope that hooks around the end of the bowstring gives them some forgiveness if they fall into bad shooting form. The rope can twist without twisting or torquing the string. These days, he says, with the increasing use of a string loop or a D-loop that lets you draw and release from exactly behind the nock of your arrow, this is not too important. Any style attachment will work fine.

Champion 3-D shooter Jennie Richardson actually started shooting the bow with a Finger Guard (also called a "No Glove") like the one sold by Saunders. The soft, molded waterproof material of the Finger Guard is perfect for use by finger shooters who don't want to use a tab or wear a glove. To install it – it actually comes in two pieces, one for the index finger above (or below if you shoot "three-finger under" style) the arrow and a longer section for the other two

fingers below the arrow – it is necessary to slide it over the bowstring and while that was relatively simple with a recurve which is designed to be relaxed when not in use, it requires a bow press for a compound bow. The Finger Guard is not recommended for today's speed bows or the newer string materials and Saunders specifically says it is for use on "strings up to 16-strand Dacron."

So, while a Finger Guard is just fine for beginners, bowfishermen and recurve shooters, Jennie soon found that she had to step up to a release. Today, she likes (no surprise) a very crisp release. "I don't want any trigger travel," she says. "I shoot a Hicks release that allows me to hold deep in my hand – I'm a little different that way. – and to adjust for tension and travel. The Hicks adjusts for pinkie or thumb triggering, too. I switched from fingers to a release when I began thinking about competing. My groups tightened immediately, from

Jeff Hopkins has been one of the hottest professional 3-D competitors in the US during the past few years. He shows excellent form shooting a Carter Colby 2 Hinged back-tension release off the D-loop on his bowstring. Jeff proudly displays the results of his superior shooting on page 145.

what I thought was an adequate softball-size group on a paper plate at 20 yards to a softball-size group on that plate at 70 yards."

BERNIE AND BACK TENSION RELEASES

Bernie Pellerite is a professional Level IV Master Coach for the NFAA. He has been a pro staff shooter, archery pro shop owner and seminar speaker. Today, he teaches professionally, writes for several archery magazines and produces videos, a hard cover book *Idiot Proof Archery*, and most recently a line of products designed to help shooters hit what they are aiming at. Bernie writes that he cured rock and roll bowhunter Ted Nugent and Pope & Young whitetail hunter Myles Keller of target panic. He describes himself as a "Type A" personality and says he has the answers. Period.

Bernie and his wife Jan own Robin Hood Video Productions. Bernie and Jan recently began production of two back tension releases and Bernie claims that if you want to win, consistently, you must learn to shoot with a back tension release. Compared to learning to shoot any other style release effectively, the learning

curve for back tension shooting, he warns, is steep, but the results in terms of winning, even at the highest levels of tournament competition, are worth the effort.

The origin of the back tension release, Bernie says, is in our human brain's programming and the sensitivity to control of the various parts (the skin, the muscles and nerves) in our body. Everything we do repetitively we remember and store in our subconscious mind. Perhaps our conscious mind selects the program – blink or draw and release, for instance – but it is the subconscious that tells the muscles how to move and the nerves what to feel. Otherwise, communicating with each of our thousands of muscles and nerves consistently and in a timely manner would make movement virtually impossible.

Different parts of the body have differing sensitivities. As humans, our fingers and our highly evolved opposable thumb are extremely agile and, with thousands of tactile sensory receptors on the tips, are very sensitive. We can typically feel the difference between holding one and two sheets of paper between our fingers and thumb, Bernie argues, and that is only a difference of a couple thousandths of an inch.

Outdoor FITA compound target champion Roger Hoyle using a thumb-triggered release shows pinpoint accuracy over a range of distances out to 90 meters.

Obviously, they can sense when the trigger on a release moves and then send the message to the brain: "Getting ready to go off! Watch out!" We anticipate and flinch, losing our sight picture. When you lose the sight picture, you lose control over the shot. Your back muscles perform gross motor functions only and are not equipped for such sensitivity.

Practicing in the back yard, we make a shot successfully time after time because there is no pressure. There may be a trophy 3-D animal staked out on the lawn, but when our target really has hair and

While becoming a better hunter is a matter involving practice, luck, opportunity and perhaps some natural abilities as well as your equipment, you can immediately become a better shot by using a release, a peep sight and a quality stabilizer. Arrowhead Archery's Bill McIver with a trophy buck from the lower Alabama Ben Pearson hunting camp.

flesh and blood or when there is money on the line, our heart pounds and our hands shake and we consciously think about what we are doing. Therein lies the problem.

If we think about our shot consciously, we anticipate it; judge our technique as we are drawing. We participate in the aiming and all the other infinite details and then we try to adjust or correct everything that does not seem perfect. We try to fix it. But perfection is a random occurrence and so in the normal course of events we freeze, we choke, we pluck the string and punch our release. We execute the shot in a manner we would never do in the back yard. The Number 4 hitter in the line-up strikes out. The 7-foot center misses crucial free throws. It is called *target panic* and every archer, whether you are a bowhunter or competitor or both, is subject to it.

Bernie's philosophy is that the archer needs to put the sight in the center of the target and keep it there. Let your active or conscious mind, what Buddhist Tibetans call *rikpa*, focus on aiming and let your subconscious mind – this is *sem*, or the stream of mental chatter – take care of the shot sequence. A back tension release is designed to perfectly fit this philosophy.

Earlier back tension models were called "mouth busters" because unless they were used almost perfectly, they released in mid draw as you were beginning to execute a shot sequence. According to Bernie, bloody noses on shooting line in the '80s were primarily due to people hitting themselves in the face with their hand when their older style back tension release went of unexpectedly.

The back tension release is designed to allow you to shoot an unanticipated shot. You do not punch a trigger with a thumb or forefinger, or even pull a lever with a pinkie. Typical wisdom says that you wrap the release rope around the bowstring, hook the rope under the open, floating jaw and then hope that you can pull straight back to position. Pausing there to aim, you pull through the shot, bringing your back muscles together. This rotates your hand just enough to allow the rope to slide off the jaw and your shot explodes, sending your arrow down range.

Bernie Pellerite says this is a gross exaggeration of the facts, but it is true that with a back tension release like Mel Stanislawski's Original Stan head on a Luxor body (now produced by Copper John) you will shoot best if you learn or develop a subconscious mental program for perfect shooting form. (That of course is not something many of us can or will do, but it is comforting to know that we can learn it from a staff of competent and NFAA certified archery coaches, a number of whom were interviewed for and are quoted in this book.)

Not many people shoot back tension releases and apparently, even fewer shoot them with continued success. They are hard to learn and it means giving up control of a critical aspect of archery, releasing the arrow. Still, for those who are interested and can persevere in learning back tension shooting, there are a number of fine releases available: the Stanislawski Releases, of course (Mel Stanislawski is commonly thought of as the father of the back tension release.), Jerry Carter's slim-line Atension (Hinge or Spike) and Colby 2 (Hinge or Spike) and Bernie Pellerite's Missing Link and ergonomically unusual E-Z Back.

Both Bernie and Stanislawski offer a Half Moon (and Full Moon for practice only, it will not "go off") as release accessories. These small disks control the movement of the independent head and are pinned between the release head and body. As the release rotates in response to increasing back tension, the clicker sounds with an audible but very quiet "click" just as it is ready to go off.

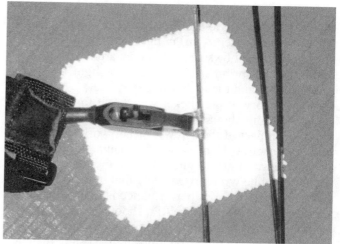

A D-loop or string-loop on a string is strictly for use with a release. It allows you to draw without having the jaws or ball bearings around the string thus eliminating a potential source of string torque. Using a D-loop may allow you to shorten your draw length.

THE CLICKER

The clicker was designed to combat the archer's number one shooting enemy, target panic. Target panic is the inability to put your pin on a target and execute a shot properly. You just can't do it.

A release aid, which gives you the classic unanticipated release, is one method of working to overcome target panic. Working with a Vibracheck SafeDraw or Bernie Pellerite's Laz-Air, a device that attaches to your bow riser and allows you to practice drawing and releasing without shooting an arrow is another.

Before the SafeDraw or Laz-Air were invented or release aids became as sophisticated as they now are competition recurve shooters and many bowhunters typically relied on a clicker. Some still do. The competition clicker was a springy metal strip that attached to the bow riser above and forward of the rest. The loose end slid over your arrow. When you drew, the metal clicker slid audibly along the aluminum arrow until you reached full draw. When you were ready to shoot, you began using back tension to pull the string another 1/8 inch or so at which point the arrow pulled back out from under the clicker. Hearing the click, the archer would instantly release the arrow.

This was a fine gadget for finger shooters, recurve shooters and competitors. It did not work for bowhunting because the clicker interfered with the broadhead and because the noise of metal scraping on metal, while slight, was out of place in the field and was discernible to game animals.

Clickety Klick made a separate style of clicker for hunting archers. It worked with any style compound, recurve or even longbows. A self-adhesive pad and chain (the same style used for light chains) attached to the upper bow riser. A string ran from the middle of the chain to the bowstring. When an archer reached full draw, the spring steel lever gave a slight, but audible snap and the archer released.

The theory of the clicker was that it forced the archer to think about his form rather than about the flight or impact of the arrow. Former world-class archery coach Al Henderson of Phoenix, Arizona now deceased, was a great believer in the mental aspect of archery and he wrote extensively that how you think, how you imagine your performance is how you will eventually shoot and score. If a shooter practiced conscientiously with more attention to how he shot rather than where the arrow impacted, Al said, then at the "moment of truth" the arrow would naturally find its way to the target. Very Zen, but Al coached Olympic medallists and bowhunters. His methods, just like the proper use of a clicker, worked.

THE STRING LOOP (D-LOOP)

When the string loop was invented, many archers slapped themselves in the forehead wondering, "Why didn't I think of that?"

The string loop is a simple and highly effective addition to your bowstring specifically for shooting with a release. The string loop gets the triggering jaws or balls or bar or string of your release off the bowstring and thereby eliminates a potential source of torque. It also eliminates the string wear some releases cause and allows you to release from directly behind the arrow. Over the course of a season or even of a series of shots, a string loop unquestionably results in better arrow flight and more precise arrow impact.

There are two types of string loop, rope and metal. Once you serve in your peep and set your sights, the very next thing a release shooter should do is attach a string loop. Of course, you can cut and tie on your own loop, simply making a knot and adding a drop of glue or melting it tight (Watch out for a flame around your bowstring!) above and below your nocking point to put your release directly behind your arrow and maintain positive peep alignment.

Metal loops like the Ultra Nok or the T.R.U. Nok attach to your string with two tiny plates and screws. These work well unless you are not particularly handy

with very small screws and washers in which case you should have your pro shop install it. Before you install a metal loop however, check to be sure your arrow nock will slide easily between the loop arms. The fit between some loops and arrow nocks can be extremely tight forcing you to sand down the sides of the plastic nock. And remember that you will lose a couple feet per second arrow speed when you attach a rigid metal nock to your bowstring.

The T.R.U. Speed Loop is a two-part loop. It has a metal nock set that clips on the bowstring like a wing folding up. The arrow nock fits into the center and is held securely. Around the metal clip is a conventional rope speed loop. The Speed Loop is designed to eliminate nock pinch at full draw, an irritating aspect of extreme string angles on short axle-to-axle speed bows that often measure no more than 32 inches long.

An option for release shooters who, for some reason, prefer not to shoot with a string loop or D-Loop are small rubber buttons or cushions from NEET or TruFire that can be placed on the string above and below your arrow's nock. Your release butts up against the bottom cushion rather than against your arrow nock and this keeps pinching and any possible interference with arrow flight to a minimum. (A word of warning about sliding these small rubber buttons on your bowstring. You need a bow press because your string must be removed and that should be daunting enough to choose a D-Loop or at least have your pro shop perform this operation.)

* Robert "Bob" or "Jake" Jacobsen is the owner of Jake's Archery Distributors in Orem, Utah. He says he did indeed win the Las Vegas pro division championships in 1974 shooting a Carroll Archery recurve and a PSE rope spike release. Bob was the last man to win the men's professional division with a recurve.

"I remember the releases we used before the rope spike came along," Bob says. "Wayne Norton at Carroll made several styles of all-plastic releases that simply held the string on a molded ledge. I think a couple of them were called the Score and the Hard Ledge. They worked great, but if they ever came off the string as you were drawing your bow, you could sure smack yourself in the face!"

SIGHT THIS!

Fred Bear's bow did not look like anything special. It was a nice take-down recurve, but in my heart, I knew it was not the bow that scored so many victories on the competition venues of the 1930s and 1940s and later brought home a parade of big game trophies from world-class bowhunts. It was not the bow that responded to every hunting challenge; it was the man behind the bow and the heart in the man. Fred had a lot of heart.

Fred was a snap shooter. He looked at a target, judged the distance mentally, drew and let fly with an arrow. It's one thing to do this with a recurve and quite another thing with a compound, but by the time compounds became popular, Fred was more than 70 years old. Pretty late in life to make a switch to new technology.

By his 70s, Fred had already survived quite a few battles in archery. One of them cost him … and still costs us … money, but Fred thought the end result was well worth it. He fought for archery equipment to be included in the Federal Excise Tax on sporting goods that automatically adds 11 percent to the cost of your bows and arrows. This tax, the result of a law called the Pittman-Robertson Act, dedicates the collected money specifically to wildlife restoration, hunter education and the development of public shooting ranges. Fred made a lot of enemies on that one.

Fred had already gone through a vicious battle – one involving rumor-mongering and infighting among manufacturers, archery organizations, archery publications and thousands of rank-and-file archers – to have bow sights legitimized for NFAA competition. Before the 1970s, not many people used a sight, but in those days everyone was shooting a recurve or longbow and, while they were just as interested in precision shooting as we are today, there were a whole lot fewer archers and the accessory boom had not yet hit. It would take the development of the compound bow and the extension of the archery game to millions of new hunters – 95 percent wanted to hunt rather than

compete – before mechanical releases, drop-away rests, coincident rangefinders and fiber optic sights were invented.

Fred Bear did not use sights on his take-down recurve although his 50-year employee and co-Archery

Fred Bear was a renowned left-hand snap shooter. He shot his Custom Kodiak take-down recurve without sights. Nevertheless, his 50-year employee and friend Frank Scott recalled that, on days when he needed just a little visual assistance, he occasionally taped a wooden match-stick to the front of his bow riser.

Frank Scott was a 50-year employee of Bear Archery having begun in the 1930s blowing up balloons for Fred Bear. Like Fred, who was his employer, mentor and friend, Frank was a dedicated recurve shooter and shot by instinct rather than with sights.

Hall of Fame member Frank Scott recalled that he would occasionally tape a match stick onto the front of his bow riser … on days when he needed just a little extra help getting the distance right. All I personally know is that Fred did not use a sight or a match taped to his bow the week I hunted with him and his Bear Archery gang at the famous Grousehaven camp near Rose City, Michigan in 1987 and by then, almost every archer used a sight.

The evidence of bow sight use from antiquity is marginal, but if the 1950s and 1960s can be considered antiquity, you can easily trace the introduction and development of sights year by year from old publications and catalogs. One of the earliest bowsights was the Folberth, which appeared in about 1954. It was a simple plastic strip with an adjustable reference spot that glued on the recurve riser. By 1955, archery pioneer Earl Hoyt had developed his Hoyt Line-O-Site and about the same time, the Doan Jiffy

BowSight, anodized red, black, blue or green, became available. These were delicate, fingertip adjustable aperture-style sights. The Hoyt could be taped on the wood riser and the Doan used a screw and a suction cup like the type used today on toy arrows. By 1963, Bear had followed suit with its Scor Mor, which had a hunter option wire with three adjustable plastic balls for pre-estimated distance shooting. These wonderful early sights offered either posts, which were identified for hunting or prism (in several angles) shooting, already recommended for competition.

The early innovation of sights that taped, glued or screwed on the riser was immediately followed by sights built into the wood riser. The high-end Bear Tamerlane cost $125 in 1964, but it was constructed with a vertical nylon cutout in the center of the riser. The arrow rest attached to the bottom of the plastic

World Champion and bowhunter Allen Conner shows excellent shooting form and a complete assemblage of the finest 3-D gear including an extended sight and scope.

plate and for an additional $19.95 the Premier Bowsight could attach to the plate directly above the rest. Fred's catalog boasted that the Premier was the "first bowsight to become an integral part of your bow." It promised that for the first time, "technically perfect arrow flight is now possible." The Premier could be equipped with a variety of magnifying prisms and one of the posts was offered with a pin dipped in fluorescent paint. Fred's Premier Bowsight was developed "for scientifically perfect alignment of string and bow center." Perhaps there is nothing new under the sun!

FORWARD!

Why not shoot with a sight? If the objective of shooting a bow is to hit what you are aiming at, you are more likely to do this with a sight than without one. Many traditionalists shooting recurves and longbows believe in or enjoy handicapping themselves more than shooting the bow already does for distance and accuracy. Except that a traditional archer shooting instinctively tends to practice more and become more proficient with his equipment, it would not be logical or perhaps even ethical to shoot without sights. In target and field competition, archers compete against people shooting with similar gear, but the archer who is hunting is only competing against himself, but still – and perhaps even more so – he needs to place his arrow precisely in the vitals of a game animal to ensure a quick, clean kill.

In a way, instinctive shooting is like shooting a shotgun. The shooter swings into his target, estimating range, wind speed and direction, angle of the shot and the movement of game without pausing to select a specific pin. A good instinctive shot is a thing of beauty, but it takes a great deal of practice, understanding your limitations, patience selecting the shot to take, and real shooting-sense to pull it off.

For most archers, sights make sense. They are a ready reference, a way of steadying us when "buck fever" might otherwise make any good shot impossible. Buck fever is a variety of "target panic" by its common hunting name and it indiscriminately afflicts competitors and bowhunters alike. Target panic is the inability to focus on what you are shooting at, exclude the extraneous, put your pin on target and execute a shot. Troops in combat, drafted grunts and Green Berets, get target panic, too. It is a human response to the mental pressure of the "moment of truth."

Just like instinctive shooting, using sights offers us a routine and when we are under pressure – when we absolutely must score a 10 or higher or lose the meet, for instance – studies show that routine is a good thing.

Sights allow us to check our facts and figures, analyze our shooting form and verify the fact that we can indeed do something right! They increase the chance that we will make good, repeatable shots.

Former individual gold medal Olympic archer Darrell Pace said that when he was shooting well, he was shooting like a machine. He meant that he had a routine and that he followed it, excluding other thoughts and possibilities. Darrell, of course, used sights on his recurve. (It is interesting that for the 80-meter shots Darrell's sight pin completely covered the gold ring!)

As with all archery gear today, there are a myriad of sight styles available and they seem to change every few days, but we are going to categorize them generally as: pin sights, pendulum sights, scopes and hybrids such as fingertip adjustable scopes with pins.

Bowhunting expert Fred Lutger proudly displays a trophy black bear. Fred's sight is a typical style for bowhunters: vertical and horizontal adjustability, machined frame, five pre-set distance pins and a battery-operated sight light.

Here is an excellent sight for a young beginner. The Phoenix from Martin Archery is all-reinforced nylon, but it features micro left-right adjustment and a dovetail attachment.

Excellent quality – durability and precision – and a wide range of prices can be found in any category.

The two dominant factors in choosing a sight for your bow are the task you need it to perform – hunting, field shooting, 3-D or Olympic-style competition – and the depth of your pocketbook. And if all this choosing and studying becomes too intense, you can always tape a matchstick to the front of your bow and if you hit what you are aiming at, you might start a trend!

PIN SIGHTS

In the old days you might have glued, taped or even screwed* a sight onto the face or back of your recurve bow's wood riser, but today, sights universally mount on your bow above and on the opposite side of the riser from the arrow shelf. This applies to all commercially made compound and recurve bows. Twin holes are drilled and tapped into aluminum and magnesium risers to accept your accessories and wood risers come with threaded brass inserts. The sight is commonly stacked, using extra-long screws, between the riser and your quiver, which mounts using the same two holes.

Pin sights come in every shape and size imaginable. Except for innovations such as the advent of fiber optic technology the basic pin sight is old technology, now. They are popular because they are cheap, easy to use and relatively effective. You can pay as much or as little for a pin sight as you want and

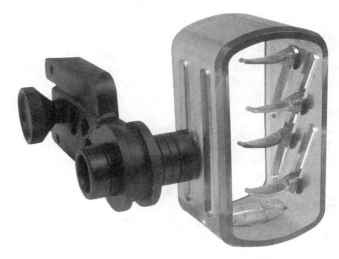

The Martin Firestar comes with two mounting styles: a dovetail and a direct or screw-on mount. The clear plastic housing is molded with three diagonal slots for very close sight pin placement. Four independently adjustable fiber optic sight pins and a bubble level are included.

they will all deliver the goods.

Except for the simplest and least expensive variety, a pin sight consists of four basic elements: the pins, the bracket that attaches the sight to the bow riser, the pin housing and the pin guard.

The simplest pin sight typically has one or more double-locking brass pins that slide up and down in vertical slots in a stamped aluminum body that bolts directly to the side of your bow. This body is not adjustable, but it will have one or two vertical slots so you can move your pins up or down for elevation. For windage, the pin is locked on either side of the slot with knurled nuts and lock washers and you move it manually in or out for sighting-in left-to-right.

A sight like this such as the ShurHit from The North American Archery Group is simplicity itself. It is a superior sight for a novice, but it will not be long before the archer finds that making fine tuning adjustments with this sight is a chore. Changing windage or elevation takes both hands and loosens the pin entirely so that it is often difficult to position it in any precise manner after you have made an adjustment. Change the left-right impact spot and you will likely alter your vertical alignment. If you take the sight off your bow when you travel, the pins invariably slip and shooting this style sight with a high energy compound bow causes the nuts to loosen. Sooner or later, you will find the pins far out of alignment. Then, it is time to move up and fortunately with bow sights, the sky is the limit.

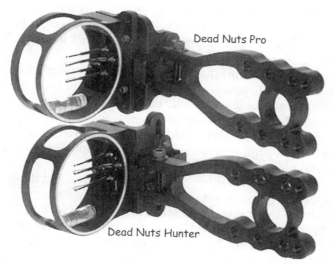

Dead Nuts Pro

Dead Nuts Hunter

The Dead Nuts Pro pin sight from Copper John vividly illustrates the recent trend toward bright, round frames around the fiber optic sight pins and the inclusion of a level, even in a sight designed for hunting and 3-D shooting. The sight pins on the Pro are .019 inches in diameter. The Pro retails for $80 or less.

Archers aiming to win on the hotly contested 3-D circuits need to study the targets and memorize shot-placement zones for the highest scores. A set of reference cards to clip on your belt as you shoot the tour will help. You need to practice distance estimation every day and invest in a bow sight that will give you the best chance of placing an arrow consistently in the 12-ring.

In Timberline's 4.6-ounce Power-Glo X-Treme, extensions of the three .040-inch fiber optic sight pins are encased in non-glare polycarbonate for an additional 3 inches of exposed fiber to gather light. (This sight is shown from the front.)

The immediate upgrade from an inexpensive Cobra double slot sight bracket and a wire sight guard is a pin sight that features a bracket with dovetail windage and elevation adjustment such as the Cobra Venom. Adjusting this sight begins with loosening the jaws gripping the dovetails and manually moving the

sight left-to-right or up-and-down. At this level of sophistication, the sight bodies will be machined aluminum and the pin guards will be much sturdier, either vented machined aluminum or a rugged (often called "high impact") plastic. The pins will probably be upgraded also to a single-locking bracket system requiring a small Allen wrench for repositioning.

By this time you will also have learned the value of dipping the tips of your pins in a fluorescent paint. A bright, distinctive pin tip will more easily stand out in the confusion of a shot out of doors and if your pins are color coded for distance, it will make it easier to avoid one common mistake at the moment of truth: "I put the pin square on his chest and missed by a mile. I used the wrong pin."

Because so many men are color blind in the red-blue spectrum, you must experiment with colors that work best for your eyes. It is common to see a set-up

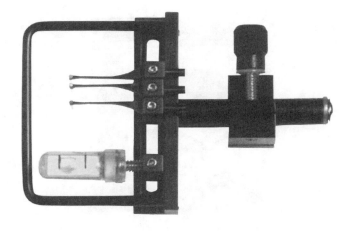

How many pins? Sure-Loc builds a number of high quality pin attachments such as this aluminum frame with .019-inch fiber optic "razor pins" to outfit a sight bar extension for hunting. Use any number of pins from one to six or seven.

From Reinhold Wirth's Mag Sight Products, the Pro-3D features a 6.5-inch aluminum bar, magnesium housing and acrylic scope housing for the single .030 fiber optic pin. At 11.6 ounces Mag Sight says, "We're not the lightest, but we are the toughest." The sight housing can be changed for three-pins for hunters and will accommodate lenses from 2x-10x. The suggested retail price of the base Mag Sight Pro-3D is $200.

like this: a white 20 yard pin, a red 30 yard pin, a yellow or lime green 40 yard pin and perhaps, at the bottom, another white-tipped 50 yard pin.

This kind of sight will give you all the shooting versatility you need for bowhunting whitetail deer, but chances are that the gimmicks and add-ons, the

advertising, the shiny packages under the counter at your archery shop, your buddy's sight and … yes, it is probably true … some real shooting benefits will soon attract you to the next level.

The problem is that the next level gets complicated because the products are so diverse and when you think about shelling out between a hundred and two hundred dollars for an archery accessory, it gets serious, too. The next level invariably involves fiber optic pins or some combination of fiber optic and metal pins.

As we have written previously, it is not a bad thing to decide before you buy just what it is you want your sight to do for you. Fixed pin sights are fine for shooting on the level or from a relatively low treestand, below 20 feet, for example – which means shooting at that height, not the height of the soles of your boots. If you go any higher, the angle of your shot can become a problem (similar to the problem with refraction when you are bowfishing) as you are shooting the longest side of the triangle, not the distance from the base of your tree to the target. Here is the problem you will face:

Your treestand platform is 20 feet off the ground. You are six feet tall. Therefore, you shoot from approximately 25 feet high.

A buck stands broadside next to the 20-yard tape you have measured from the base of your tree.

The Browning Lightning is a durable, lightweight injection molded sight with three plastic fiber optic pins. It provides gross windage and elevation adjustment.

The Timber-Glo Crosshair sight from Timberline Archery Products. The vertical crosshair helps stop bow "cant" or lean. Jim Sherman at Timberline says the crosshairs help you pick a spot because they divide the game animal with the vertical crosshair lined up behind the front legs and the horizontal dissecting the lower third of the body.

Your shot must cover 65 feet or 21-2/3 yards accurately.

Do you compensate for that extra distance by placing your 20-yard pin on the top of the deer's back or below the chest? Or do you shoot a bow that is so fast that one pin effectively covers 15 to 30 yards?

At this point in your archery development, you will invariably wonder how many pins you really need. Simple slotted pin sights allow you to put about as many pins in the sight as you want. Most archers use three or four and typically adjust them for 10 yard distance increments, from 10 to 40 or 50 yards. If you launch a super fast arrow, 250 fps or faster for bowhunting however you may only need one pin to cover your comfortable shooting range, setting it for example for 25 yards and just holding a little high for 30 yards and a little low for 20 yards. When you are studying sights, check just how close the pins can be set. Fast bows need very close pins because the trajectory of the arrow will be flatter than for slow bows. In this case, look for "zero gap" pin spacing. If you are comfortable with a slower bow, something in the AMO rated range of 220 fps to 230 fps; you should have plenty of room with almost any sight to adjust your pins for best shooting performance.

The StarForce X-Treme from HHA Sports is a good example of the upgrade to a double dovetail sight with fiber optic pins. The body and bracket are CNC machined aluminum. The five pins are .030-inch diameter fiber optic pins that are micro-adjustable for windage and set in angled dual tracks for zero gap pin spacing and alignment. The guard is a tough clear Lexan plastic.

The types and styles of fiber optic pins – and although some archer believe they are brightest when you need the brightness least, they do not work in the dark – available on sights is astounding. There are at least a dozen different ways to mount the fiber optics in your sight. The objective of them all is to protect the fragile fiber optic filament and still gather as much light as possible to give you an aiming or reference point even when the light conditions are poor. The cords of fiber optic are fairly delicate, so these days it is not enough to simply offer fiber optics. They must be protected but still have a lot of the fiber showing to collect light.

Some of the most popular of the current model fiber optics are from Trophy Ridge. Their FlatLiner Xtreme is today's top-of-the-line pin sight, even thought much of the sight frame itself is plastic and archers have, as a rule, preferred the rugged, go-anywhere durability of machined aluminum to the lighter weight of plastic. (The term "ultralight" is a sure give away that something is plastic.)

The FlatLiner Xtreme is completely adjustable without the need for tools. You will believe that with all of the advertised features you have purchased a tool designed for work on the international space station rather than simply for hunting:

- The vertical in-line fiber optic sight pins are micro-adjustable with a gear drive and a cam-lock pin holder
- Dual-action vibration dampening system means the unique pin slots are cradled in an absorbent rubber gasket
- Mounts quickly with thumb screws
- Has an incremental elevation and windage adjustment calibration.

Five things are of special note regarding the Trophy Ridge FlatLiner and other superior pin sights of its genre such as the Toxonics Hybrid V. These elements suggest definite new trends in sight development and use.

- First, of course, is the archer's apparent acceptance of the plastic guard and housing that we have already mentioned.
- The second is the included level that has for years been thought of as an accessory for target shooters and an affectation for bowhunters.
- Third is the use of camouflage on the sight body and housing. Sights have "always" been black. Camo is nice, but as we know in our brains if not in our hearts, it is unnecessary here. If you

At Sure-Loc, Steve Gibbs' Lethal Weapon sight series feature .0015-inch windage and elevation adjustments. The Lethal Weapon 1 is available with 3- or 6-inch extension bars and four fiber optic pins with steel mountings.

purchase a sight with camouflaged parts, you are paying more. Just recognize that camo is a vanity expenditure. The deer truly do not care.

• Fourth, the sight pins are "stacked" vertically. Traditionally, all sight pins are horizontal.

• Fifth, the sight body is round, like a target sight. Traditionally, a sight body is rectangular or boxy.

• Finally, there is a movement toward totally independent secondary adjustability. As we have mentioned above, the first couple of sights you buy will probably not be fingertip adjustable. You will have to hold the pin and loosen and tighten it directly. With these new sights, you twist a knob, which turns a screw that moves a pin. It is indirect adjustment.

The cross-hair sight is only a variation on the pin sight. Still, it is easy for gun hunters who are accustomed to looking through scopes to adjust to them as their aiming picture feels "right."

Jim Sherman's Timber-Gloss Crosshair Sight from

This little light is designed to outfit most PSE sights and many others as well. It's blue light highlights the recent trend from red lighting to blue for early morning, evening or cloudy day conditions.

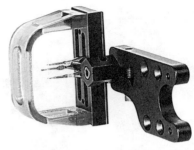

The PSE Infinity Sight features a machined aluminum body and dual-track – for zero-gap pin spacing – sight bar. The guard for the three metal .030 fiber optic pins is clear, high impact plastic. Windage and elevation adjustments can be made independently.

Timberline Archery Products is a fine example of this style. "Crosshair sights have many advantages over pin sights," says Jim. "The vertical crosshair helps to stop bow cant, a bow leaning to one side and not shot in a vertical position. Bow cant can be a serious problem when shooting on hillsides or even from a treestand. Lightweight bows with a quiver attached throw your bow balance off so you tend to twist a little, almost unconsciously, to correct and this throws off your balance completely. Certainly, a bubble level can help and many archers use them successfully, but it is slow to use and even the slightest movement makes a bubble move back and forth. That can be pretty distracting if you pay more attention to the bubble than picking a spot on what you are shooting at. Anyway, shooting with a crosshair, you just line the vertical crosshair up with the animal's legs and your bow is vertical. That makes it fast, easy and accurate to cure bow cant problems."

Crosshairs also help you pick a spot on a big game animal because they divide the animal with the vertical crosshair lined up behind the front legs and with the horizontal dissecting the lower third of the body. According to Jim Sherman, "That makes using a crosshair easier than trying to place a single pin on the side of a deer."

Sherman argues, "Everyone knows that a small aiming point increases accuracy. A typical fiber optic sight has a fiber end that is about .062 inches. In addition, most pin blocks that hold the fiber end are about .080 inches and that covers a lot of a target. You can't hit something if you can't see it. That's why the crosshairs in the Timber-Glo are only .016 inches in width. That's the smallest aiming point in the industry. The light gathering crosshairs are easy to see, even under low light conditions."

The fully machined Tru-Site from TRUGLO with .029-inch ProWrap fiber optic pins is fully micro-adjustable. It is also available with a tritium pin.

These unique sight and accessory vibration dampeners from Global Resource can be applied in places which no other dampener can fit. They will prolong the life of your sight and reduce the chance that accessory items will rattle loose in high speed bows. They are compact and a light-amplifying insert inside the pin guard will enhance the visibility of your pins.

The crosshairs in the machined, double-slot Timber-Glo are supported on both ends so they will not sag and they stay parallel. This also reduces crosshair vibration. The double slots allow all five crosshairs fit within a half inch. Additional crosshairs can be added and are inexpensive to purchase for this superior dovetail sight.

HOW TO ADJUST YOUR SIGHTS

Longtime bowhunter and recreational archer Don Friberg, an Assistant Regional Director for the US Fish & Wildlife Service, says that adjusting your sights is a key to hitting what you are aiming at and the quicker you can make your arrows fly to the bull's eye, the more fun you are going to have.

Don teaches young people to stand close to their target and get a feeling for where their bow shoots before they move out to 20 yards, the distance at which a more experienced archer frequently starts. "I get them to shoot at five yards before we move out to ten yards," he says. "This gives them confidence that they won't miss the bales and that they can hit what they are shooting at. Sometimes, we'll move back a few yards every couple arrows, depending on their attention span."

The basic rule is that your pins follow your shot. If your arrows are hitting to the left of what you are aiming at, move your pins left. If your arrows are

hitting to the right, move your pins to the right. The same rule applies for vertical or elevation adjustments. The pins follow the shot. While it may at first seem counter intuitive – If your arrow hits to the left, shouldn't you move your pin right? – adjusting your sight pins will quickly become second nature.

After they have a good feeling for their bow and their impact point, Don starts novices on their 10-yard or 20-yard pin. "We shoot a group of three before we make adjustments and if they have a peep sight, we get that set up first."

When his archers can hit the bull's eye consistently at 20 yards, Don lets them set up their other pins, working back to 30, 40 and even 50 yards. All pins must be vertically aligned.

WHAT IS A FIBER OPTIC?

A fiber optic sight pin is a little miracle of human luck and ingenuity on the end of your bow and it is, in some small sense, a capsule summary of human history.

Obsidian or silica glass formed during the extreme heat of a volcanic eruption has been made on the earth as long as there have been flowing rivers of lava. When humans began to build stone tools some few hundred thousand years ago, obsidian eventually came to be highly prized because of its sharp, brittle properties. Cutting tools flaked from a chunk of obsidian would hold an edge. It has only been recently in terms of man's tenure on the earth, perhaps around 2,500 years BC, that man imitated nature and made glass himself.

According to Jeff Hecht's *City of Light*, it took another 2,500 years for the Romans to learn to produce glass fibers and another 1,700 before glass fibers could be spun in about the same manner that Rapunzel spun gold.

Over the next three centuries, scientists discovered that light could be channeled through water and glass and by the early 1900s "light guiding" through bent quartz rods became a useful tool to help dentists see inside their patients' mouths.

Researchers also realized that certain materials (streams of water or glass rods then, special spun plastic or extruded glass fibers now) would best transmit light if they were clad in another material that did not transmit light quite as well. Hence, today's technical term, "cladding" which means nothing more

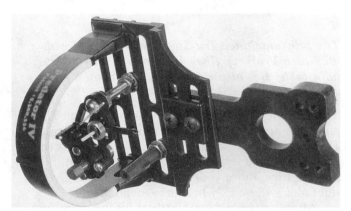

The Predator IV is a pendulum sight with adjustment possibilities for windage, arrow speed and elevation. A cushioned bumper and lighted TRUGLO sight pin are included.

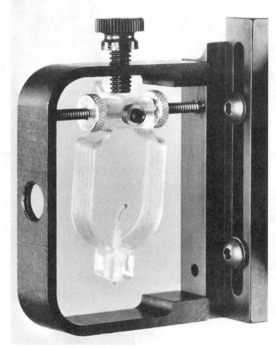

The Pendulum Sight was not invented by Savage Systems, but the company has offered many styles and options from fixed brass pins to fiber optics and even long-life, glow-in-the-dark tritium pins.

than clothed or cloaked as in, "Ye olde lad is clad in the same raiment for poaching the king's deer today as he was yesterday for church."

Anyway, optical fibers are tiny, transparent rods of glass or plastic that are spun or extruded and then stretched, dyed and bundled together. The fibers become very long and very flexible and, given the proper machine design, can be built in almost any diameter imaginable.

Light, whether it is a particle or a beam or a ray or something entirely unique in the universe, travels along a fiber optic rod because the rod has a property called "total internal reflection." That means it transmits light better than air and while the idea is a hard one to wrap a non-scientific mind around, it may be one of those things archers just have to accept on faith. It is sort of like living inside a mirror.

Most of the light in a fiber optic rod is confined inside by the cladding, which has a lower refractive index – meaning it does not transmit or carry the light as readily – and therefore tends to confine it to the rod. A very small percentage of the light is lost as it travels along the fiber optic rod and that makes it glow slightly along its length. The remaining light is what you see on the melted – and hence slightly larger in diameter at the tip than along the length of the rod – tip of your fiber optic pins.

What this all means to archers is that when folks like Paul LoRocco, president of TRUGLO, could not see his sight pins while bowhunting on dark evenings back in the 1980s, he began to look around for some way to bring light to his eyes. Because, as we get older, we all experience some degradation in our optical abilities Paul tried the solutions available then, such as the molded plastic Saunders T-Dots. The T-Dots helped, but for Paul and many others, they were only a small step forward and then he came up with the fiber optic solution.

Today, extruded TRUGLO fibers are patented and the formula for their composition is proprietary. Paul's company has become a major supplier to other archery and shooting sports companies. According to TRUGLO Vice President Lorraine Hellinghausen, the

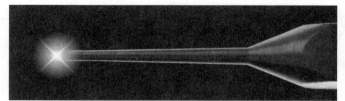

The Tritium/Fiber Optic Sight Pin from TRUGLO. When the light fades or the shadows make sighting too dark for fiber optics, the tritium keeps the brightness level up. Tritium is a radioactive element.

TRUGLO fibers are essentially the same type used in telecommunications and today, fibers used to carry light and bits of electronic information, fibers very similar to the ones you hold on the 12-ring of a 3-D deer, are used in everything from the family car to add-on shotgun sights to the space shuttle.

WHAT SIZE FIBER OPTIC?

If you hunt in the evenings when you get home from work, you may want a sight light and the largest diameter fiber optic possible. On the other hand, a smaller pin covers less of the target.

If the 3-D competition bug bites you, you may want the smallest diameter fiber optic because your ultimate target is a circle on a 3-D target not much larger than a silver dollar.

Of course, the size of the block that holds the fiber optic and the size of the fiber optic itself are different. Manufacturers may advertise .040 inch, .030 inch or .020 inch optic cords, but the ends of these is always melted back so the actual fiber you see is usually about .015 inch larger than the actual fiber. Think about it before you buy and then splurge for the best sight you can afford.

PENDULUM SIGHTS

Pendulum sights are a cooperative effort between manufacturers – to invent and successfully market a device that solves a problem – and hunting archers who have difficulty shooting their bow at downward angles from a treestand. The higher you hunt the less chance of being detected by a deer, but the more difficult to identify the correct aiming point and make a pass-through shot. The idea of the pendulum is that no matter what the distance to your target, assuming it

Savage Systems was one of the first manufacturers to make a commitment to pendulum bow sights for use by archers hunting from treestands. These type sights, which usually cover the range archers shoot, from 10 to 30 yards, are quiet, fully adjustable and may be locked down to use on the ground.

is within your effective shooting range (and that range is about 30 yards), you can sight dead-on the vitals without having to make split second pin and gap decisions. It almost sounds too good to be true.

Pendulum sights work and they are much improved from the pendulums of the 1980s, which were noisy and not the easiest sights to keep in adjustment, either. If you want to purchase a pendulum, wiggle it to check for noise and ask about effective shooting distance. Its operation must be silent and you should be able to shoot out to 30 yards. One of the difficulties pendulum manufacturers have is to provide a free-swinging pendulum, but one that will not jiggle every time your heart beats. Read the instructions and, if you have a chance, try before you buy.

The people at Keller Pendulum Bow Sights have been experimenting with pendulums for years and their black, all-metal Series 2000 exhibits the benefits of a quality pendulum. A slot in the pendulum bracket allows the sight swing to slide up or down for help sighting-in your arrow. This pendulum uses a single sight pin floating on an axis and this helps eliminate any confusion associated with multi-pin sights. There is no guessing distance, treestand height or arrow speed from dead-on zero yards out to 30 yards. The Series 2000 comes with two extra sight pins for ranges beyond 30 yards. A removable, battery-powered LED light can be screwed into a drilled and tapped receiver above the floating pendulum.

The pendulum innovator in recent years has been Savage Systems, which began as an arrow rest manufacturer and fell into the pendulum business when the first commercial Savage design began selling – a lot! Huey Savage's pendulums are cushioned so

The Elite Micro II from Bob Closson's SightMaster is an 8.4 oz. fingertip adjustable bow sight. The sight includes a bubble level and a seven-position scope plate that makes this sight superbly adjustable. You might miss, but with a fingertip adjustable single-pin sight, you will not miss because of pin confusion.

The Savage QC Ranger is a fingertip adjustable sight that is keyed to bow speed.

that even if you move your bow quickly, the floating sight bracket will not make any noise. His up-pin Feather Weight Pendulum offers a variety of pin options, too: a tritium pin, a fiber optic pin, a "dually" or twin fiber optic for extra distance shooting, a FiberGlo pin and a tritium powered fiber optic called the Night Hawk.

Huey, who passed away suddenly in 2003, said tritium is a low radiation gas that, for archery purposes, is contained into a sealed capsule requiring no regeneration. "It provides more than five years of illumination," he said, "and can be used in a stand-alone, ball tip up-pin or to provide illuminating power to a fiber optic aiming point in low light conditions." Illumination is warranted for ten years and that is probably far more than you will ever use.

The interesting FiberGlo pin is designed to provide aiming for up to two hours on a very dark day when the sealed power source is fully charged. The FiberGlo pin is rechargeable in minutes with ambient or UV light.

Whatever type of sight pin you use, Huey said, you just sight-in your Savage pendulum on the ground at 20 yards and you are set to shoot accurately from almost directly beneath your tree to 30 yards. Faster bows will get further distance while slower bows may get less. Pendulum sights like the Feather Weight can be outfitted with a standard bracket with a set of ground pins for "off-season" shooting.

TRUGLO says it is the only archery company licensed by the Nuclear Regulatory Agency to handle tritium, a radioactive isotope of helium. Tritium comes as a gas that is packaged in a small glass bulb or vial for use as a sight pin or in combination with a fiber optic rod. Because it glows or emits beta particles continuously and will do so through its "half life" of 10-to-12 years, tritium is an independent, but tiny light source that can really power up a fiber optic rod. Lorraine Hellinghausen at TRUGLO says a tritium-powered fiber optic is the ultimate sight pin and, "Yes, it is Pope and Young legal, too."

FINGERTIP-ADJUSTABLE SIGHTS

Everything grows out of pin disorientation … or so it seems. Bob Closson was a truck driver and when he and Sarah moved from California to Montana, she bought him a bow. By 1980, he had fallen in love with archery and at Bob's "moment of truth" he chose the wrong pin and missed badly on a record book bull elk. Every red-blooded American knows what happened next. Bob figured there had to be a better way and went into his workshop to begin tinkering. It took him five years, but in 1985, he patented the sliding, up-and-down motion of a fingertip adjustable bow sight. That is essentially the story of archery in America.

Bob formed SightMaster and sold 1,000 fingertip adjustable bow sights that year. Every one of them was completely manufactured by hand. That 1,000 was all he had. "Bowhunters," Bob says, "went nuts over them."

Today, there are a dozen fine fingertip-adjustable sights available and they are all designed to give hunting archers quick and easy sighting versatility with a single, moveable pin in a round aperture. Typically, they bolt directly onto your bow and, with an offset block, your quiver attaches to your bow on top of them.

Bob Closson's new Elite Micro II is an excellent example of the state of the art fingertip adjustable sight. The Elite Micro II weighs 8.4 ounces. Fully extended, it is 6.38 inches long and 3.5 inches high. It is a smaller, lighter version of the sights Bob has been marketing for more than 15 years and features a fiber optic aiming point and black, non-reflective wire crosshairs behind the fiber optic. Each sight comes with a bubble level on a clear, polycarbonate scope ring. The yardage arm can be locked in place with a brass knob. The scope plate has seven positions for the threaded scope rod and this lets an archer make large

Here is a FITA-style sight with Isogrid frame for recurve shooters only from Sure-Loc. The Quest-X has a 5 1/2-inch sight frame, a 9-inch extension and an 8-32 single up-pin aperture holder.

Copper John is a recent entry into the target sight field. Their innovative, curved frame ANTS windage block unit on their Field & 3D sight eliminates the occasional binding of earlier styles because the fiber optic pin in the scope always points directly at the archer's eye for a clear round dot at any distance. This unit features 3.25 inches of vertical travel and weighs 7 ounces.

initial adjustments before he begins fine-tuning. The frame is machined aluminum and brass offsets are available for mounting a quiver on or above it.

Setting your yardage is relatively easy with the Elite Micro II. Choose one of the seven positions on the scope plate, mark off 20 yards for example and shoot a group of three shots. If there is difficulty with clearance between your arrow and the bottom of the polycarbonate scope, move the scope arm up until there is room. You will need to adjust the hole selection so that your shortest and your longest shots will all clear and will all have sufficient placement on the back of the mounting plate for yardage reference stickers which are provided. If you change arrows, increase your draw weight or significantly alter your broadhead, for example, your yardage reference marks may change, but it easy to peel the old ones off and stick on new ones.

When you see your target, whether it is a pronghorn or a 3-D mountain lion, you must estimate the distance to the point where you want it to meet your arrow. Then, you must know or quickly decide exactly what that distance is and move the sliding brass indicator arm exactly over your pre-determined yardage marker on the back of the sight. When your deer steps onto that spot or when you draw on the 3-D target, you will know exactly what the distance is.

The benefit to an archer in the field is obvious. With a quick adjustment you can gauge precisely where you want to place the arrow. There is only one pin so you can not get confused. "You don't need more than one pin," Bob says, "because with this type sight, the one pin will cover distances from dead-on to 80 yards."

There are some drawbacks to most fingertip adjustable sights. While they may look complicated, Bob says, they are not really hard at all. Nevertheless, at the "moment of truth" you are just as likely to fumble with the yardage adjustment lever as choose the wrong sight. And for a hunter, fiddling with the yardage knob means there is additional movement, albeit very small, that a big game animal can pick up on. Finally, today's high energy bows need a lot of noise and vibration damping to keep from damaging the rod that holds your sight on the bracket. Breakage of this rod was a common event until manufacturers learned to use a thicker and therefore sturdier support rod.

Perhaps the single most curious and potentially fatal flaw with fingertip adjustable sights was pointed out by the man who started it all nearly 20 years ago. Bob Closson says that high-speed bows and curious riser configurations may be the death of the fingertip concept. He has always been proud that there was plenty of vertical adjustability built into his SightMaster sights. Today, a lot of archers look for zero-pin-gap sights for bows shooting 300 feet per second and that means that one pin can just about cover from 10 to 30 yards. Whereas bow sights in the

The "Western Bowhunter" Doug Walker.

'80s may have needed two to three inches of adjustability for yardage markers, the hot bows of today may only need one. "The fingertip adjustable concept may eventually be doomed by our technological advances," Bob concludes.

Whether it is or is not doomed, several companies are offering fingertip adjustable sights. The Electra Slide from Cobra and the HHA Model OL-4100 feature built-in, battery-operated sight lights that brighten the glow of the fiber optic pins inside the 2-inch acrylic aperture. TruGlo has tried to simplify the mechanics and number of parts with their Magnum Ranger Rover, which also features three fiber optic pins.

Most fingertip adjustable sights such as Toxonics' Hybrid 1 or the Bull's Eye Simplex can be outfitted with a magnified scope lens and thereby increase the ability to place your pin – and hence your arrow – perfectly in any lighting situation.

By far the most complex and interesting of the new fingertip adjustable sights is the Savage Quick-Click Ranger. Huey Savage designed the Quick-Click to double as a hand-held chronograph to show you the speed of your arrow. It allows you to shoot from 20 to 70 yards with just a "quick click" and the fingertip adjustable sight lever does not need to be locked down before you shoot. The yardage reference marks are laser engraved so there is no need to place a yardage reference tape on the sight or to mark distances with a pencil. You move the sight manually by lifting the end of a projecting bar with your fingertip, just like with any other sight, but the Quick-Click has an "automatic" distance yard stop so that you can both feel the clicks and hear them – if you listen carefully – which you can preset for one, five and ten yard increments. The unique Quick-Click will accept a Savage pendulum cradle, fixed pins or a round target-style scope. The key to the Quick-Click is the speed indicator knob on the yardage lever arm.

The benefits of this innovative sight are obvious. Once you establish and program in your arrow speed, it is extremely versatile. On the other hand, it may be a little heavy, bulky, complex and expensive for most hunting archers.

TARGET SIGHTS

Not many people who pick up a bow ever need a FITA-style competition sight. Still, they are used at the highest levels of world archery competition, the Olympic games and the professional levels of 3-D shooting where being out of the quarter-sized 12-ring on a target at 38-1/2 yards can cost $10,000. So, this style bow sight is used by perhaps one or two percent of all of the archers in North America.

A target sight, in contrast to a sight for hunting archers, is made of about five parts. There is an adjustable mounting bracket which is smaller than for a modern four pound compound bow because it attaches to the riser of a lightweight, precision machined recurve. The mounting bracket holds an extension bar because competition shooters want the sight as far in front of them as is legal as long as they can still see their sights. Attached vertically to the fore-end of the extension bar is the micro-adjustable sight bracket and mounted on that bracket is the FITA pin sight or a scope or a specifically designed set of pins because yes, some people do use these for hunting.

Al Coons at Copper John says one of their ANTS style target sights was used by Vic Wunderle to win the silver medal at the 2000 Olympics. The farthest distance Olympians shoot today, 90 meters, is with a recurve bow and a finger tab. The sight has to be good – and right on, because at 90 meters the target looks about the size of a half dollar and the bull's eye, 11.4 centimeters in diameter, is only a pinpoint at the range which the archer's sight pin covers.

Copper John target sights are equipped with their specially curved sight bracket that they call their ANTS system, for Always Normal Target Sight. ANTS gives the shooter a sight picture that is totally consistent because it is designed with a curvature to fit the natural curvature of the eye. According to Al, when you adjust a "normal" target sight bracket for distance beyond your base or zero yardage – which may for instance be 20 yards – you begin to see more of the fiber optic pin in the scope rather than the dead-on aiming dot. "Our curved frame ensures that the fiber optic pin in a scope always points directly at an archer's eye," Al says. "Thus, you have a crisp, clear round dot at all shot distances." The curved frame also ensures that the lens is perfectly square to the eye at all times, thereby eliminating distortion caused by tilted optics.

The Copper John target sight weighs a very light seven ounces. If you plan to mount a scope and shoot 3-D or perhaps even hunt, purchase the frame with 3-1/4 inches of vertical travel. If you plan to shoot in Olympic-style competition (FITA is the Federation International de la Tir a l'Arc, the governing body of international target or Olympic competition.), you will want to select the sight frame with 4-1/2 inches of vertical travel because you will need to be absolutely world class proficient at great distances and because the recurve arcs an arrow toward rather than drives an arrow toward its target.

Each of the Copper John models comes with the unique 3rd Axis Leveling System incorporated into the quick disconnecting scope carrier. The system lets the archer remove and later remount the scope without having to re-level each time. Al says this means an archer can set up multiple scopes prior to a tournament to be changed at will during a tournament without worrying about leveling the scope each time.

Doug Walker, "The Western Bowhunter"

Doug Walker, called The Western Bowhunter, is a member of the Bowhunter's Hall of Fame and has hunted and written about hunting with the bow and arrow for half a century. He has shot almost every bow, arrow and sight combination possible. Doug's learning curve began even before he met the legendary Fred Bear.

You've got a bow in your hand, Doug says, so what's next? How do you draw it, aim it, and shoot it? Do you just pull back and concentrate on the target spot, release, and expect the arrow to hit that target? Do you use the above plus a point-of-aiming spot? Or do you just simply put a sight pin on the target and expect to hit it? There are many variables these days and they all matter to your overall success.

With more than 50 years of bowhunting – and he is still at it – and 53 big game trophies in the record books, Doug Walker has tried everything from longbows to the latest, most advanced single-cam compounds. He has shot both fingers and a release and just about every type of sight that has ever come on the market.

Most open-minded bowhunters are "curious creatures," Doug maintains, and most will try anything to increase their chances of hitting what they are shooting at. "After 50 years," he says, "I still haven't found any sure way to hit precisely where you want to every time; you actually have to dig down deep into your gut of knowledge and experience, and then settle on that special method you have developed, and then quite simply stay with that method.

"The problem is that you will have good days and bad days. You will have days when you can drive nails and days when you can't hit an elephant's butt from 20 yards. As soon as you have a bad day, you will want to begin tinkering with your gear and your technique. That is going to get you into deeper trouble."

During his first years of archery, Doug was something of an instinctive shooter, much like Howard Hill, the famous longbow shooter. In those days, he remembers, everybody said, "just concentrate on the spot you want to hit … and you will hit it." Very Zen-like. Most competitors would claim something like, "I look at the target and see nothing else; by concentrating intensively on the target spot, I hit it."

Doug says he wishes he knew then what he knows now. "I learned this method of shooting, but I also learned that it was only good up to about 10 yards! Just like throwing darts, it was eye-to-target-spot and then training your body, arms, shoulder, etc. to correctly coordinate your muscles to get that dart into the spot. Beyond 10 yards however, good shooting boiled down to actually knowing what you were doing, learning some fundamentals – just like today – and this is where I got much better with a bow and you can, too.

"Howard Hill called his method using split vision or an indirect imaginary point-of-aim. He not shot this way himself and wrote many articles explaining how he did it. Howard would say, 'If you know your indirect imaginary point and place the tip of your arrow on it and then shoot high, then by moving that indirect imaginary point lower you would hit true with your second arrow.'

"Howard was a hunter foremost and a tournament archer second. He used his method to win several tournaments and I doubt he ever missed an animal on his second arrow using this method. He didn't miss many shots with his first arrow!

"When I say this about Howard Hill, I may will bring some Howard Hill advocates to ask, 'Hey, how about his shooting dimes and aspirins out of the air?'

"Well, you must remember, all this trick shooting was done at less than 20 feet. Howard practiced a true form of instinctive shooting. It takes a rhythmic coordinating of the eye, mind and body that only Howard and a few others have ever developed to such a high pitch of ability in their lifetimes. All the trick shooting that he did, and that he did so well, was at a very close range."

Doug Walker developed his own point-of-aim or split vision or imaginary point shooting system in the 1950's. He took "his share of game and won a few tournaments," Doug says, but in the mid-1950's, he read about the early American bowhunter and film maker Art Young, the man whose film Alaskan Adventures also inspired Fred Bear.

"If you ever noticed his pictures at full draw, Art Young drew his bow with three fingers under the arrow. I started experimenting with this method and became extremely accurate, especially with my high anchor. Nocked at full draw, the arrow would be just 2 inches or so under my eye, giving me an imaginary point-on point-of-aim, say at 40 yards. That meant that for a target at 40 yards, I would put the tip of the broadhead directly on the spot I wanted to hit.

"In those days, I canted my bow and I soon discovered that by setting up a wood die to nock and point my arrow, that I could plumb my two bladed broadheads or the top blade of a three-bladed broadhead so that it would resemble the front sight of a rifle. In other words, the top blade would be vertical, even though my bow would be canted. So, using the top tip of that broadhead, I found it was point-on at 15 to 20 yards; halfway down the blade, 30 to 35 yards; and, as I've said, about point-on at 40 yards. With most of your shots at big-game animals 40 yards or less, you can see how such a system could work. It was deadly accurate up to 40 yards. I ended up calling it shot-gunning, as it was just like looking along the top barrel of a shotgun."

In the 1960s, Doug began shooting with fixed sight pins, but he maintained his high, above the corner of the mouth, anchor point. With sights, he sighted in for 20 to 50 yards in 10-yard increments. "I believe in making a yardage decision on first eye contact with an animal," he says, "because I have always been good at judging distances. Once I make a decision, I stick to it, as studies show that your first good impulse is often correct. If I felt it was a little more than say, 40 yards, I would mentally call that a hard 40. If I felt that it was a little less than 40, I would hold slightly higher, but still keep that pin on the animal. If I figured it was a soft 40, then I would hold the pin a little lower, but never take the deciding pin off the target.

"I think a lot of archers using pins think the same way, but if they feel the shot might be over, say, 40 yards, they will hold that pin above the back of the animal and that's where the arrow will go for a miss. That's why I never take the pin off the animal. A lot of people might say, 'Well, that requires a lot of split second thinking,' but I can tell you that, with practice, you can do all that thinking as fast as pulling your bow to full draw.

Doug prefers keeping both eyes open when he draws, concentrating on the part of the target he wants to hit. "As I draw," he says, "I see my sight in what you might call my secondary line of vision. When I see in my secondary line of vision on the spot I intend to hit, I release. With just a little practice, you can do the same, and do it as fast as anyone using any technique. I can testify that after 50 years of bowhunting, it's the most accurate and fastest way of getting an arrow off and on its way to a big-game trophy."

One of the most important tools Doug says he uses setting up a bow for a hunt is a Potawatomi Bow Square. "It is an absolute must that your fistmele (brace height), nocking point and limb tiller do not slip or move out of place, after all the time you spend tuning up your bow and sights and properly marking the bow square accordingly. Don't forget to take that bow square with you. When you're miles from home at a bowhunters' camp, all you'll have to do is slip it out, and in seconds you'll be able to make you're your bow is set up properly.

Doug believes strongly that a bowhunter should use "everything at his disposal, and out of respect for the animal he is hunting, he should do everything in his power to kill that animal as quickly and humanely as possible."

SCOPES
AND
TARGET SIGHTS

As far as archery is concerned, a scope is a sight with a round aperture. It may accept a variety of lens with magnification from 2x to 8x or it may be used without a lens. A scope can have from one to three fiber optic pins or may have a dot or some other aiming point in the center.

Indoors at the highest level of competition, a scope is required for archers who want to get a check or win prizes, but as top pro shooter Evan Baize knows, your sight needs continual checking and maintenance. Carrying no quiver or backpack, a heavier, higher quality porro prism binoculars such as the one hanging from Evan's pocket, will give you a finer image of the target than will a lighter and probably less expensive roof prism.

Not many years ago practically every sight for hunters was rectangular. Sure, Olympic competitors some elite NFAA archers used round sights and, but 99 percent of all shooting with sights took place with pins inside a rectangular bracket: sight frame and pin guard. Well, today there is a general movement toward round apertures by hunters, competitors, and manufacturers. The general idea of course is that when you shoot through a peep sight, you can more readily align your front and rear apertures. This makes it easier for your eyes to focus and to place the pin in the center for a balanced, un-torqued shot.

Clyde Hartsell of Bull's Eye Sights (Archery Promotions) has owned a pro shop and coached his daughter Stephanie to state shooting championships. He believes the human eye "naturally centers on circles easier than any other shape." Subconsciously, it is easier to center a round peep on a round sight aperture. Clyde believes the average hunting archer is between 35 and 40 years old, maybe older, and their eyes have "matured" which means they are flattening and the focal point is changing. In other words, they are not getting any better. These days, a 2x or 4x lens will help these older archers acquire their target faster and this time to settle down into a shot – breathe, draw, aim, release and follow-through.

The adjustable PSE Infinity Sight is sturdy and offers two pin tracks for its fiber optic pins. It is an excellent sight for hunting or club shoots. Note the squarish design of the bracket and pin guard.

"With a square sight," Clyde says, "the tendency is for the eye to float or wander and that is terrible for an archer."

There are two schools of thought about scope apertures, which have a secondary function as a pin guard. One point of view claims you want a clear aperture to let as much light into the glowing fiber optic strands as possible. The more the better. You will find these clear apertures on the Sniper from Pro Hunter or the three-pin Ace Saturn from Archer's Choice. But you find the opposite viewpoint expressed on the black housing for lenses on the Bull's Eye Simplex Hunter and the camo painted aperture on the Trophy Ridge Flatliner. A dark aperture suggests that the pin guard has a responsibility to keep out some of the ambient light (as well as rain) because too much light causes glare on a lens and actually makes it more difficult to see your pins.

Carbon Impact makes scopes with camera-style sun shields on the front end in black and silver for 3-D and target shooting. The machined aluminum housing for the 3-D version is larger than the target version, 1.75 inches to 1.375 inches. These fine housings are developed with screw-in lens retainers for use with Feather Vision lenses from zero power (non-magnifying, but center-drilled for an optical fiber aiming point) to 8x. The center-drilled lens can be ordered with three sizes of optical fibers: .019, .029 and .039, or for an up-pin kit.

The standard aiming point in a scope is a fiber optic pin. The usual configuration is a single pin called an "up-pin" which rises vertically from the aperture. A second style is a three-pin scope with additional pins from the off-bow side and dropping down from the top.

It is common to see scopes with bubble levels and battery-powered sight lights. These small sight lights are screwed into pre-drilled locations and, in the past, have typically given off a red light, which has a longer wave length and is therefore harder for a game animal to notice. Today, sight manufacturers are offering blue lights because archers have discovered that the shorter wavelength blue glow is more intense and causes a different optical effect on your optical fibers. Big game animals will probably not notice whether it is blue or red, because unless it is pitch dark – in which case you

TRUGLO has taken current trends on standard sight brackets to another level with the Glo-Brite 3-Pin Sight using very long fiber optic strands to wrap around the round pin guard.

The new TRUGLO Hy-Site shows an intermediate step between the design of the composite pin guard from squarish to circular. This is a rugged three-pin sight that offers zero pin gap on a composite, glass-filled nylon frame for lightweight on a machined aluminum mounting bracket.

are hunting illegally – they will not be able to detect it.

THE SCOPE LENS

Aside from the obvious shape, the lens is the heart of the round scope idea. There are three areas you need to be knowledgeable about before you decide to put a lens in your scope – and because scopes come in numerous diameters, not all lenses will fit all scopes, so be sure to ask before you buy:

- Do you want a plastic (called polycarbonate) or an optical quality glass lens
- What magnification, if any, do you prefer and how does that relate to the objective standard of "diopters?" (It varies because not all manufacturers adhere to an accepted standard.)
- What size scope aperture do you need and what kind of aiming point is best for your shooting interests.

You measure lenses by their power in diopters, by their diameter and by the type of material they are ground from, but their "index of refraction" is also a key element to understanding their quality and capabilities. The key words are:

- "Diopter" which is the "ability to magnify at a certain rate" (the basis of establishing a lens or scope "power").
- "Refractive Index" (RI) which compares the speed of light through some transparent medium such as a lens versus the speed of light through air. Generally, the higher the RI the thinner the lens and the better the quality of light transmission because there is less material to slow up the beam or ray of light.
- "Power" is the understood magnification versus the so-called "naked eye" and the measure is pegged to diopters. Customarily, a two-power or 2x lens would be understood to give you twice the magnification as your unaided eyes, presumably with 20-20 vision. Because the industry has struggled however to develop and adopt a standard that archery scope lens manufacturers will adhere to, the term "power" is not an absolute. It actually varies from one manufacturer to another. Archers who also shoot firearms with scopes understand and expect that a calibrated 4x Bushnell scope will give the same magnification as a calibrated 4x Burris. This is not yet the case in archery.

Feather Visions' Vice President Chuck Cooley is

The Martin Slick Sight illustrates the move to round, clear apertures for archers, whether they are hunters or competitors. It is easy to move and sets up quickly. A single fiber optic aiming dot is suspended in a 1 $\frac{1}{2}$-inch frame in clear crosshairs.

both an outstanding archer – he has twice won the NFAA Outdoor shoot at Redding, California in the Men's Open C Class and is planning to "turn pro" – and an optician who is also, he says, on pace to become a certified "Master Optician."

According to Chuck, Feather Visions manufactures about one-third of all the scope lenses used in archery. Chuck grinds and polishes lenses from four materials – polycarbonate, optical plastic, composites and crown or optical quality glass – but optical plastic is fast becoming the standard. "We get them directly from the factory and they look like a hockey puck," he says, "only they're clear, not black."

Although polycarbonate has been around since the 1950s, its use in high quality lenses is relatively recent. Polycarbonate has a 90 percent light transmission rate and a 1.59 index of refraction. The relatively high, 1.59 refractive index means that light bends very little as it passes through the lens (the greater the curve, the lower the RI). Because it takes less polycarbonate material to make a lens for any given prescription, Chuck says, polycarbonate lenses are therefore thinner and lighter than other materials. For an archer who is depending on a polycarbonate lens for a clear picture of his target, this can present a problem around the edges in the early morning or late evening, though. Still, polycarbonate is impact resistant and the industry recommends it for "active people" … and archers are, by and large, active people. Polycarbonate naturally blocks 99 percent of the sun's ultra-violet rays, UVA and UVB.

With a 1.498 refractive index, optical quality plastic or "hard resin" lenses (CR-39 or allyl diglycol carbonate if you are taking notes) are the most common archery lenses sold today. These are the closest to crown glass in quality and consistency of image. Hard resin lenses are lightweight, versatile and, if you wear glasses, chances are those lenses are made from this material now. You will experience little interference or distortion with a lens made from optical quality plastic. This material blocks 93 percent of ultra-violet rays and has a relatively light transmission rating of 92 percent.

The standard lens material against which the others are measured is glass, specifically crown quality or optical quality glass. This is glass made with no imperfections (realistically, with extremely minimal imperfections), no dust and no air bubbles. The RI of crown glass is 1.523 and the light transmission rating is nearly 100 percent. Glass is traditional. It is precise and provides a stable optical image unaffected by most chemicals. When our dads were kids, their "glasses" were really made from glass and this caused two paramount problems when they climbed trees and played sandlot baseball: permanent dents on the side of the nose because their glasses were heavy and screaming parents who would be forced to purchase new glasses every time a dad fell out of a tree, slid into home plate or got punched in the nose.

An ultra-high index plastic is available for specific lenses with refractive indexes as high as 1.9 which means light passes even faster through this lens material than through glass or polycarbonate. High index plastic lenses are expensive however and although they are very thin, are relatively heavy because the plastic used is extremely dense.

Two types of scope lens grinds or shapes are currently used by archers. The standard and still most common is the plano-convex lens; the newest is a composite aspheric lens. The plano-convex lens is a curved lens that gives magnification from its depth or thickness and the curve of the lens. The greater the curvature, the greater the magnification. Unfortunately, the thicker and more curved the lens, the greater the potential distortion of the picture from the edges inward. This is called "chromatic aberration" and it defies the needs of outdoorsmen who primarily want a clear, precise image regardless of the weight.

The durable, lightweight aspheric lens gives a more optically correct image than a plano-convex lens. An aspheric lens has the near flatness of glass with the superior optics of a corrected curve. It is the design used today in higher quality telescopes. Computer designed, the aspheric lens is programmed to focus light rays at a single point. Aspheric lenses deflect rays

The Bull's Eye Simplex Hunter fingertip adjustable sight was developed for hunting archers. The 1 3/4-inch diameter aperture is composite and comes with a single fiber optic, but can be fitted with a level, additional pins and magnifying lenses. A beefed-up connecting rod in a special sleeve prevents rod breakage from stress.

striking the outer edge and focus them toward a common image point. The ultimate result is a significantly sharper, higher-contrast and more detailed image that is smooth and precise right out to the margins. A pair of binoculars equipped with high quality aspheric lenses can be designed with thinner and fewer lens elements. This means less overall length, several ounces less weight and improved low light visibility.

Even though the difference is minute, traditional lenses have multiple points of focus – close, but not precise – and that makes the image less than crystal-clear. This means that light hitting the lens farther from the center does not necessarily come back to true focus and this causes blur in the image. The closer to the edge of the field of view you look, the worse it gets. To compensate, traditional optical systems group several lenses, but that makes for a larger, heavier instrument and a loss of light transmission since each of the lenses blocks some of the light available.

With an aspheric lens and a single or much tighter focal point, there is less distortion around the periphery and enlarged objects appear more natural at any power.

Even though archers need weight forward – as in a stabilizer – to balance their shooting form, lighter is better when it comes to scopes because with a high-

Light and strong, Sure-Loc has developed a name for machining precision target sight brackets and frames. The Supreme 400 is micro-adjustable in accurate and repeatable .002-inch increments. Most competitors and many hunters are mounting scopes on this type frame for ultra-accurate shooting. Now, Sure-Loc is building scopes with matched sets of concave and convex precision-ground Swarovski lenses bonded together leaving the outside surfaces flat. These lenses feature anti-reflective coatings and are available, not in power ratings, but in industry objective diopters ratings.

speed bow, the strain or shock on the lens-mounting rod can be extreme. In past years, a considerable amount of breakage or worse, the slight metal fatigue that causes a scope rod to bend unnoticeably out of position throwing your aiming point off just slightly, has been a problem for 3-D competitors and manufacturers alike. High-speed video shows scopes vibrating wildly during and following a shot.

The rod is still the weak point in archery scope systems. Not only is the rod subject to bending and breakage, but also unless it is tightened almost to the breaking point, the scope is prone to twist or rotate on the rod, a rather obvious problem.

So, what kind of scope lens should an archer choose? Chuck Cooley says it depends on the game: 20-yard dots, 3-D, field or hunting. Most 20-yard shooters – and this takes place primarily indoors – prefer a general purpose, low-magnification scope. Because of the close distance and the poor quality of indoor lighting, something in the 2x to 3x works well. When these archers step up to a higher magnification scope (Feather Visions makes lenses up to 10x.), they can watch their aiming point wobble – some shooters are astounded to watch this because they see the natural wobble magnified for the first time ever – and this can be a cause of target panic. A 4x magnification (.50 diopter) is common among 3-D and field shooters who often must concentrate on targets at 40 to 45 yards and even longer on some venues.

Feather Visions' Chuck Cooley believes many hunters can shoot well with a round scope out in front of their bow, but whether this is really better than a square or rectangular sight frame is a different matter. He doubts round is any better than rectangular. The theory is that someone sighting with his or her round eye through a round peep will … just naturally, perhaps by magic … adapt better to a round sight frame, one they can frame into the peep. But what happens when the sight pin they select is not in the center? Chuck asks. If the sight pin needed for the shot is not in the center of the sight then the whole theory becomes problematic.

Probably, Chuck says, the average hunter will want to avoid magnifying lenses in scopes, whatever their geometric shape. Every lens, even the toughest polycarbonate, can scratch and fog-up and attract dust and streak with water when it rains. Plus, as we have already noted, the armature or lens-mounting rod holding the scope on the bracket is prone to turn if it is bumped and if it is bumped hard enough, it will bend or even break. Any of these difficulties can be a disaster on a bowhunting outing. In addition, a magnified lens is illegal for hunting in some states.

All of the potential difficulties in the above paragraph are especially inherent in a peep "clarifier," a tiny magnifying scope insert in a peep sight. "When the peep lens and the lens in your scope are properly matched, you have a wonderful, clear sight picture," Chuck says, "but if they are not precisely right, this item or archery gear can cause more problems than it solves."

Magnification inside a peep sight is an excellent idea for some sets of eyes that need the extra enlarging and focusing ability. For indoor competitors in air conditioned, controlled environments they can be wonderful except that the clarifier and the peep negatively affect the amount of light reaching your eye which, indoors, is usually not as good as ambient outdoor light anyway.

For hunters or 3-D shooters who are outside in the weather, a clarifier can be more of a problem than it is worth. The tiny, replaceable lens is negatively charged with electrical ions and, just like your glasses, attracts dust. Plus, grit inside the peep means a cleaning job since just trying to blow the dirt out with your breath may work but always adds humidity to the lens and peep and in the long run makes the problem worse. Imagine cleaning your peep and a lens the size of the tip of your little finger in the field, especially when your hands are dirty or you are wearing gloves.

LENS COATINGS AND LENS ACCESSORIES

It is important that you purchase a lens that is coated for maximum protection against any number of problems.

- Anti-fogging coatings prevent your lens from filming over if you accidentally breathe on it or if you are standing on the shooting line one summer evening and the air conditioner goes off.
- An anti-reflective or anti-glare coating will eliminate most surface and interior reflectivity so you can shoot at any angle to the sun.
- Anti-static coatings help keep dust and dirt from adhering to your lens and this obviously promotes a clean sight picture.
- Of course, high scratch resistance is especially nice because you are going to lean down toward that 3-D javelina to retrieve your arrow and your scope is going to try to impale itself on any stick or branch or even the arrow nocks in your competitor's hip quiver.
- A hydrophilic lens coating is useful outside because it causes water to spread evenly over a surface rather than beading-up or forming refractive and reflective droplets. (Optics manufacturer Carl Zeiss refers to its Clear Coat as a "self-assembling, high performance, transparent top coating.")

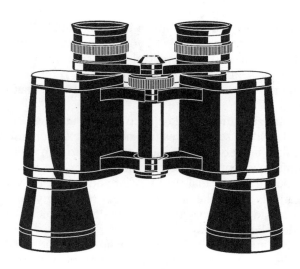

In the porro prism binocular, the objective or front lens, is offset from the eyepiece. Porro prism binoculars provide greater depth perception and generally offer a wider field of view.

In roof prism binoculars, the prisms overlap closely, allowing the objective lenses to line up directly with the eyepiece. The result is a slim, streamlined shape in which the lenses and prisms are in a straight line. Roof prism binoculars are usually lighter and more compact than comparable power porro prism binoculars.

The scientific jargon describing lens coatings goes something like this: TSP Duravane 2000 is a "high-resistance anti-glare hardcoat that optimizes display readability by reducing the coherence of reflected images while maintaining exceptional character resolution." Whew.

Custom tinted scopes are not usual on the 3-D or NFAA circuits, but Feather Visions, Bull's Eye and others can apply them in numerous colors and intensities to eliminate specific wavelengths of light. It is just like trying on shooting glasses of different colors and seeing how amazingly the world changes. Amber, blue and red are common tints for indoor shooting while light gray is typically selected for bright light conditions.

Most serious 3-D competitors have used a Clip-On Blinder such as the metal one offered by Feather Visions or the plastic one from Bull's Eye. A blinder is a solid sheet about the size of a playing card that attaches to the bill of a cap. It helps keep glare down from your non-dominant side and prevents "wandering eye," the tendency for your non-dominant eye to distract your focus on the target.

A variety of lens cleaning solutions and even some disposable sheets are available. Be sure, before you use them, that they are clearly marked indicating that they will not damage or streak the coatings on your lens.

In the lens coating secret jargon manufacturers use in their advertising and brochures, here is the low-down on understanding what it all means:

- Coated lens systems have a single coating layer on at least one lens surface. These are usually

A set of compact, camouflaged, rubber armored Bushnell 12 x 25 roof prism binoculars is fine for most whitetail or bear hunting in the woods of the eastern US and Canada. Fully coated lenses with a 240-foot field of view at 1,000 yards these inexpensive (retail around $25) binoculars weigh 11.3 ounces.

cheap lenses for scopes and sights and if your budget is a heavy consideration, these may be for you. Expect to have some performance objections

At the high end of the Bushnell line and absolutely suitable for outdoor use is their waterproof roof prism Elite 8 x 42 mm, but it retails for between $900 and $1,000. The Elite weighs just less than 2 pounds, but it offers fully multi-coated optics and an upgraded quality of BaK-4 barium crown glass.

in the field, however.

• Fully Coated lens systems have a single coating layer on all glass-to-outside air surfaces. This coating system is found on basic, economy model binoculars and spotting scopes, for instance, and is sufficient for most uses in good weather and stable lighting conditions.

• Multicoated lens systems have multiple, complementary-function coating layers on at least one lens surface: anti-scratch plus anti-glare coatings, for instance. The quality here is good for midlevel binoculars and scopes.

• Fully multicoated lens systems have multiple coating layers on all glass-to-air surfaces. All premium-grade binoculars are fully multicoated. In the long run, optics that are fully multicoated will give you the very enjoyment in all weather and in low light conditions.

The complementary coating inside a pair of binoculars is called phase-coating. High-quality instruments coat the internal prisms, too.

THE BINOCULAR

Given equal magnifications and objective lens sizes, the sharpness, brightness and detail resolution of

the image you see through a binocular depends most on the optical quality of the glass the manufacturer uses. The higher the grade of glass, the more expensive it is, too.

There are two different kinds of glass objects in a binocular: lenses and prisms. The lenses are the round, flat things stacked at the eyepiece and objective ends. The prisms are funny-shaped chunks inside that bounce light around so you can have usable magnification, focal length and a right-side-up image without the instrument being two feet long.

There are two basic types of prisms. Porro prisms are offset and route light at 90-degree angles. Roof prisms are overlapped and route light at more acute angles and are more lightweight and compact. Porro prisms binoculars have the classic stepped offset look. Roof prism binoculars have a slim, sleeker, straight-tube look.

Roof prisms are more sensitive to "stray light" or light bouncing off the interior surfaces and lens housings of the binocular itself. They require phase-correction coatings for premium resolution and contrast. In catalogs, these are called Phase-Coat, P-Coat, PC-3 Coat and similar terms. Also, because roof prisms route light at sharper angles, they require higher-grade glass to equal porro prism performance. Premium roof prisms typically employ barium crown glass. BaK4 is the most common grade.

Porro prisms and less premium roof prisms commonly employ less expensive glass, so roof prism binoculars generally cost more than porro prism binoculars of equal magnification and optical performance.

Similar quality issues apply to lenses. When light passes through any piece of glass, it is dispersed into component colors and must be brought precisely back together for a sharp image. Binocular makers use precisely selected multiple lenses of different glass types with precisely calculated curvatures to create a chromatically corrected (an achromatic) system.

Even achromatic systems will have small residual color aberration if they use "ordinary" glass and that can become fatiguing at magnifications of 10x and stronger after long viewing periods and in extreme light situations. The solution, in premium grade products is to use a more expensive and somewhat heavier extra low dispersion (ELD) or anomalous partial dispersion (APD) glass. Depending on the brand, this glass is also called ED Glass, Fluoride glass, HD, EDX or APO. Such systems are termed "apochromatically color corrected" or "super-achromatic." These are all good keywords to look for when you are shopping for a pair of binoculars in your price range.

Here are three basic classes of binoculars – compact, midsize and full size – that archers may want for the 3-D circuit or for bowhunting. Commonly, archers like to carry compact binoculars because they are small, lightweight and, at the distances archers usually shoot, these units are excellent. Unfortunately, when you go to British Columbia for sheep or North Dakota to hunt high plains mule deer, you will discover that they are woefully inadequate. We will look quickly at two binoculars in each category, a cheap and an expensive set. Basically, more expensive equals a better picture in any conditions, a wider field of view and some bells and whistles.

- Compact Cheap: The Celestron 8x21mm Mini costs about $30. It is 4-1/4 inches long and weighs 5 ounces. The field of view at 1,000 yd. is 367 ft. for this ultra-light roof prism, ruby 15-layer coating binocular.
- Compact Expensive: The Khales 8x32mm Close Focus costs about $510. It is 4-3/4 inches long and weighs 21 ounces. The field of view at 1,000 yd. is 399 ft. for this rubber-coated, armored binocular.
- Mid-Size Cheap: The BSA 10x42mm Cross Country costs about $90. It is 6 in. long and weighs 20 ounces. The field of view at 1,000 yd. is 315 ft. for this roof prism, waterproof, center-focus, right-eye diopters adjust and multicoated model.
- Mid-Size Expensive: The Swarovski EL 10x42mm EL costs about $1,450. It is 6-1/4 inches long and weighs 27-1/2 ounces. The field of view at 1,000 yd. is 330 ft. for this magnesium-alloy frame, three-lens objective with the ability to focus as close as 6-1/2 feet.
- Full-Size Cheap: The Bushnell 12x42mm H2O costs about $100. It is 8-1/4 inches long and weighs 27 ounces. The field of view at 1,000 yd. is 299 ft. for this economical porro prism, nitrogen-purged waterproof binocular with contoured eyecups.
- Full-Size Expensive: The Leica 12x50mm Trinovid costs about $1,245. It is 7-1/4 inches long and weighs 40-1/2 ounces. The field of view at 1,000 yd. is 325 ft. for this roof prism, phase-coated, multicoated lens with sliding eyecups that is waterproof to a depth of 5 meters.

SCOPE TERMINOLOGY

MAGNIFICATION: This is also called "power." Essentially, magnification is the extent to which objects appear larger when they are viewed through optical instruments. Power is commonly expressed by the number (or the numbers) preceding the "x" in optical specifications. Horton's 4x32 crossbow scope, for instance, makes objects appear four times larger, while a 1.5-6x32 variable-power shotgun scope makes objects appear anywhere from one-and-a-half to six times larger. Optical systems accomplish this by changing the angles at which image-forming light rays enter the viewer's eyes. Low-power scopes provide the most effective light management and produce a brighter sight picture and wider field of view than higher power scopes, even in low light conditions.

OBJECTIVE LENS: The front lens is measured in millimeters (mm). It is the number after the "x" in optical specifications. Larger objective lenses collect more light from viewed objects than smaller lenses. Increasing the objective lens diameter, from 32mm to 64mm effectively quadruples your scope's light-collecting ability.

EYE RELIEF: This is the distance in millimeters (or sometimes in inches) between the eyepiece lens and the point where your eye needs to be positioned to see the full field of view. When you are shooting a crossbow, expect recoil and never put your eye directly against the back of the scope.

EXIT PUPIL: This is the small disk of light that can be seen behind the eyepiece from a distance of about 1 foot. Generally, the larger the exit pupil the brighter the image in low-light hunting conditions. You can determine the size of the exit pupil by dividing the objective lens diameter in millimeters by the magnification. So, the Horton 4x32 crossbow scope has an 8mm exit pupil and that is about as good as it gets.

PARALLAX: With telescopic sights, parallax occurs when the image of the target and the image of the reticle are on slightly different focal planes within the scope. When present, parallax causes the target to shift laterally relative to the reticle as the eye is moved from side to side. This can be a mechanical problem with the scope or it can be a problem with eye positioning relative to the eyepiece lens. Some high power scopes have special knobs that allow you to correct for parallax, as refocusing the eyepiece will not do it.

Antireflection Coatings: Antireflection coatings improve light transmission and contrast by reducing image-degrading and light-robbing reflections that occur at each of the 14 or more glass-to-air surfaces that exist in expensive optical instruments such as the expensive Leica spotting scope you will need when you go Dall sheep hunting in Alaska. Coating qualities vary greatly, ranging from single-layer coatings to multiple-layer coatings on some or all surfaces. "Fully Multicoated" is the highest designation.

FIELD OF VIEW: Often abbreviated FOV, this is the maximum width of the area that can be seen through your scope.

DIOPTER ADJUSTMENT: The knob found on most binoculars that allows you to correct for the visual differences between your eyes.

RESOLUTION: The ability of a pair of binoculars to produce separate and distinct images of closely spaced objects. Measured in "seconds of angle."

TWILIGHT FACTOR: This is a mathematical formula for comparing the low-light performance of different scopes or binoculars. Calculate your scope's twilight factor, multiply the diameter of the objective lens by the magnification and extract the square root of the product. Okay, let's try this for the Horton 4x32 crossbow scope. (Diameter of objective lens is 32mm) x (Magnification which is 4) = 128. The square root then would be approximately 11.3 and that (I think.) is the Horton's twilight factor.

The archer who wants to go west for big game in the mountains or on the plains will want to take a spotting scope. A scope will not only help you find the ram hidden in the rocks, but it will help you field judge the trophy potential of a distant pronghorn buck. For competitors and their families and coaches, nothing beats viewing the point of impact at extreme FITA distances through a spotting scope. The Spacemaster Kit includes a camouflaged, rubber-armored 15-45 x 60 mm scope, a backpack carrying case and an adjustable tripod. The retail price is about $300.

THE PEEP SIGHT

Peep sights preceded the compound bow, but with the increased energy presented through a shot and the increased arrow speeds involved in today's hot bows, a peep is absolutely necessary for precision shooting. Experienced riflemen who shoot with "iron sights" rather than optical scopes understand the need for a peep sight, its relationship to the front bar sight and ultimately to hitting what you are aiming at.

A peep is a nothing more than a hole or an aperture. It can be round or square or even oblong. It is a hole in a machined piece of metal or a molded piece of plastic that fits into your bowstring above the nock.

Close-up of the Perfect Circle peep showing the string grooves in the plastic peep, the peep hood, aperture and tubing that attaches to your cables.

When you draw, you pull the string to your anchor point and, if you have everything set up properly, the peep centers its hole in front of your eye, blocking out the area around it. In the exact center of your peep, you want to center the proper distance pin or the correct pin gap. For a right-hand shooter, you draw to your right eye, left-handers to the left eye.

Most shooters serve their peep, which means they tie it in place with string above it and below it to make sure it will not move. Once served, a bowstring on a compound bow is so tense that barring an accident, the peep will remain perfectly in place until you remove it or the string is relaxed. When you remove the string and relaxing a recurve, you may want to exercise some caution to make sure the peep stays in place.

Pearson professional 3-D shooter (Men's Open Pro Division), bowhunter and former archery pro shop manager Jeremy Blackmon of Pensacola, Florida says that quite frankly a peep makes the difference between winning and losing. "I have been shooting a bow for 24 years," Jeremy says. "I never get tired of it and my only trouble with archery is that I don't have time to shoot more." This guy, who placed third for ASA "Rookie of the Year" honors when he first turned pro, is dead serious.

"If you want to be competitive, you have to use a peep," Jeremy says and he uses one for hunting and competition. "The average guy who shoots a five to six inch group at 35 to 40 yards can install a peep sight and cut the size of his groups in half."

Basically, the peep works like the rear sight on a rifle or shotgun. Put it in proper alignment with the front sight and, all things being equal, you will hit what you are shooting at. If the rear is out of alignment, even by millimeters, it can cause a miss of feet or yards, depending on the distance to your target, even if your front sight is right on. You can quickly sketch this out on a piece of graph paper to see the difference an in-line peep or rear string makes. This means that even in a 20-yard indoor club shoot finger shooters can vary their shot several inches to the left or right of the bull's eye if they smile or grimace!

Essentially, a peep sight does two things, says Ken Johnson, manufacturer of the unique Nite Hawk Peep Sight. "A peep serves as a rear anchor and it helps you pick a spot," he says. "In the old days when everyone shot a recurve, archers understood that the anchor point was extremely important. People practiced drawing to a consistent anchor at the corner of their mouth, or with their thumb touching the lobe of their ear or the string touching the tip of their nose, for instance. These days, with fast compounds and release aids, you hear archers talk about a 'floating anchor point' – not coming to a precise rear spot each time they draw – as if that is a good thing. It isn't."

Ken says a peep helps solve left-right shot placement problems that are the result of the famous "floating anchor" because it helps the shooter focus their vision in the center of the hole in the peep. These days the peep is often the most accurate part of an anchor point. "Ninety percent of the time," Ken claims, "a peep sight will improve your accuracy. Guaranteed."

Both hunters and competitors will benefit from a peep because that moment when you just have to make a shot, when you have to execute perfectly, is the most difficult of all. Anyone can stand in the back yard and take a deep breath to relax and shoot a 3-D deer in the

Ben Pearson staff shooter Jeremy Blackmon says that using a peep sight makes all the difference between winning and losing. "If you want to be competitive on the 3-D competition circuits, you have to use a peep."

Release shooters like World Champion Randy Chappell have an easier time with independent peep alignment than finger shooters who typically twist the string and must be conscious of peep alignment. With a release, the string comes back to your anchor perfectly every time.

vitals time after time. It is another thing when the pressure is on and there is hair on your target. Things go wrong: you have to hurry before the deer goes behind the tree and out of your shooting lane or your hand unavoidably shakes in front of the grandstand at the shoot-out. A peep sight will help keep Murphy's Law from becoming a prohibitive factor at your moment of truth.

Jeremy agrees with Ken Johnson's assessment of a peep for hunting and competition. "I use a non-reflective black, machined aluminum Fletcher Tru Peep," he says. "Like most archers, I use a smaller aperture peep for competition – a small or micro hole, about 1/16 inch in diameter – and a larger aperture for hunting – a large or super hole, about ¼ inch in

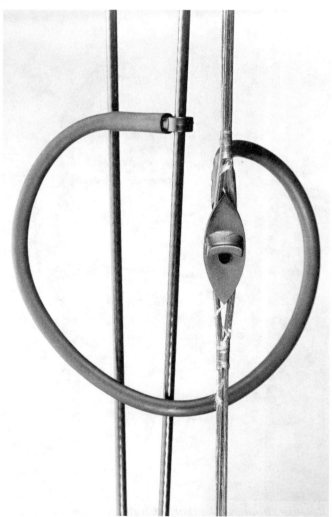

The classic, self-aligning Zero Peep from Fine Line now attaches to the bow's cables, eliminating its original anchor post and the connection to the bow's upper limb. The aperture is hooded and the string grooves are deeper to accept 18-strand strings.

diameter – because you can never tell what the weather will be like. Trophy deer are most often taken when the day is at its dimmest, in the early morning or late evening, so I usually want the larger hole for bowhunting."

A potential difficulty using a peep for hunting is that it will not align when you draw. Release shooters have a much easier time with this than finger shooters who typically twist the string and have to be conscious of peep alignment. With a release, the string comes back to your anchor perfectly every time. When they twist the string, finger shooters run the risk of staring at the side of the peep and then must think, consciously, about twisting back so the string and peep come into alignment. When a trophy deer is moving through your shooting lane, you do not want to have that problem, so a self-aligning peep may be the correct choice of equipment for most finger shooters.

Another difficulty using a peep is string stretch. Synthetic strings may be stronger than steel, but when they are warmed or continually stressed, they will elongate. When this happens your settings can change. It is always a good idea to draw and check peep alignment with your sights before you climb into your treestand. Surprise is less of a problem for competitors because 3-D archers typically shoot a few practice targets before they step up to the first shooting stake.

The Pensacola archery pro feels that the Fletcher peep works especially well with his choice of front sights. His three-pin machined aluminum TRUGLO Eye Sight has a curved guard to keep the fiber optic pins safe in the housing and the curved aperture and curved guard work well in tandem. His secret is that he uses three different diameter pins in the front sight to compensate for the size of a target at a given distance: his 20 yard pin has a .040 inch diameter head, the 30 yard pin a .030 head and the 40 yard pin a .020 head. Jeremy's three-power target scope from Shrewd Precision Products also fits the curved peep aperture thus affording him relatively easy alignment.

THE SELF-ALIGNING PEEP

For years, the only self-aligning peep archers used was a Fine-Line Zero Peep. The peep was molded black plastic and had a tiny hood over the hole to help eliminate glare. It was served directly into the string. A latex tube fit tightly over a post on the rear of the peep; the other end of the tube fit over a post on an adhesive anchor pad that stuck to the inside of your top limb. Over the years, Fine Line has made numerous refinements to the basic Zero Peep. Their Pick-A-Peep, has a slotted receiver so that you can easily switch different size apertures. One optional style simply ties the black latex tube to the cables. This successful peep and its many imitators give you an almost perfect view every time even if you twist the string slightly.

Several other manufacturers are marketing self-aligning peeps with distinctive features. The Ace Clearview is angled through the string so that at full draw you look straight through the opening. The

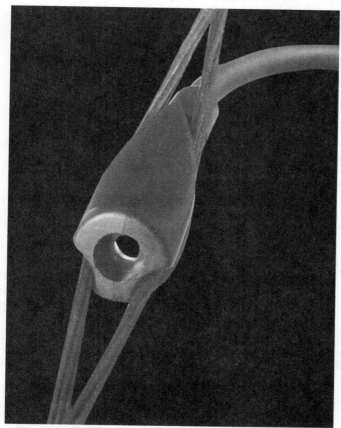

The self-aligning Centra Peep lets you line up your peep with the curve of your pin guard and the rubber tubing automatically positions the peep. The aperture is 1/8-inch in diameter.

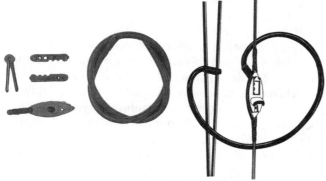

Elements of the Pick-a-Peep, a non-rotating peep sight that attaches easily by a latex tube to your bow cables. Two slide inserts give seven aperture sizes.

Golden Key Total View Line-O-Peep does not need to be served into the string, because tightening a small screw tightens a self-locking clip into place. The hole for this peep is drilled to ¼ inch diameter and the surgical tubing locks onto the cable. Although it is not in their catalog, Savage Systems makes a unique fiber optic self-aligning string sight. Using this sighting aid, the archer sights between two fiber optic fibers that are encased in clear polycarbonate, rather than through a hole.

The only nock on self-aligning peeps is with the rubber tubing. It has been known to slip off the posts or to snap when you are drawing or at full draw. This can cause a serious problem if it slaps you in the eye. Also, high-speed photography proves anecdotal user reports that the latex tubing becomes hyperactive and can cause slapping noise as it gyrates wildly before the stray energy in a bow dissipates.

The new C-Peep from Inglewing is one of the most unusual of the self-aligning peeps. Its bracket fits through the string, but the peep itself is actually to the side. One open side and three triangular aiming posts make this a very distinctive looking sight. Its designer says that the open slot on the side allows more light to enter and thus gives hunters 10 to 15 more minutes of quality hunting time. Plus, the molded plastic sight itself is angled, thus allowing the sight to "square-up" and give you a clear hole to look through when you draw. Finger shooters should love this style peep and for perfect alignment, release shooters who use a D-loop will also be impressed.

THE INDEPENDENT PEEP

Most peep sights are simply served or clamped

In low-light conditions, TRUGLO's GloBrite Peep uses a fluorescent green insert for three separate settings to augment low light conditions. The included rubber tubing automatically positions the peep to your eye.

into your bowstring. Some will fit vertically in the string and may be thought of as free-floating. Others fit horizontally so that when you draw the string the hole presents a relatively clear oval picture; peeps that tie in at an angle are designed to give you the complete hole for perfect centering of your pins.

The Shurz-A-Peep and Pro Hunter Peep have three slots in their machined sides. This gives you a lot of flexibility dividing the strings for perfect rotational balance, but this particular style of independent peep gives you an aiming oval that will not hamper your vision no matter how the string rolls. Usually, you can twist the string tightly and with the new synthetic materials such as Fast Flight from Brownell, you can stabilize a peep well.

The Fine-Line Ultra-Glo is a fiber optic peep sight. Four small fiber optic sections are inset around the hole and, according to designer Sam Topel, this helps the archer concentrate on the aperture.

Specialty Archery Products has the most "accessorizable" machined aluminum peep sight made today. Not only is its Specialty Peep offered in five different hole sizes, but also it has several tiny Zeiss clarifier lenses for magnification. Its Super Peep Kit includes the peep housing, three size apertures and a special aperture wrench. While the use of magnifying lenses so close to your eye can be a terrific assist for some archers, it can cause problems for others. Lenses seem to attract dust and moisture. This is one situation where you must try before you buy.

Ken Johnson's Nite Hawk Peep is made with a peculiar X or + style hole in the middle. Ken's theory is that diffused light bending around the edges of a peep, especially in low light situations, is a big reason archers miss their target. Therefore, the light coming through the four arms of the peep is diffused or appears to be hazy to our eye, but the light passing directly through the tiny square center cannot be diffused because the center has no edges. Therefore, the tiny square hole works exceptionally well in any

If you work on your bow often or help your archery buddies, you will want one of the E-Z String Separators, which allows easy installation of peep sights. Vinyl coated, it will not damage your strings. Beats screw drivers and dull knives!

hunting or competition situation.

No discussion of peep sights would be complete without a mention of the venerable plastic PaPeep. This old-line peep sight is available with four angled hole sizes and features a large hood to help cut glare.

NOW, MAKE YOUR PEEP WORK

The two archery accessories that will make you a finer shot – after you tune your bow and select a properly spined arrow – are your peep and a release. Each has its pitfalls, however. If you are not attentive to the release, you can torque it and twist the string even though this is much harder than when you shoot fingers. A peep sight cannot just be screwed onto the riser like your front sights. It has to be tied securely into place in your bowstring. This is called "serving the peep" and it must be done right. If it slips or is improperly positioned on the string, it can cause you to miss.

After you select your peep, you must insert it into the string and fix it in position. You will see archers try to do this with their fingers, but it is difficult with a high poundage bow that stretches the string extremely tight. Erring on the safe side, most manufacturers recommend that you relax your bow weight in a bow press, insert the body of the peep between the strings with strands divided evenly to a side (the Bull's Eye Expert Peep or the RedHawk Low Light Peep) or to the appropriate slots. There may be three (the Shurz-A-Peep) or even four (the Fine-Line Ultra-Glo) for some horizontal peeps.

Using a bow press to relax the strings so you can insert a peep is fine if you have a bow press or have access to an archery pro shop, but most archers in the world do not. When the string is relaxed it is easy, but lacking a bow press, you can carefully spread the strings with an EZ String Separator or even a dull screwdriver. (The author has seen several archers use a knife for this purpose, but this is NOT recommended.)

With the strings separated and held apart, you can manually insert the peep into the string and position the string's strands in the appropriate grooves.

The next step is to adjust the peep so that it lines up perfectly in front of your eye when you are at full draw. You can do this yourself, but it is tedious. A helpful friend can position the peep for you quickly. When you draw, make sure it is the way you draw when you are actually shooting. Think of good form and come to your anchor naturally. The test is whether you can naturally look through the peep and see your pins or your scope. When you sight-in on a target, you want your chosen pin in the exact center of the peep's hole. Some retailers test the set of the peep by having you close your eyes and execute your draw. Then, when you open your eyes, the peep should be perfectly positioned to help you make a shot.

Experienced archers make a record of everything. At this point, you will want to make a written note of the distance from the top of your nock set along the string to some point on your peep, the bottom or the center of the hole. Then, if you have to re-set the peep and do not have a friend to help or want to set up a spare string for an emergency, you can do it quickly by yourself.

We are going to talk about three methods of string serving, the easiest way, the easy way and a more difficult but more common way:

EASIEST WAY: Use double nock sets above and below your peep. This is easy and it works, but it is not recommended to have potentially loose brass buttons so close to your eye following a shot. Plus, this method adds weight and cuts down on your arrow speed. If you use this method to install your peep, make sure the nock sets are so close to the body of the peep that it is impossible for the peep to pop out of the string, even if your bow is dry-fired or shot without an arrow on the string. Most archers who use this method, cover the nock sets with tightly tied-on serving material and then add a drop of glue on top of that. In this case, your peep should never move or pop out.

EASY WAY STEP 1: Lay your bow on the workbench or better yet, stand it upright in a bow press so you can work on it without having to keep it balanced between your knees or on your lap. Tie a dozen or so knots of any variety around the string just above the peep using a braided serving thread you can buy from any pro shop. Bowstring material will work. Heavy dental floss will work although, before you use it, it is typically white. Now, alternate the knots on each side of the string and finish it off with a square knot because that will not slip.

EASY WAY STEP 2: Secure the last knot you tied, the square knot with a drop of glue. Cut off the loose string ends.

EASY WAY STEP 3: Now, just below the peep, tie a second series of knots in the same manner as those you tied above the peep.

EASY WAY STEP 4: Finally, slide the servings you have just tied tight against the top and the bottom of your peep. This will normally hold the peep in place. If you need to adjust the peep, the servings can be slid up or down with your fingertips.

The Easy method can slip and while no method is foolproof, the Standard method may be best in the long run. According to archery coach Bob Ragsdale, the basic archery question he hears – five-to-one over all others he says – is "How do I tie-off a serving end?" The Standard method of peep serving takes care of that question.

STANDARD WAY STEP 1: Lay an inch or so of serving string along the bowstring and, holding it in place, wrap around it. This is called the "over-wrap" start. Wrap tightly. Now, pull on the still exposed end to tighten the first couple of wraps. At a point about an inch from where you want the served section to end, begin what is called the "reverse back-wrap."

STANDARD WAY STEP 2: (It takes some manual dexterity to accomplish this, so do not get frustrated if it does not come out right the first time.) Wrap the serving string several times around the bowstring both above it and below it. Most good peeps have a safety tie-in-groove today. This is the time to wrap that as needed.

STANDARD WAY STEP 3: Continue now below the loop with a little more than an inch of tight wrappings. Now, hold about a 2-inch "slack loop" with one finger and then, three or so inches down, start wrapping the tail portion inside the loop from the opposite side in the opposite direction! The end of the slack loop will be on the top while the other end will come from the bottom side. Wrap a dozen times tightly inside the slack loop back in the direction of the peep inside the loop with the tail end of the wrapping string placed under the last original wrap. Now, make more wraps in the normal direction. The back-wrapped loops will actually unwind to provide the material needed to complete the serving.

STANDARD WAY STEP 4: While you hold the final wrap tightly, gently pull the trapped and exposed tail enough to tighten up the entire back-wrapped section. Clip off the tail excess. At this point, you may glue or melt the end of the serving to help keep it tightly in place.

NO-PEEP ALTERNATIVES

One of the most interesting sight options is one that offers both front and back posts or pins and apertures. The EZ Bow Sight from Scrape Juice Products, for instance, uses the same aiming system that firearms shooters have used successfully for hundreds of years, mounting adjustable front and rear fiber optic sights (Tritium sights are new for 2003.) on a single, lightweight sight bracket.

The EZ Bow Sight eliminates the need for peep sights, kisser buttons and, Dennis Lewis claims, even levels. "This sight reduces and in many cases eliminates bow torque," he says, "it allows you to shoot more accurately at moving targets, helps you acquire a target faster and hold steady on it longer and dramatically improves your low light shooting, helping frame the target naturally."

The EZ Bow Sight uses twin fluorescent red fiber optics in the rear aperture to horizontally bracket a fluorescent green fiber optic in the front aperture, just like many firearms sights. When properly aligned at full draw, the rear aperture perfectly frames the front aperture. This makes target acquisition fast and helps eliminate bow torque. The camouflaged bracket and 1-1/2 inch (inside diameter) apertures are machined aluminum. The threaded .1875-inch front and rear posts are easily adjustable and the knurled adjustment knobs are large enough to make quick adjustments on the coldest day.

A similar sighting system to the EZ Sight is the X-Cel from Simpson Quality Designs. Front and back sight brackets are independently adjustable and a single fiber optic occupies the front sight frame. A fluorescing "X-style" crosshair is employed as the rear sight to rapidly center the eye on the front pin bead. Designer Dave Simpson feels his sight has applications for both bowhunting and bowfishing when archers must acquire a moving target fast. The X-Cel retails for about $70.

The No-Peep from Timberline is a very different peep alternative to help you achieve a positive and consistent anchor. The No-Peep is an "eye alignment device" rather than an additional or rear sighting aid, explains Jim Sherman. Mounting on a rear-facing bracket the 2.2-ounce No-Peep houses a lens with a dot. Behind the lens is a ring. You adjust it so the dot is inside the ring when you are at your anchor point. Draw while looking at your sight pins and target and you will see the No-Peep in your peripheral vision.

"The optics of the No-Peep magnify misalignment," Jim says. "The principle works with any type sight: pins, crosshairs, pendulums, you name

it. The bracket has four mounting positions so you can mount the No-Peep either above or below your sight pins. Because you can only see the No-Peep with the eye behind the bowstring, you can shoot with both eyes open and that always helps target acquisition."

THE KISSER BUTTON

The kisser button is a small disk of plastic that is clamped onto a bowstring and gives you a ready reference each time you draw. Typically, archers will clamp or serve the button onto the string in such a manner that when you come to full draw, it touches the same place on your lips – hence the name "kisser" – every time. It essentially performs the same function as a peep sight, but has most commonly been used by competitors instead of hunters.

Although kisser buttons have fallen in favor with the advent of many new types of peep sights and release aids, any competent pro shop can attach one to your bowstring – or, certainly, you can do it yourself. Roger Grundman's Flex-Fletch, Tom Rowe's Granpa Specialty, Saunders and U-nique make kissers. Lacking a peep sight, the kisser is the next best thing to a consistent rear sight. Clamped or served securely in place, the kisser button will work with a high-speed bow.

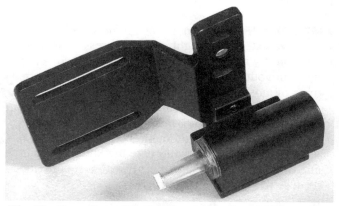

The No-Peep from Timberline is an "eye alignment device" rather than an additional or rear sighting aid.

STABILIZING YOUR SHOT

When you read advertising copy about archery stabilizers and leaf through magazines and company catalogs, you should be prepared for a great deal of "English language shock." The ideas typically presented are so convoluted as to be almost incomprehensible without a Ph. D. in Engineering and some would make a Ph. D. chuckle – or cry. Here are just a few recent examples:

- Special powder filled chambers suppress and stabilize multi-directional oscillation
- Momentum inhibitors
- Truly 360-degree active vibration reduction units,
- Let you tune the balance and harmonic reduction,
- Uses IPPW, Inverted Pivoted Piston Weight technology,
- Command the responsibility of functionality, durability and aesthetics and
- Energy entering the chamber is converted to heat via a patented visco-elastic polymer that kills noise and vibration with brute efficiency.

Archery stabilizers really came into vogue at about the time 3-D shooting became popular, in the early 1990s, because cams changed from soft to hard (in some cases radically hard), one-cams with idler wheels began to replace radical twin cam wheel designs and most risers for hunting were designed to be reflex (bending in or back toward the shooter) or straight. Deflex risers (the older style riser that bends out and away from the shooter which gives a longer brace

height and is thought of as "forgiving") were reserved for novice archers and inexpensive bows.

Sure, stabilizers were available before 1990, but

Few archers have had as much success on the national 3-D tournament circuits as Utah's consistent, professional Randy Ulmer. Attending the opening ASA 3-D shoot in Florida in February 1995, Randy displays the long aluminum stabilizer that has been used in competition for more than a generation. These hollow stabilizers are part of the equipment options allowed in the open, unlimited (professional) classes.

The ultra-versatile Pack Rat Stabilizer available through Martin Archery features a broadhead puller, string tracker and roomy, watertight storage compartment.

One-piece black steel stabilizers are still available and can be used as a front stabilizer or a back balance. This 12-ounce solid stabilizer from Martin will fit any bow with standard 5/16-inch threads.

they were primarily of two varieties. The first, a hollow aluminum tube about 30 inches long with a light weight on the end, was used by spot shooters at indoor tournaments for bow balance and – frankly – to lean or rest on between shots. The second type was, more often than not, simply a short, solid chunk of steel that a bowhunter had been talked into buying even though "balance" was not in the serious bowhunter's vocabulary in those days.

Times change. First, you are going to purchase a stabilizer because you want to find the perfect balance for your bow given your shooting form. Second, you want to reduce the resultant noise and vibration (the shock) of a shot. Balancing your bow will let you keep your grip loose and minimize the torque most archers tend to twist into the riser and thus into your arrow. Reducing the noise will diminish the chance that your shot will disturb game although if we hit what we were shooting at more often, this would not be a big problem.

Shock and vibration can have numerous detrimental effects in your shooting system, and that includes your hand, wrist and arm:

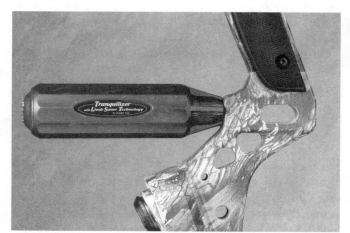

The Tranquilizer Mini stabilizer from Golden Key-Futura is built with Sims "LimbSaver" technology to reduce shock and vibration. Threaded end caps allow the archer to add extra weight or even a string tracker.

- Causing hand and arm fatigue,
- Contributing to painful joint inflammation (bursitis) and
- Causing intense vibration in the mechanical system and thereby shaking loose your sight, pin settings and arrow rest. This is straightforward wear and tear and, with any modern high-energy bow, you have a thousand dollars wrapped up in it and the accessories and thus you have an investment to protect.

Today's stabilizers incorporate several different types of rubber and aluminum and wrapped carbon housings. They are filled with springs and oils, gels, powder and sand. And for those who just cannot give up the "old days," there is good news. You can still purchase a solid steel stabilizer.

A good stabilizer is part of a silencing and vibration damping system that will make shooting more comfortable and therefore more accurate. You will be able to feel the effects of a good stabilizer, because you will not feel "riser buzz" in your hand and arm. (Riser buzz is similar to that uncomfortable

The new 4-inch Doinker Camo Hunter in Realtree and Mossy Oak camo patterns is designed to increase accuracy and dampen vibration. Doinker says its distinctive rubber coupler uses patented "active-vibration-dampening technology."

The Lore stabilizer from Carolina Archery Products illustrates a trend in incorporating steel rods with a vibration dampening rubber insert and a fluted rubber end element. The Lore is 6 ?-inches long and weighs five ounces.

TRUGLO's Deadenator Stabilizer combines precision machining with Doinker technology: 4-1/2 or 6-1/2 inches.

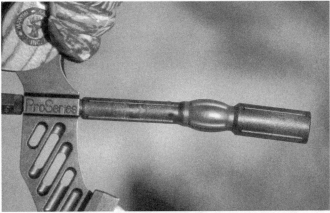

The one-piece Doinker Hunter (SH7) is 7 inches long. The purpose of any stabilizer is to eliminate noise and vibration and to help balance a bow in the archer's hand. With bows becoming shorter and lighter, this is a more critical task than ever.

feeling you get when someone strikes the blade of your crosscut saw with a hammer or runs their fingernails down a blackboard.) You will be able to orally detect (to hear) the effects of a good stabilizer too, because the after-shot noise will be considerably diminished.

When you hold your naked bow balanced in your shooting hand, the top of the bow drops back toward your face because your grip is below center. The proper weight and length stabilizer on the front (and perhaps extending to the sides and rear as well) of the bow will help keep it in a vertical position. After a shot, an effective stabilizer will help the bow swing slowly forward allowing you to catch or steady it with your wrist sling rather than clutch it in your grip. A good stabilizer helps with follow-through and in that regard archery is no different than tennis or golf. The shot is not over until it is over – and follow-through is part of the shot.

Of course, most archers do not use a wrist sling – and most archers grab and twist the bow riser. In spite of years of teaching by archery coaches, most archers still draw to or beyond their peak holding weight and

the pressure on their string hand and on their shooting hand naturally causes them to twist the riser. String burn on the inside of the arm is an occasional, visible sign of this effect. And still, we wonder why we miss! A quality stabilizer can help you correct these shooting form errors.

The increased weight from a stabilizer should provide some additional inertia and help keep your shooting consistent. With most "loaded" bows (bows with sight, quiver, arrows and silencing devices) already weighing as much as a loaded shotgun, between six-to-eight pounds, an additional six-to-ten ounces is probably insignificant. The position of the stabilizer below and forward of the grip is correctly positioned for other shooting benefits, too.

DOINKER

Before Bill Leven, owner of Leven Industries and inventor of Doinker stabilization products, emerged on the archery scene, there were two types of bow stabilizers and most archers would not give you a so-called "plug nickel" for all of them. Bill's advent was timely and archers, by and large, were wrong headed about the need for effective stabilization … at any speed. BB – Before Bill – as we have said, there were these types of stabilizers:

- Solid steel for bowhunting. What most archers understood to be a stabilizer was a solid chunk of steel. Unless they were competitors, they also believed this solid chunk of steel was an unnecessary drag, something heavy and relatively useless, because no one – in those days, before the rise of 3-D and speed bows – was taking the time to explain what stabilization was all about.
- Hollow aluminum tubes for competition. Competitors, of course, understood the concept of bow balance because, gripping their bow lightly, they did not want the bow to fall back and hit them in the eye after they shot. The sling would not prevent that. At indoor tournaments such as the prestigious Las Vegas Indoor Championships, every archer used a stabilizer, but it was mostly to lean on after a shot and because it looked cool, rather than for any widely understood benefit. If they were hunters, their use of stabilizers for competition did not carry over.

Bill Leven actually entered the stabilization market slow and low. The achievable speed of bows (arrows, actually) climbed dramatically during the late 1980s and early 1990s and for a while it seemed that every archer wanted to shoot a super-fast bow. A bow that only propelled an arrow in the 210 to 230 fps range was no longer acceptable except on the "value-priced" (cheap) bow rack. The increasing size and well publicized cash awards in 3-D shooting competition also helped make a faster, lighter arrow with a flatter trajectory desirable. When America's couple million bowhunters bought into the high energy, fast bow, light arrow syndrome, manufacturers had to do something to ease the strain, the shock and noise of a shot, because little of that potential energy was being delivered to the arrow. Instead, it went into the bow, the sight, the rest and the shooter's hand and arm. Ouch!

By the early 1990s, the old archery concept of a "forgiving bow," one that would allow you to make a mistake in shooting form and still deliver its arrow on target, was temporarily forgotten in the rush to faster arrow speeds. But archers soon found that their new bows, although faster than ever before, were very hard to handle, and almost impossible for finger shooters.

At that point, America's free enterprise entrepreneurial drive took over and dozens of individuals began to study how they could lessen the shock and noise of a shot from a high-energy speed bow. The general idea was to add a shock absorber to the bow – somewhere, somehow. It was easier said than done, but at first the obvious place was the stabilizer.

Potential manufacturers quickly realized that the hollow tube and solid steel concepts, of what seems from today's perspective to be an almost ancient era, were not getting the job done. They looked at existing shock absorbers on automobiles and machinery, and begin filling the hollow tubes with weights and springs, oils, sand, powders and eventually, viscous gels. Almost all of these were – and are – more effective than the earlier stabilizers.

Then, in the mid 1990s, Bill Leven began to promote his Doinkers. His ads were simple black and white efforts that looked like they had been done by his kids or in a high school art class. But the concept caught on. Bill's secret was to isolate, to mold the metal attachments at the ends inside thick rubber boots. It was a simple idea and it worked. In a sense, it was the break-through, the one that had everyone else slapping themselves on the head and asking, "Why didn't I think of that?"

Today, Doinker has a large line of vibration and noise dampening products. Like every other stabilizer manufacturer, Bill's products are endorsed by professional archers and well-traveled bowhunters. Bill offers hats and decals and he, himself, has become a curiously recognizable, avuncular figure in his ads and his catalog.

The basic Doinker is unchanged although Bill now has four sizes and several strengths of rubber available

to hold different forward weights. Numerous combinations of Doinkers and stabilizers, some in camo, take up several pages of his catalog. In his enthusiasm to deaden your shooting, Bill has teamed up with IBO World Champion Burley Hall to extend the product line and its good looks into graphite bars, a curious but effective rubber Doe-Nut collar that slides forward and backward on a stabilizer to customize balance, and a line of adjustable V-Bars and V-Bar mounts.

Giving credit where it is due, Bill notes that product designer Billy Godfrey has developed a unique vibration elimination attachment that screws directly on to a scope thread. Vibration of the forward-placed scopes on high speed bows, especially on the IBO shooting circuit, caused many scope mount failures before the mounting bolts were beefed up and IBO began to take the idea of an arrow speed limit seriously.

It is safe to say that if there is a spot on your bow and accessories that can successfully hold a shock and noise deadening unit or a silencing item, Doinker, Sims or one of the numerous other companies in the field are working on a specialized attachment to make it more secure and more effective.

THE STABILIZING ALTERNATIVES

Not content with solid steel, the North American Archery Group has at last diversified its stabilizer presentation. Like many other companies that use Doinker or Sims Vibration Lab technology, North American uses Doinker rubber sectionals between or at the ends of its solid steel tubes. It also sells an adjustable, black 6-inch carbon tuning rod stabilizer.

One of the big dogs in the stabilizer and arrow rest market, Golden Key-Futura has basic stabilizers in practically every length, weight and configuration you could need. The ECO is powder filled. The Ace Hydraulic is filled with viscous oil and a spring-mounted internal piston. The Tranquilizer series uses an internal Sims LimbSaver. Golden Key offers a

From Sims Vibration Laboratory, the Modular Stabilizer System comes with three modules and a stem extension allowing you to customize stabilizer length while reducing noise and vibration. Weighs 8 ounces and is 5-1/2 inches long. Additional 2.3-ounce modules are available.

The value of a long stabilizer says Ohio's Jack Wallace, who is a consistent high performer on IBO 3-D competition venues, is not just to lean your bow on … although it does that, too. A long, lightweight stabilizer lets you shoot with a relaxed grip thus reducing torquing forces on your bow riser. Riser torque is a primary source of inconsistent left-right arrow strike.

variety of weights for the tips of their aluminum rod/steel weight stabilizers and a lightweight bracket – the Balance Beam – that allows you to offset your stabilizer to balance a heavy sight or a quiver full of arrows.

Many companies have taken two distinctive paths in presentation of stabilizers. Carbon Impact's camouflaged (or black) gel-filled series uses carbon impregnated fiberglass tubes in one inch and 1.5 inch diameters. They call these their Fat and Super Fat stabilizers respectively. Mounting a rubber Sims Limb Saver to the front outside of the tube increases its shock dissipating abilities.

For archery competitors, who are more interested

The 10-inch V-Flite stabilizer from Hi-Tek Sports Products is filled with powder and is unaffected by weather. It is available in black or in camouflage.

in perfecting their bow's in-hand balance than decreasing the noise or shock of a shot, the second Carbon Impact approach to bow stabilization uses carbon rods in multiple configurations and lengths. You can easily position one or more built-in sliding weights along the four rods or even angle them to the rear with a Sliding V-Bar.

Dating back to the time of its founder, the intense, perhaps brilliant, but amiable Chuck Saunders, Saunders Archery has a history of "complexification," adding twists and turns, buckles, bolts, swinging arms and hidden mechanisms to almost every archery accessory. The Saunders "shock and sound deadening systems" are outstanding for their apparent intricacy … and for archery construction, surprisingly polished good looks. And certainly, the Saunders claim to have started the trend to deadening shock with the 1985 introduction of the Torque Tamer stabilizer is a stretch.

If you begin with the basic Saunders ShockTamer; then add the twin chambered, screw-on Pro-Tamer or single chamber Tamer SS; and then "top off" your stabilizer with a Pro-Bandit and add a Bandit to your sight bracket, you have a system of a dozen or so metal and rubber parts.

In typical Saunders fashion, their Pro-Angler knuckle has a whopping 312 total settings – 13 vertical and 24 rotational – to counter-balance your bow quiver and any torque you add to your system.

Vibracheck (R&R Enterprises) offers a number of stabilizer lengths and weights for archers who hunt or shoot competitively. On the hunting side, Ron Gilley – himself a hunter and a former competitor – has responded to the archery community's increased interest in quiet, vibration-free shooting by incorporating a thickened gel which he calls VibaSORB into its stabilizer line-up. A free-floating aluminum weight on the front of gel-filled Vibracheck stabilizers is molded into the gel, not attached to the outer, metal shell of the stabilizer. When you shoot, vibration is transmitted to the weight, which flexes and rotates inside the gel – it in effect stirs the absorbing gel – and this helps dissipate vibration. The 1-3/8-inch diameter Isolator is rubber-coated, filled with the gel and available in multiple lengths, weights and camo

Short stabilizers like the new Icon from Ron Gilley's R&R Vibracheck are designed primarily to dissipate vibration and reduce the noise of a shot.

The new ShockFin stabilizer from Global Resource is tunable for weight distribution and features a carbon tube.

The purpose of a V-bar such as the Vibracheck Vbar Deluxe System (two 6-1/2-inch Hydraulic or gel-filled Strikewave stabilizers and bracket: 15 to 19 ounces.) is to help the archer distribute weight evenly. Hunting archers rarely uses v-bars, but for the highest level of precision shooting, the bow's center of gravity should be straight down, below the shooter's bow hand and a V-bar system helps accomplish that.

patterns. Vibracheck's hydraulic stabilizer uses a central piston with a spring on either side immersed in a viscous fluid.

For competition shooters, Vibracheck offers a variety of handsome stabilizers anodized in bright black and silver. Although hunting archers prefer short stabilizers for easy maneuverability on a treestand or in tight situations, archers shooting indoor competition prefer a long (up to 32-inch) stabilizer so they can rest their bow on the floor between shots without having to put it in a rack or hang it awkwardly from a belt sling. The same gel-filled stabilizer principle works on the 3-D and spot shooting venues as in bowhunting. For competitors, Vibracheck offers several styles of rear-facing stabilizers, both single and double, to offset the forward weight of the bow sight and allow your bow to sit dead in your hand.

TRUGLO, best known for its fiber optic sight pins, recently entered the stabilizer market with three styles. Not wanting to leave anyone out or to seem partial, TRUGLO stabilizers are available in Mossy Oak Forest Floor or Break-Up and in Realtree X-tra Gray or

Hardwoods HD camo patterns. The aluminum Solidifier is old-fashioned, solid aluminum. This inexpensive stabilizer provides weight forward for balance, but does little for shock absorption. At 4 or 6 inches long, the Nullifier uses an internal weight in a fill of gel. The top-of-the-line TRUGLO Deadenator is one of many new stabilizers using a popular Doinker between a forward weight and an aluminum tube filled with shock-absorbing gel. The Deadenator is available in sizes from 3.5 inches and 4.3 ounces to 6.5 inches and 9.3 ounces.

The Lore Stabilizer from Carolina Archery Products features six steel rods set into the outer perimeter of an anodized aluminum base. Wedged in the center is a sculptured rubber plug. Ike Branthwaite at Carolina says the rods act like tuning forks and effectively transmit the vibration of a shot into the rubber core. Advertising copy calls this a "multiphasic fluted damping element matched to a system of opposed linear springs." The Lore is 6.75 inches and weighs 5 ounces.

New to the archery game, Global Resource has come out swinging with several new products. Their ShockFin stabilizer begins with a wrapped carbon housing. Inserted securely into the housing is a stiff rubber insert to absorb vibration. Adjustable, modular aluminum weights are inserted in the center of the stabilizer to absorb and dissipate the vibration.

Numerous other companies have excellent names in the archery stabilizer business and, if you try before you buy, it will be hard to go wrong with products from any of them: Cardoza, Cobra, Easton or Specialty Archery Products.

STABILIZER NOTES

Many manufacturers offer stabilizers with ends fitted so that one to two ounce stackable weights can be added. This lets you customize weight distribution and vibration damping. Vibracheck, for instance, builds its gel-filled 6.5 inch, six ounce rubber coated Strikewave with a tip so that additional weights can be added to help you find the perfect balance as well as deal with "stray" vibration not absorbed by the arrow.

Another handy stabilizer-related item is a quick disconnect. Screw this short, light connector into the stabilizer bushing and leave it in place. Then screw or clip the disconnect plug onto the stabilizer. The Muzzy and Carbon Impact disconnects let you add or remove a stabilizer in one, quick twist rather than screwing it all the way in and out each time you prepare to shoot or take down your bow. Vibracheck also has a 10-degree angled (downward) disconnect which, Ron Gilley believes helps lower the center of gravity of your bow and thereby helps you hold it steadier.

COMPETITOR & BOWHUNTER

Dan Massimillo has been shooting a bow for 38 years. He is an avid bowhunter and, when he has had time, has shot in the NFAA Bowhunter Freestyle Division, winning 17 Florida State Field Championships and four southeast sectional titles. Among Dan's nine Pope & Young whitetail bucks is a 187-point whopper from Kansas that the Buckmasters organization filmed him harvesting in 2002. It is one of the largest free-ranging deer ever taken on video with a bow.

While Dan does not claim that a stabilizer changed his life, he does say that it has definitely contributed to an increase in his shooting effectiveness. Would he shoot or hunt without a stabilizer? "Not if I could help it," Dan says.

Dan shoots the Doinker with Sling from the North American Archery Group, a company that has also been his employer for 15 years. Essentially a couple chunks of steel on either side of a rubber Doinker; this 6-inch stabilizer weighs 8.4 ounces. "It is the only stabilizer available with a built-in sling," says the left-hander.

"Bows are getting faster and lighter, but I like a little weight in my shooting hand. I shoot 80 pounds for hunting. A high-poundage, high-energy bow needs a little more weight to help eliminate noise and shock. The stabilizer adds weight forward where I need it to keep it out of my face after I shoot and I feel the increased steadiness. My bow doesn't rock as much – unless I get tired or there is a strong breeze – and so it is easier to hold on the target. That's as important for a bowhunter as it is in competition. Plus, I like my bow to fall or rock forward after a shot. Placing weight forward causes that to happen and the sling gives me the assurance that I can maintain control without grabbing the bow in my shooting hand."

A quick disconnect helps attach your stabilizer to the "converta accessory insert" – now usually referred to as the "stabilizer insert" – below the grip on your bow. With one quick turn you can remove a stabilizer for storage or shipping. The 1-1/4-inch-long Quick Disconnect from Vibracheck is available with a 10-degree angled face, pictured here with a 6-1/2-inch, 6-ounce rubber-coated, gel-filled Isoflex stabilizer)

Dan Massimillo, a manager at the North American Archery Group, has won 17 Florida State Field Championships and has taken nine Pope & Young whitetails. With the trend in bows toward lighter and faster, Dan says he would not enter a shoot or hunt without a stabilizer and a sling.

TIPS ON TARGETS AND SHOOTING AT TARGETS

Every archer should have a couple of sturdy foam or bag targets available for shooting practice, even if there is a convenient range nearby. Private ranges (except at some archery pro shops) are practically nonexistent and public ranges get crowded in the weeks before the opening of hunting season. Given the continuing miserable state of local finances, these may not be in good shape for a practice session anyway.

A conscientious archer who hunts or competes seriously will practice year-round. The quality of his practice should be self-determined and not subject to municipal budgets or someone else's entrepreneurial instincts.

The social and political climate in America and Canada has changed in the past quarter century. Twenty-five years ago, there was little or no public debate about hunting or the shooting sports: they were widely accepted. Today, with population and urbanization trends continuing to distance the public as a whole from any personal responsibility for acquiring its own food through hunting or even gardening, a lot of care needs to be taken when you are shooting recreationally or just practicing. Shooting has become a more private affair and practice is more serious now than ever.

Taking care of your shooting and your sport means, in some measure, being familiar with the targets available and then finding a safe and appropriate place to practice. The *Archer's Digest* will help familiarize you with the targets, but finding a good place to shoot may be the easiest ... or most difficult assignment. For that, begin with the phone book's "Yellow Pages" and sporting goods stores in

Professional archers such as Alabama's Pete Works believe that only continual practice will reap trophy rewards in competition or bowhunting.

Practice from a level position to set your sights, tune your rest and make sure your equipment functions properly as a system.

Practice from an elevated position is a superb way to warm up for bowhunting season if you plan to hunt from a treestand.

traditional. You can usually shoot in your back yard, on a public range or at a local archery pro shop. Shooting "on the level" helps you discover problems with shooting form (Are you gripping the riser too tight and applying torque to your bow riser?); find out if your arrows are properly spined (Do they fly erratically, without grouping?); listen for riser buzz (Is there excessive noise or vibration caused by stray energy?); and discover any loose or poorly fitting connections. This is all a necessity before you go to the field to hunt or to compete.

If you are a hunting archer, you need to practice from a treestand or some elevated position. It is the rare archer who hunts from a ground blind, although it can be done successfully for almost any big game species from whitetails to black bear. In some special cases, such as pronghorn hunting, ground blinds, pits and level shooting are common, but even then, hunting from an elevated windmill can sometimes be a better way to go given the pronghorn's phenomenal eyesight.

Shooting from a treestand, from the roof of your garage or even a stable ladder secured to your house, will give you an excellent sense of your ability in a real hunting situation. In some ways, shooting from an elevated position is a lot like bowfishing: your target may not be exactly where you are aiming. You have to learn how gravity and the angle to your target affect the flight of your 400-500 grain, 200 mph broadhead-tipped arrow.

Practice from an elevated position is not the same as practicing from the ground. Hanging in the air 20 feet off the ground is not the time to wonder if your equipment is tuned; it is not the time to make a decision to replace your plastic fletching with feathers; it is not the time to fumble around in your fanny pack for a set of Allen wrenches to tighten the quiver against your sight's side-plate. Figure out or fix all of those things on the ground. You practice from "on high" for one reason only: so that you can put your arrow into the vitals of a game animal below you and ensure a quick, clean kill.

Whatever target you use, whether you are shooting at ground level or simulating treestand shooting, here are some guidelines for effective practice:

• Set up, test your gear and make basic equipment adjustments on the ground, not when you are "in the air." It's a lot safer to take your bow apart on the ground than while you are on a treestand. (When I adjust my equipment on a treestand, Murphy's Law inevitably causes me to drop something vital, like my release.)

• Vary the angle and the distance of your shot and your shooting position (seated, kneeling, standing, twisted to the right, etc.), except while

your area. Do not despair. Resources, instruction and archery friends are available in every corner of North America and around the world.

How to Practice

Pete Shepley, president of Precision Shooting Equipment and Steve Spurrier, coach of the National Football League's Washington Redskins say how you practice is how you will perform under pressure. Not "practice makes perfect," but "Perfect Practice makes Perfect." In this respect, it is no longer sufficient to mark off 20 yards to a pie plate and shoot for an hour, although that kind of shooting can certainly be fun and beneficial. With the advance in equipment sophistication during the past 25 years and the general public's increasing, and often critical, awareness of our hobby, you must be proficient. That means making your practice as sophisticated as your shooting at "the moment of truth."

You need to practice from a level position to set your sights, tune your rest, make sure your equipment functions properly as a system and become proficient at basic range estimation. This shooting is easy and

Bowhunting for big game may be a solitary activity and bowfishing on a beautiful spring day may be as much fun as archers are legally allowed, but for sheer excitement and practice shooting when you feel pressure, nothing beats 3-D competition.

you are performing basic and essential set-up: initial pin setting, rotating your arrow nocks for rest clearance, or determining centershot, for example. A varied approach to your shot will be more challenging, will more closely replicate actual situations in the field and will be more fun.

• When shooting from an elevated position, have someone move your target if possible, to simulate different angles of presentation and approach. Deer will occasionally enter your shooting lane at exactly 20 yards and stand broadside with their eyes closed, but do not count on it. More often than not you will have to shoot down and either around the tree or twisted to your most awkward side (to the right for a right hand archer and to the left for a left-hander). The more you practice, the better you become estimating the angle of

penetration into a big game animal's kill zone and the more comfortable you become with your ability to make the shot count.

• If you make an effort to simulate the pressure you would feel making a trophy hunting shot or shooting for the grand prize in your archery club's 3-D shoot, you will take a big step forward in making your practice more realistic. Think about making your shot under pressure. Think about your mother in-law arriving for an extended visit or how little you are saving for your kids' college education. If that does not cause your blood pressure to rise, nothing will!

Here are a few additional tips that may provide the edge for better shooting:

• Trigger your release by surprise (no punching!) to avoid target panic.

• Allow your pin to float through the vital zone. Do not "lock-on." Your pin will make the classic "figure eight" patterns in the target zone and when you refuse to over-control, your arrow will find its proper place in the target.

• Make your practice as close to shooting under pressure as possible, whether you hunt or shoot 3-D or both. Realistic practice relieves the strain of the "real thing."

• Relax. Breathe. Accurate shooting is difficult enough without adding torque by holding your riser in a death grip. When you are relaxed, focusing on the process of the shot rather than the outcome will naturally cause your sight pins to settle into a smaller, tighter group. "Trust the force, Luke."

• Concentrate. Pick a spot. Focus not on the antlers or the body of the deer, but on the muscle moving beneath the hair. Like a baseball pitcher who looks at the catcher's mitt, look your arrows into the heart of your target.

The most popular archery target during the past ten years has been the 3-D foam animal target, but many other styles are available: a screen target for indoor shooting with blunts (perhaps in the basement during a long winter); an outdoor do-it-yourself hay bale target with paper target faces; simple blocks of foam with spots painted on their sides; a variety of bag targets filled with shredded paper, particles of foam or sawdust … and even a shooting device that attaches to your bow and allows you to practice without a target … or an arrow!

WHAT TO LOOK FOR IN A TARGET

There are only a few essential features to look for when you want to purchase a practice target: price, size

A target that looks like a big game animal such as this finely painted and heavy-antlered fallow deer from McKenzie Targets makes practice fun and shooting interesting. McKenzie big game targets typically break apart into three sections for easier handling and storage.

Today's 3-D targets such as this red boar hog from Longhorn have scoring zones that conform to the two national competition circuits – ASA and IBO – molded into the sides.

THE 3-D TARGET

The advertising for most 3-D targets usually says they are "crafted with head-turning, realistic detail." If your only experience with a 3-D foam target is five to ten years ago, this may seem misleading. Today's 3-D animal targets are superior in every category to targets built even five years ago: accuracy of their looks, design and all-around durability. This is why game wardens use them to trap poachers.

Today's 3-D animal targets by and large have superb arrow retention and easy arrow removal qualities. With nearly 20 years of research, beginning with waterfowl decoys, manufacturers have developed formulas for foam that allow their targets to stop any

and weight (portability and storage), and style of shooting practice you are performing.

- For $100-$200 an archer can purchase any target manufactured anywhere in the world, including shipping, except for those super-extra large 3-D space alien targets designed for club events or pro shop walls which obviously take an enormous pounding every day.
- How portable do you need the target to be? Look for overall size and weight or, in some cases, size of its component parts. Portability and storage are issues here as is (be honest!) your ability to hit the target. Unless you are a crack shot, larger targets are preferred to smaller targets.
- If you are primarily a bowhunter and/or a 3-D competitor, you will certainly want an animal target. But several block targets offer versatility and options you should consider, too.
- FITA or NFAA competitors will prefer grass matt targets and paper faces of the same style they will face in competition.

Taking a sensitive and sharp-eyed wild turkey with a shotgun is not easy and trying to take one with a bow can be downright frustrating. Before you head to the field, you will want to practice the draw-aim-release sequence to minimize your movement. A 3-D foam turkey target will help you "get your mind right!"

Shooting 3-D competition is an excellent way to stay in shape for bowhunting because you shoot at realistic, life-size big game targets; you can use your bowhunting gear; and you must practice distance judging to score.

launched arrow, even the fastest, small-diameter carbon shafts and many have been designed for broadhead practice as well.

To build a 3-D target, several ingredients are needed: a fiberglass mold, an inert foam expander and an activating agent. When these two ingredients are poured – by a precise formula – into the mold, a chemical reaction (heat and pressure) takes place and the now-activated foam expands to fill the cavity. Once the foam cools, it is removed from the mold. The mold lines are smoothed, the target is drilled for supporting hardware and it is painted. The result is a dense, flexible, self-closing (self-sealing) 3-D foam target that resembles a game animal.

The largest 3-D manufacturer in the world, McKenzie Targets produces several foam lines that help make archery fun and hunting practice realistic. In spite of what you may think, the evolution of 3-D targets did not begin with or for bowhunting. Beginning in 1989 and growing with the 3-D boom in the early '90s McKenzie has supplied targets for all major competition venues, including the National Field Archery Association (NFAA) 3-D Championship.

With its recognizable three-section design, a McKenzie is highly recognizable. This design makes shipping and storage easier and the center section, the section with an animal's marked vitals, can be replaced or repaired after you have done a lot of shooting. In conjunction with the Archery Shooter's Association (ASA) and the International Bowhunting Organization

Innovator and manufacturing leader McKenzie Targets has life-size deer, bear and turkey targets with exposed anatomy for teaching proper shot placement. McKenzie sculptor John Witalison worked with the National Bowhunter Education Foundation's Tim Pool and Wayne Trimm to create realistic and anatomically accurate instructional models.

(IBO), both of which manage extensive national 3-D competitions, McKenzie pioneered molding competition scoring zones in their targets. A typical 3-D target weighs between 50 and 70 pounds.

A variety of animals are represented in the McKenzie Natra-Look Series, from whitetail bucks to wild turkeys. Their Medium Alert Whitetail measures

Professional outdoorsman David Hale says Morrell's Bionic Buck target is "the best there is" for practice. The solid foam Bionic Buck is designed to allow one-finger arrow retrieval. Its burlap-wrapped center section, which covers the deer's vital area, can be replaced for about $10.

33.5 inches at the shoulder, is 44 inches in body length and represents a live weight of about 135 pounds. The unique Gobbling Turkey is 20 inches high and represents a 20-pound bird. Perfect for practice shooting, these targets are painted in excellent detail and the molds are sculptured to show muscle and wing feather configurations. They are anatomically correct and weather resistant. McKenzie says the foam formula is mixed to allow for easy one-hand arrow removal.

The unique McKenzie Quartering Deer has 3-D scoring zones marked so that shooters can practice quartering shots on a 160-pound buck from the ground or from a treestand at a 45-degree angle. One side is marked for a ground shot and the other side is marked for a treestand shot from 15 feet high and 15-20 yards away.

3-D target manufacturers like McKenzie, Morrell, Rinehart and Longhorn have antler kits that can be set, more or less securely, into the head. Mule deer antlers are available for the mule deer buck target. The same is true for exotics like fallow deer and black buck and even larger game like elk and caribou.

Bowhunters yearning for some fun on the range or perhaps looking forward to a trip to a ranch to hunt non-native or exotic species should check out McKenzie's Exotic Series. Five targets are available, from Fallow Deer to a 10-inch high, 9-foot alligator in

three-piece construction. Complete with jagged white teeth and gleaming, beady eyes, this rowdy reptile represents a 250 man-eater.

The McKenzie Safari Series expands the 3-D challenge for practice and for club shooting. Featuring anatomically correct hyenas, leopards, impalas, warthogs and huge, 325-pound black-maned lions, the Safari Series is ideal to shoot before a dream hunt in Africa or just for fun.

McKenzie's line is extensive. Bears, bighorn sheep, bull elk, mountain goat, caribou and a 1,000-pound bison make up the HD Target Line. The Rock Rascals are smaller, one-piece critters – raccoon, fox and woodchuck, for instance – molded on freestanding bases. All of the Rock Rascals have approved IBO scoring rings on both sides. The Aim-Rite series has a special removable core for heavy practice. Replacing this core rather than the entire target is very cost effective and McKenzie says this target series is excellent for field points or broadheads. The economical TuffBuck is made from urethane foam and is molded with the vitals and bones marked right on the target.

Even with an automated assembly line and 600-700 molds on hand, McKenzie remains innovative and responsive. The company recently teamed up to produce two life-size 3-D targets with exposed anatomy for instructing proper shot placement. McKenzie sculptor John Witalison worked with National Bowhunter Education Foundation Executive Director Tim Pool and nationally recognized artist Wayne Trimm to create realistic and anatomically accurate instructional models for whitetails, bear and turkey. The whitetail target is scaled to represent a 135 to 140 pound animal with one side having expertly sculpted and painted exposed vitals.

Delta, Rinehart, BlueRidge, Longhorn and Morrell also build excellent 3-D targets. The unique Delta Elite Grizzly Bear is sculptured after a full-grown boar grizzly roaring and standing braced against a three-foot stump. Its mouth is wide open and full of teeth. This huge (60 x 61 x 22 inches) 3-D target ships in three boxes. The BlueRidge Monster Whitetail features a slide-in replaceable vital zone. The Longhorn Warthog is molded in such detail – including gleaming white trophy tusks – that it will literally make you want to shoot first and ask questions later. Morrell's Bionic Series is especially durable because the center or vitals section is covered by a formed, but inexpensive burlap mat and filled with compressed cotton. Dale Morrell claims this allows his bionic Bucks to be shot three to five times longer than conventional foam targets.

After you shoot out the center of your 3-D target you may either repair it or purchase a new section from the manufacturer or your local archery supplier. Longhorn and Cherokee Sports both market inexpensive 3-D repair kits. The Cherokee Magic-Fix self-healing formula fixes all 3-D targets and contains both black and brown coloring. Additional colors are available and, according to Cherokee, one kit will normally make two to three repairs. A larger, Club Kit contains enough material to repair 20 to 25 targets. Holes repair in about 15 minutes.

Buck Screw has a 3-D target cover to help you protect your investment from the weather and to disguise it during transportation or when not in use. The durable, rip-stop camo cover is treated to prevent deterioration from ultra-violet exposure and will fit most standard target styles.

BLOCKS AND BAGS

Bag and block targets – easy to carry, easy to shoot, easy to store – have been popular with archers for many years. The continuing innovation is what materials are used for filler and how they are designed to make shooting practice better.

Lots of advertising has promoted The Block layered field tip and broadhead target from Field Logic. One of the unique aspects of The Block is that, because of its layered, self-healing foam design, it is even useful with expandable broadheads. Built with layered foam strips, arrows tend to slide between the

The Carbon Block from McKenzie Targets is a weatherproof, layered target designed to stop any carbon or aluminum arrow quickly by friction-pinching the arrow shaft. Arrows slip between compressed layers of high-density foam with minimal target damage and remove easily with one hand. This target can be shot on all four sides.

compressed layers and are stopped by heat and friction that, Field Logic says, literally "grabs" your arrow. Wrapped in thick black plastic with a handle and painted black aiming dots, The Block is a simple and effective practice tool for any archer and block targets do not require a separate stand. The Block is waterproof and will not freeze.

The Cube from American Whitetail sells against The Block. The Cube can be shot by broadheads on all sides, not just two. The Cube's solid bonded laminations produce less slivering and its solid foam construction requires no boards or metal bands to hold it together. Plus, The Cube is lighter and easier to carry than The Block. So, look at each and make up your own mind!

A bag target such as Magic Stop's MS II is light and easy to store and set up. Plus, you can shoot it from any angle or direction. Of course, the 6-1/2-ounce UV coated polybag cover is imprinted with aiming dots on one side and a stylized vitals aiming scene on the back. All four corners of this bag are sewn with nylon straps so the bag can be hung on a branch or frame. Replacement covers are available. Velcro seals the stuffing sack inside the cover.

Long an industry standard, Hips foam targets have been commercially available for 20 years and are always distinctively marked with his yellow and black "happy face."

Morrell's Eternity Target is the official warm up target for IBO, NFAA and ASA shooting competition. It is stuffed with compressed, high-grade fiber with a cardboard frame to maintain shape. The large, outdoor Range Target measures 32x32x12 inches and can hang on a special stand made of heavy gauge steel. A weatherproof cover is available. Dale Morrell says he wants a target that stands up to continual pounding from high-speed bows and still offers easy arrow removal. These targets are not for broadhead shooting.

Third Hand offers an interesting bag target the company calls the Rag Bag. Third Hand sells the 32-inch by 34-inch durable outer poly bag – you fill it with old clothes, sheets, towels or even plastic bags. The bag face is printed with five aiming points on one side and 18 on the reverse. The 18-spot side helps you keep arrows from hitting one another. Obviously, this is an economical approach to practice, but archers shooting high-performance bows may need to be certain of their stuffing before they cut loose.

In addition to its 3-D animal targets, McKenzie offers a variety of lightweight block and bag targets in its TuffShot Series. Its Tuff Block (24x24x12-inch) and CarbonBlock (large or small) will take thousands of shots. The Tuff 24 sets up like a 3-D deer target with rebar support rods provided. It has aiming dots on one side and the muscle structure of a deer raised in relief on the other. This helps bowhunters learn to pick a spot for best shot placement.

MISCELLANEOUS TARGETS AND ACCESSORIES

Saunders Archery has sold many thousands of its SACO Blunt Target. The face of the target is a tough screen that hooks and stretches, with grommets to a lightweight, flexible frame of rods. When the arrow hits, the target collapses and then springs back into shape, dropping the arrow in front. This target is designed to be shot with large blunts only. Field points and broadheads will quickly destroy it. Four blunts and a carrying sack are included with each target purchase. The SACO target is ideal for inside shooting during the winter or in inclement weather.

Saunders is known around the world for its Indian Cord Target Matts. Pioneered by founder Chuck Saunders, the Indian cord grass is cut on Saunders property and wound into a mat in its plant in Nebraska. These tough, heavy mats are covered with resilient burlap and hand sewn. While they are not recommended for broadhead practice, mats are long lasting, relatively economical and traditional. The Indian cord holds the arrow at its flight angle, revealing how well the bow is tuned and especially revealing with fletchless arrows. These mats are excellent for straight-ahead practice with any bow and

The Outdoor Range target from Morrell will stand up to thousands of shots from field and target points. Morrell targets are the official "warm-up" targets for most 3-D shooting competition. This large bag-style target measures 32 x 32 x 12 inches.

arrow combination, but because they are heavy they do require a stand or easel.

Archery International or AIM produces a different type of target matt and stand. The AIM mats are produced from woven rice grass and stitched into recognizable blue polymer covers. The 2-inch thick matt is recommended for recreational use and bows shooting 50 pounds or less. The 4-inch matt will handle any weight, size or speed arrow.

For anyone with a dense straw or hay target butt available, a paper target face will be in demand. Fortunately, dozens of styles are available. They are inexpensive and attach to a target butt with target pins or even bent sections of coat hanger. Morrell makes three popular paper faces: the blue and white single spot and the five-spot and three-spot Vegas face. If you shoot a lot, purchase these in packs of 100. Maple Leaf Press offers a wide variety of paper target faces for all uses featuring various animals and rings.

If your target grabs and holds your arrows, either because it is new or because it is particularly dense, you will benefit from using an arrow puller. You can use any flexible piece of rubber. The one you use to help you twist off jar lids in the kitchen is fine, but if you want a specialized tool that is designed to fit carefully around an arrow shaft, Third Hand makes the

Pro Puller. The molded Pro Puller has finger grips and a V-tapered compression channel to handle any size arrow.

Introducing a youngster to archery will be beneficial for him and gratifying for you. Senior Division Champion Denny Stiner worked with grandson Evan Klaves, four years old, and they both won trophies in the May 2002 Central Illinois 3-D Challenge.

If you are a 3-D competitor, you will eventually want a reference card that shows the scoring zones for competition targets. A number of companies such as Bull's Eye and Third Hand offer these, in color or black and white. These are available for either McKenzie or Rinehart targets.

Whatever your archery interest, whether you are a competitor or a bowhunter, if you shoot actively a tool like the Recover to help you find lost arrows will pay for itself quickly. Nothing is more frustrating than to shoot at small target and miss or a large, well used target and get a complete pass through, and then not be able to find your arrow. And if you are practicing with broadheads, an arrow that has hit and run under the grass is a "must recover!" The Recover is a 6-ounce, compact metal detector that operates on a nine-volt battery. With its arrow attachment, you can scan for arrows while standing. It is excellent for aluminum arrows and will help find the inserts, outserts, field points and broadheads on carbon arrows.

From archery products newcomer Global Resource comes a tool to help you estimate the distance to your target. RangeAid is a collection of 22 clear plastic cards put together to open like a fan. Each card is imprinted with one of 33 McKenzie 3-D animal targets in four sizes with scoring zones. You can quickly select the appropriate silhouette. It's a handy reference tool for competition, says Rebecca Kronfeld of Global Resource, "you will immediately know where to place your arrows."

"Dad! I found it!" Target practice is better when you can find arrows that tend to slide beneath the grass and disappear if you miss or shoot through your target. The Recover Arrow Detection System operates on one nine-volt battery and can help locate aluminum, carbon or wood arrows.

TARGET SHOOTING – WITHOUT A TARGET

If you ever sweated out a week of lousy weather when you should be outside practicing and could not get to an inside archery range, either before hunting season or a major 3-D tournament, you understand the frustration of not being able to shoot. You also know the danger and care needed when you fling arrows between the cars in the garage. Now, several companies have devices that allow you to practice safely with your own bow and shooting set-up, but without an arrow or even a target.

The Vibracheck SafeDraw is a sophisticated pneumatic system that allows you to practice with your bow, your sight and your release - anywhere, anytime - without ever sending a projectile down range. The pneumatic chamber is a 33-inch red tube attached to your bow with a black clamp at the stabilizer hole. The new-for-2003 clamp allows you to shoot the SafeDraw

The SafeDraw from Vibracheck is a sophisticated pneumatic system that allows you to practice without ever sending a projectile "down range." Attached properly to your bow, it is safe to shoot and ideal for keeping the muscles in shape between seasons.

with your arrow rest in place. (When it was introduced in 2002, you had to remove your arrow rest before clamping the SafeDraw in place at the Berger buttonhole through the riser.) A black rod, which serves as the drive shaft for the pneumatic piston, attaches securely to your bowstring, like an arrow. With the SafeDraw properly in place, you can safely draw your bow and practice your complete shot sequence without fear of a dry-fire, or causing damage to the bow or injury to yourself.

Because of the ability to draw, aim and release with the exact same equipment you will use in a tournament or a hunting situation, without loosing an arrow, the SafeDraw could prove instrumental in the treatment of target panic. Vibracheck President Ron Gilley says, "Target panic commonly stems from a fear of missing. By taking away the possibility of missing, an archer can feasibly re-program his or her shot sequence without the anticipation that creates target panic. Using the SafeDraw is more effective than blank-bale shooting because you can properly re-program your entire shot sequence, including aiming."

A separate model developed by archery coach Bernie Pellerite is called the Laz-Air Shot Trainer and marketed through Bernie's Robinhood Video Productions, projects a laser dot where your arrow would have gone. "Using this corrects most aiming and form flaws," Bernie says. "It helps you program your shot sequence and back tension until they are automatic. Finally, our Laz-Air will help you cure target panic. And don't think that target panic is only something that competition shooters get. I've helped such internationally recognized archers as Ted Nugent and Myles Keller get back on target. This works!"

George Chapman, Director of Precision Shooting Equipment Schools and a world-renowned archery coach, says, "This is the finest shooting aid I've seen in archery in 58 years. There is nothing else out there that comes close to being this good for safety or for learning to shoot with a release."

THE INTERNATIONAL BOWHUNTING ORGANIZATION

The IBO did not begin as a national 3-D competition shooting archery circuit. It just turned out that way.

IBO began over a Midwest kitchen table in 1984 with the grandiose direction to "promote, protect and advance bowhunting." For years, no one had a clue how to put that idea into actual practice. The "Triple Crown of Bowhunting" 3-D shooting events began as something of a stepchild. Now, that schedule of events is the engine that runs the organization. Most IBO members are barely aware the IBO has any other specific goals than promoting archery through unmarked distance 3-D shooting competition.

The IBO organizes and runs three-day 3-D tournaments from February until August. More than a

Men and women mount podiums as 3-D target champions, taking home a variety of cash and prizes. Payouts are usually based on formulas that take into account total sponsor fees, donations and membership entry fees. Some archers have won more than $100,000 in a year of 3-D shooting.

thousand archers who are divided into competition classes by sex, age and equipment choice typically attend tournaments.

3-D shooting is popular because many archers see it as a tune-up for hunting seasons or a way to stay in shape for bowhunting. The majority of bows on any IBO 40-target venue are their owner's camouflaged hunting bows. Archers universally enjoy the unmarked yardage feature, the 3-D animal targets used and the opportunity to shoot for cash and prizes. IBO President Ken Watkins says the IBO returns about 40 percent of its entry fees (which can range as high as $250 per tournament for a professional archer) to winners in most categories including the 3-D Triple Crown in the US northwest.

IBO shooting has several features that make it unique and distinct from all other unmarked yardage venues:

- With one foot against a shooting stake, shooters have two minutes to make a shot,
- The greatest distance is 50 yards
- Scoring zones are 11 – 10 – 8 – 5 – 0,
- No cameras, rangefinders or binoculars over 8-power magnification are allowed,
- Shooting is regulated by arrow weight (5 grains per pound of an individual's draw weight), a speed limit (280 fps) and a peak draw weight per category: compound shooters = 80 pounds maximum draw weight, traditional shooters = 90 pounds, female and youth shooters = 60 pounds and cub (9-12 years of age) shooters = 40 pounds.

To shoot an officially sanctioned IBO tournament, you must be a member of the IBO. Annual membership currently costs $25 for an individual and $30 for a family, the IBO's Ken Watkins says.

For additional information about the IBO, contact: IBO, P.O. Box 398, Vermilion, OH 44089. The telephone is (440) 967-2137 and the Internet site is www.ibo.net.

THE ARCHERY SHOOTER'S ASSOCIATION (ASA)

The ASA was founded in 1993 to organize and run a successful, national 3-D tournament circuit during the months when there were no archery hunting seasons. That is its single goal and when it recently teamed up with Cabela's the name of the national circuit changed officially to the "Cabela's – ASA Pro Am."

Valdosta, Georgia entrepreneur and video producer Wayne Pearson founded ASA in the late 1980s as the Outdoor Trails shoot. Wayne promoted his tournament vigorously and it grew in enjoyment, popularity and cash payback. By the late 1990s, Wayne's ASA became the first national competition venue where archers could – and have! – win enough money to make a living shooting a bow. Almost no one thought Wayne could accomplish that. The nay-sayers were wrong.

Today, Wayne is long gone, but ASA President Mike Tyrell says the tournament circuit is in excellent shape with seven national Pro-Am tournaments typically beginning in Gainesville, Florida in February and ending with a National Championship in August. The ASA has also worked hard to develop a Federation Tour, a club-state-region structure to build 3-D archers and promote long-term interest in 3-D competition.

There are obvious similarities with IBO, but the differences are important even if they may be subtle. ASA is a for-profit enterprise while IBO is a 301-3c non-profit corporation. ASA tends to be a more southern circuit while IBO tends to have a more northern flavor. On a tournament for tournament basis, IBO tends to host a greater number of archers. ASA now uses Rinehart 3-D targets while IBO has always used McKenzie. Like IBO, ASA shooters must stand at a stake, but targets will not be farther away than "about 45 yards," Mike Tyrell says. "We give tournament organizers some leeway for terrain."

The shooting venues are essentially the same. ASA typically shoots two 20-target days, but the scoring zones are 12 – 10 – 8 – 5 – 0. The 12-ring is low and off center and archers who shoot for the 12-ring risk missing the target entirely. This makes any shoot-off exciting. Paybacks are in the 80%-of-entry fee range and a group of four competitors needs to budget about 3.5 hours to shoot the course. Except in a couple special cases, bow speed pegged at 280 fps. Cameras are allowed during shooting and there is no restriction on binocular power.

To shoot an officially sanctioned Cabela's-ASA tournament, you must be a member of the ASA. This may not be true for the ASA Federation tour at the club-state-region level. Annual membership currently costs $25 for an individual and $35 for a family.

For additional information about the ASA, contact: ASA, P.O. Box 399, Kennesaw, GA 30156. The telephone is (770) 795-0232 and the Internet site is www.asaarchery.com.

KNOWN DISTANCE FIELD SHOOTING

There was no such thing as a 3-D foam target when the National Field Archery Association (NFAA) was organized in 1939. There were no plastic vanes; there was no compound bow; there were no aluminum arrows; and states were still experimenting with bowhunting seasons. Still, there were however thousands of hard working and committed archers who wanted to enlarge their opportunities to shoot the bow

If you and your buddies are taking archery too seriously, perhaps it is time you livened up your practice with some fun and highly challenging Rinehart targets!

and arrow. The result of their labor is the largest archery membership organization in the world.

Although many knowledgeable sources place the "actual paid" membership much lower, NFAA Executive Secretary Mary Helen Rogers claims the NFAA has around 20,000 members. There is no question however that the NFAA does have a functioning grass roots organization in all 50 states. In addition, she says, more than 1,000 archery clubs and pro shops are affiliated with the NFAA.

The NFAA hosts archery instructor training courses and certifies archery coaches. It supports many archery activities and gets politically involved locally and at the state level, the levels at which non-migratory big game wildlife populations are typically managed. And because most NFAA members are bowhunters and field shooters, it contributes to the defense of bowhunting. The NFAA's primary goal though is to organize and manage the hundreds of marked yardage tournaments, both outdoor and indoor, held each year at club, state, region (the NFAA calls these sectionals) and national level. This shooting calendar includes the prestigious Las Vegas and Atlantic City indoor championships.

At a field shoot, participants stand with one foot against a stake and shoot at a paper target placed downrange at a known distance, from as close as 10 feet to as far as 80 yards. Twenty-eight target stations are scored 5 – 4 – 3 – 2 – 1. Archers shooting different styles of equipment compete only against each other. Women compete with women: men with men. Everywhere an NFAA-affiliated field tournament is held, the rules and structure are the same. Bows are restricted to 80 pounds draw weight, arrows to 280 fps. The NFAA is member of the world field organization, the IFAA or International Field Archery Association, and has strong ties to the National Archery Association (NAA), which sponsors the American Olympic team.

For additional information about the NFAA, contact: NFAA, 31407 Outer I-10, Redlands, CA 92373. The telephone is (909) 794-2133 and the Internet site is www.nfaa-archery.org

WHAT IT TAKES

Royce Armstrong, the publisher of *3-D and Bowhunting Times* has been following and reporting on the national 3-D circuits for a dozen years and he knows most of the top archers, manufacturers and archery coaches personally. "It takes an enduring interest," he says, "the ability to keep at it until it works. Of course, some natural talent helps, too.

"Sure, good equipment and focused practice are vital, but at the very highest levels of international competition, I'm convinced that these are not the elements that separate the winners from those who are just very good. I'm convinced that at the top, it is all mental."

Royce believes that so-called average archers can shoot immensely better if they work with a professional archery coach. For the price of a new bow, they can step out of the milling crowd into the ranks of superior competitors and archers. "Most top shooters use coaches to perfect their game," he says, "and these are the very people you believe would not need a coach. A good coach won't necessarily tell you what to shoot or how to shoot it, but will keep you at the top of your game mentally."

LOTS OF EXTRAS: STUFF YOU JUST GOTTA KNOW

Getting into archery is a lot like going to the store for ice cream. You can get a scoop of vanilla instead of the other two or three dozen flavors, because you know you have a choice of so many toppings and extras and cones and cup styles. A scoop of plain Jane vanilla becomes a magic carpet for your taste buds to slip you off to nirvana.

Buying a bow is the same way. It opens horizons to learn about and use accessories of virtually all shapes, sizes and benefits. Much of what is reported in this chapter will be required, but some of it will just be interesting or even simply curious. We will try to let you know the difference between what you must have, must learn about – and what will just interest you or take you to that next archery step.

RELEASING THE STRING WITH YOUR FINGERS

Let's face it. Ishi and his cousins and thousands of years of archers before the Ice Man was discovered in northern Italy with an arrowhead in his chest, shot a bow with their bare fingers. Or did they? The evidence is mixed because something like a leather shooting tab or a glove is highly perishable. Mongolian thumb rings made of bone indicate that at least some earlier generation archers fully understood that they could shoot better if they cushioned the bowstring on their fingers with ... well, something.

The leather shooting glove is a very good way to shoot the bow and most traditional archers who shoot longbows and recurves rely on a glove (or a tab) for hunting and competition. A leather glove is almost the "nothing can go wrong" solution for finger shooting – until it rains and the leather gets wet – or until it is used so much that you wear permanent creases deep in the fingers and have to provide that extra "oomph" to actually let go of the string.

In spite of the name "glove" an archery shooting glove from NEET or Wyandotte Leather only covers the tips of your three middle fingers, the ones that actually grasp the string, and a bit of the back of your hand. The small leather cases slip over your fingertips

The mechanical release aid is an outgrowth of archers realizing that even as children they were wrapping more of their fingers around the string than was strictly necessary to draw the bow and this extra friction and torque on the string often prevented a smooth shot.

This top grain, leather shooting glove lets you feel the string through soft, form-fitting, closed-end fingertips. An elastic insert between the leather finger cups and the wrist attachment allows the glove to stretch as you flex your hand.

Here's a no-pinch tab that has three layers – slick calf hair on the string, a rubber center insert and a felt cushion – plus a rubber finger separator to help you keep from pinching the arrow nock.

The two No-Glov molded rubber finger guards provide perfect finger positioning around your recurve nock and arrow. Once popular among hunters with recurve bows, today they are primarily used by bowfishermen.

and attach to an elastic strip that holds these small cases on your fingers by providing a little tension to the Velcro strap around your wrist.

The glove is simple and effectively protects your fingers from the stress of drawing, holding and releasing the string. On a 70-pound draw weight bow, that stress can be significant – even painful – and it only takes a few shots with bare fingers to appreciate the padding provided by a soft leather glove. Being stiffer and slicker than your fingers, the leather glove also eliminates some of the torque and friction of a release. Gloves are available in four sizes from small to extra large, so be sure to try it on before you buy.

An improvement over the shooting glove – at least from the point of view of a clean release – is the finger tab even though it does not look quite as macho. A good number of the traditional fraternity looks down on the tab as slightly effeminate, but that is certainly a false attitude. In many ways, the finger tab is better for its job than the glove. When you slide your middle finger through the hole of a tab, you will realize that your above-arrow finger has one protective pad while the two fingers that usually hold the string below the

arrow (this is the normal set-up, anyway) share the larger one. By having two fingers share a single protective pad below the string, the finger tab reduces some of the variability of your release.

The finger tab provides a more consistent release and perhaps better finger protection than a glove because it is normally multi-layered. Tabs are typically made from an inner (next to your fingers) layer of heavy felt and an outer (the side in contact with the string) layer of hair-on clipped calfskin or elk skin (Wyandotte or Kan't Pinch) or suede leather (NEET) or even thick plastic (Saunders). Some tabs include a third, inner layer of rubber to provide adherence between the outer layers and add to the cushioning.

Tabs, like gloves, usually need to be broken in but can certainly be taken out of the pro shop and directly into the deer woods. Because they are simple and lightweight, not much can go wrong unless, in your excitement to make a shot, you inadvertently slip the string between the layers. That will be a problem, but you will realize what you have done as soon as you draw. Of course, a tab can get wet and it may even freeze if it gets wet when the temperature drops. Still, a tab is a simple, effective and inexpensive solution for finger shooters. Remember to discard it in favor of a new one when it takes on a folded or worn aspect, however.

The more expensive tabs will have a finger spacer to prevent you from squeezing the nock of your arrow when you come to full draw. Obviously, just as with a mechanical release aid, if you pinch the arrow nock you can negatively affect arrow flight. The relatively expensive Cavalier Elite Tab features an anodized aluminum plate with an adjustable ledge for sure placement against your cheek or chin at full draw. This tab is highly effective in FITA shooting, but not a hunter's tab.

The old-fashioned No-Glove or the Saunders Finger Guard needs to be mentioned here as an option

Competitors in top national and international tournaments use this Elite Finger Tab because it has an adjustable plate and ledge that provide solid draw positioning.

for protecting your fingers when you draw. You must remove your string before you can slide these two-piece rubber finger protectors – the smaller section above the nocking point for your index finger and the larger section below for your other two fingers – in place over the string. With a recurve, which you relax when you are through shooting, that's not a problem although it will probably require that you use a piece of wire wrapped through your string loop to pull the bowstring into place through the No-Glove. It is easy … and not easy to install. So, if you use a No-Glove for bowfishing where things are routinely wet and slimy, for instance, dedicate that string to bowfishing rather than taking the No-Glove off each time you go to the range or out bowhunting.

It is not advisable to use a No-Glove with a compound bow unless it is a low-energy, low-speed bow used by a novice or youngster.

Protecting Your Arm

It seems like such an old fashioned thing, an armguard, like something from the days when folks drove Model Ts to shoots, shot clout and really understood what the word *fistmele* meant. Do not kid yourself. This is one small piece of archery equipment that you must use. On the other hand, once you get an armguard that fits and that you remember to put it on each time you pick up your bow to shoot, there is not much reason you should ever give it much thought again, either.

You need an armguard because the forward lunge of the bowstring after you release can do a lot of damage to the inside of your bow arm if it hits there. And anyone who has shot more than a few arrows has eventually been reminded of the necessity of this insignificant bit of gear with a brilliant and painful blue-black-purple bruise that seems to take forever to

Many archers, especially for cold weather, prefer a large armguard such as this one from NEET that helps keep their clothing well out of the way of the bowstring.

go away. Only indirectly does the string cause the bruise. You have a bruise because you shoot with improper form, by twisting your bow arm so that the meaty part of your elbow and forearm makes a bulge in toward the bow … and it will happen when you least expect it.

You can easily see how this happens by holding your arm out to the side, but straight as if you were holding your bow and then rotating your elbow back and forth. That is exactly where the armguard should be strapped. (The other interesting thing to note here is how difficult it is to keep your hand straight, without twisting. Now, imagine the possibilities for torquing your bow riser!)

Of course, the armguard protects your arm, but it also protects your shot. If you are hunting in more than one or two layers of clothing or you hunt the coldest part of the second rut, you understand down-filled jackets and the concept of "layering." Wearing this much you will not have a problem bruising if you get hit by the string, but you will still need your armguard to keep the clothing out of the way of the bowstring.

Once you understand the need for an armguard, the possibilities are boundless – even in this simple and unimaginative bit of gear. Try a few on and see what you like. Think of your shooting situation, too, and then buy one or buy a couple. They are cheap. If possible, shoot with them on your arm. Armguards come in numerous lengths, just like archers' forearms

In most cases, a lightweight ventilated armguard will be a perfect hunting and shooting companion.

At the highest levels of 3-D and international competition archers shoot without armguards, but these are the finest archers in America ... and they still risk a serious bruise.

and if one is a bit too short, you can adjust it, but if it is a bit too long it will forever be an irritant.

Finally, is it important to purchase a camouflaged armguard? Does a camo armguard work better than a black armguard? What if the camo on the armguard does not match your camouflage clothing? Do not worry. Your chances of encountering Martha Stewart in the deer woods are slim.

The simple, effective armguard for most situations is a light, vented style from WRI-Vista. These fasten around your forearm with Velcro straps and, after you get used to wearing it, you will hardly know it is there – until the moment you make a thoughtless release and your string slaps against it or worse, snags on its trailing edge! These are excellent all around armguards: light, comfortable and easy to use.

Saunders makes a ventilated armguard with plastic mesh protection. These have the same benefits as the Vista armguards. Two or three straps. Easy and cool in the summer. The Saunders armguards tighten with a metal hook and the strap is adjustable elastic. On a warm day north or south, you will appreciate a lightweight ventilated plastic armguard.

NEET and Wyandotte Leather make most of the solid, non-vented armguards on the market. They come in a variety of price ranges, from $8 to $30, and a variety of lengths, widths and materials. A standard length is six or seven inches. There are 13-inch armguards, too, for archers with real shooting form difficulties! Most of these are leather or some leatherette like Cordura. Internally, they will have tough strips or staves of plastic so they will remain resistant and keep their shape.

BuckWing makes an interesting 8-inch armguard called the Saveyur II. It is actually a tubular knit fabric that slips on without hooks or fasteners, like a sock, that fits from your wrist to about your elbow.

And there are "traditional" armguards, also, for archers who just cannot settle for simple. Wyandotte and NEET both make lace-up leather armguards that look very good in pictures with longbows and fringed buckskin shirts, but must be a pain to put on and take off.

THE CHEST PROTECTOR

The chest protector is a simple, adjustable garment that has two functions: it protects ladies chests from a poorly executed shot and it keeps loose clothing and other personal items out of the path of the bowstring. Essentially, it performs the same function as an arm guard. Picture the chest protector as half a vest that is held in place by an adjustable strap around the back. The NEET chest protector is adjustable, comfortable nylon mesh with a self-adjusting back strap with Velcro fastener.

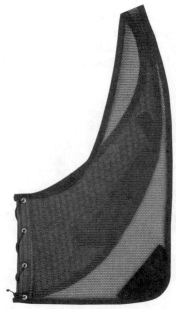

The chest protector is designed to keep the bowstring from hitting your chest and any loose clothing.

204 *LOTS OF EXTRAS: STUFF YOU JUST GOTTA KNOW*

In the field, anything can happen and often does, says world-class bowhunter Randy Waddell. Randy took his 9-foot, 900-pound Alaskan brown bear at 22 yards! Note the armguard on his left forearm.

WRIST STRAPS OR SLINGS

Good shooting form requires that you shoot with a relaxed bow hand. If it is not relaxed, you inevitably twist or torque the bow and this causes erratic, left-right arrow impact. Technically, you only want your hand to hold the bow up, to provide a steady bracket against which you can draw and release. Although it would detract from the archery experience, a metal bracket held in your hand so that you could not touch the bow at all might be ideal.

The loose grip is a difficult concept, because our natural inclination is to grab the bow, wrap our fingers around the handle and squeeze it tight. After all, the bow together with your accessories weighs 5 or 6 pounds and you are trying to hold it out at arm's length. So, when we release the string, all of the energy of the shot is moving away from us and the bow is going to try to jump forward, out of our hand. We do

not want to drop the bow, so we hold on tight. For most archers, this becomes a paradox. A sling or strap can help solve the problem because it will catch the bow, but it takes some getting-used-to, some shooting with it in place to build confidence that it will actually work.

The standard sling strap is leather or braided nylon. Typically, it is designed to fasten beneath your stabilizer (the stabilizer holds it in place) and adjusts for comfort with a Velcro tab or a light buckle. Most slings, including many of those from Cavalier, Gibbs, NEET and Paradox, can remain attached to the bow with some variety of stabilizer mount. It is important that they remain in the raised or up position, because if you need to make a quick shot, you want to be able to slip your hand into the sling and onto the grip without fiddling around or having to use two hands.

One of the simplest slings, the Super Sling from

Cavalier, is a double nylon loop. To use it, place your hand on the bow riser in your natural shooting position and one of the loops slides onto your thumb and one over your middle finger. Easy to use and adjust, this

finger sling works like the Chinese thumb puzzle. The bow cannot fall out of your hand and the tighter you pull – unless you try to wiggle out of it – the firmer it holds. Many archers will like the simplicity, but others will find the feeling unnatural and annoying. Paradox makes a similar sling from braided nylon.

Whatever sling you use, it is important that it is comfortable and remains in the up position when your hand is not on the bow. The Cavalier Speed Sling is rigid tubing that attaches to a metal stabilizer mount. While this rubber tube design works well, it does not look terribly comfortable and to compensate, Cavalier offers an optional soft fleece sleeve to slip over it.

A fully adjustable bowsling made of 1-inch wide polypropylene webbing for strength and durability. This sling features an adjustable buckle and butterfly bracket.

BOW HOLDERS, HOOKS & SLINGS

There will occasionally be times when you do not want to hold your bow in your hand or lay it down on the ground. A tuned bow, equipped with matching accessories is a fine tool and can be quite expensive (easily more than $1,000 for high end equipment) so you want to keep it out of the dirt and away from careless boot steps. A bow holder attached to your belt or around your waist and an over-the-shoulder bow sling can help you protect your investment and take some of the weight (and tedium in a treestand) off your hands when you need them either for other tasks or just to be still.

A bow holder attaches to your belt and lets your place your bow riser in it at the grip. If you are stopping to score a 3-D target or glass a ridge for elk, the PSE or Bateman bow holders can work just fine. Because archers who hunt and shoot competitively design them, these bow holders will not scratch your bow. They are usually a rigid piece of aluminum or even plastic covered with sturdy nylon or some other soft synthetic material and some of the cups are covered in a faux fur for softness. One variation is the

A wrist strap fastening beneath the stabilizer gives archers the security that they can shoot with a relaxed grip and not lose control of their bow after their shot.

An inexpensive but workable bow holder slides over your belt and leaves your hands free for binoculars.

An elaborate and adjustable bow holder such as this one from NEET slips over your belt and has a drawstring to keep it from flopping when you are on the trail. This style bowholder will also work in treestands.

A kisser button is used primarily by finger shooters and competitive recurve shooters. When the string is drawn, the kisser button touches a precise position on an archer's lip and this lets him know that his anchor point is secure.

rubber-coated Hip Clip, which is designed to hold your bow by its string or cables.

Bow hooks attach to your belt and let you rest your bottom eccentric in them. Useful while stalking or standing on a treestand, they hold the bow in the ready position and take the weight off your bow arm. The Bateman hook threads over your belt. It is made from two inch black poly webbing and is very lightweight. The NEET Bow Rest just snaps over your belt and has an elastic tie-down cord, gunslinger style. The Vista Bow Hook is fleece lined to keep your cam or strings from scratching.

Vista's Bow Toter is designed to free your hands and take the weight off your bow arm. The long adjustable strap has a loop at each end that slips over your bow's cams. Just sling it over your shoulder, adjust the buckle for comfort and you are good to go. The Flex Foam Bow Carrier is padded and has an elastic chest strap to keep the sling on your shoulder. The Gibbs Easy Sling/Case includes a bag or case for your bow to protect it from the elements while you have it slung over your shoulder.

THE KISSER BUTTON

Kisser buttons are still used by finger shooters and FITA shooters who attach them to the bowstring above the nock point locator. It was always rare to see a kisser button on a compound bow, even a light draw weight compound, and most are used on recurves. The purpose of the kisser button is to give archers a specific reference point to which they draw the string each time. The only problem is facial contortions as a result of weather or even a shooter's mood swing. The kisser will not touch the same part of your nose or lip if you are smiling or frowning. The soft, slotted kisser from Saunders Archery slides over the string and is

fastened in place with a cushioned brass nock point locator.

TRAVELING BOW CASES

If you are at all serious about archery, whether you are an avid bowhunter or a dedicated 3-D competitor, you need a quality hard-sided bow case AND a padded soft-sided case. You can take your soft-sided, lightly padded bow case across the country in your pick up truck, but just try to fly to Alaska with it. The airlines would not accept many soft-sided cases anyway and their baggage handlers, men who are able to put major dents in high impact, industrial plastic luggage, would have a veritable "field day."

There are actually a variety of hard-sided, high impact plastic cases for archery gear. MTM Case-Gard makes a broadhead case with a built-in broadhead wrench that carries a half-dozen assembled and sharpened heads. Plano offers a variety of archery tackle boxes with hinged and lift-out trays similar to your fishing tackle box. MTM also has a unique Bow Maintenance Center (okay, it is technically not a case) with a maintenance and travel rack that positions your bow upright for all adjustments – setting nocks, reserving strings, waxing strings, making tiller adjustments, etc. – that do not require the bow to be disassembled. It also serves as an "excellent way to transport or store a fully assembled bow," MTM says.

A soft-sided case is easy to pack and takes up so little room in the trunk of the family car that when you get to the 3-D shoot, you may wonder where you put it. NEET is the leader in soft-sided case design with a dozen or more styles and designs to choose from. First however, their non-padded Camo Cover is an inexpensive poly-cotton sleeve designed to cover the bow, with the quiver and arrows attached, to meet state cased law requirements. The Camo Cover features a full-length zipper and folds or rolls up to pocket size when not in use or when you need to stuff it out of the way in your daypack. This non-padded sleeve is great for states with laws that require bows to be cased before daybreak and immediately after official sunset.

NEET's line of padded cases is extensive and cases are available in a variety of camo patterns, solid colors and interesting Southwest style designs. Most of them feature a full-length zipper and an inch or more of egg crate padding on both sides, sandwiching your bow in comfort. When you buy your case, look for outside carrying pouches for miscellaneous gear and full-length arrows, wrap-around web handles and a D-ring hanger on one end for the "off season." NEET, Methods, SKB and others also make padded cases for takedown recurves.

There is a lot to choose from in the hard-sided case field, but in this gear zone as in so many others, you get what you pay for. My first hard sided bow case featured lightweight, key-locking metal latches that looked sturdy enough, but soon bent and tore up completely, apparently from the stress and bangs of ordinary travel. The case weathered thousands of miles of airplanes and pick-up trucks, but those latches did not last the first year. Thank goodness for duct tape!

Flambeau ("We bring plastics to life.") builds a high impact plastic Safeshot bow case that is oversized with plenty of room to accommodate most compound bows and quivers (although since the trend to shorter bows, length should not be a problem with any case). Two adjustable Velcro straps are included to securely hold your bow in the foam-padded interior. Up to a dozen arrows with broadheads attached, can travel without any chance that they will damage the bow, string, cables or your accessories. Look for multiple locking points and a piano style hinge on this black model.

The Winchester Bow Case is aluminum sided with reinforced corners. A pair of combination locks and key locks helps keep it doubly secure. Wheels on one end and a handle on the other end let you wheel this through airports just like luggage. Because it has an all-metal exterior, it will be heavier and more expensive than molded plastic models, but it peace of mind should be worth the extra price.

SKB builds a variety of molded plastic and handsome soft-sided cases that are actually designed for traveling. Their double cases are designed to carry two bows with up to 18 arrows or a bow and a rifle. Their double recurve case features a combination of rigid and soft foam compartments for two takedown recurves and accessories.

SKB's bow bags are as handsome (and manly, yes)

as affordable bow cases get. They are completely padded and the interiors feature suede leather at high friction points to prevent abrasion. The handles are reinforced with leather. The problem with this style case is that you will need to find a good way to secure them although SKB says that the oversized, self-repairing nylon zippers will accept customer added luggage locks.

The SKB compound roller bag has a top side handle and bottom side rollers and legs for waiting in long lines at airports and then rolling along without breaking a sweat to check in. The exterior fabric is a heavy "600 dernier" and a shoulder strap is included.

An excellent name in hard-sided bow cases, Doskocil has been building high impact plastic cases for 20 years. Their Deluxe Bow Guard case features hard plastic two-piece riveted handles and "airline approved" key locks.

Sizes of bow cases are variable and you can find cases designed for the largest compound bow you want to carry (the Doskocil Field Locker Single Bow Case is 52 ½ x 21 ¾ x 6 inches or 4 cubic feet) or designed precisely to minimize the space taken up while still providing full protection to your gear (the SKB Deluxe Short Bow Case is 40 ½ x 15 x 4 inches or 1.4 cubic feet).

Kolpin calls their new water repellent Double Edge a "bow gear bag" rather than a case. It carries two bows and extra gear in a case with padding and protection on all sides. One exterior pocket and five internal pockets keep your gear from rattling around when you are packing and traveling. It measures 45 inches by 7-1/2 inches by 16-1/2 inches and includes a shoulder strap.

ARCHERS AND TREESTANDS

Ancient human hunter-gatherers must have realized that when they hunted on the ground, vegetation and terrain limited what they could see and consequently limited the effectiveness of the cooperative hunting they could plan. Even stereoscopic vision, large eyeballs, sensitive ears and a nose perched on top of a neck that could rotate 270 degrees could not prevent them from occasionally falling victim to lions and packs of wild dogs while they were on the ground.

To increase their safety and their effectiveness as hunters, early humans must have sought out and even fought for the high ground. In many places, open grassland for instance, this certainly meant scrambling up trees. Even with primitive spears and pointed rocks, the elevation afforded by climbing a tree would every now and then give a hunter the immediate advantage of striking down at otherwise wary prey wandering beneath him. Probably however, assuming that deer and hogs and buffalo were just as suspicious 10,000 or 20,000 or even 100,000 years ago as they are now, the principal advantage of height would have been for planning and safety.

Today, we take up the bow and arrow in a radically different world than the one in which our distant ancestors lived, but the three reasons for hunting from an elevated position are just as important now: safety from other predators, including other human hunters; planning and coordinating a stalk or a cooperative effort; and especially the advantage of striking down or, with today's vastly superior equipment, of striking down and out with speed and efficiency.

TYPES OF TREESTANDS

Today's hunting archer can choose from three basic treestand styles – climbers, fixed-position or hang-on stands, and climbers – and one style that mimics the stand and the tree, the tripod which is regionally popular in the U. S. southwest.

Most archers, virtually all of whom are Daniel Boone in their heart, climbed trees as children. Our ancestors climbed trees and our closest biological relatives still do. One could argue that climbing is in our genetic make up. So, is this why is there an entire industry devoted to helping us get up off the ground? Can't we do this by ourselves? There are three answers.

- Unlike our ancestors who hunted and foraged for a living, we are accountants and house painters, doctors and mechanics. We are part-time hunters and outdoorsmen. As a species, we are larger, heavier and less physically adept than ever before and we have generally lost the need for and interest in climbing.
- American comedian George Carlin says we take our "stuff" with us everywhere. Certainly we do haul a lot of gear into the field when we go

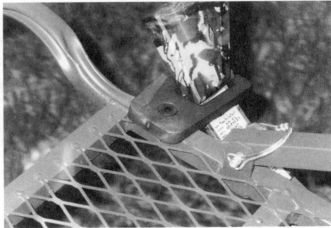

Archery lends itself to innovation and "accessorizing" in all forms, from hunting to competition. Here, an add-on bow holder of high-impact plastic from High Point Products has been added to the steel platform of a climbing stand from Professional Hunting Products. A bow holder allows an archer to keep his bow at the ready with an arrow nocked without having to hold it in his hands throughout the hunt.

hunting. That stuff, of course, is designed to help us part-time hunters take home full-time game animals.

• Finally, a commercially manufactured treestand offers us advantages in comfort, safety, efficiency and flexibility that we could never realize without one, certainly not with the stands we build in our garage or nail to trees in the deer woods.

Treestand design has evolved enormously since early commercial models became available in the 1970s. Today's designs are attentive to comfort, safety and versatility. They allow us to scale a variety of trees and to enjoy and appreciate our limited time in nature.

FIXED-POSITION STANDS

The classic treestand for archers is a fixed-position stand. Using the natural branches of a tree or steps that screw into or strap around the trunk, the archer climbs until he has reached the preferred shooting height. Once he is sure he is securely attached to the tree with a safety belt or harness, he pulls up the stand with a rope and attaches it securely to the tree. When the stand is stable, he steps onto it, first carefully transferring the safety line or harness, and then pulls

ALL-STEEL HANG ON SECURITY

SUPERIOR COMFORT

FOLDS SNUG AGAINST TREE

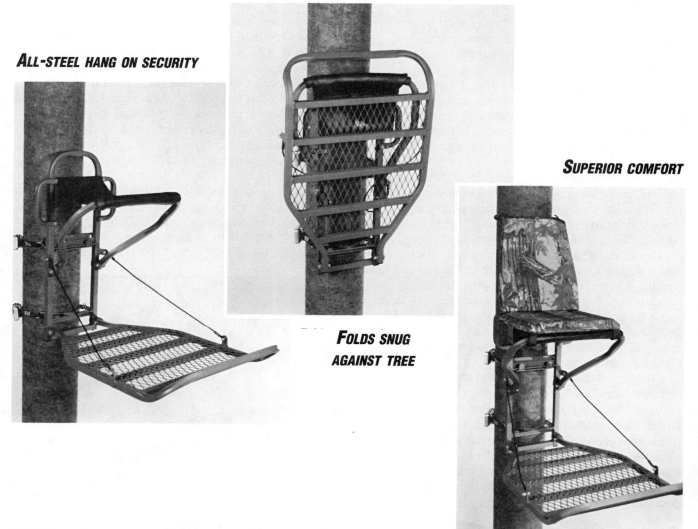

This lightweight hang-on stand illustrates several points about recent treestand development. First, it folds up against the tree to minimize its silhouette. This helps prevent theft, unauthorized use and potential liability when you are not present. Second, the basic design of many stands now includes such features as a foot rail to help you keep from becoming fatigued on stand. Third, the stand can be removed from the tree leaving the bracket attached. You can purchase several inexpensive brackets, but may only need a single stand. Finally, the obvious comfort of the optional padded seat and seat back contrast sharply with the mesh of the folding seat.

The classic fixed-position or hang-on treestand will fold flat against a tree when not in use. Secured in two positions by ratcheting belts, this fixed position stand sets up quickly and can be moved by one person.

up his bow and perhaps a fanny pack stuffed with hunting accessories.

Fixed-position stands have been commercially available for about 25 years. The "Lem" from Loc-On, now part of Consolidated Treestands in Magnolia, Arkansas was one of the earliest successful designs. With its fastening chain, the aluminum Lem weighs only 13 pounds and offers an angled 27- by 20-inch standing platform. It has a fold-down seat and a 300-pound weight rating. Like so many early designs, the Lem was produced to meet the minimum functional needs of the budget-conscious climbing archer. Although the Lem is definitely priced attractively, the round bar on the front of the fold-down seat tends to put your legs to sleep. A good, thick cushion is highly recommended.

Like all archery and hunting equipment, even basic

fixed-position stands have undergone redesign for comfort, safety and versatility. "The Cedar" from Warren & Sweat, now part of USL Outdoor Products in Minneapolis, Minnesota is a 14-pound welded-aluminum stand with a rectangular 36-inch by 20-inch standing platform. The seat is removable and thickly padded. "The Cedar" attaches to a tree with a quiet, lightweight 1-1/2-inch ratcheting strap and the platform leans tight against a tree with serrated blades for extra grip. A safety video, featuring recognized Minnesota bowhunting expert Myles Keller, and a heavy-duty nylon chest restraint are included with the stand.

Archers considering the purchase of a fixed-position treestand should understand their advantages and disadvantages. First, like the aluminum 10.5-pound "Wildcat Lite" from Hunter's View in Peoria, Illinois fixed-position stands are typically light in weight. They vary from 10 to 20 pounds, depending on platform size and whether they are constructed of aluminum or steel.

Fixed-position stands usually fold up conveniently for carrying and come with backpacking straps. Because the platforms are built in some type of grid, it is easy to attach your pack and accessories to their frame. The stand acts like a natural backpack frame. The 13-pound aluminum "Z-Loc" from Ol' Man in Hattiesburg, Mississippi is sold with backpack straps. The lightweight and quick folding nature of fixed-position stands mean that they are highly portable and relatively easy to move from tree to tree.

Finally, because fixed-position stands are smaller overall than other stand types, they present a low profile in the woods. For an archer, who has to move his body and equipment significantly to get off a shot, these stands offer a lot of freedom. Look for a fixed-position stand that will fold up against a tree and, secured with a chain and lock, can be left in place from hunt to hunt. (To prevent theft or the use of your stand by an unauthorized person, you will want to remove your tree steps.)

Responding to hunter's needs for multiple hunting locations depending upon the time of day or the prevailing wind direction, manufacturers like Trax America in Forrest City, Arkansas produce fixed-position stands that can be moved from tree to tree and mounted on brackets which are be left permanently in place. Trax' 15-pound "Hooker" comes with one bracket assembly. Additional brackets are much less expensive than purchasing an entire stand assembly.

While the advantages of fixed-position stands – lightweight, portable and low-profile – make them seem like the perfect treestand for an archer, they also have distinct disadvantages. Because of these advantages, fixed-position stands must be relatively small. Consequently, they offer little room or comfort for larger, heavier bodies.

Few hunting archers enjoy putting up a hang-on stand in the dark of early morning. While they may only weigh a dozen pounds, fixed-position stands are irritatingly awkward and it is the rare or accomplished archer who can hang a fixed-position stand in silence and without working up a good sweat. On a cold morning, the sweat eventually means trouble as your body cools.

The final disadvantage to using fixed-position stands is that the archer must carry steps with him or rely on a tree's natural branches. Relying on natural branches seems to be the logical and obvious choice, but most trees the archer wants to climb, relatively vertical trees of medium diameter in exactly the right position for a stand, will be deficient in branches or certainly deficient in branches at the right height and interval for a climb. In addition, a 200-pound man either carrying or pulling up another 25 pounds of gear needs to be very careful where he steps.

Manufactured climbing aids come in three styles: screw-in and strap-around steps or a strap-on ladder. Several manufacturers such as Gorilla, in Flushing, Michigan offer machined screw-in tree steps and, to

Today's treestand is often part of an outdoor ensemble that allows you to be comfortable while you are hunting. Many argue that if you can wait quietly, you are a more effective hunter. Still, a stand that is equipped with many comfort and shooting features can be large and heavy. Add this to the weight of a fully set-up bow and a complete daypack and you may need an ATV to get to your chosen hunting location.

climb to hunting height, an archer should plan to carry and use at least a dozen. Because steps weigh about 9 ounces each, that means carrying an additional 6 to 7 pounds of cold steel in your backpack. Screwing your dozen steps into a tree, even in states where it is legal to use tree-damaging steps on public land, and repositioning your safety line and gear haul-up line up the tree as you go, is laborious and time-consuming.

Strap-on steps or ladder sections are increasingly popular alternatives to screw-in steps. "EZY Climb Folding Rope" (or Hang-On) Tree Steps from Cranford Manufacturing in Mocksville, North Carolina are machined from heavy, 11-gauge steel and attach around a tree up to 17 inches in diameter with a polyester tire-cord. They are easier to hang, but just as heavy as and much more bulky than their screw-in cousins.

An alternative to using individual steps is a lightweight climbing pole or stick. Climbing poles, typically built with four or five steps per section, are now seen more frequently in the woods. The "Po-Jo Pole" from Amacker in Sondheimer, Louisiana is a three-section alternative to conventional tree steps. The three, 4-foot "Po-Jo Pole" sections snap together quickly and fasten to a tree with webbed nylon straps as you climb. The complete "Po-Jo Pole" weighs 9 pounds.

CLIMBING STANDS

With untold millions of pine and hickory trees and not a single limb to stand on for 60 feet straight up, it is no wonder that the climbing stand is thought of as a southern innovation dating from the 1970s. The first climber used by most experienced archers was a Baker from Valdosta, Georgia. Today, climbers are used everywhere, primarily for deer, but also for elk and bear.

The typical climber is a two-piece treestand. Thought of as a "stand-up, sit-down" device for climbing a tree, a climbing stand offers distinct advantages over fixed-position stands, with few drawbacks. Early climbers were uncomfortable, prone to slip dangerously – especially on the smooth bark of a pine tree – and noisy. Those problems have largely been solved.

To use a climbing stand an archer fastens the back strap, bar or rigid chain of both the upper or seat section and the lower or platform section around the tree. He inserts his boots into the straps or under a bar on the platform and, gripping the upper section with his hands while resting his forearms on the side rails, proceeds to hang on to the rails while he lifts his feet and the platform several feet. He then shifts his weight to the platform, taking it off the seat section and lifts

Even today's "stripped down" welded aluminum or steel treestand is a product of more than a quarter century of experimentation and trial and error. Simple in appearance, this new climber from Tree Lounge in Cumming, Georgia, is a highly refined tool designed and manufactured for lightweight portability, safety, comfort and effectiveness.

Because the hunting archer must be very close to game for a successful shot, classic stand-up, sit-down climbing stands have become an important tool. They can be repositioned quickly to take advantage of shifts in wind currents or to move from feeding to bedding trails. Equipped with optional accessories such as padded seats, backs and arm rests; a foot rail or gun rail, and even various camouflaging and weather mediating devices, today's climbers offer comfort and security for all day hunting.

the seat until it is comfortable to repeat this process. In this manner, alternately standing, lifting and squatting, the hunter works his way up a tree. In practice, it is both easier … and more difficult … than it sounds, but with just a few minutes of actual practice, the hunter quickly becomes proficient in the self-climbing process.

Today's climbers offer three advantages over fixed-position stands. They are typically larger, more comfortable and safer. (The last point is arguable because most hunting accidents are climbing related.) The API "Grand Slam Super Mag Supreme" made in

Tallulah, Louisiana lives up to its billing on all three counts and is typical of the "souped up" climbers designed for all-day or 10-minute use. This stand's 350-pound weight capacity will safely accommodate practically any archer. The seat is thickly cushioned and a long, padded backrest is included. Of course, the arm rests, front safety bar and optional shooting rail are also camouflaged and padded. API's "Power Gripping" rubber covered chains wrap around a tree and hold the stand secure providing silent, no-slip climbing on trees from 6 to 24 inches in diameter. Every API stand comes with a full-body safety harness and safety video.

The better designed, and of course costlier climbing stands offer small extras that are well worth considering.

- Bungee-style tension cords strap around the back of your boots to keep your feet from slipping out from the climbing bar or straps.
- True platform dimension means that you can use all of the advertised platform width and that the sidebars or suspension wires or ropes that wrap around the tree will not keep you from shifting position as a long hunting day wears on.
- Bow holders should fasten to the platform without the necessity of drilling holes.
- Optional footrests will help you stay comfortable and alert, and shooting rails will accommodate the two-season, gun and bow hunter.

• Swivel seats allow smooth, silent turning and shooting practically 360 degrees.

Because there is significantly more metal exposed on a climber than on the typical fixed-position stand, archers considering the purchase of a climbing stand need to remember that the bow can be an awkward shooting tool. Hence, there is more potential for game-alarming noise and interference with movement for a clean shot. You should always practice drawing your bow at a variety of angles to see if you will be satisfied with a stand's clearance before buying it.

A second consideration for archers is size and weight. Although climbing stands offer greater comfort and ease of movement (portability) when you change from morning to afternoon locations for instance, these benefits come at the expense of increased weight. Normally, a climbing stand will weigh twice what your fixed-position treestand weighs, but if you consider the weight and bulk of tree steps or climbing sticks with your fixed-position stand, the weight difference may not be all that much. The decked-out, welded aluminum API "Grand Slam Super Mag Supreme" mentioned above weighs 30 pounds (without a foot rest or shooting rail). Fortunately, padded carrying straps are an available option!

LADDER STANDS

The third style of treestand is the ladder stand. The concept is extremely simple; a seat is attached to the top of a ladder. Typically, these steel or aluminum stands are sold as a platform/seat unit with two or three ladder sections; the sections join by simply sliding crimped section ends into the un-crimped ends of the adjoining section. The pressure of a person climbing and the friction of metal-to-metal contact keep the parts in place. Following assembly, one lifts the stand and positions it against the tree. Ladder stands attach to a tree in the same manner as fixed-position stands, with a ratcheting belt, rope or chain. Mid-way up the ladder however, and within reach of a person standing on the ground, there is typically an additional brace to steady it and provide rigidity. With a secure grounding, the ladder stand thus has three points of steady support.

The bulky, unnatural profile of ladder stands is highly visible compared to fixed-position or climbing stands. For gun hunters, this may not be a problem, but for archers who shoot comparatively short distances (most record book deer are taken at less than 25 yards), a ladder may not be the optimum solution to treestand hunting. Additionally, ladders are relatively heavy and can be difficult for a person to erect and secure alone.

Ladder stands are extremely useful however when you plan to return often to a hunting location, over a planted field, for instance. If responding to the vagaries of the weather or the phase of the moon or wind direction is important for stand positioning, then a ladder stand should not be the only treestand in your inventory. Typically though, ladders are safe and easy to hunt from once they are in position.

An excellent example of the minimalist and inexpensive style ladder stand, the style that allows hunting archers the greatest flexibility and freedom to move from place to place, is the "Ranger" from Remington by USL in Minneapolis, Minnesota. The "Ranger" weighs 38 pounds. Once stood against a tree, it is 15 feet to the seat. The platform, made from expanded metal decking, doubles as the seat. The top step is also the foot platform. This stand separates into 3-foot sections for carrying. It is bare, but highly utilitarian.

Ladders can be equipped with swivel seats like those in your fishing boat or even purchased with a bench seat for two people to use at a time. There are a variety of foot rests, gun rests, railings, padded seats and back rests, even complete wrap-around camouflage drapes and awnings available.

For teaching someone else to shoot from an elevated position, the unique "Me and My Buddy" stand from Trax America is designed for two people to sit or stand comfortably from tandem upper and lower seats. This is an excellent stand for teaching a novice archer to hunt or to just enjoy the outdoors. A superb stand concept, the "Me and My Buddy" stand weighs only 35 pounds, but it advertises a load capacity of 400 pounds. Got a kid? Get a buddy!

ALTERNATIVE STANDS

The ingenuity of independent people in a free-market economy was never more evident than in the treestand niche in the archery and hunting marketplace. Several dozen manufacturers offer excellent fixed-position stands, climbers, tree sticks or climbing poles and ladders. There is an also an abundance of alternatives to the three traditional manufactured styles.

Tripod stands give archers an excellent opportunity to rise above otherwise level landscapes. With their modern origin in Texas and the southwest, where tripods will elevate a hunter into or, in many cases, above the tree canopy, tripods or quad-pods can provide 10 to 15 feet of elevation and relatively comfortable 360 degree shooting.

Tripods from companies like BBK in San Antonio, Texas offer features the hunting archer will want to consider before making a final purchase. One feature is the seat belt, thoughtfully included, because hunting on a tripod usually means hunting in full sun and that leads to warm relaxation, drowsiness and an increased opportunity to take a spill. A buyer should look for some additional rigidity and stability such as leg pads that are drilled for ground spikes and perhaps mid-height crossbars, too. Check its maximum weight restrictions, as more is generally better than less. Getting onto the platform of a tripod can be tricky so make sure access is easy and that the platform will be wide enough for comfort. Typically, this means that the tripod platform will be equipped with some style trap door. With practice, one person can assemble and set up a tripod stand in just a few minutes.

Archers have experimented with a variety of hanging seats for years, but Trophyline's "Tree Saddle" is a unique step in perfecting that idea and, with a 500 pound weight rating, this Jasper, Georgia bag should accommodate the heaviest climber. One simply straps on the leather saddle and uses a conventional means to climb. Once you have reached your preferred shooting height, you securely attach the safety belt and quite literally hang in position, braced by your feet and legs, with the ability to shoot 360 degrees. The "Tree Saddle" or the "Tree Suit" from Chariton, Iowa will take some getting used to as it is an unusual concept and does place your feet and knees under a strain.

TREESTAND SAFETY

The development of the compound bow in the late 1960s and 1970s encouraged a generation of new archers by making bows a little easier to shoot and arrows travel a little faster. Increasing participation caused increasing demand and the growth of the treestand industry. At some point, archers realized that

All wrong! The days when archers climbed and hunted from trees without the security of a full body safety harness should be long gone.

Just right! With a properly attached harness, the archer is a safer and more proficient hunter. No hunter (gun or bow) should consider climbing a tree or sitting in a treestand without a safety harness attached at all times.

homemade nail-and-wood stands were not the answer to their hunting needs. Along the way in those 30 to 40 years, thousands of people were seriously injured and hundreds were killed in hunting related tree climbing accidents.

When archers began climbing seriously in the '70s, little thought was given to safety. That's of course no longer true, but back then if someone looped a rope around his waist and tied it to the tree behind him, that was considered "safe enough." It was also unusual. Because the rope would occasionally snag on the stand seat or on a branch, archers complained that safety lines limited their freedom of movement (It's a free country, right?) and it does take a considerable amount of movement to pick up a bow, then draw, aim and release at a target. Unfortunately, it took many thousands of accidents for participants and manufacturers to understand that the danger of climbing trees in the woods was serious.

Today, climbing safety is taught as part of hunter education programs. Manufacturers like Summit Specialties in Decatur, Alabama offer not just a safety belt with every treestand purchase, but a full four-point safety harness. Summit's "Seat-O-The-Pants" safety harness will hold you upright if you fall and it features a shock-reducing tether that acts as a brake should you spill over the side of your stand.

Even manufacturers that do not offer a high quality safety harness or fall restraint system with their stands offer videos promoting climbing and treestand safety. Too often, a simple belt or chest restraint has proven to be inadequate or even compounded error with tragedy when a climbing archer was squeezed to the point of suffocation or found that he was unable to maneuver sufficiently to rescue himself.

Safety can no longer be considered an "issue" for debate among climbing archers. The use of a high quality fall restraint system must be a cold, accepted fact, both on a stand and climbing to and from a stand. The intelligent archer would no more climb without a safety harness than he would jump out of an airplane without a parachute.

"SO, WHAT CAN GO WRONG?"

"If a person is at all aware, he should be able to twist around while he's in the air so he doesn't land on his head." Six hours later, Bill was in a hospital emergency room and this is a true story.

"It looks like you fell out of a treestand. You did, didn't you?" the nurse asked in dismay. "You're the third one this week."

The 4 x 4 buck only ran a hundred yards before piling up. "It was a wonderful evening," Bill recalls, "so I wasn't in a hurry to get down from the stand."

The archer was experienced and well traveled. Married late in life, he never took off his wedding band, though. It was as much a part of his wardrobe as shoes and socks.

Eventually, he attached his bow to a cord and lowered it from his seat 30 feet up. Methodically, he stood and faced the tree, making sure of his equilibrium. Then, he reached his foot out for the first step. With his boot on that first screw-in tree step and a good grip on the trunk of the tree, Bill released his safety harness. That first step is the most dangerous so he was careful. His screw-in steps were built with a slight lip on the outside end to help keep a carelessly placed or dirt-caked boot from sliding off.

It was that little flange though that was going to force the archer to sleep sitting in a chair for six weeks because on the third step down, his wedding band hung up on it. Without thinking, he jerked his hand to shake it loose from the step.

Bill fell nearly three stories, landing upside down on his right shoulder.

"As careful as I am, I refuse to believe I fell out of a tree," he thought. He did not know whether to go for help or hide in embarrassment.

Settling comfortably into a state of shock, he gathered his equipment as well as he could and walked out to check his buck. There was not much pain, not much more than what he would later refer to as "discomfort." He was surprised and angry with himself for falling.

Because he could not manage to hold anything in his right hand, he thought his injury might be worse than just a strained shoulder. Feeling "pretty sore" he half zipped his coat for a sling and walked out.

Bill's recuperation was arduous. The fall had been painless. It was the sudden stop that broke his right arm below the shoulder and cracked the knuckle of the joint. The latter injury and the subsequent swelling, proved to be painful and it healed slowly.

For six weeks, he slept or tried to sleep, sitting up in an easy chair. Lying down hurt too much. Bill went through eight weeks of three-times-a-day supervised rehabilitation.

The therapy worked. Six months after his fall, Bill was in Alaska, hunting black bears. "I did everything the doctor told me to do," he says. "I was faithful to the exercise and rehab schedule. It wasn't fun, but I wanted to shoot again as soon as possible.

"My fall happened so fast I don't recall a thing. There wasn't time to think or react. So, I was wrong. When you fall suddenly, like out of a treestand, you can't protect yourself. It happens too quickly. We think, it can never happen to us, but it can. It happened to me."

After 30 years of hunting with the bow, the 6-foot, 195-pound bowhunter says he has more respect and care in a treestand and when climbing than before. "I don't wear my wedding band hunting now. They had to cut the one off at the hospital after my fall. I didn't get a new one until the next Christmas.

"The best protection while climbing and in treestands is to go slow. Make sure of every little movement of your hands and body. Maybe your best protection is fear.

A quality, secure stand and confidence in a properly executed shot should be enough to bring home wall-hangers every year.

THE TREESTAND MANUFACTURER'S ASSOCIATION

An archer who is preparing to purchase a treestand should know about the TMA, the "Treestand Manufacturer's Association." Understanding what those initials mean and watching for them on the side of a box or in treestand literature, could literally mean the difference between life and death.

The TMA is an organization of manufacturers that have banded together to establish internationally recognized standards for safety, materials and construction techniques to help ensure that your hunting is as safe as it can possibly be. TMA was organized in the early 1990s when Michigan's Jeff DeRegnacourt, an avid bowhunter and insurance agent, began discussing safety standards with a group of treestand manufacturers: Ray McIntyre, of Warren & Sweat, John Woller of Summit, Paul Meeks of API, John Louk of Ol' Man and Spencer 'Bear' Dunn from Trax America.

Today, a treestand bearing the TMA insignia tells you that similar stands have been submitted to an independent engineering facility for testing. Among other things, stands are graded on construction methods, quality of materials, load capacity and stability. A passing grade at all levels is meaningful for your safety in the field. A TMA committee reviews the reminder or warning labels on stands and the clarity and comprehensiveness of instructions.

Membership in the TMA also insures that if you do have a problem or become injured when using a stand, there is sufficient product liability insurance to cover your claims as a result of your injury.

A Note About Shooting From Treestands

These days, some archers and manufacturers claim that shorter bows are more practical for shooting from treestands because they are more maneuverable. By this logic, a 30-inch axle-to-axle PSE Firestorm would be a more desirable bow for most Eastern whitetail hunters than a 39-inch PSE Mohave. Certainly, a

Archers who are successful year after year like to climb high and while this means carrying a lot of gear into the field, the safety of a strap-on ladder like the Sure Foot from Ol' Man, is worth its weight in broken bones and doctor bills.

With a little practice, you can shoot a bow effectively from a treestand. According to the Pope & Young Club, the private records keeping organization that records trophy North American big game taken with the bow and arrow, most whitetail deer killed east of the Mississippi River are shot from a treestand.

continue on next page

THE TREESTAND MANUFACTURER'S ASSOCIATION _continued_

shorter, lighter bow is more maneuverable than a longer, heavier bow. Using a shorter bow also reduces the chances that you will bang it accidentally against the treestand just when game is in sight. On the other hand, shorter bows are much less forgiving of errors in shooting form and this fact is critical. Short, fast bows can be as difficult as a nagging spouse. If you shoot the bow that best fits your style, all other factors are negligible.

Whatever length or style bow you use, shooting from a treestand requires that you use proper form. Perhaps it is even more critical than shooting on the range. Your body should be relaxed and at 90 degrees to your target; feet spread for comfort and stability. Expect game to approach from difficult angles and practice twisting in the "wrong" direction (deer typically appear at the four o'clock position for a right-hander, for instance, and they probably have their nose and eyes in the air watching you). When shooting down, keep your head aligned over the center of your torso and bend at the waist. If you do not practice good form when you shoot from an elevated position, you run a high risk of missing an easy shot or worse, wounding game.

You will probably tune and sight-in your bow over a flat surface. Realize that shooting within your comfort zone from a treestand increases the distance to your target. Using the formula for determining the long side of a right triangle ($C^2 = A^2 + B^2$) you can figure the actual distance you need to shoot. If you mark 20 yards (60 feet) on the ground and shoot from (the height of your arrow on release, not the distance from the ground to your stand) 25 feet high, the actual distance to your target is 21 2/3 yards (65 feet).

The rule of thumb – after plenty of practice shooting from your stand – is to aim low whether you are shooting down from a treestand, downhill or even uphill. The tendency is to overshoot. Hunting videos clearly show deer "jumping the string" or dropping down (they tense their legs to spring away, just like a

human sprinter getting ready to burst out of the starting blocks) when the sound of a shot reaches them or when they detect your movement, so without good practice, expect to be doubly penalized. Your arrow is traveling at 200 mph or less while the sound of the shot reaches a deer at 750 mph.

Chances are that you will sight-in your bow standing on the ground and shooting over a relatively flat course. When you climb a tree however, the dynamics of shooting change and, according to Murphy, anything that can go wrong will! Only practice from different positions and at different angles makes perfect shots happen at the "moment of truth."

ARCHERRY TOOLS FOR THE WORKBENCH AND THE FANNY PACK

ARROW SPIN CHECKER

To hit what you are shooting at, your arrows and the points attached to them have to be straight. Technically, you would like them to be absolutely in line with the force on the back of the arrow exerted by the string. In the "old days," archers rolled arrows on the edge of a table or, placing the point in the palm of their hand and the middle of the shaft between their thumbnail and a fingernail, blew on the fletching to check for even spinning rotation. Those methods were far from foolproof though and today, following the explosion of arrow shaft and head styles during the past 10 years, they are just not good enough.

Apple makes several inexpensive Spin Check instruments that let you place your arrow in grooves on the top and then roll or spin it to check for shaft straightness, nock alignment, vane or feather balance and broadhead balance and alignment. If, for instance, your broadhead wobbles, meaning its tip will not be squarely in-line with the kinetic energy in the arrow, you will notice and can adjust it immediately.

ARROW NOCK ALIGNER

This handy gadget lets you check the positioning of your fletching with mathematical precision simply by standing your nocked arrow in the aligner and verifying, on the nock aligner's 360-degree scale, the degree of fletching placement. Sure, you can eyeball nock position every time you make up a new arrow or install a new arrow rest on your bow or you could use the nock aligner tool from Specialty Archery Products. It is cheap. It is small and lightweight enough to carry in your tool box … and it works.

BOWSTRING WAX

It is a myth that new synthetic bowstring and cable materials like S4 or 450 Premium do not need lubrication. After all, as a form of plastics, they are made from oil which, as we all know, is just dead

Every string needs to be waxed. This unscented string wax from Brownell will increase the life of your bowstrings and protect against broken and fraying fibers. String wax is easy to carry in any fanny pack (it will soften in warm weather) and should be on every archery workbench.

dinosaurs, right? Okay, yes and no. To err on the safe side, let's lubricate all bowstrings.

Browning makes a Bowstring Wax formulated specifically for high-performance strings. No matter what kind of bow you are shooting, recurve, fast (hard) cam bow or crossbow, keep your strings AND your cables well lubricated as this will prevent them from becoming brittle and prevent the detrimental effects of changing weather conditions. (On crossbows, you also want to keep the arrow track lubricated to minimize friction over the flight surface.)

PORTABLE BOW PRESS

Chances are, you do not have the space for a heavy-duty bow press on your work bench and, even if you had one of the big pro-shop Apple units, it would gather an inch of dust because you would use it only a couple times a year. Still, there are times when an archer needs to relax his compound bow to replace or twist the bowstring, insert or adjust a peep sight in the string or even change a cam or idler wheel. Not many years ago, the most common method was to take your bow to a pro shop and let a certified archery mechanic take care of that for you, but despite the growth in popularity of archery and bowhunting, there are fewer pro shops today than there were 10 years ago. Although, it is true that archers would also ask a buddy to lean down on their bow, thereby compressing it a little, so that they could rotate a peep sight! How dangerous to your bow and your buddy was that? Fortunately, there are a lot of small, portable bow presses today that take the danger out of making quick adjustments.

The patented Feather Visions Psyclone Porta Press is designed for one-person operation. Two models are available, one for split limbs and one for solid limbs. The idea is to insert rigid, rubber-coated pressure arms between the limbs, lock the Psyclone in place and, when you draw your bow, the Psyclone automatically takes up the slack in its own stretched string and thereby holds the limbs relaxed and in check.

Other portable bow presses by Cardoza and Bowmaster work in essentially the same manner. Others operate using brackets to fit over the limb tips. For safety purposes and for assurance that you will not damage your bow limbs, a press that compresses the limbs away from the tips is generally preferable – although it is harder for it to do its job there – to one that operates at the extreme ends of 12 or 14 inch limbs.

HAND-HELD BOW SCALE

This could be classified as a toy and chances are you have something like it in your fishing tackle box, but Cardoza Creations offers a hand-held bow scale. It measures items from 15 to 90 pounds on a scale marked in one pound increments. Two indicators make this tool useful. The first measures peak weight and the second measures let-off.

To use the Cardoza scale to measure bow weight and let-off, simply attach the metal pig-tail hook to your bowstring and, with your hand around the cross-bar (the scale will be inside your grip so it is hard to watch it as you draw a bow), pull your bow to full draw as you would if you were going to shoot an arrow. The scale's internal spring will compress and when you let down, the plastic indicators that were pushed forward by the string will remain in place. It is simple, useful and inexpensive.

Set the scale to zero, hook your bowstring in the pigtail and then draw to your anchor or the bow's valley if you are a release shooter and this little scale will give you an accurate reading to 90 pounds draw weight.

NOCK PLIERS

It goes without saying that archers need nock pliers. Any time your set-up changes – new arrow rest, increased draw weight, tweaked draw length, different

TRAVELING BOW PRESS

COMPOUND BOW PRESS

Two different styles of bow press for two situations. The portable press is perfect for an archery home workshop or even for a long trip. The more substantial unit is found in pro shops and perhaps at the home of archers who make a living at the sport: top ranked money winners on the national 3-D circuits and full-time product analysts and writers.

Archers need extra nocks and nock pliers. Any time you make an adjustment to your bow's weight or draw length, you will need to recheck nock point location and shoot a few arrows to verify that your bow is in tune.

arrow spine or fletching – you may need to adjust your nock set. And yes, you do need the special pliers because just any old set of hardware store pliers is not designed to apply even pressure around the nock and string and will – not can, will – damage your nocks. Standard steel pliers have straight, hard machined edges that easily cut and rough up brass nock sets and your string too, if you are the least bit careless.

Game Tracker's Universal Nocking Pliers have two size holes for nock installment on all size strings and a tapered wedge located on their nose to open nocks for adjustment without damaging the nock or the string. (Yes, it is unfortunately all too common to see experienced archers try to loosen nocks with a screwdriver or even a knife blade. Please do not imitate this bad habit.)

BOW SQUARE

If you are going to work on your bow, crest arrows, tune for arrow flight, you need a bow square. Game Tracker makes a 6-1/4-inch-long aluminum bow square with dual string clips for precise nocking point measurement and positioning. It works without batteries or having to move or remove any other bowstring accessories (peep, nock point locator, silencing whiskers, etc.) that you may have installed. Two spring steel clips hold the square in place on the string with the arm lying on top of your arrow rest while you make adjustments. The bow square is useful for checking and setting tiller (whether this is truly important is discussed elsewhere) as well as

Here is a handy and inexpensive bow square from Saunders Archery with a 5/16-inch extension rod that sits on your rest just like an arrow. You need this tool to position your nock sets and hence, your arrow.

positioning your nocking point.

BPE builds a unique, orange plastic mini-square complete with a built-in standard 5/16-inch nock. Remove the arrow point and screw this mini-square into the arrow point insert to use it for an instant visual check of your arrow nock in relation to the nock locator on the string. This Bow Square is especially handy for a day pack.

CENTERSHOT GAUGE

If you shoot in competition or are obsessed with accuracy – as most archers should be – or shoot with a mechanical release aid, you want to maximize the direct energy of your release to the center of your arrow. This will help minimize porpoising, the vertical bending of the arrow shaft as it zooms off your string and arrow rest, and begins to stabilize.

Golden Key-Futura makes a popular and very specific tool for centershot determination called its TruCenter Gauge. "For many years, archers have been eyeballing centershot," says Freddy Troncoso of Golden Key, "but our TruCenter Gauge does the work for you."

Game Tracker's EZ CenterShot Tuning Tool is quite different from the Golden Key tool. Game Tracker's EZ CenterShot mounts to the hex key of your bow's limb bolts and suspends a small gauge on top of your arrow for calibrated adjustments.

HEX WRENCH SET

Every archer needs one of these and fortunately they are cheap and available through any pro shop. The hex keys (Allen wrenches) themselves will help you adjust draw weight and set up almost all of the accessories on your bow. Without a hex wrench set, you are practically dead in the water for making any adjustment or alteration to your bow. The Bear Hex Wrench Set has nine keys and the Pine Ridge Allen

One handy tool will allow you to change the weight you are shooting and attach and remove most accessories. A hex (or "Allen") wrench set is cheap and a must in every tool kit.

Wrench Set has 12. Fletcher's Field Tool includes eight hex keys plus a standard screwdriver, a Phillips screwdriver, an open-end adjustable wrench and a three-blade broadhead wrench!

If you are a traditional shooter, this is the cord-and-cup arrangement that will help you string your recurve bow safely and without twisting your limbs.

RECURVE/LONGBOW BOWSTRINGER

Do not use the step-through method for stringing your recurve or your longbow. Eventually that is going to result in a twisted bow limb or, if your hand slips off while the bow is bent over your knee, you could lose an eye or the limb could break your jaw when it snaps back. Isn't it really easier and safer to toss a NEET Bowstringer or Saunders No-Twist Bowstringer in your day pack? They weigh practically nothing, take up no space and the sturdy, braided nylon string and black end cups are useful for recurves and longbows.

To use for stringing, simply slip your bowstring over the limbs – making sure that the string is oriented so your nock point locator is positioned properly – and then stretch one end into the string grooves cut into the bow at the limb tip. The other end will be relaxed about mid-way to the opposite tip. Now, put the end cups of your bowstringer securely over the tips and, while you hold the bow tight, lift it with one hand while your foot is over the bowstringer. Next, take the hand that is not holding up the bow and slip your bowstring into the limb tip grooves provided for the string. Make sure the string is fully seated before relaxing and removing the bowstringer.

SAW

This, you gotta have. Get one. A bowhunter scouting or setting up a stand or just still hunting through an area without a saw … well, you might as well leave your bow at home. There are branches to cut, twigs to clear and sneaky little limbs on bushes that need to be trimmed. Unless you are climbing a smooth-bark tree like a pine, in which case you will need some turpentine to get the sap (with one "p") off

your hands and your stand, you will not be able to put a climber up a tree to good shooting height without taking off some limbs. Some you can break off and bend, but on the way down, those are going to cause a problem and it is far better to cut them close to the trunk, especially when you are hunting 20 or 30 feet in the air.

The best-all-around saw for a bowhunter's pack is a folding saw and you can buy on in any sporting goods store or hardware store. Coughlan's makes them and Bear markets them. The Bear Folding Saw has a sturdy 6 ¹/₂-inch steel blade that, according to the company "never needs sharpening." Un-clip the blade and it folds, teeth first, into the handle. It is lightweight and compact. Judging by the torn jeans and a few nasty cuts I have self-inflicted from carelessness, it is sharp enough. These saws usually have a hole in the wood or plastic handle for a lanyard. Good idea! Once you have a deer down, you can also use this saw to help with field dressing chores. An active bowhunter will get a couple years of use from a single blade and a relatively expensive model like the $40 Browning Model 900 will slice through green limbs the size of your wrist in eight to ten strokes.

Some folding-blade saw models have a hollow handle that will accept a broom handle and some have an extension that lets you reach out and cut something beyond what you could ordinarily reach. Obviously, you will not carry a broom handle into the woods on your hunting days, but this is an extremely useful idea for clearing out shooting lanes and putting up treestands.

If you are in the outfitting business, you probably need a bigger saw, like one of the Wyoming Saws with long, replaceable blades. These come in numerous editions and lengths and are used more for boning out meat (be careful if Chronic Wasting Disease is affecting your area) than sawing through branches. Outdoor Edge makes a variety of excellent non-folding saws, but because they are so sharp and the design is not of the folding-blade variety, you will need to keep them inside their hard Delrin sheaths when you are not working with them.

A note of caution about using a saw in the woods. It appears that unless we are experienced outdoorsmen, our natural tendency is to clear two or three times what is necessary. Think about the old carpenter's "saw" before you cut: "Measure twice, cut once." Animals will notice when an area in their home range has been altered so, if you can get by with less cutting, the recommendation from here is to do so.

- A saw mounted on a long broom handle or else the special limbing tool you find at the hardware store (awkward to carry into the woods) will extend your reach.

- Earlier selection of stand sites and clearing shooting lanes is better than later.
- Think about using cut branches to form a funnel for game – that wants to stay hidden, but will take the path of least resistance – if that is appropriate where you are hunting.

FIND YOUR WAY

An important concept that most archers ignore because they hunt familiar river bottoms and woodlots is the ability to see "the big picture." Of course, scouting the terrain to become familiar with the territory you are hunting is the best way to guarantee that you will not (don't say never!) become disoriented, but the second best way may be to have in your backpack a good map that details the terrain. Thousands of true-life stories attest to the importance of possessing and understanding maps when you are hunting outside your familiar surroundings or in the less populated areas of Alaska or Canada.

Maptech's Terrain Navigator offers topographic (topo) maps for the entire US packaged as 30 "Super Regions." Each Super Region contains 3,500 or so US Geological Survey (USGS) topo maps and costs less than $150, about four cents per quadrant. Maps covering smaller areas cost less than $50. Maptech has also recently launched its new Pocket Navigator software that turns a Pocket PC into a terrain map or nautical chart. Hook up a GPS and you have a portable chart plotter.

If you prefer to stay with paper-based maps, Maptech has teamed up with MyTopo to offer waterproof topo maps. Log onto www.maptech.com and select an area. The advantage of using MyTopo maps is that you can enter your chosen area and possibly eliminate the need for multiple maps of regions that lie along the edge of a standard USGS topo grid and the cost is only about $15 per map.

YOUR PERSONAL BLIND

There are two types of personal blinds for the hunting archer. By "personal blind" I am suggesting that you can carry it or even wear it into the woods rather than build it from natural materials available on site or construct something semi-permanent out of – well, you have seen dozens of styles with an incredible thoughtfulness of resources – wood or tar paper or sheet steel or tree branches or camo cloth nailed between two trees.

Double Bull Archery sells a variety of ground blinds for archers. The $300 T2 has a peaked roof and, like all of the Double Bull blinds, it has a unique CamLock System for stretching the outer poly-cotton

fabric and preventing it from flapping in the wind. The interior is black-backed and you shoot through windows hung with a very lightweight netting on all of the T2s and the T5s. The netting is, of course, cheap and replaceable. Double Bull says it takes 20 to 30 shots through the netting before you need to replace it.

Double Bull's blinds do not have floors and the company recommends that archers brush out the inside and pile the duff against the bottom edges as that is the location that allows your odor to escape via natural breezes, there and the net-covered windows. (Double Bull says it consulted with ScentLok about the possibility of adding a layer of activated charcoal to cut human odor, but it was just not economically or practically feasible because activated charcoal needs occasional reactivation in a dryer to get rid of the captured odors – and Double Bull blinds, especially the T5s are too large for conventional home dryers. The larger, flat-roof T5 blinds range in price from $389 to $446. (This blind also allows you to unzip a quarter of the roof for waterfowl shooting.)

AmeriStep offers a 10-pound tent-like camouflaged portable blind called the Doghouse TSC (for Total Scent Containment). This nylon blind has two layers of cloth: a black, glare-free inner layer that corrals human scent and other non-natural odors inside

The Doghouse Pack-In Blind from Ameristep pops up fully in 10 seconds and packs down into a 2-inch by 24-inch disk in just 15! The Doghouse weighs 10 pounds and pops up to 5-1/2-feet high by 5-feet square. You can shoot right through the lightweight and replaceable mesh curtains.

and the camouflage-dyed exterior. The windows of the Doghouse are covered with a lightweight see-through, shoot-through membrane that also helps hold human scent inside. Consequently, you can shoot while remaining completely unnoticed from the outside. AmeriStep says this 12-pound blind will fold and pack into a 2-inch by 24-inch pack for easy carrying. Fully deployed, this blind has 25 square feet of floor space and is 5 feet, 10 inches high. AmeriStep President Robert Ransom says the blind sets up in 10 seconds and break-down time is only 15 seconds. The zippered door is large enough for a wheelchair, too.

The portable, flame-retardant InvisiBlind sets up in about six seconds and offers a patented shoot-right-through-the-windows design that lets you move about inside while remaining unseen to game animals. Plus, InvisiBlind says its waterproof polyester layer holds your scent inside, too. The shooting panels on each side are replaceable. The InvisiBlind measures 6-1/2 feet long by 5 feet wide by 6-1/2 feet high. This means it has 32.5 square feet of floor space and with 6-1/2 feet of head space, the InvisiBlind has enough room for two hunters to hang out for most of a day.

Rancho Safari offers a variety of Shaggie 3-D Cover Systems for unique personal concealment. Think of the famous "Ghillie Suit" used by snipers. The Rancho Safari suits may not be that one, but they are not that different, either. The Shaggie Longcoat gives you head-to-toe invisibility. It comes in three sizes, is made with a variety of materials and – for the two-season hunters among us – is available in blaze orange. It weighs 10 pounds and costs about $150. The Shaggie Special costs less than $200 and weighs 13 pounds. Strips of cotton, burlap and jute are sewn onto the mesh shell. A variety of headgear and face masks is available. The Rancho Safari Shaggie suits will work for archers, but are perhaps best for riflemen or even paintball players.

Certainly you can cover up with leaves and lurk inside a blind or you can try a fitted suit like one of the 3-D Leaf camo and bug suits from Bug Tamer. These patented, double mesh suits provide head to toe camo and allow you to hunt (or fish) in comfort in the buggiest environments. Hundreds of center-stitched leaves on the outer, no-see-um proof micro-mesh are free to flutter in the breeze and provide shifting patterns of light and shade. The thick, inner mesh provides a stand-off that lets you wear a Bug Tamer without needing potentially harmful and game alarming insect repellents. The suit allows you to make small movements without being detected by game.

COMPASS AND WHISTLE

You may never need either one of these outdoor

Do not even think of going into a difficult outdoor environment without a flashlight, a compass and a whistle. A 25-cent whistle will save your life when all of your high-tech gadget's batteries fail.

survival tools, but there are literally hundreds maybe many thousands of hunters, hikers, campers, boaters, bird watchers, photographers and fishermen who have passed through the "pearly gates" because they did not have them when they needed them … and died as a result. They are cheap. They are effective. Get one of each and carry it with you, even when you believe you know the lay of the land or perhaps especially then, because pain can quickly cause a total fog of disorientation, even when you are hunting in your back yard.

A whistle can save your life. It should be your number one survival item and it should be in your pocket where you can reach it easily if you become injured, not in your backpack or even in your fanny pack. Most archers take their fanny pack off and store it under the seat of their treestand. They leave a larger pack on the ground, perhaps scratching leaves and sticks over it. So, when they fall, the fanny pack is 20 feet over their head and it will not be any help. The piercing scream of a good little whistle can be heard many times as far as a human scream. When you run out of breath screaming or run out of energy after you have fallen out of your treestand or gotten lost, you will still be able to blow that whistle.

The compass is your second survival item. Compasses are fun too, and fun to teach your children how to use. (Chances are they know how to blow a whistle without your help.) In imitation of Fred Bear's set up, Bear Archery has installed small compasses in the wood recurve bow handles in the Commemorative Series: Super Mag 48 and Super Kodiak recurves and Montana longbow. They look good, but rely small, inexpensive compasses on these only as a last resort.

Brunton and Silva make excellent lines of compasses that they market to outdoorsmen. The

Brunton watch band compass is compact and filled with liquid which dampens the spin of the free-floating needle. Their pin-on ball compass has luminous points for night use (handy if you get lost!) and comes with a non-magnetic safety pin.

Compasses hardly cost anything, so get a good one. Brunton's Classic 8040G mirror compass weighs 1.6 ounces. and this plastic model includes: anti-static, clinometer (measures angles up or down hills), declination adjustment from the magnetic and "true" north pole AND a lanyard, protective cover, sighting mirror, thermometer, waterproof jeweled bearing and two-degree graduations on the compass scale. All this for about $30. For the price, you just cannot go wrong. You can buy a metal body, liquid dampened lensatic model for just $15. At that price, you can afford to buy two and give one to an archery buddy!

Whatever style you buy, look for liquid dampening or the needle will rotate like mad with the least little disturbance or if you bring your knife blade near it. Look for all of the features above but if you are traveling, look for a plastic compass base with gradations that you can place on top of a topo map. The dial must swivel of course and I like the mirror or lensatic feature that lets you plot a course, more or less accurately, through unknown territory.

One word of warning about compasses. We all believe – because we were Boy Scouts or in the Army years ago – that we know how to use a compass. It's like driving. Everyone believes they are a good driver. Well, do not count on it. A few minutes of study with the directions could be the refreshing difference that saves your life.

Bow Rope

Do not climb a tree with your bow in one hand or even slung over your shoulder. You have undoubtedly heard that a hundred times, because archers still go outside and do it and they still get hurt needlessly. For less than $5, you can buy a rope that takes much of the happenstance and potential for accidents out of tree climbing. Hook one end of the rope to your belt. Pull on your full body harness. Climb the tree and then draw your bow and fanny pack up to your stand.

Face it. Climbing trees is dangerous. The days of climbing trees with an awkward bow over your shoulder should be long past.

A 30-foot section of camouflaged, rot resistant nylon rope with a quick release hook is available from your local hardware store, any archery pro shop or from Third Hand Archery. A rope in the woods is handy for lots of uses. It weighs practically nothing. End of preaching. Thanks for listening!

Trail Markers

Toward the end of his life, Daniel Boone was credited with saying, "I never got lost in the woods, but once I was bewildered for three or four days."

Well, if you have ever been lost or even briefly bewildered in the woods, especially at night, you know what a creepy feeling it is. Everything looks different at night. Very different. The familiar trail disappears. Distance judging becomes more difficult. Your flashlight is not as strong as it was just a few weeks ago and finding those thumb-tack-size reflective markers is more of a challenge than you want to admit. You are tired, cold and ready to be home.

The Fire Tacks solution is a set of larger trail marking units which they call 3D, 4D, Hot Dots and Fire Tape. These are very highly reflective (with "prismatic technology" they are "Retro Reflective" says Wild Tech, the manufacturer) and sizeable enough that your flashlight will really have to be dim to miss them. The 3D markers are triangular; the 4D markers are a little cube; Hot Dots is a hexagonal reflector; and the flexible Fire Tape – which uses the same reflective technology as the rigid plastic markers – has a small strip of hook and loop material sewn on each end so that you can simply loop it over a branch or bush.

Unlike the blaze orange but non-reflective surveyor's tape (or pieces of white toilet paper!) we used to mark our trail for so many years, Fire Tacks trail markers are larger, more permanent and impervious to weather. They come in three colors: Blaze Orange, Ice White (neutral by day) and Stealth Brown (brown by day, but orange by night). Fire Tacks claims that in tests at the 3-M laboratories, their Tacks were 10 times as bright as trail tacks and, in inclement weather, were 500 times as visible. That is a lot! A pack of 25 3D or 4D Fire Tacks costs about $10 while a combo pack in a plastic carrying case (25 3D tacks, 25 4D tacks and 10 sections of Fire Tape) costs $30.

Knives & Sharpeners

Sometimes it seems like the only reasons to hunt and fish are to get away from (fill in the blank), to eat candy bars without having to ask permission or share with the kids and to carry a knife. You can go for weeks and not catch or shoot anything worth a hoot and then when you do and the adrenaline has washed out of your system after your buddy takes pictures, the neighbor kids gawk and the local anti-hunter vegan fumes and stomps away, you've got to gut the fish and clean the deer. Don't worry. You will get some sleep tonight. It just won't be much.

The first archer I remember seeing in the woods about 25 years ago was wearing a sheath knife on his belt that practically hung down to his knees. And that

For archers, knives are tools ... and toys. It does not matter what quality of steel is in the blade or what type of grind the blade holds or what kind of handle material the knife has. What matters is that it is sharp and that you do not wait until the minute you have to field dress a big game animal to become accustomed to it. This Dave Davis custom bone-handle knife looks good and it is excellent for all-around camp chores.

was before Rambo made big knives popular. Popular, but not practical.

The second archer I remember was my hunting mentor who had a folding pocket knife about as big as my little finger – okay, not even that big – who taught me how to dress out his big buck that day and then helped me dress out my little doe, too, with the same blade. That knife was tiny, but it was sharp and it did the job on those two Minnesota whitetails. Then, all we had to do was drag them a mile and a half uphill out of the river bottoms to the car.

If this were not a family book, I would say, "Oh, screw the research and buy some knives. Buy a bunch of them. Some are pretty and some are deadly looking. Whatever. Knives are just fun." I do not make a nickel more of income one way or the other if you buy one knife or 100, but I personally kind of like having one in my pocket to open boxes, gut a deer or ... yep, toss in that little donation box inside airports these days when I have forgotten to pack it and have already checked my bags.

You might have guessed that I am not a big fan of research and complicated study when it comes to buying a knife. Buy the one that looks good to you and chances are, you will make it work just fine. The only real tip is to keep it as sharp as you are able. Studies show there is less chance you will cut yourself with a sharp knife than with a dull one. Really! That is research you can trust.

There are practically as many different kinds and styles and weights and blade grinds and materials compositions of knives as there are archers. Practically speaking, none of this matters for the simple act of field dressing a deer.

SEVERAL KNIFE COMPANIES AND THEIR KNIVES

Benchmade is the exclusive manufacturer of the "Axis Lock," a very strong folding knife-locking mechanism. Interestingly, for the minority of left-handers among us, the Axis Lock is equally effective for both right-handers and southpaws. Benchmade builds some great looking knives and some of the most functional blades for archery chores. Their 814 Realtree Hardwoods is a modified liner-lock with a handy drop-point. When closed, this 3-ounce, $120 (suggested retail price) knife is 4-2/5 inches long. The 3-1/4-inch blade length is just about ideal. The 410-Rockwell stainless steel liner resists corrosion and the stainless steel blade sharpens relatively easily, for stainless. A black Teflon coating retards corrosion and adds a custom finish.

Case or W.R. Case & Sons markets a variety of high end and low end knives. The Case name has long been associated with interesting knife styles like the Ridgeback Hunter. Designed by knife-making guru Blackie Collins, the Ridgeback Hunter has a 3 1/2-inch up-swept skinner blade forged from Tru-Sharp surgical steel. This fixed blade sheath knife with black Zytel handle measures 8 1/2 inches overall and weighs 4 1/5 ounces. Purchase includes a leather sheath.

Imperial Schrade has a huge catalog of knives for outdoors use. The D' Holder carries an incredible $300 price tag if you do not find it on sale, but no knives (or bows for that matter) are actually sold at full suggested retail. This sheath knife was designed in collaboration with knife maker D'Alton Holder. The blade is polished stainless steel and the handle is "stabilized" maple burl. It features a full-tapered tang and a leather sheath complete with basket weave stamping on the outside and black fabric lining.

SHARPENING

"You could sharpen a knife or broadhead blades on the curb outside your house," says John Anthon, president of GATCO Sharpeners. "I don't recommend it, but it is our view that sharpening – especially with older tools like whetstones – is a lost art."

The key to honing a good edge on a knife is consistency. No matter what you use, it is critical to run the blade across the implement at exactly the same angle each time and with the same number of strokes on each side. That is why Arkansas stones, once the most common sharpening tool, have fallen out of favor

A crock stick from Lansky or GATCO will apply a fine edge to your knife or resharpenable broadhead. Dozens of styles are available: V-sticks, folding sticks, double-row sticks and others. Ceramic sticks are brittle and need care to prevent snapping, but are easy to carry in protective cases and take into the field for touch-up when you are in the middle of an elk or moose.

with hunters. Almost every sharpening product designed works in the hands of a patient practitioner, but some, like whetstones, are more difficult to master.

Certainly, there has been a change in the steel used in knives, too. Twenty years ago, Anthon says, all but the most expensive blades were made from soft steel which was easy to work into a good edge, but then dulled quickly. Modern knife blades are much stronger and the steel is considerably harder than it was just a few decades ago. Harder steel takes much more effort to sharpen.

Anthon reminds us that no two knife blades have the same geometry, but a "good rule of thumb" is to sharpen a blade at a 30-degree angle. "A blade will sharpen more quickly and it will hold an edge longer at a higher angle," he says.

To figure out if the sharpener you want to use is the right one for the job, run your finger down the sharpening surface. The coarser the sharpening implement, the faster it will put an edge on a very dull knife, although it won't be a very smooth or durable edge. It's a good start, however, and only one step in the process. Smooth sharpeners, butcher's steels, fine-grained stones and ceramic rods, for instance, typically only put a finishing touch on n already sharp knife, so attempting to put an edge on an extremely dull knife with one of those products will take a long time. Use those only after you have used a coarser sharpener.

Anthon says that a multi-step, angle-guided sharpener like those from GATCO will put a razor's edge on any knife, even serrated blades, with minimum effort. For a quick fix out in the field, pocket-sized sharpening sticks that have a diamond-impregnated rod will put a quick and workable edge on an otherwise dull knife.

Lansky Sharpeners says its system will sharpen practically any blade and it couldn't be easier. First, attach the blade to the symmetrical, ambidextrous, 360-degree multi-angle clamp. Then, select the color-coded sharpening hones with the coarse, medium or fine grits you need to use and attach them to a guide rod. Finally, select the proper angle to bevel, sharpen or polish the knife blade and insert the guide rod in the angle hole. This system keeps the plane of your grind on the blade consistent (at 17, 20, 25 or 30 degrees) for the best possible edge. Begin sharpening with one side of the blade then flip the clamp over to sharpen the other side.

Apparently, everything you need comes in a convenient, molded hard plastic storage and carrying case. Lansky also makes the popular "Crock Stick" sharpeners and also carries Natural Arkansas (novaculite) Bench stones in their line. These stones have been prized for centuries for their unique sharpening properties. Novaculite stones are much treasured by those whose livelihood depends on the sharpness of their knives, axe blades and tools. Formed of pure silica under intense heat and pressure below the earth's surface, novaculite has the additional ability of polishing as it sharpens.

Lansky's Natural Arkansas Bench stones are cut from novaculite and mounted to a solid walnut block, elevating the stone for greater sharpening ease and hand protection. These stones are available in two grades, soft and hard. The soft Arkansas stone is used to do the initial rough cutting and smoothing to achieve a sharp edge. The Hard Arkansas then follows up with the final smoothing and polishing.

When you become interested in putting a good cutting edge on your broadheads or your knives, you will need the proper tools and that little kit includes a honing oil like Nathan's Natural Honing Oil from Lansky. Highly refined, such honing oils are essential in keeping your hones lubricated to achieve the best sharpening results. Just a few drops will protect the hone and give you the professional edge you desire. Nathan's Natural Honing Oil is available in 4oz. (120 ml) plastic bottles.

SHARPENING FIXED-BLADE BROADHEADS

The biggest single mistake many bowhunters make when filing their fixed blade broadheads, heads like the Zwickey Eskimo and the Bear Razorhead, is that they try too hard. Fred Bear believed in a broadhead that had a slightly rough edge, feeling that it cut better and left a hole that would not seal quickly. Frustration getting a good edge often forces you to remove unnecessary amounts of metal, especially with the older heads, which are made of softer steels. (Heads like the Bear Razorhead and the Razorhead Lite are stainless steel and it takes some effort to sharpen them.)

Initial strokes are used with moderate pressure, but always finish filing with very light strokes, rotating the broadhead regularly. Many archers count their strokes for even filing as they rotate their broadheads. You may want to use a ceramic stick after using the file to help polish your blade's edge.

Start working with a clean file. If your file is new, here is a sharpening tip. Use chalk to save wear on your file's teeth and to prevent "pinning," the buildup of small metal chips in the teeth of your file. These metal chips seem to clump or bind to the file and are difficult to get out later. Filling the space between the file teeth with chalk will increase the effectiveness of a file because it extends file life and produces a smoother, more professional finish. Metal removal from your broadhead edges is faster and easier this way, too.

The teeth on your file are only meant to cut in one direction. Sliding a broadhead back and forth on a file will prematurely wear down teeth. Keep your files clean except for file chalk. Most archers tend to use their files too long. You cannot fix worn teeth. Files are cheap. Throw it away and purchase a new file. It may sound like country music, but no file lasts forever.

TOYS FOR ARCHERS

TWO-WAY RADIOS

Commonly thought of as two-way radios, these Family Radio Service (FRS) units eliminate some of the shouting and jumping up and down you used to do with a hunting partner, especially if you were out west looking for elk or in British Canada scouting for sheep or desperately signaling your guide for more toilet paper. Hand-held radios can help your guide warn you of a grizzly approaching from your backside. They can help you collect a "gut and drag" detail after you have a big game animal down. And you can certainly use an FRS radio to call for help if you are hurt or in danger. You may even want to look for a radio with a specific, continuously broadcasting weather channel!

The advantages of a FRS radio are many. They come with 14 channels or public access frequencies and they can be used by anyone. By simply pressing a button and talking, you can communicate with anyone who is dialed into the channel you are using and within hearing range. They do not require any training or permits to use and need no towers to relay the signal. Like beepers, some even have a vibration mode that lets you select the call you will take, and earphones that allow you to listen in silent mode.

These radios will work where battery operated cellular phones are useless. For all of the built in benefits and possibilities, they are inexpensive – cheap – especially in an emergency.

Some FRS units are made specifically to appeal to outdoorsmen. This concept suggests that they are especially lightweight and rugged, but in reality, this may just be packaging and promotion because "lightweight and durable" would describe practically the entire FRS radio family.

On the other hand, unless you leave the FRS in your backpack, it is doggone certain to go off with a staticky voice – "Hey, I just saw a marmot!" – at just the moment you are coming to full draw on a trophy brown bear and you are guaranteed to not appreciate it

then. All FRS radios are limited to line-of-sight range and work best in open, flat surfaces, because a range of about two miles is about their maximum, although this will vary with battery strength, the weather and other factors, but price does not give you stronger communications. In rough terrain – on your sheep hunt, for instance – they may or may not be the answer to your communications problems unless you climb high.

On the disadvantages side, what you say on the air

Archers who take to the trail will appreciate the ability of an FRS radio to keep in touch with their guide or hunting buddies back at camp. FRS radios are inexpensive and come with a multitude of options. Vista even makes special camo holsters for them.

Is this what the "well dressed archer" wears into the field in the 21st Century? GPS unit and cellular phone with a custom camo case designed by NEET.

can be heard by anyone listening who is tuned into that channel and, with "atmospheric skip," some ham radio operator in your home town is sure to tell your wife he heard you on the radio. So, beware! For privacy, look for models that offer channel codes which allow you to engage in communication a little more selectively.

Something to think about before you buy is how you plan to use your FRS radio units. (They usually come in pairs and, if you only had one, who would you talk to?) Make sure they are legal in your state for the type of hunting you are doing before you begin coordinating party stalks on deer, for instance. Each archer who is considering using an FRS radio should ask himself whether these radios are ethical for hunting. Perhaps the answer is yes ("Help! I'm hurt.) … or perhaps the answer is no ("Get ready, its coming your way!"). For most situations, including the emergencies mentioned above, ethical hunters would use FRS radios to excellent personal advantage without disadvantaging his quarry. That should be the standard.

Garmin has a GPS (Global Positioning System) unit and two-way radio in one compact unit it calls its Rino Series. You can talk and transmit your exact position at the same time. It weighs just 8 ounces and is water-resistant. Check out www.garmin.com

Motorola's TalkAbout T6320 has a wide range of options such as 38 interference eliminator codes, a scrambler with three settings and a rechargeable battery with drop-in charging unit. This Motorola model has a built-in digital compass, barometer and thermometer, altimeter, clock with alarm and a stopwatch with a lap timer. Like your cell phone, a removable plastic belt clip is available. These small radios come with a one-year warranty. But will it make coffee? Check out www.lenbrook.com

For a range up to five miles, Motorola and others offer a radio with a more powerful battery, but a little less sexy styling. Their rectangular TalkAbout Distance DPS radios have a voice-activated, hands-free operating switch and an audio accessory jack for an earphone. A rechargeable NiCad battery is recommended although the unit is alkaline battery compatible.

Cobra Electronics offers the Micro-Talk series. These have auto squelch, back-lit LCD screen and water resistance for an affordable price. www.cobra.com

The compact Audio-Vox FR531 has a lock key and power-saving circuitry. It is simple and inexpensive. www.audiovox.com

RANGEFINDERS

With the fast, minimal trajectory compound bows we are shooting today, who needs a rangefinder? Well, if you are a hunter whether it is with a bow or a gun, chances are you will benefit from one (and you can use it on the golf course, too). Even professional archers have to practice continually to keep their distance estimating skills sharp and the US Army regularly proves this to young recruits on a relatively open field with camouflaged figures at various distances and in various postures, behind trees and kneeling behind bushes. Practically no one gets the distance right without extensive practice.

Have you ever wondered what that guy from down the street is doing when he seems to be pacing off distances from his mailbox to various spots on the block? He is not the neighborhood nut. He is probably an archer practicing distance estimation skills. The more you practice, the better you become, but distance estimation is a skill like weightlifting. The benefits of a single session are transitory. You must stay in shape on a regular program of lifting or estimating distance, because if you do not, the part of the brain responsible for this function apparently takes a siesta.

The neighborhood system of pacing and estimating when you walk the dog is fine except that when you are in the woods and that trophy appears suddenly, trees will obscure your view, and bushes and vines. Perhaps a ravine and a stream will lie between you and your trophy. If it is foggy or raining or cold, you are definitely in trouble. That's why you need a rangefinder.

Archers take most big game animals within 30 or 40 yards, but exact distance estimation is still critical.

The Ranging TLR 75 from American Visionwear is a non-electronic coincident rangefinder that is perfect for archers. It ranges distance manually from 10 to 75 yards with an accuracy of plus or minus 1 yard at 50 yards. The unit weighs 7 ounces.

Perhaps it is especially critical with a broadhead-tipped arrow, because there are matters of ethics and pride at stake. A rangefinder will keep you from having to pace off distances from your treestand to mark shooting locations. It prevents those bright ribbons from fluttering in the brush around your stand, marking 20 or 30 yards, and allows you to judge distance accurately without leaving your scent throughout the area.

Most laser rangefinders are shaped like binoculars. When you gaze through the eyepiece a superimposed crosshair aids in aiming. Just press a button and read the LED distance display. Depending on the make and model, a number of options can be called on such as changing mode to accommodate weather conditions or the subject's light reflectivity.

A laser rangefinder operates by emitting a laser light pulse that strikes the object in your crosshairs and is reflected back to the unit's receiver at around the speed of light. Since laser light travels in a straight line and a constant speed, the time it takes the pulse to leave and return is calculated internally and a distance in yards or meters is displayed.

Rangefinders are prohibited on 3-D courses and distances are already marked on NFAA and FITA venues. So, this is strictly a toy for bowhunters (golfers, backpackers, timber cruisers, etc.) and four companies are in the business: American Visionwear builds the Ranging coincident series, Nikon builds the Buckmaster Laser series, Leica the Rangemaster and Bushnell builds the Yaradage Pro series (having apparently recently discovered that the brief market appearance of its bow-mounted BowPro rangefinder was, for some reason, not well accepted by archers).

There is some distance measuring error in a laser rangefinder. The closer you are the better for your laser is the rule. Checking distances beyond a few hundred yards, we discover that the greater the advertised distance a laser estimates, the greater the error.

[Archers need to understand the archery and bowhunting level in the commercial mix to appreciate why battery-operated laser rangefinders are essentially designed for riflemen with effective operating distance out to half a mile. There are 16 million gun hunters and, realistically, about 2.5 million archers.]

American Visionwear's Ranging coincident rangefinders are a non-electronic throwback to simpler times, optical (non-electronic) rangefinders, but these handy, pocket-sized rangefinders do not need batteries and they can easily be operated and readjusted if they are dropped. "Coincident" means that dual mirrors give you a split image through the viewfinder and when you align the image correctly with the finger-operated focus wheel, the distance can be accurately read from the internal scale. Distance can be determined in any weather and the ranging function is not affected by hand tremor. This rangefinder will even work through windshields! With a 98 percent accuracy level and a price tag much less that of a battery-powered laser rangefinder, these are great values.

The Ranging TLR 75 is the unit most in use by bowhunters. It features a dual yards/meters scale and a two-power magnifier. Its minimum range is 10 yards and maximum range is 75 yards with an advertised accuracy of plus or minus 1 yard at 50 yards. The unit measures 6 x 3 x 1-1/2 inches and only weighs 7 ounces. For archers, most of whom take game at less than 25 yards, this is the ticket. A Ranging Model 75 costs about $60 for a unit in matte black or $75 in

The 6-power Bushnell Yardage Pro Scout laser rangefinder is accurate from 10 to 700 yards. A laser rangefinder is a distance-measuring device capable of instantaneously measuring distances to any target plus or minus 1 yard accuracy.

camouflage. A soft carrying pouch is available for an additional $20 direct from Ranging. www.ranging.net

Leica offers a laser rangefinder called the Rangemaster (LRF 1200). Well known as a high-end German optics supplier, Leica says the Rangemaster is effective to 1,200 yards and features "lightweight, compact, one-button operation and an LED display with automatic brightness control." Look through the 7x monocular port and the LED display is self-adjusting for brightness. The Rangemaster will accurately measure distance in meters or yards from as close as 10 meters (33 feet) out to 800 m (874 yards) with a factory-established accuracy of plus or minus one yard. The 21mm front lens offers a field of view of 367 feet at 1,000 meters. Leica's Rangemaster measures 4-3/4 x 4-1/8 x 1-9/16 inches and while the size and power will be excellent for two-season (gun and bow) hunters, archers will find that the 7x magnification is a little high for shooting tasks within bow range. Check them out online at www.leica-camera.com

Bushnell's Yardage Pro series is excellent for hunters and outdoorsmen of all kinds, but because the magnification ranges from four- to eight-power, its

Bushnell's 4x Yardage Pro Sport laser rangefinder is accurate from 5 to 800 yards. Distance readouts are displayed in the magnified monocular for a true view of the field. The adjustable eyepiece compensates for an individual's eyesight.

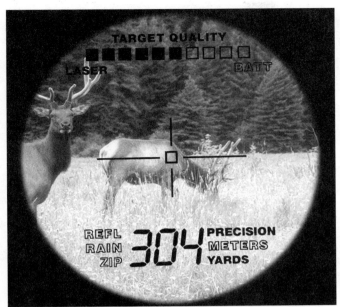

The view through Bushnell's Yardage Pro gives a precise estimation of distance to your target plus or minus one yard.

advantages for archers are limited. The Yardage Pro series takes a three-volt battery, a nine-volt battery or four AAA batteries.

The Bushnell Yardage Pro Scout has a six-power magnification and only weighs 6.8 ounces. At 1-1/2 x 2 x 2-3/4 inches, it will easily fit in your pocket. With so much to carry into the field and fumble around with already, archers will find that the Scout's one-hand grip and one-button operation are a plus. Bushnell's larger laser rangefinders take two hands to operate and, when you are measuring distances out to hundreds of yards, a tripod or some secure brace is necessary to trust the feedback you get from the laser's LED display. The Scout is accurate to plus or minus 1 yard from 10 yards to 700 yards in any weather, including rain or snow, the company says. It is water-resistant, comes with a case and strap and its plastic body is available in black or Realtree HD Hardwoods camo. A "low-battery" indicator is standard.

Bushnell attempted to sell a bow-mounted laser rangefinder called the Bow Pro a few years ago, but it was met with a peculiar lack of enthusiasm by archers who apparently still prefer the hand-held variety. The Bow Pro ranged from about 10 to 90 yards.

Of special interest to prospective purchasers of laser rangefinder is the method it uses to give you a reading. Take the Bushnell Scout, for instance. It is advertised as accurate to plus or minus one yard out to 700 yards. Of course, a laser rangefinder only works because something is reflecting the laser directly back into the objective lens of the unit. The fine print for the

Bushnell's Digital Compass comes in a handheld unit or to be worn on the wrist like a watch. The Wrist-Top DNS is a compass, calendar, watch, alarm clock and thermometer. The upgraded DNS Pro includes a barometer, altimeter and weather forecaster and the handheld unit includes a map light!

Scout thus accurately notes that the laser is accurate depending upon the nature of the target. At www.bushnell.com the following targeting information can be discovered about the Scout (and it is indeed a plus that the company provides this information):

- A reflective object (an automobile, for instance) is accurate to 700 yards.
- A hard solid object (a tree trunk) is accurate to 570 yards.
- A soft solid object (a deer or an elk) is accurate to 300 yards.
- A fluttering or moving object (a running, hopping mule deer or even a flag, for the golfers among us) is accurate to 250 yards.

Several companies offer rangefinders that allow

you to move or scan distance with moving game animals, assuming you can keep the red dot or crosshairs centered on a buck meandering in your direction that's still 279 yards away. The Bushnell Yardage Pro Legend is a palm-size digital laser rangefinder that accurately measures distances from 10 to 930 yards in rain or snow and, Bushnell claims, "right through brush and branches." In the Legend's scanning mode, you can keep continuous track of moving game up to 450 yards away!

Nikon's Team Realtree Laser 800 measures 5 x 3-3/4 x 2-1/4 inches and weighs 9-1/2 ounces without batteries. The multicoated monocular comes with a huge, 8x magnification standard. Nikon offers five modes of operation depending on your target and the weather: standard, rain, 150, scan and reflective. The objective lenses are 28 mm and the field of view is 236 feet wide at 1,000 yards. The Laser800 can focus on an object at a distance of only 16 feet. The Laser 400 is advertised with an accuracy of 1/2 yard.

The unique feature of the Opti-Logic Laser Rangefinders is that their XT series is "tilt-compensating." Theoretically, it will measure both line-of-sight and horizontal distance to a target at the same time. Although they are a little large, with their 4-yard minimum range, these red-dot aiming systems could be ideal for archers.

STAND LOCATOR

One is never sure whether a new archery gadget is a toy or a practical advancement that is going to make our lives easier, our distance judging more accurate, our hunting more successful.

If you have ever stumbled around in the dark looking for your treestand at oh-dark-thirty in the morning, having missed the trail of tiny tacks that seemed so obviously placed in broad daylight – and most of us have – the Lem-O-Ward visual stand locator might not seem so doggone silly. Simply place the palm size, visual locator on your stand and set it for the time you will be approaching the area. The gadget's high intensity light will come on at that time and stay on for one hour or until you shut it off manually.

The Lem-O-Ward costs about $25, but before you fork over the cash, consider your ability to schedule and follow through. How well are you able to make plans and carry them through with children, dogs, rainy days, church attendance and cold, frosty mornings when it is often easier to roll over and, well, hunt next week? That little light exploding in intensity for an hour may not bother any big game animal … or it just might. What do you think?

TRAIL CAMERAS

Why not put a camera in your shooting lane and record everything that comes by when you are not in your stand? The archery magazines are full of photos taken by these cameras: families of raccoons, trophy bucks, coyotes, stray housecats and other hunters. Now this is fun! The only problem with these units is that unless you have a well-concealed location, your camera could be in trouble if an unscrupulous individual passes by and sees it.

Sure, these cameras can be expensive – the Cam Trakker, which claims it is the best and thereby justifies its advertised $429 price for the camera (with optional panoramic mode), infrared motion detector, mounting bracket and camouflaged, weatherproof mounting box – and you need film and batteries. The infrared sensor detects heat in motion within a conical area directly in front. The camera is an Olympus QuartzDate 35mm model with six photo delay options.

The Digital CamTrakker ($1,175) uses a Yashica Micro Elite Digital Camera with 3.3 mega pixels and 2x optical zoom. The strobe flash can take reasonably good pictures of objects up to 75 feet away. Delay options are available from 20 seconds to 45 minutes. 65 photos are available on one digital card.

Phantom Hunter calls its black-cased camera a "no-frills scouting camera" and it gives a discount off the normal price of one ($320) if you purchase two ($599). The company says you have more than one spot to scout so obviously, you need more than one scouting camera. This is an economy-minded scouting camera: no microprocessor, no switches, no complicated programming and no exposed wires. This

Trail Timer's EZ-Cam 35 mm film camera (shown open) has a date and time stamp for each photo taken, a self-timer, panoramic view option, auto flash (including night scene flash and red eye reduction). In addition the 35 mm camera unplugs from the EZ-Cam for use as a standard camera.

The TrailMac Game Camera from Trail Sense Engineering uses batteries that will last for months. Selective infrared sensor settings adapt to different terrain and temperature and allow you to capture motion out to 60 feet. It features 24-hour operation with date and time imprinting.

unit comes with a Yashica Impression 35mm camera which can imprint the date and time on the film and operates on two AA batteries. The weatherproof case is impact resistant ABS plastic. The solid state infrared detector is pre-set for a three minute delay between photos, but runs 24 hours a day. Independently battery operated, the camera sensor runs 24-7.

At the lowest end in terms of price ($280) is the DeerCam, the official scouting camera of the Quality Deer Management Organization. Simply remove the DeerCam from its box, install the batteries and set the adjustable delay when you strap it to a tree. You can set the delay from 15 seconds to one hour and the counter will record up to 2,500 events. (Wow!) It is ready to go, as is. In Professional Mode however (requires the

optional Xpander System) it will record up to 475 events – even without film in the camera!

The DeerCam includes a password theft control system and the enclosing plastic box can be padlocked. DeerCam operates with two nine-volt batteries and has a low battery indicator. The Olympus Infinity XB 35mm camera inside the molded camo container has a date and time stamp for each frame of film shot.

Finally, there is the "no film" Game-Vu Digital Trail Camera from Nature Vision. Because it is digital, there is no film, no flash and no noise with this camera. Unlike cameras with film that has to be processed ($5 for the 24-picture roll of film and $7 for processing, each roll), the Game-Vu provides 64 images that can be downloaded into a computer and even viewed in the field with an optional shirt-pocket-size monocular for continuous 24-hour viewing. The monocular eyepiece is adjustable to your eyes and it attaches to the camera with a lanyard. The infrared strobe on the Game-Vu Digital Trail Camera is not as powerful as a standard camera flash – operating successfully out to just 15 feet at night, 25 feet by day – and it takes six AA batteries to operate this camera for a week. Click on its "Sleep" button and then in "Capture" mode you can expect up to 150 hours of

continuous operation.

TRAIL TIMERS

Here is the original. The single-event Trail Timer has been around for almost 20 years. Tie it around a tree at about chest high to a deer – 1-1/2 to 2 feet off the ground – pull the cord out and tie it lightly to something on the opposite side of a trail. A deer or bear or some other hunter walks down the trail and brushes the thin cord aside. The spring-activated

Turkey hunters can use inflatable birds like this jake from Delta. You could inflate a whitetail decoy or even an elk, but would you want to?

The unit that started it all, the patented Original TrailTimer single-event game monitor. String the spool of thread across a trail and when a game animal trips the string, the monitor records the time and date. It is pocket-size and battery-operated.

retriever in the Trail Timer box pulls the cord back and stops the clock. You simply read the time and date the cord released. Simple. At $18, it is cheap enough. But, that is the end of the information, too.

Trail Timer (www.trailtimer.com) has added two upgraded systems to its original inexpensive trip-cord unit. Its "Plus Five" five-event infrared timer ($72) has five re-settable clocks that record time and date of the most recent activity on a trail or at a scrape. Its range is approximately 60 feet and the cone of sensitivity at that distance is three feet. Their new "Plus 500" event infrared timer ($135) is ideal for high activity trails, bear baits and scrapes. These infrared units are compatible with camera systems and operate on a nine volt battery. Trail Timer recently developed a trail camera, its $250 Photo Hunter and, for hunters who already have a compatible camera and one of their infrared units, a case with internal rigging into which you insert your own automatic 35mm camera.

DECOYS

Not too long ago, an effective big game decoy was thought of as a white handkerchief tied to a barbed wire fence in pronghorn country. Supposedly, the four-footed critters with that extra-keen 9x eyesight would become so nervous or curious about that waving flag that they would just have to go and find out what it was all about. As a hunting archer, that was your chance.

Then a guy out on the High Plains named Mel Dutton thought up a portable pronghorn decoy that actually worked. Mel's pronghorn decoy is still available and probably better than ever. Made out of ABS plastic and painted to look like the real thing (except that live goats do not come with those little handles), Mel's pronghorn can do double duty. With its center post, you can set it up near your blind and let it do its decoying job alone. If you are trying to stalk within range of a goat that will not come to you (watch out for that cactus!), place your hand through the slot and edge forward with the decoy. You actually can – if you are careful and the wind is right – crawl within bow range. Getting the 46 x 41 inch decoy stuck in the ground, nocking an arrow, coming to full draw and crouching over the decoy to shoot before the antelope's extraordinary eyes send it whirling off at 45 mph is another matter. Mel's pronghorn and his larger (46 x 60 inch) rear view cow elk decoy fold for easy carrying and storage.

Today, decoys are available for almost anything you want to hunt although with grizzlies, extra caution is advised. Decoying is fun and once you get the hang of it, you will certainly increase your odds of bagging deer or pronghorn (or wild turkeys and surely ducks and geese). Using a decoy is fun and, for deer, America's most sought-after big game animal, a decoy can provide that extra bit of spice needed to keep you attentive during a suspiciously uneventful day.

Could you use your 3-D target from McKenzie or Rinehart or Blue Ridge as a decoy? Absolutely. After all, this works for a lot of game wardens catching poachers. The three-piece Full Body Whitetail Deer from Blue Ridge, for instance, would make an excellent decoy. Just set it up where deer can see it from a distance and make sure the wind is blowing from the decoy to you. Otherwise, you are probably wasting your time. This is a full-body deer that resembles a real deer in size and in its paint job, too. If you sprinkle it with the right deer lure … well, what could be better except having a tame deer on a leash?

Well, there are problems with using a 3-D target as a decoy. First, one of these deer targets will weigh more than 20 pounds. They are bulky and even broken down into their sections are difficult to carry (just like a real deer). They have rather obvious section lines and scoring zones that a deer may or may not care about. No one really knows for sure and the anecdotal evidence is mixed. Finally, unless it is new, you have probably shot the heck out of your 3-D practice deer and wild animals may feel more pity for it than curiosity.

While some of the following are not especially designed for archers, but for turkey hunters, most archers are two-season hunters. In other words, we are hunts first and our choice of a gun or a bow is second. So, here is a mixed selection for your shooting enjoyment.

Feather Flex offers two inflatable turkey decoys, a hen and a jake that has a short rubber beard. These stand on one post and are designed to move on that post in a breeze. A whole flock will fit in your backpack and each one weighs less than a pound.

Feather Flex also makes a variety of foam duck, goose and turkey targets. Their Elk Silhouette is a unique and interesting "headless design" that lets you use it with any type of call as long as you make sure the missing head is behind a bush. This elk is designed to be suspended between two trees with an adjustable shock cord. The Feather Flex bedded whitetail deer is made from a soft rubber that weighs about a pound and rolls up for easy carrying into the field.

Of special interest to predator hunters are their whitetail fawn and the clever "Rigor Rabbit" that is designed to quiver as if it were injured. Rigor Rabbit is operated with four AA batteries on a set sequence of 15 seconds on and 15 seconds off.

Delta's 3-D Deer Decoy features a unique storage cavity inside the body that holds everything needed for set up: legs, antlers and stakes. This decoy is made with soft foam that is lighter (less than 13 pounds) than a full size 3-D deer target and it comes with an orange strap for safe carrying. Most experts agree that for most effective shot presentation, archers should face a buck decoy toward your stand and a doe decoy away from it. An aggressive buck will want to confront the head or sides of another buck while he will want to

A decoy is not a sure-fire way to get a shot at a big game animal, but it does add another dimension to your hunting strategy. These 2-D decoys are enlarged photo images of actual game animals and, while they may not be as good as a 3-D decoy at interesting a trophy buck, they are much easier to carry and set up.

You could use a full-size 3-D deer as a decoy or perhaps even tie a live deer near your stand, but this Delta whitetail is specifically designed as an easy-carry decoy. Everything you need for set-up fits inside the body cavity.

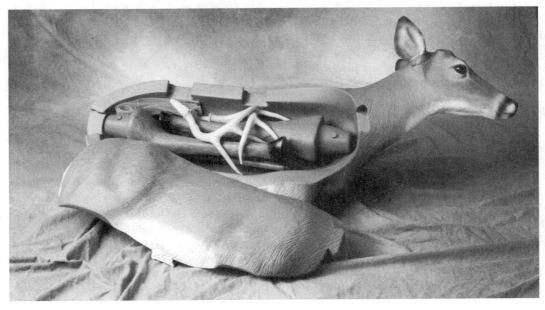

mount a doe. And remember to be conscious of the wind, too. If your scent covers a decoy, you should not expect that it would attract other deer.

If you use a Carry-Lite deer for instance, many experienced archers recommend you spray it with an odor neutralizer like the Super Odor Eliminator from Scrape Juice after you set it up. This will help eliminate human odors and if you have your favorite deer attractant handy, something like REALDeer from Shannon Outdoors that is distilled from fresh deer tarsal glands, splash some of it on a stake or even on the ground beside it, making sure that you do so with an eye to your shooting lanes. Should you place deer attractant directly on the decoy? Most archers who have successful experience with decoys recommend not.

The more realistic it is the better the decoy will work. If you can equip it with motion or even apparent motion, you will probably increase your odds. Custom Robotic Wildlife (www.wildlifedecoys.com) makes a full-body mount of a buck or doe that wildlife officers use to catch poachers and illegal road hunters. The tail and head move by remote control. If this proves to be too expensive – standing bucks start at $1,200 and bedded bucks at just $850, try the Tail-Wagger from Come-Alive Decoy Products (www.tail-wagger.com). "Would you fish with a lure that did not move through the water?" asks Come-Alive Manager Eric Lenz. The $50 battery-activated tail attaches to full-body Flambeau or Carry-Lite deer and gives them realistic motion. For just $100, you can buy the Tail-Wagger attached to the rear-end of a 3 ½-pound foam deer designed, at 24 inches high and 10 inches wide, to simulate a 90 pound deer.

The only note of warning with taking a deer decoy into the woods is to beware other hunters. We know from experience that we can be our own worst enemy when we carry capes with antlers or sometimes full-size decoys in or out of the woods. That caution makes the orange strap and carrying cavity of the Delta deer an interesting and useful safety feature.

GLOBAL POSITIONING SYSTEM (GPS) UNITS

So, you are on an elk hunt in the mountains of Montana, but you live in a suburb of Montgomery. Everything in your environment from the trees to the ground under your feet to the peaks soaring over your head and the big game you are hunting looks odd, exciting. It can be easy to get turned around – lost. If that happens, a Global Positioning System (GPS) unit will seem more like an essential survival tool than a toy.

A GPS unit is an enormously sophisticated device, but it has been simplified so that we non-scientists can

The Magellan SporTrak Color from Thales Navigation is the only handheld GPS receiver with a full, 16-color sunlight viewable display and a three-axis electronic compass. The SporTrak Color is waterproof and carries 32 MB of total memory. It operates on the field on two AA batteries and will interface with a personal computer. Suggested Retail Price is about $500.

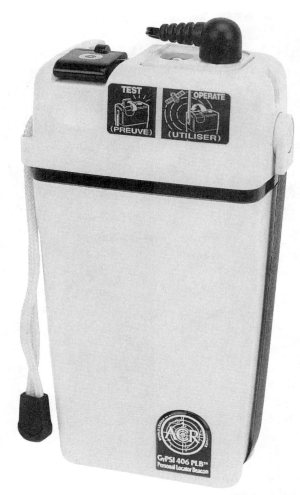

The GyPSI 406 Personal Locator Beacon from ACR Electronics transmits a 406 MHz EPIRB (emergency position indicating radio beacon) for search and rescue (SAR) situations. You can hunt, fish and hike in remote areas in North America and, if a bear attacks or you break a leg, you can alert SAR by pushing a button. A satellite will pick up the signal and relay your location to the nearest SAR team. At just 17 ounces, ACR's 406 floats and is totally waterproof.

use it successfully to determine such things as our position anywhere on the surface of the earth, our direction if we are moving, the time of day and our position relative to some object such as our parked truck or camp.

GPS is a satellite-based navigational system that works over any terrain, on land, on the ocean or in airplanes. It was developed by the US Department of Defense and the figure of $12 billion seems to be a widely accepted figure for start-up costs. What we taxpayers got for that money was a system of 24 satellites, each carrying an atomic clock and positioned

in highly predictable orbits 11,000 miles over our heads. Those satellites broadcast coded radio signals in microwave band lengths that travel (in a vacuum) at the speed of light. Signals are then "heard" by a GPS receiver, which mathematically triangulates or locates position in three dimensions and gives you other information as well. It takes three widely spaced, but simultaneous signals for general positioning, four signals to ensure that you are getting entirely accurate information. The most advanced units can measure position to within one centimeter!

The Magellan Sportrak Pro hand-held GPS from Thales Navigation is ideal for archers in the field and, without accessories like a jack to the accessory outlet (cigarette lighter) in your truck or a carrying case or a special antenna, costs about $270. This unit will give you your location to within three meters! Its shell is tough, high impact plastic and it is waterproof. Do not try this in the bathtub, but the Sportrak Pro floats! Because it is about 1 1/4 inches wide and weighs just a little over six ounces, hand-held units like this one fit in your shirt pocket, but are powerful enough to guide you back to camp in a blinding snow storm. The SportTrak Pro has a 2 1/3 by 1 2/5 inch screen, a bright backlight, a quality antenna and 9 MB of memory expandable to an amazing 23 MB. This GPS shows major roads, highways and waterways and can download additional maps. It has a zoom feature and a nine-button keyboard that give you options such as your compass bearing, speed and the distance remaining to reach a programmed objective

For even more power, consider adding the Mighty Mouse 2 GPS Antenna from GPS Outfitters. It offers a 29 dB gain over other antennas and plugs into GPS receivers with a simple 2-1/2 to 5 volt DC external antenna jack. It includes a screw-on mounting plate and multiple connectors.

Garmin's Rino 110 combines a hand-held radio with a GPS unit! It has 22 voice channels and 38 squelch codes. Retailing for about $195, the Rino 110 lets you communicate up to five miles on select GMRS channels and, within two miles on one of its FRS frequencies, will beam your location to your buddies in the field. The unit is waterproof and submersible. The Rino has individual "pages" on the operator's screen for the radio; for information about "best" hunting and fishing times at your location; for a map of your area; for navigation information including your speed, distance to your objective and estimated time of arrival; for miscellaneous "Points of Interest;" and for a Trip Computer. One of the coolest features is a tracking log that shows you not only the location of your friends in the field, but their path or track to their destination. Just tell your unit to "GoTo" and it gives you a path directly to their location.

Sometimes the best is listed last, but while the Lowrance iFinder is a superb GPS unit costing about $190, it does not have a radio. Still, if you want to learn about GPS, visit the Lowrance Internet site at www.lowrance.com for a tutorial. It is very good. There, you will not only learn about the iFinder and other GPS units, but you can learn that the US military recently discarded its SA or "Selective Availability" mode which allows us civilian operators to find our location much more precisely than just a few years ago. And what you learn on that site about the initials WAAS that you see in many advertisements may scare you! (WAAS stands for Wide Area Augmentation System and it was originally developed to allow civilian airliners to fly closer together. As if boarding a 20-year-old airliner that is going to fly six miles high at 400 mph for four hours with a snoring man who has body odor on one side and a woman with a screaming child on the other while you eat airline pretzels was not scary enough!)

The Pack Rat acts as both a stabilizer and a string container for archers who want to attach a line to their arrow to help track it after a shot.

DOWNED GAME FINDER

Golden Key-Futura markets the battery-operated Game Seeker that operates on the principle that every living creature gives off heat. Even after death, it takes a certain amount of time for the body's heat to dissipate. Chances are that if you hunt at all, you have or will one day be faced with an extremely difficult blood-trailing situation. The new Game Seeker uses a sensor to detect slight amounts of thermal heat emanating from downed game. Using a laser pointer, the black-cased Game Seeker pinpoints the location of downed game, Golden Key says, as far away as 200 yards. The digital bar graph displays the detection of heat waves and gives off an audible sound that can be detected through the unit's earplug. Of course, it will also point to live game, other bowhunters – who will not be happy when you stumble into their blind – cars in the parking lot …. Suggested Retail Price about $275.

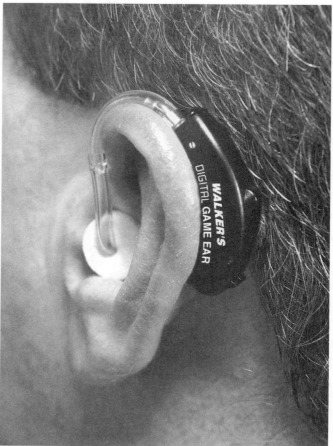

The Digital Game Ear slips around behind your ear and has a cushioned earpiece that fits inside your ear canal like an earplug. A tiny 1.4-volt button cell battery that is rated for an average life of 160 hours powers it.

HEARING AID

Yes, there is a way to amplify the minute noises in the woods and still protect your ears from muzzle blast. Okay, for archers this is not a problem, but if you are a two-season hunter (gun and bow) or enjoy a day at the shooting range, the Walker's Game Ear can be just what the hearing doctor ordered. If you are solely a bow and arrow hunter, it still works just fine – without the muzzle blast!

Bob Walker has produced a variety of sound amplifying units for hunters and shooters, but we are going to talk about his Game Ear that he advertises as "Better Hearing! Better Hunter!"

The Game Ear now comes in four versions. The original or #I, offered hearing enhancement and safety from extremely loud noises. How it does this is a puzzle to a non-engineer – something called a sound "compression circuit" that protects you from sounds greater than 110 decibels (dB) – but these devices are

Bob Walker's Digital Game Ear weighs less than 1/4-ounce. Bob says it can amplify the sound of a deer walking through the brush or even a panting lion ready to pounce.

powered by a tiny 1.4 volt button cell battery (included with each purchase) which have, Bob claims on his Internet site at www.walkersgameear.com, an average of 160 hours of life.

The plastic-cased Game Ear slips around behind your ear and has a cushioned earpiece that fits inside your ear canal like an earplug, but this plug is connected by a plastic tube to the circuitry behind your ear. The plastic case has a numbered dial so that you can re-tune it to your own ears without experimenting every time you wear it. It looks just like grandpa's hearing aid! The Game Ear weighs less than $\frac{1}{4}$ ounce and, according to the testimonials on the Internet site, can amplify the sound of a deer walking through the brush toward you or a panting leopard getting ready to pounce. Not bad!

The Original Game Ear costs about $175. Game Ear II includes adjustable frequency tuning and costs $228. The Game Ear III is the real beauty though, as it includes both adjustable frequency tuning and a couple channels for close range two-way communications – like a walkie-talkie! Game Ear III is $325 and there is a new digital Game Ear that is supposed to give you ultra-clear hearing that costs $490.

Is it a deer or a squirrel? How will you ever be able to get comfortable and take a nap on stand again?

STALKER SHIELD

Your first instinct is to laugh when you see the Stalker Shield, but on second thought, it occurs to you that this thing just might work!

The Stalker Shield is a mirror blind that accurately reflects or mimics the hunting surroundings. Use a Stalker Shield and you may never have to change your camo again because, behind it, you can hunt or stalk in total invisibility. The mirror surface has 100 percent surface reflectivity. It is fully portable and sets up quickly. It can be used in almost any terrain and for any game animal.

The Stalker Shield is available from Ruffolo Enterprises in two sizes: small is 40 oz. and measures 30 by 50 inches. The large size is 50 oz. and measures 40 by 67 inches.

A Shield includes its own flexible fiberglass rods and handle. To use it, you crouch behind it and angle it slightly toward the ground so that it reflects ground cover to any game animal. The Stalker Shield actually works quite well, but it has a down side or two: crouching behind the Shield, which sits on the ground, is tiresome, even on a stool. Wind causes the flexible mirror to move or shimmer and, while it may not be noticeable to a deer or turkey, rain will streak the surface causing distortion in the reflected image.

WHAT IS A LASER ANYWAY?

Generation X thinks of lasers like Baby Boomers think of transistor radios. "Cool, but so what." Like a lot of things we take for granted, they are little miracles of nature and since we archers are outdoorsmen, naturalists, we need to know just a wee bit about them because we use them at work and in our recreation.

Albert Einstein is thought of as the father of the laser because he postulated photos or light particles in 1917. Bell Labs research scientist Arthur Schawlow is credited with the invention of the laser in 1958 and for this he won a Nobel Prize in 1981. Schawlow said, "... when the first lasers were operated, I and other scientists close to the research were surprised about how easy it turned out to be. We assumed that since lasers had never been made, it must be very difficult. But once you knew how, it was not at all difficult. Mostly what had been lacking were ideas and concepts." Easy for him to say.

The word laser is short for Light Amplification by Stimulated Emission of Radiation. Basically, you energize a light emitting substance like an artificial ruby with energy (the Bushnell Yardage Pro Scout uses a three-volt battery for this) and it sets up a chain reaction funneling photons through a polished and highly reflective tube, lots of photons. A laser is, after all, an intense, monochromatic (usually red in our rangefinders) beam of light where, unlike from sunlight or from a flashlight, all the crests and troughs of the light waves are precisely identical, uniform and unidirectional.

Rangefinders are regulated by the Food and Drug Administration (FDA), which sets accessible emission standards for radiation. The tools we use have built-in FDA Class I (of four total classes) lasers. That means we cannot have access to the laser during use and that it is eye and skin safe. You could stare into it during operation, but just to be safe, no one would ever recommend that. Class II lasers, by the way, can be an eye hazard if you chronically look at them directly. Class III lasers pose an acute hazard from direct viewing or prolonged contact and Class IV lasers pose an acute hazard from direct or even indirect viewing. Beyond that, we are in Star Wars territory and we only want to kill our game efficiently, not kill and cook it on the spot.

The unique Stalker Shield is a mirror blind that accurately portrays its surroundings – swamp or snow – to any big game animal because the flexible mirror has 100 percent reflectivity.

BOWFISHING AND BOWFISHING GEAR

Some archers argue that bowfishing is the most fun a person can have with a bow and arrow. They reason this way.

- When you are bowfishing, you are, by and large, fishing for finny characters that are not considered game fish. Your quarry is not a bass or a trout or a walleye. In fact, most states prohibit bowfishing for native game fish. You are fishing for carp and gar in fresh water and sharks and skates or small rays in salt water and the carp is an introduced, exotic species.
- You will not be expected to keep and eat everything you shoot, or perhaps any of it. Many bowfishermen head straight to the dumpster with their haul of trash fish. People who are aware of population dynamics generally appreciate your removing these fish from the water.
- There is no pressure to fill a tag and there is not a record book, certainly not one that anyone takes seriously. Unless you are participating in a bowfishing tournament, whether you take one or a hundred carp out of your favorite lake or whether the largest one weighs two pounds or thirty pounds, it is pressure free.
- The equipment, unless you absolutely fall in love with bowfishing and build a specialized boat, is inexpensive.
- Whether you fish from a boat or from shore, you are outside having fun in sunny weather in the spring and summer, not huddling silent and immobile on a treestand in the fall and winter. Get a tan. Go for a swim. Have a good time.

If these are not enough reasons to convince you that bowfishing is a real archery treat, consider yourself "fun challenged."

Bowfishing is different from all other archery games in one very important respect. You tie one end of a line on the arrow and the other end on a bow-mounted reel. After you shoot, you retrieve the arrow and get ready to shoot again. How you gear up to do

this safely and successfully is the subject of this chapter.

YOUR BOW

Almost any bow will do for bowfishing: a compound, a recurve or, in special circumstances, a crossbow. (Although I have never seen a longbow used by a fishing archer, it is certainly possible.)

Because it is designed with cams or wheels and hence has a let-off, a compound bow allows you to hold at a lighter weight than peak while you track a fish through the water or perhaps adjust your aim to the movement of a boat. A compound will give you plenty of power to reach fish swimming several feet below the surface and will extend your range from shore or from a boat deck.

The ability to hold after you draw is a benefit because in bowfishing, what you see is not what you get. Fish in water are subject to an optical effect called "refraction" because water is denser than air. This means, light moves at different speeds when it travels between mediums of different density: it is slower in materials of greater density. Therefore, it is slower in water than air.

The result of refraction is that the fish is not where it seems to be, because you are looking from one, lighter medium – air – into another, denser medium – water. You must compensate for this both mentally and physically.

In the beginning, bowfishermen shoot over or above fish. To adjust for refraction, aim lower or closer to the boat than the fish seems to your "naked eye." You must aim and shoot beneath a fish to hit it, because remember that what you "see" – what your brain recognizes – is not light entering the water, but light reflecting back to your eyes from an object in the water. The deeper a fish is swimming, the greater the difference between its apparent and its real positions and hence, the "lower" you must shoot.

At this time, there are no bowfishing sights

Shelby Cass, daughter of Bowfishing Association President Chris Cass, shows good shooting form on a bright summer's day outing. Unlike hunting, bowfishing is a gregarious archery activity that is most enjoyable in the spring and summer when the weather is bright and warm. Chris confesses that he is a bowfishing "addict," and takes his sport and his daughter Shelby onto the ice to fish for carp during a harsh Wisconsin winter!

available to help with the triple difficulty of bowfishing: movement, distance and refraction. Effective shooting is still trial and error – old fashioned learning! The more you do, the better you become. Even though AMS sells a simple single pin sight for bowfishing, archers who have shot more than a few fish usually remove their bow sight because it is useless on the water and because it will inevitably become entangled in your line.

Because it shoots a faster arrow than a recurve, with a flatter arrow trajectory, a compound will also help deliver an arrow accurately on more difficult distant shots. Even with a compound bow, shots beyond twelve to fifteen yards are rarely successful (unless you are shooting at a hundred-plus pound alligator gar) because so many variables are involved: movement of the fish through the water, movement of the boat, the difficulty of accurately estimating the angle of refraction, and the weight of a heavy bowfishing arrow and fish head trailing a spool of line behind it. The smaller the shot angle, the greater the chance that your arrow with its barbed, harpoon head, will plane erratically through the water.

Even the largest reptile on the North American continent, the American alligator, can successfully be taken by bow with a proper bowfishing set-up.

Your choice of a bow is virtually unlimited for bowfishing. Many tournaments are won with a recurve because they typically can launch arrows quicker and smoother, but a compound delivers more energy on target and that is especially useful for fish that are not cruising on the surface. This stingray was taken in brackish water on the Gulf of Mexico.

The knock on compound bows often reported by experienced archers who bowfish is that when the cam(s) rolls over, the shooter loses time and concentration and the heavy arrow jumps off the special rest. This is because of the bump or jump when you draw the bow into the valley of the draw force curve. Unless you hold the arrow on the rest with your finger, it almost always falls off, not only because of the sudden drop in holding weight, but because you are moving and aiming downward, too.

Weighing four-to-five pounds without the reel, line and an arrow, a compound bow with machined aluminum riser can tire you out during a bowfishing tournament or a long day on the water. Imagine that you performed a hundred curls in the weight room or that you hefted and shot a 60-pound compound bow a hundred or more times. Which activity would give you the most exercise?

For bowfishing, the kinetic energy your bow

delivers and thus, the weight you shoot is practically irrelevant. An old, 45-pound recurve will stick and hold most fish. So, unless you are stalking monster alligator gar in Texas or Louisiana, you can safely leave your elephant bow at home.

That said, fishing archers will testify that the scales on large gar and carp can be thick and horny, so a little more power is better for these fish than a little less. Hit them broadside in shallow water and this will not matter, but that is like having a whitetail buck walk broadside into your shooting lane, stop and look in the opposite direction. This doesn't happen very often, because usually the fish are moving, they are sensitive to your movement and you are shooting down at an angle.

When an archer takes up bowfishing, he learns that many of his equipment concerns evaporate. Tuning, tillering, arrow speed, sights, release aids, hard cam, soft cam, stabilizing, silencing — none of these things are of particular importance. In fact, the archery accessories essential for bowfishing are a reel with a line and a harpoon-tipped arrow. If you get into a lot of shooting, you may want to experiment with an old fashioned leather glove or a finger tab because your fingers can become extremely sore from continual shooting and you will find that using a release, while it certainly can be used for bowfishing, is slow and cumbersome.

Many bowfishermen like the old fashioned, three-finger molded rubber No-Glove from Billy Armentor's

This excellent haul of carp gets favorable reviews from knowledgeable fishermen who are aware of the damage this bottom-feeding exotic fish does to spawning beds of native species. The carp and related species such as buffalo fish are usually considered "trash" fish and it is not required that sportsmen consent to eat it after they have killed it.

Cajun Archery or from Saunders Archery. The padded No-Glove allows you to shoot without a glove or tab, which get wet and then become practically useless anyway (except for a cheap plastic tab). To use it, remove the string from your recurve or compound and slide it up through the center hole of this two-piece accessory: the smaller, one-finger section goes above the nock and the larger, two-finger section goes below. Remember. You are not shooting for a record book. You are having fun.

Bowfishing action can be exciting. For fast shooting, a recurve is smoother than a compound bow and can usually deliver sufficient power, even for really big fish which you will want to hit a couple times anyway and perhaps get a drag float on as soon as you can to tire them out. A recurve does not need to be pulled completely back to full draw to be effective and can be drawn and released quickly. Small fish or spawning carp on or near the surface, for instance, may just as effectively be speared by plucking the recurve string rather than going through the complete breathe-draw-aim-release sequence like you would bowhunting or at a competitive 3-D shoot.

Recurves are lighter in weight than compound bows and not as much can go wrong. Averaging a pound or less without attached gear like reels and rests

(You will not need a quiver for bowfishing.), the recurve is a relatively simple tool to operate successfully when you are hauling in 20 or 30 yards of soaked, braided Dacron string and a fish fighting for its life. All that time you are trying to maintain your balance on a moving boat or tip-toeing to keep the water below the lip your hip boots while you are holding your bow out of the water.

Unless you snag your recurve string on the motor mount or step on it repeatedly when you put the bow down to haul in a fish, a recurve may prove to be the best-all-around bowfishing tool. Separating it from a spaghetti-like mess of line once you have boated a fish is certainly much easier than untangling a compound.

- A crossbow can easily be used for bowfishing and it has many advantages for an archer who is confined to a wheelchair or for someone going after alligators or giant alligator gar. Whether from a boat deck or from a dock, a crossbow built by Horton or Excalibur or TenPoint will provide plenty of power. Crossbows are easy to sight-in on a fish and hefty enough so that if the line is tightly fastened to the reel, fighting a fish of almost any size, even while seated in a chair with wheels should be manageable.
- There are four difficulties with crossbows when used for bowfishing: strength, speed, design and weight.
- A crossbow is not an instrument designed for rapid shooting. If it is cocked by hand, lifting the string to snap into the receiver can quickly become a chore and a prescription for a backache the following day.

If a cocking device is used, it will take you several minutes to "reload," even if you shoot and miss.

- Because the crossbow is a "horizontal bow," your bowfishing arrow must pass across and in close proximity to the crossbow's cables. Knowing this, it is important to make sure your bowfishing line is very tight and well out of the way of the cables before every shot. Interference by your line with the moving cables could spell disaster.
- Finally, the very stability of an awkward eight-pound crossbow is prohibitive for an outing of any significant duration or action, much less a 24-hour bowfishing tournament.

BOWFISHING REELS AND LINE

Archers have been fishing with bows and arrows for thousands of years. Archaeologists have documented harpoon-style fish points made with fish bones on every continent and throughout Polynesia.

An early Fred Bear film shows him bowfishing from a canoe on the Great Lakes. He is shooting a

Doug Bermel is wheelchair-bound, but used a Horton crossbow equipped with an AMS Retriever Reel to take a superior alligator gar during a trip to Texas. "Bowfishing is a lot of fun," Doug says, "and is a great mixture of bowhunting and fishing. It gives you a great reason to get out of doors during the spring and summer season."

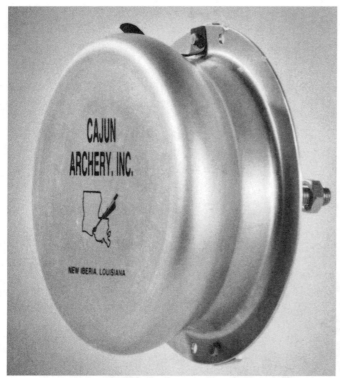

This wrap-around bowfishing reel is still manu-factured and sold by Cajun Archery. It is inexpensive, simple ... and effective. The standard reel screws into the stabilizer insert and is held tight with a nut.

The AMS Slotted Retriever Bowfishing Reel is filled with line. The action end is tied to a bowfishing arrow and the other to a lightweight float. If you arrow a truly large fish, such as a shark or ray or hundred-plus-pound alligator gar, this rig will help you keep track of it.

recurve, of course, to which he has taped a wooden block and around this block he has wrapped his fishing line. At the time the film was made, in the 1940s and '50s, there was no manufacturing standard for accessories such as inserts for mounting stabilizers or bow reels, so black electrician's tape had to suffice. Equipment development has come a long way since Fred's time.

As a fishing archer, you need a reel to retrieve the arrow after you shoot. Three reel styles are used for bowfishing: a circular wrap-around reel, a closed-face spinning reel and the specially designed and very popular Retriever reel from AMS.

For 30 to 40 years, a circular wrap-around reel was used by practically every bowfisherman. This style reel is both functional and lightweight. After a shot, you simply pull in your line by hand, wrapping it around the reel as you go. These reels work equally well for left- or right-handed shooters. A small, but important safety element that actually helps you shoot better is the tiny key or clip attached to the spooling edge of the reel. This clip holds your line securely in front of the bow so that it will not tangle as you shoot or scout for our next shooting opportunity.

The Retract-O-Blade bowfishing reel screws into the accessory mounting hole on the front of a bow's riser. It only weighs about five ounces, even with line attached. The aluminum construction is durable and it can be used for any bow drilled and tapped with a standardized accessory insert. Retract-O-Blade sells its reels with 50 feet of 80-pound test braided nylon line. That weight should be sufficient for small sharks and alligator gar weighing several hundred pounds, because bowfishermen chasing these fish try to hook them more than once. Rather than fighting them and bringing them to the boat, they then attach the end of the line to a bright float, which they can follow in their boat until the fish gets tired. Because so many archers use old or non-standardized bows to fish, Retract-O-Blade also sells this same reel with a bracket designed to tape onto the handle of a bow.

The circular bowfishing reels snug against your riser with a simple jam nut for exact positioning and advertise smooth line feed, an important consideration for retrieving a fish that is racing away at top speed. Grayling Outdoor Products makes a lightweight molded plastic reel that is sold with 50 feet of 88-pound line. Cajun Archery also manufactures lightweight, aluminum five-inch tape-on and screw-on reels. The Game Tracker version includes two clips on the back (between the reel and the bow) to hold spare arrows, but in practice this is cumbersome because when you are shooting or furiously reeling in line, additional arrows hanging down in front can make for a mess. The most interesting design is the open mesh 6.5-inch diameter reel engineered in heavy-duty plastic from Saunders.

The least used, but still completely functional of the three principal types of bowfishing reels is the closed-face reel. A good example is the Zebco 808 Spincaster. It is made specifically for bowfishing with modified bearings and internal components of brass and stainless steel. The reel handle is oversized for high-leverage cranking and it features a lock-down drag for tough fights. It comes with a spool of 70-pound braided Dacron line.

A spincast reel like the Zebco 808 is not designed to attach directly to a bow, but to a special adapter rod or reel mount. Cajun offers an aluminum fishing reel mount that screws into the 5/16" x 24 stabilizer bushing hole on the front of your bow. The mount has a clever, two-part adjustable footed holder that allows you to snug the reel tight. You can even screw a solid fiberglass rod onto the front of your reel mount for a 17-inch overall length for playing fish to the boat. This short rod is tipped with a standard stainless steel guide.

The most popular style bowfishing reel is the Retriever from AMS. The Retriever mounts directly to your bow riser's sight holes. Its mechanical theory is superbly simple. After you shoot, squeeze the trigger on the frame of the Retriever with a finger from your bow hand. This locks the durable urethane retainers around your line and as you turn the extra-large crank with your shooting hand, the retainers rewind your line into the attached bottle. It is a convenient system with no drag and no bail to release. The Standard Retriever comes with 35 yards of 130-pound test braided Dacron line installed. AMS offers a mounting bracket for offset risers or for mounting on recurve bows.

The only caution with a Retriever is to make sure you do not grasp the trigger when you are ready to shoot. This can happen through inattention from lack of activity or on those frantic hundred-shot days. Holding the trigger when you shoot could cause the arrow to snap back in your face and injure you.

AMS builds their reel with minor modifications for attaching a float for large fish like 200-pound alligator gar or big salt-water rays and sharks. Called a Slotted Retriever, the end of the line is tied to an external float. When an alligator or shark zooms off with your arrow, it quickly pulls the Retriever's 35 yards of line out of the bottle and your float zooms off following it. Just remember to keep the bow pointed in the direction of the streaming line until it all plays out and then follow the float to locate your fish.

For most bowfishing chores on carp and buffalo, tilapia and dogfish, a lightweight line works well, but specialty lines are available in a variety of materials (Spectra, Fast Flight, etc.), colors and test strengths for bigger game, alligator gar and alligators. For alligators, heavier line is obviously an excellent choice and braided lines suitable for bowfishing are available up to the 600-pound test Brownell Gator Cord. Your reel should come with line test recommendations and if not, a call to the manufacturer will give you a range of acceptable options.

YOUR ARROW

Not many years ago, fishing archers simply tied their line to a hole in the base of the arrow, ran the line up to the front of the arrow near the harpoon point, and held it there with a rubber band. When you shot, the line pulled out from under the rubber band and the line flowed away with your arrow. Even 50 years ago, it was understood that the line had to run free from the front of the bow – and the rear of the arrow – after a shot. As equipment has become more complicated and with the development of powerful compound bows with extra cables and a cable guard, it is more important than ever to make sure your line does not foul in the process of shooting.

"A fellow bowfisherman was killed while practice shooting in his backyard early last year (2000)," says a release from AMS in Stratford, Wisconsin. "His line was tied to the tail of the arrow and upon release, the line tied itself to his bowstring. The bowstring absorbed all of the arrow's energy and brought the arrow back nearly as fast as it left his bow and fatally injured him."

This fiberglass fish arrow has durability, flexibility and strength. Monofilament line with a heavy swivel line guide allows the line to slide up the shaft when used. It is equipped with a double-barb fish point that unscrews for fish removal. Note that the black plastic fletching-sleeve has been removed and the arrow is ready to hook up and shoot.

A major difference between bowfishing and any other archery event is that for fishing, you want to keep you arrow attached to your bow with a fishing line. Numerous methods for attaching your line to the solid fiberglass fish arrow abound and AMS has developed the Safety Slide specifically to keep fishing line away from the arrow rest at full draw. If the line should become entangled with the rest or reel when you shoot, it will jack-knife back into your face and this situation is extremely dangerous.

The essential problem and one that has been recognized for years is that your line needs to be secured to the nock end of the arrow. Attached to the front or the middle, the line would quickly stop your arrow in flight. Attached to the end, it trails along behind and serves as a stabilizing influence (one with a whole lot of drag) on the arrow's flight. The problem is that attached at the nock end of the arrow, the line can hang up on your bow's string or cables or even the arrow rest.

Several companies offer kits that allow you to attach your bowfishing line to your arrow in a manner to help ensure that you will get smooth, safe flight. Called "cabling," for the cable that runs the length of the arrow, a kit typically includes a length of braided steel wire or heavy monofilament that is attached to your arrow through holes drilled near the tip and nock ends. After a swivel is slid onto the cable, it is crimped securely at both ends. You simply tie the line from your reel to the swivel and, when you are ready to shoot, make sure the line and swivel swing free in front of your bow.

Responding to the death of the bowfisherman mentioned above, AMS developed a new cabling system called a Safety Slide. The AMS system consists of a collar that slides along your arrow shaft. Your line attaches to the side of the collar. If tied correctly, the line trails your arrow practically on-center, promoting true arrow flight. A urethane "shock pad" affixed to the arrow shaft with a screw prevents impact damage when the arrow plays fully out and begins to pull line behind it.

Bowfishing arrows are specialized instruments designed only for fishing and they are not interchangeable with hunting arrows. Hunting arrows, whether aluminum or composite, are too light to pull line from a reel, plow through the water, carry a heavy harpoon head, and impale fish. This task requires a solid fiberglass arrow.

Fiberglass bowfishing shafts are the bowfishing

standard. They are strong enough for carp or gators and the fiberglass has a "memory" that allows it to return to straight after bending. Aluminum is heavy enough, but at the usual 11/32-inch diameter, it can bend and this immediately renders these shafts unusable. Muzzy Products also sells a composite bowfishing shaft.

Bare fiberglass shafts are usually sold in 32-inch lengths in a standard 5/16-inch diameter. The tip is blunt for attaching an adapter and a screw-on fish head. The nock end is tapered to five degrees for a glue-on nock or nock adapter and normally the arrows are pre-drilled at both ends for cabling. Manufacturers drill holes in adapters that exactly match the holes in the shaft. Shafts are usually white, but may also be available in blue, green, black and orange.

If you purchase a bowfishing arrow already "made up," and that is not a bad idea if you are a novice, are strapped for time or are "all thumbs" in the workshop, it will have black rubber Lay-Fletch sleeve with molded fletching at the nock end. Fletching is used to stabilize an arrow in flight, but at the short distances involved in bowfishing and with such a heavy arrow, there is some reasonable question whether this fletching is either necessary or effective. Experienced bowfishermen often remove it.

Every fishing arrow, like every hunting arrow, must be equipped with a nock so you can hold it on the bowstring and so the bowstring can propel it forward at a target. A variety of conventional plastic nocks and Uni-Nocks with Adapters is available.

BOWFISHING POINTS

The job you require a fish point to do is penetrate and hold so that you can reel in your trophy. Many styles are available and virtually all of them will work. They either glue directly onto the fore-end of your shaft or screw into an adapter that is glued on the shaft.

Retract-O-Blade builds stainless steel (or nickel-plated) heads with spring steel blades in single- or double-blade versions. These heads are advertised at a whopping 475 gr. The Retract-O-Blade head is designed with a collar at the base to make it easy to remove the fish from your arrow. Push the arrow tip completely through a fish (Bowfishermen are not usually squeamish characters.), squeeze the retractable blades together and slide the sleeve over them. Then you can easily pull the arrow back through the fish.

Retract-O-Blade's Garpoon comes with either a hardened steel "rock tip" or a chisel tip and weighs 562 grains!

Muzzy's Quick Release Bowfishing Point has a hardened steel tip. The Gar Point uses the characteristic Muzzy Trocar Tip and the Carp Point has a multi-faceted machined steel tip. This head is designed to hit-and-hold. Removing the arrow from a fish is easy by simply shoving it completely through and reversing the barbs with your fingers. The Mohawk, Shure Shot and Wee Stinger heads work in a similar manner.

The venerable Sting-A-Ree fish point assumes three positions and shoots similar to a mechanical hunting head. The barbs are closed, folded against the arrow in flight. During penetration, the barbs fold open. To remove your arrow from a fish, simply twist the arrow slightly to partially unscrew the head from its ferrule and when you pull the arrow out, the blades unlock and fold forward.

You will see several other head styles on retail shelves. The Lil' Stinger is an inexpensive, fixed wire-arm point. After harpooning a fish, push this head through and unscrew the point from the adapter to remove it. The Talon features a single wire arm and its manufacturer says this reduces arrow planing in the water. The Warhead's distinctive flat, twisted barbs are designed to help your arrow rotate, thus improving underwater accuracy. The Warhead is not the most aerodynamic head, but its short pyramid head is supposed to grab and hold fish after only 2 ? inches of penetration.

Top 10 Bowfishing Accessories

1. Polarized Sunglasses: Polarized sunglasses cut glare and help you see beneath the surface of the water. Look for side panels, a top shield or a wrap-around style to block reflected light. You can buy inexpensive glasses at any bait and tackle store or you can look for a pair of glasses with the right features and some styling, too. Bushnell's H2Optix line features several frame styles and three polarization qualities. You can purchase Bushnell's

"Lido" sunglasses for instance with amber, dark gray or dark gray with silver, top gradient flash coating polycarbonate lenses. Be sure to attach the adjustable floating sport strap to keep these sunglasses on the surface, because when the action gets hot, they will go overboard!

2. Roller Rest: Carefully remove the exotic, programmable arrow rest you use for 3-D competition and bowhunting. Now, jam a broken pencil stub into the rest attachment hole above the arrow shelf in your bow. If this seems too basic or too drastic, try a Muzzy Wheel of Fortune Rest (brass wheel and stainless shaft), a Cajun Roller Rest (Delrin roller and brass shaft), Hi-Tek Spear-It Roller Rest or a simple Muzzy Tri-Loop Rest (for unfletched arrows). Designed to help an exceptionally heavy arrow (compared to a hunting arrow, that is) achieve flight, these rests are total simplicity. The roller style rest is easy to mount, fits right- or left-hand bows and is easy to adjust for centershot on offset riser bows. Hi-Tek notes that the low friction, precision machined roller in the Spear-It rest never needs lubrication.

3. Armguard: Sure, they are hot and "experienced" bowfishermen scoff at them. Still, if you misalign a shot even slightly and your string hits your bow arm, your painful new four-inch by three-inch black and blue bruise will make you wish you were wearing arm protection … for about a week.

4. Protection from Sun and Bugs: The higher the SPF sunscreen protection, the better. During a good day on the water, you will tan and burn, so staying lathered with sun block will help prevent skin damage from ultra-violet rays. If you are active or the day is hot, you will sweat so you may need to reapply your sun block several times. The peak bowfishing months are during the spring and summer and that is exactly the time of year when

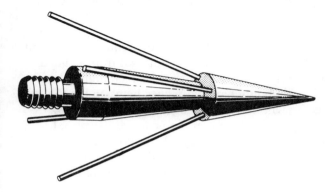
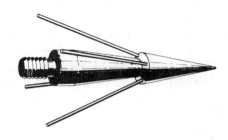

The Lil' Stinger Fish Point from Cajun Archery comes in a two-harpoon-wire and a four-harpoon-wire configuration. This style of point is highly effective fore retrieving fish, but must be pushed through and unscrewed before the fish can be removed from your arrow.

mosquitoes hatch. With so many mosquito-borne diseases current now in America, from West Nile Virus to Encephalitis to Dengue Fever, it is important – and may be critical – to protect yourself. If you live in a state where it is legal to bowfish at night, your boat's lights will attract biting bugs as well as fish. Authorities now recommend that a chemical repellent with a DEET concentration of 35-percent (or less) is as much poison as the adult human body should be exposed to and children should not be exposed to DEET at all. An excellent alternative is to wear a bug suit like the patented, double mesh Bug Tamer, in which case you will not need chemical repellents. (Protect yourself, but be aware that the chemicals in sunscreens and insect repellents may, in some cases, damage the finish on your equipment or the outer mesh of a bug suit.)

5. Fish Bopper: "Stop 'em from floppin'," Muzzy says. Once you have them in the boat, apply the coup de grace quickly with this small baseball bat and get on with business.

6. Fishing Floats: Big fish will not roll over and die just because you have stuck an arrow in them. You will have to stick sharks, alligator gar and alligators numerous times before you can pull them to the boat or to shore.

7. 3-D Carp: Muzzy markets a foam, 3-D carp bowfishing target. At two feet long, it can be anchored on heavy cord and moved around underwater for realistic shooting practice. You will want to remove your harpoon tips and replace them either with a heavy screw-in field point or the Muzzy 4-D Practice Point, which is sold specifically for use with the carp target.

8. Bowfishing Camo: If you cannot locate your fishing partner out on the water, he might be wearing what Muzzy calls their Midnite Tiger Camo. This Viet Nam War-era tiger-stripe pattern comes in multiple shades of blue, rather than wartime green and black. Check your aquarium. Fish see movement and they do look up, just like deer!

9. Wide-Brim Hat: Keep the sun off your face and the back of your neck. Grow long hair or wear a hat that keeps your face and neck shaded. It may be hot and you may sweat, but a wide-brim hat helps prevent sunburn and skin cancer.

10. Bowfishing Videos: Stay sharp for carp. Enjoy the total bowfishing experience at any time of year with *Bowfishing The Big Waters*, Impale A Scale and *Gator Safari*. These videos are available from your local retailer or from most manufacturers of bowfishing equipment.

BOWFISHING ASSOCIATION OF AMERICA

When you catch bowfishing fever, you will look for additional opportunities to get out the water with your bow, to extend your fishing experiences, and to hang out with others who enjoy this aspect of archery. At this point, it is time to get in touch with your inner bowfisherman and call your state archery association for information, state regulations and contacts or to call the Bowfishing Association of America (BAA). The BAA is a small non-profit association that helps maintain a schedule of tournaments and other get-togethers throughout the US and Canada.

"Bowfishing is not only archery," says BAA President Chris Cass, "it's fishing, stalking, boating, hunting and genuine outdoor fellowship all wrapped up in one."

A family membership in the BAA costs $25 per year. For additional information, contact the BAA at: Bowfishing Association of America, 470 Mohawk Rd., Janesville, WI 53545 (608) 756-5605. The BAA Internet site is www.bowfishingassociation.com.

NOW THIS IS A BOAT!

Mark Land is Director of Bowfishing Development for Muzzy Products in Cartersville, Georgia. He has built a boat – essentially from the "ground up" – just for bowfishing.

"I finished it the night before the third annual Muzzy Classic bowfishing tournament," Mark says. "We hold the Classic on the last weekend in April on Lake Guntersville in northeast Alabama. We had 46 two- or three-person teams in 2002. Many bowfishing tournaments award prizes for total number of fish, but we found that people in airboats won all the time because airboats are more effective at getting into the shallows. So, we changed our tournament to Heaviest 20 Fish, with a limit of five grass carp. We had a grass carp last year that weighed over 71 pounds! People who haven't tried bowfishing can think about wrestling that one into the boat!"

Mark began building his bowfishing special with a custom-built 18-foot aluminum boat from Legend Craft in Alexander, Arkansas: 28-inch high sides, 70-inch wide bottom and 96-inches between the top rails. It came with dual center consoles and a shallow "V-into-flat" hull. To power the boat and its special accessories, Mark employs three motors:

- a 115-horsepower (hp) Mariner outboard. (He plans to upgrade to a 200-hp Mercury before the 2003 season.)
- A 24-volt Minn Kota Maxxum electric, bow-mounted trolling motor that delivers 65-pounds of thrust and will operate smoothly in a foot of

water. "I use it for moving slow and quiet in the shallows," Mark says. He has modified it with a 74-inch hand control so he can move and watch for cruising fish at the same time.

• A stern-mounted, three-blade 42" composite aircraft propeller for moving in water less than one foot deep and through thick beds of grass. The variable-pitch propeller or fan operates with a 20-hp twin cylinder Briggs & Stratton Vanguard motor and is shrouded with a wire cage on the front. "This particular style of fan is used to inflate hot air balloons," Mark says. "It will push my boat over stumps and things in the water that would otherwise hang us up."

To move this heavy boat (Mark can do 38 mph when he get cranked!) and keep him powered-up day and night, Mark has installed a 24-gallon gas tank, two heavy-duty 12-volt marine batteries and a red and black, 7.8-hp Generac 4000XL generator with a 6,600-watt surge rating. The generator slides conveniently under the boat's rear deck. With its own four-gallon tank, the generator provides eight-to-nine hours of electricity, depending on the load.

Because bowfishing tournaments can mean all-night operation, Mark installed eight 300-watt halogen floodlights on the bow and two 500-watt floods on the stern. For driving lights, there are two 7-inch, 100-watt stainless steel headlights with high-low capabilities. Of course, the boat hull is modified for standing archers with heavy-duty diamond-plate aluminum decks, raised 20 inches in the front to provide a clearer view down into the water. Around the front of the deck is an 18-inch aluminum railing. "It isn't necessarily for safety," Mark says. "I use the rail to brace against when I shoot and fight a fish."

Mark's bowfishing boat has all the extras that tournament bowfishermen need to compete successfully: a Magellan Global Positioning System (GPS), a Hummingbird depth finder, dual bilge pumps and a 2,000-pound capacity tub with a two-inch drain to hold fish.

"I can fish in salt or fresh water in this rig," Mark says. "All I need is my archery gear and a fishing license." Plus coolers, seats, sunscreen …. Actually, it is not all a person needs. Mark concedes he needed a 4,000-pound-rated TrailMaster trailer with electric disk brakes to haul the boat and a 300-hp Chevrolet V-8 truck "with the extra towing package" to pull it. No counting the truck, his fishing licenses, archery gear, gas and time off from work, Mark estimates he has more than $25,000 invested in his hobby.

"Sure, but I can fish as many as six people," he says, "four off the front and two off the back!"

A new bowfishing video from Mark Land and Muzzy Products called *Impale A Scale* provides more than an hour of action footage from a seven-day fish-hunting odyssey through Alabama, Louisiana, Mississippi and ending on the Gulf of Mexico. This video, which features Mark's remarkable boat and a dozen species of fish, is available from Muzzy Products in Cartersville, Georgia (800) 222-7769.

It is not unusual for "hooked" bowfishermen to spend thousands of dollars outfitting their boats with generators and extra lights for night fishing, high-powered fans to cruise in shallow water and big outboards to move all this weight across the water.

Tips and Tactics From The Experts

Bowhunters' Digest
Advanced Tactics, 5th Edition
Edited by Kevin Michalowski
Learn advanced bowhunting tactics from more than twenty top bowhunters including Greg Miller, Bryce Towsley, M.D. Johnson, and Gary Clancy. They'll teach you how to hone your hunting and shooting skills to increase your success. Become familiar with the latest equipment and accessories and find out how to contact archery manufacturers, dealers, and other resources with the state-by-state list.
Softcover • 8½ x 11 • 256 pages
300 b&w photos
Item# BOW5 • $22.95

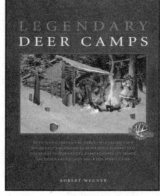

Legendary Deer Camps
by Robert Wegner
Travel back in time to experience deer camps famous Americans such as William Faulkner Aldo Leopold and Oliver Hazard Perry. Rediscover classic hunting traditions such a freedom, solitude, camaraderie, rites of initia story-telling and venison cuisine through a s of famous deer camp biographies and rare h torical paintings and photographs. This is th second book in the *Deer and Deer Hunting* Classics Series.
Hardcover • 8¼ x 10⅞ • 208 pages
125 b&w photos • 75 color photos
Item# DERCP • $34.95

Modern Whitetail Hunting
by Michael Hanback
Don't rely on luck to harvest a big deer this fall. With advice from one of the foremost hunting writers in the world today, learn where mature bucks live and what triggers their movements, best early and late-season strategies, up-to-date tree stand, rattling, calling, and scent tricks, how to hunt huge deer on small lands, and much more. Get the advice of Mossy Oak's top big-buck hunters. More than 100 photographs and illustrations set into motion today's latest and greatest whitetail strategies!
Softcover • 6 x 9 • 224 pages
100 b&w photos • 8-page color section
Item# MWH • $19.99

Whitetail Rites of Autumn
by Charles J. Alsheimer
Discover what a typical day is like for a rutti buck during November! This exquisite pictor of the whitetail species provides new insight understanding of the rut: the seeking, chasing, breeding, beyond the rehashed information a serious deer hunter already knows-or should know. This all-color volume is both entertai and educational, displaying an intensified, well-edited file of deer images, while offering considerable insight into America's favorite game species, including chapters on fawns birth, the time before the rut, and dominant behavior of the male whitetail deer.
Hardcover • 9 x 11½ • 208 pages
175 color photos
Item# RTSAU • $34.99

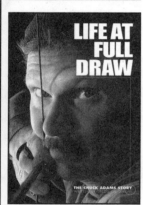

Life at Full Draw
The Chuck Adams Story
by Gregg Gutschow
Live the life of a legendary bowhunter as he makes and breaks hunting records and revisits his greatest conquests. Read how Chuck Adams has successfully bowhunted just about every game animal in the world. You'll get a true sense of adventure, as well as learn some of the best secrets of the world's best known and most widely published bowhunter.
Hardcover • 6 x 9 • 304 pages
80 b&w photos
Item# CHKAD • $24.95

Giant Whitetails
A Lifetime of Lessons
by Mark and Terry Drury
Leave it up to the high-adventure outdoor te Mark and Terry Drury to reveal hidden secret others would not tell! From how to hunt rare October cold fronts and utilizing ultimate dee funnels, to hunting mature bucks in their ow bedroom, Giant Whitetails discloses revealin facts on consistently harvesting trophy buck The Drury's share observation tactics and tip for hunting by the moon, as well as methods successful ground hunting, non-intrusive hu and using rattling antlers effectively. Compris 10 individual accounts of hunting trophy buc from start to finish, each chapter tells a new inspiring story, and for your benefit, finishes a "lessons learned" section.
Hardcover • 8¼ x 10⅞ • 240 pages
340 color photos
Item# WWDH • $29.99

Rub-Line Secrets
by Greg Miller
In Rub-Line Secrets, Greg Miller takes deer hunters to the graduate level in teaching them proven tactics for finding, analyzing and hunting a big buck's rub-line. No one has enjoyed more rub-line success than Miller. His straight-forward approach to hunting rub-lines is based on more than 30 years of intense hunting and scouting. The book is illustrated with photos and diagrams that help Miller explain his proven rub-line tactics.
Softcover • 6 x 9 • 208 pages
100 b&w photos
Item# HURU • $19.95

Mapping Trophy Bucks
Using Topographic Maps to Find Deer
by Brad Herndon
Remain one step ahead of the competition! T next time out in the field, the odds will be in favor if you have a topographical map. With new guide, you will learn the basic concepts topographical maps and implementing sound terrain hunting strategies. From inside corne and double inside corners to the perfect funn and mastering the wind, get a better concept using the wind and understanding topograph maps. Illustrations show details of how deer move, where to place your stand, and how to the wind to ensure a successful whitetail hun
Softcover • 8¼ x 10⅞ • 192 pages
150 color photos
Item# TRTT • $24.99